Film Noir **Reader 2**

D1075726

Also by Alain Silver

David Lean and His Films
The Vampire Film
The Samurai Film
*Film Noir: An Encyclopedic Reference to the
American Style*, Editor
Robert Aldrich: a guide to references and resources
The Film Director's Team
Raymond Chandler's Los Angeles
More Things Than Are Dreamt Of
What Ever Happened to Robert Aldrich?
Roger Corman: Metaphysics on a Shoestring
The Noir Style

Also by James Ursini

David Lean and His Films
The Life and Times of Preston Sturges, An American Dreamer
The Vampire Film
*Film Noir: An Encyclopedic Reference to the
American Style*, Editor, 3rd Edition
More Things Than Are Dreamt Of
What Ever Happened to Robert Aldrich?
Roger Corman: Metaphysics on a Shoestring
The Noir Style

Film Noir

R E A D E R 2

EDITED BY

ALAIN SILVER & JAMES URSINI

LIMELIGHT EDITIONS

NEW YORK

First Limelight Edition   July 1999

ISBN 0-87910-280-2

The Library of Congress has catalogued the preceding volume as follows:

Film noir reader / edited by Alain Silver and James Ursini
        p.   cm.
    ISBN 0-87910-197-0
    1. Film noir--United States--History and criticism. I. Silver, Alain, 1947-
II. Ursini, James.
PN1995.9.F54F57 1996
741.93'655--dc20   96-11102
                                                                CIP

The editors are grateful for permission to reprint copyrighted material as
detailed in the Acknowledgments.

Contents

Part Three: The Evolution of *Noir*

Acknowledgments

As with the first volume, the root idea for an anthology on *film noir* goes back to fall of 1974, so we continue to acknowledge our prospective collaborators from that project as well as two co-editors of *Film Noir: An Encyclopedic Reference to the American Style*, Elizabeth Ward and Robert Porfirio (who contributed directly to the research for this volume by supplying a copy of the Nino Frank article).

Our criteria in supplementing the first *Film Noir Reader* began with the missing seminal articles by Frank and Chartier and spread outward from there. We are grateful to all the authors whom we contacted personally about reprints or new pieces for their enthusiasm about the project. For the rest: the Shearer piece from the *New York Times* was discovered during an internet search on a site maintained by Christian Clark and Jason Delgado. As usual other research was done at the Academy of Motion Picture Arts and Sciences Library in Beverly Hills.

Permissions editors were Ouardia Teraha (Éditions de l'Étoile) Marci R. McMahon (University of Texas Press), Mary Jaine Winokur (Heldref Publications), Robin Wood (*CineAction!*), Arlene W. Sullivan (The John Hopkins University Press), and Suzanne Regan (*Journal of Film and Video*). Linda De Martinez typed portions of the manuscript; and, of course, Mel Zerman at Limelight Editions again made the entire endeavor possible.

Stills and frame enlargements not from the editors' personal collections, were loaned by David Chierichetti, Janey Place, Robert E. Smith, James Paris, Lee Sanders, and the Robert Porfirio Collection at Brigham Young University administered by James D'Arc. Film stills are reproduced courtesy of Columbia, ITC, MGM, Miramax, New Line, Orion, Overseas, Paramount, RKO, Sovereign, 20th Century-Fox, TriStar, United Artists, Universal, and Warner Bros. Other illustrations: Willem de Kooning, *Woman, I*, photograph © 1999 courtesy of The Museum of Modern Art, New York; Franz Kline, *Mahoning*, reproduction © 1995 Whitney Museum of Modern Art; Edward Hopper, *Night Shadows*, photo courtesy of Terra Museum of American Art, Chicago; and Weegee photos, Liaison Agency Inc.

While we have again attempted to reproduce the original pieces as closely as possible, some formal or practical considerations resulted in a few changes. While film titles may have been all caps or underlined in the original, for the sake of stylistic consistency we have chosen to italicize them as well as the term *film noir*. Except for this, any other underlining or italics in the text is that of the original authors. Most of the authors used end notes, so we have adopted that format throughout. We also changed the punctuation of the titles of some of the pieces previously published elsewhere when it differed from the style used here.

With regard to the illustrations, we have again as far as possible reproduced images identical to or from the same films as those used with the original article, without duplicating photos which appeared in the first **Film Noir Reader**. As before we have taken the liberty of occasionally injecting our own viewpoint in the captions.

"Crime Certainly Pays On Screen" by Lloyd Shearer, originally published in the *New York Times Magazine*, August 5, 1945. Copyright © 1945 by the *New York Times*. Reprinted by permission.

"Un Nouveau Genre 'Policier': l'Aventure Criminelle" by Nino Frank, originally published in *L'Écran Français* (August, 1946). Translation Copyright © 1999 by Alain Silver.

"Les Américains aussi font des films 'noirs'" by Jean-Pierre Chartier, originally published in *La Révue du Cinéma* (November, 1946). Translation Copyright © 1999 by Alain Silver.

"Évolution du film policier" by Claude Chabrol, originally published in *Cahiers du Cinéma*, No. 54. Copyright © 1955 by *Cahiers du Cinéma*, Éditions de l'Étoile. Reprinted by permission. Translation Copyright © 1999 by Alain Silver and Christiane Silver.

"Three Faces of Film Noir" by Tom Flinn, originally published in *The Velvet Light Trap*, No. 5 (1972). Copyright © 1972 by Tom Flinn and the University of Texas Press. Reprinted by permission of the author and the University of Texas Press. All rights retained by the University of Texas Press.

"Film Noir: The Society. Violence and the Bitch Goddess" by Stephen Farber, originally published in *Film Comment* (November-April, 1974). Copyright © 1974 by the author and *Film Comment* Publishing Corporation. Reprinted by permission of the author and the Film Society of Lincoln Center.

"The Filmic Transaction: On the Openings of Films Noirs" by Marc Vernet, originally published in *The Velvet Light Trap*, No. 20 (Summer, 1983). This version copyright © 1983 by Marc Vernet and the University of Texas Press. Reprinted by permission of the author and the University of Texas Press. All rights retained by the University of Texas Press.

"Film Noir: Style and Content" by Dale E. Ewing, Jr., originally published in *The Journal of Popular Film and Television*, Volume 16, No. 2 (Summer, 1988). Copyright © 1988 by Heldref Publications (1319 Eighteenth St. NW, Washington, D.C 20036-1802). Reprinted by permission of the Helen Dwight Reid Educational Foundation.

"Whatever Happened to the *Film Noir? The Postman Always Rings Twice* (1946-1981)" by Robert G. Porfirio, originally published in *Literature/Film Quarterly*, Volume 14, No. 2 (1985). Copyright © 1985 by the author and Salisbury State College. Reprinted by permission of the author.

"Creativity and Evaluation: Two Film Noirs of the Fifties" by Robin Wood, originally published in *CineAction!*, Nos. 21-22 (Summer/Fall, 1990). Copyright © 1990 by the author and *CineAction!* Reprinted by permission of *CineAction!*/Robin Wood.

"Fragments of the Mirror: Hitchcock's *Noir* Landscape" by Alain Silver, originally published as "The Fragments of the Mirror: the Uses of Landscape in Hitchcock" in *Wide Angle*, Volume 1, No. 3 (1976). Copyright © 1976 by the author and the Athens International Film Festival. Reprinted by permission of the author and the John Hopkins University Press.

"The Unintended *Femme Fatale: The File on Thelma Jordan* and *Pushover*." by Elizabeth Ward, ASUCLA Program Notes, Spring, 1974. Copyright © 1974 by Elizabeth Ward. Reprinted by permission of the author.

"Translate and Transform: from Cornell Woolrich to *Film Noir*" by Francis M. Nevins adapted from **First You Dream and Then You Die** (Mysterious Press, 1988), Copyright © 1988 and 1999. Reprinted by permission of the author.

"*Film noir* and Samuel Fuller's Tabloid Cinema:Red (Action), White (Exposition) and Blue (Romance)" by Grant Tracey. Copyright © 1999. Printed by permission of the author.

"Dark Jazz: Music in *Film Noir*" adapted from *The Dark Age of American Film: A Study of American* Film Noir *(1940-1960)* [doctoral dissertation, Yale University] by Robert Porfirio. Copyright © 1979 and 1999 by Robert Porfirio. Printed by permission of the author."

"Mad Love is Strange: More Neo-*Noir* Fugitives" by Alain Silver and Linda Brookover, a portion of which was originally published as "Truffaut's Allusive Sirene" by Alain Silver in the *UCLA Summer Bruin* (August, 1970). That material, copyright © 1970 by the author and the Associated Students of the University of California, Los Angeles. Other material copyright © 1999 by Alain Silver and Linda Brookover. Reprinted by permission of the authors.

"Film Noir: Today. Son of Noir" by Richard Jameson, originally published in *Film Comment* (November-April, 1974). Copyright © 1974 by the author and *Film Comment* Publishing Corporation. Reprinted by permission of the author and the Film Society of Lincoln Center

"Writing the New *Noir* Film" by Sharon Y. Cobb. Copyright © 1998. Reprinted by permission of the author.

Film Noir **Reader 2**

"There's no mystery...they do it for sex or money or both." Screen versions of James Cain's characters include the hapless brunette Mildred Pierce (portrayed by Joan Crawford, above) and Phyllis Dietrichson (portrayed by Barbara Stanwyck) reaching for her gun at left.

Introduction

Alain Silver

> It's just that producers have got hep to the fact that plenty of real crime takes place every day and that it makes a good movie. The public is fed up with the old-fashioned melodramatic type of hokum. You know, the whodunit at which the audience after the second reel starts shouting, "We know the murderer. It's the butler. It's the butler. It's the butler."
>
> James M. Cain

James M. Cain also told *New York Times* writer Lloyd Shearer in 1945 that he had "never written a murder mystery in my life. Some of the characters in my novels commit murder, but there's no mystery involved in them. They do it for sex or money or both." Like the filmmakers who defined the classic period of *film noir* and some of its prototypes, Cain never uses the word *noir*. This seems natural enough for an English-speaking writer; but no doubt some will interpret this as more proof that *film noir* was invented by a bunch of Frenchmen catching up on American movies in the Parisian cinemas of 1946. This issue is addressed in depth in the introduction to the first **Film Noir Reader**, and there is no intention of covering the same ground in this companion volume. However, as the perspective of the editors regarding *film noir* remains the same, some background comments seem appropriate.

The seminal essays in this volume are designed to complement those of our earlier anthology and include several pieces from the 1940s. While it is undeniable that the filmmakers of that era were most, if not all, unfamiliar with the term *film noir*, it seems also undeniable to us that they were familiar with the concept. In **Film Noir: An Encyclopedic Reference** and the first **Film Noir Reader**, classic period cinematographer John Alton is quoted on the subject of style. But the perception of a style also underlies James Cain's comments. Writing in 1945 and disdainful of a *noir* cycle, which he calls "hard-boiled, gut-and-gore crime stories, all fashioned on a theme with a combination of plausibly motivated murder and studded with high-powered Freudian implication," Lloyd Shearer certainly perceives its existence more than a year before either Nino Frank or Jean-Pierre Chartier thought of giving it a name. Half a century later, it is chilling to realize suddenly that some readers of the *Times* must have been digesting Shearer's comments de-

3

ploring Hollywood violence at the exact moment that, half a world away, most of Hiroshima was being vaporized. What might Shearer have made of the theory that audiences were numbed to violence by World War II just one day later?

The underpinning of Shearer's dismissal of *noir* starting with his anecdote about Producer Joe Sistrom and *Double Indemnity* is his old-fashioned, New York style Hollywood bashing. At the end of the article, Shearer also quotes Raymond Chandler about the Hays office and escapist entertainment. For our purposes, a more useful quote from Chandler is found in his letter to Joe Sistrom, written two years after the Shearer piece:

> Back in 1943 when we were writing *Double Indemnity* you told me that an effective motion picture could not be made of a detective or mystery story for the reason that the high point is the revelation of the murderer and that only happens in the last minute of the picture. Events proved you wrong, for almost immediately the mystery trend started, and there is no question but that *Double Indemnity* started it.... The thing that made the mystery effective on the screen already existed on paper, but you somehow did not realize just where the values lay. It is implicit in my theory of mystery story writing that the mystery and the solution to the mystery are only what I call "the olive in the martini," and the really good mystery is one you would read even if you knew somebody had torn out the last chapter. [letter of December 16, 1947 to Joseph Sistrom excerpted in *Raymond Chandler Speaking*, p. 130]

While Chandler's prose is typically hyperbolic and may overreach in his comment about tearing out the last chapter, clearly what defines the "mystery trend" that is *film noir* for him is the style. While Shearer's antagonism towards Hollywood makes him use Cain and Chandler like literary clubs, Nino Frank understood what Cain and Chandler were saying when he wrote about the old and new kind of American police dramas.

The sensibilities of Hammett, Cain, and Chandler were integral to what Frank called a "new kind" of film, which he was the first to dub *"noir."* Frank probably never read Shearer's piece and the Cain quote and certainly could not know what Chandler wrote to Joe Sistrom; but he was clearly on the same wavelength as them in discussing an outdated style of novel and film when he affirmed that "I don't know of any enlightened devotees of the genre who could not nowadays plumb the mystery from the first fifty pages or the first two reels..." For Cain, Chandler, Frank, and others to follow, plot mysteries were old hat, stale and predictable long before creaking to an end. Style and character were now the key.

They still are. There are plenty of plot twists in classic period *noir* and the best of neo-*noir* as well, but those twists are designed to surprise the protagonist not the viewer. The self-assured deductions of Holmes and his ilk still have no place in the *noir* sensibility.

As before the definition of that sensibility is the purpose of this collection of essays. And as before the writers herein may approach that definition either directly (what *film noir* is) or indirectly (what it is not). Either way, the range of their opinions derives from a common perception that goes back more than fifty years to Shearer, Frank. and Jean-Pierre Chartier, that, whichever they may be and whatever makes them so, some films are *noir*.

The journals in which Frank, and Chartier first called *noir* films *noir* are long defunct. And it may seem that, other than the fact that they coined the term, their insights into *film noir* are limited. But, as with Shearer, their perspective and their significance as seminal articles is unique in that it is contemporaneous with the height of the classic period. And there is a key perception, that Shearer either does not see or does not care about, which Frank and Chartier simultaneously have: that these films are something new, not mysteries in the detective tradition going back to Poe and Doyle, but psychological dramas, grimly naturalistic, sordid, despairing, and exciting to watch.

As the classic period wound down, Claude Chabrol and others writing for *Cahiers du Cinéma* and *Positif* sustained the critical discussion of *film noir* culminating with Raymond Borde and Étienne Chaumeton's book-length, French-language study in 1955 (see the first *Film Noir Reader*). And it is still remarkable that no English-language critics would enter the discussion for more than a decade when the early, overview pieces of Raymond Durgnat and Paul Schrader (see again *FNR* I) finally appeared. While he warns that he "in no way attempts to trace the limits of *film noir*," Tom Flinn's 1972 piece is one of the first in-depth articles on particular aspects of *noir*. Two years later, Stephen Farber's social analysis (and Richard Jameson's piece in Part III) appeared in a special *film noir* section of *Film Comment* in 1974.

As was clear from the selections in the first *Film Noir Reader*, although commentators generally agreed on when the classic period began and ended and which pictures were most significant, what defined *film noir*, whether it was genre or movement, content or style, emerged as and has remained the key issue. Marc Vernet's 1983 article redefines the thrust of French criticism under the influence of semiological and structural methods. Vernet's close inspection of six classic period films (*Maltese Falcon, Double Indemnity, The Big Sleep, The Lady from Shanghai, Out of the Past,* and *The Enforcer*) moves from Borde and Chaumeton's concept of ambiguity to the chaos that underlies the noir universe. Because *film noir* is resistant to a straightforward semiological deconstruction, Vernet concedes that its "sense of disorder and reversal, however, is in every case relative." But when he concludes that "a hero cannot be both strong and vulnerable, the woman good and evil," Vernet seems to fall off the structuro-semiological deep end. His search for oppositions using Propp or Levi-Strauss becomes a search through enclosed texts where "each functions perfectly within the context of its own system"; but this ignores the critical context, that viewer expectations are derived from the emphasis on character over plot, from the evolution of *film noir*, as first described by Frank, Chartier, and Chabrol. Vernet seems to echo Chartier's analysis of the Dietrichson/Neff dynamic when he types the femme fatale: "the woman is made guilty and, despite her protestations, she is either abandoned or killed by the hero." But Chartier understood that it was Neff's outlook, not Dietrichson's, which was the linchpin of *noir*, a paternalistic outlook which dichotomizes women into destroyers or saviors. Vernet is seeking designating structures in a film movement that often depicts extreme, even cataclysmic events, what Frank called a "change in background from a vast and novelistic treatment of nature to a 'fantastic' social order." In this context, a better guiding principle might have been an observation analogous to Frank's by structuralist Maurice Merleau-Ponty: "the dialectic proper to the organism and the milieu can be interrupted by 'catastrophic' behavior."

In 1978 James Damico (see *FNR* 1) proposed the idea of a narrative model for *film noir*, which Dale Ewing revisits ten years later in "*Film Noir*: Style and Content." Ewing bluntly asserts that "the fact that analysts have made generalizations about *film noir* from its stylistic qualities does not necessarily invalidate their conclusions; it only forces them to take into account basic objections to their method." What Ewing does not seem to grasp is that the overemphasis on style in the early work of Durgnat and Schrader was heavily rhetorical and designed to counterbalance those who would have made *film noir* into a genre. Still, in addressing the style/content issue, Ewing's piece closes out Part One with a solid recapitulation of this issue that goes all the way back to Chartier and Frank, who, as it happens, saw no conflict in valuing equally the naturalistic dialogue and "the meaningful glances in *Laura* or *Double Indemnity*."

As with the first *Film Noir Reader*, Parts Two and Three of this volume put the *noir* phenomenon in closer focus through Case Studies and review its evolution within and after the classic period. Our selection criteria for the reprinted material in Part Two, such as Robin Wood's close analysis of creativity and authorship through *the Big Heat* and *Kiss Me Deadly*, Francis Nevin's survey of Cornell Woolrich, and Robert Porfirio's consideration of two adaptations of Cain's *The Postman Always Rings Twice* evolved from the Case Studies in the first *Film Noir Reader*, where our editorial prejudice was that the detailed consideration of individual works and individual authors would help elucidate what critics call the texts and viewers call the movies. Elizabeth Ward reflects on the impact of *Double Indemnity* on subsequent classic period *noir* films starring Barbara Stanwyck and Fred MacMurray, and I revisit the darker expectations of landscape in Hitchcock. New pieces include Grant Tracey's study of director Sam Fuller's extravagant contributions to *film noir* as "tabloid cinema," Robert Porfirio's consideration of jazz and classic *noir*, and more neo-*noir* fugitive couples.

Part Three of this volume delves further into the consideration of the boundaries and influences of classic *film noir* as evidenced not only by the on-going vitality of neo-*noir* as a genre in the U.S. and throughout the world but through other cross-generic style and content. The beginnings of neo-*noir* are revisited in the reprint of Richard Jameson's 1974 "Son of *Noir*" and there is a glimpse at its possible future in the newest reprint: Sharon Cobb's internet article for would-be screenwriters in the *noir* tradition.

Several all-new essays consider *noir*'s relationships to other types of films and other types of art: James Ursini considers science fiction and *noir*; Tony Williams, British *film noir*; Kent Minturn, abstract expressionism and *noir*; and Linda Brookover, crime photography and *noir*. Another new piece by William Covey tracks the evolving relationship of *film noir* and women both as neo-*noir* protagonists and as filmmakers. Finally, mindful of the fact that the first *Film Noir Reader* was well received as a reference text for survey courses, we have concluded with Philip Gaines' recent schematic for such a course.

Those familiar with the first *Film Noir Reader* or other of our director or genre studies will know what comes next: the admonition that all these texts are secondary documentation, that what counts most are the films themselves; or as Claude Chabrol wrote in 1955: "successes, popular styles, genres are all mortal. What remains are the works, good or bad." So, as before, we have tried to select pieces that range widely across the subject and that support a broad range of associated film viewing. From the contemporary pieces written when the classic period was still developing to the new articles written for this volume, as editors we have tried to be inclusionary and to fill in gaps. Of course, if the reader has never seen a key *film noir* such as *Double Indemnity*, now would be a good time to put down this book, go to the local video outlet, and fill in that gap. None of the following essays require any introductory comments for full understanding. All of them do require a perception of *film noir* that can only be obtained from films themselves, which fortunately are more readily available than ever before. Taken together *Film Noir Reader* and *Film Noir Reader 2* are still far from exhaustive. But hopefully they will provide the reader with a ready reference to the heart of that particular darkness known as *film noir*.

Above, Barbara Stanwyck as the scheming Phyllis Dietrichson helps her "injured husband," Fred MacMurray as Walter Neff, board a deadly train in *Double Indemnity*.

Crime Certainly Pays on the Screen

Lloyd Shearer (1945)

The Growing crop of homicidal films poses questions for psychologists and producers.

Of late there has been a trend in Hollywood toward the wholesale production of lusty, hard-boiled, gut-and-gore crime stories, all fashioned on a theme with a combination of plausibly motivated murder and studded with high-powered Freudian implication. Of the quantity of such films now in vogue, *Double Indemnity*, *Murder My Sweet*, *Conflict* and *Laura* are a quartet of the most popular which quickly come to mind.

Shortly to be followed by Twentieth Century-Fox's *The Dark Corner* and *The High Window*, MGM's *The Postman Always Rings Twice* and *The Lady in the Lake*, Paramount's *Blue Dahlia* and Warner's *Serenade* and *The Big Sleep*, this quartet constitutes a mere vanguard of the cinematic homicide to come. Every studio in town has at least two or three similar blood-freezers before the cameras right now, which means that within the next year or so movie murder–particularly with a psychological twist–will become almost as common as the weekly newsreel or musical.

Fortunately most of the crime films recently released have been suspense-jammed and altogether entertaining and it is entirely possible that those which follow will maintain the standard, but why at this time are so many pictures of the same type being made? This is a question which the average screen fan would like answered.

Hollywood says the moviegoer is getting this type of story because he likes it, and psychologists explain that he likes it because it serves as a violent escape in tune with the violence of the times, a cathartic for pent-up emotions. These learned men, in a mumbo-jumbo all their own, assert that because of the war the average moviegoer has become calloused to death, hardened to homicide and more capable of understanding a murderer's motives. After watching a newsreel showing the horrors of a German concentration camp, the movie fan, they say, feels no shock, no remorse, no moral repugnance when the screen villain puts a bullet through his wife's head or shoves her off a cliff and runs away with his voluptuous next-door neighbor.

Moreover, the psychologists aver, each one of us at some time or other has se-cretly or subconsciously planned to murder a person we dislike. Through these hard-boiled crime pictures we vicariously enjoy the thrills of doing our enemies in, getting rid of our wives or husbands and making off with the insurance money.

In short, the war has made us psychologically and emotionally ripe for motion pictures of this sort. That's why we like them, that's why we pay out good money each week to see them and that's why Hollywood is producing them in quantity.

Of course this is just one school of thought and you may skip school or enroll in it, as you like. You may simplify the entire problem and say that you see crime movies simply because they happen to be showing at the time you attend the theatre, and that you enjoy them not because they afford you the opportunity of vicariously murdering our mother-in-law or projecting your own repressed emo-tions but because they're well paced, exciting and interesting. If you say this, how-ever, you may be admitting at once that the war has not altered your sensitivity to death, that you are not profound, that you are subnormal in homicidal instinct, and—worse yet—you are repudiating the psychologists. And who wants to repudi-ate psychologists? Let's face it. They have to live too.

Another school of thought (there are always at least two schools of thought about anything in Hollywood) subscribes to the belief that the main reason behind the current crop of hard-boiled, action-packed cinema murders is the time-hon-ored Hollywood production formula of follow-the-leader. Let one studio turn out a successful detective-story picture and every other studio in the screen capital follows suit. Result: a surfeit of motion pictures of one type.

Take, for example, the Paramount picture *Double Indemnity*, generally ac-corded the honor of being the first of the new rough, tough murder yarns. How did this movie come to be? Did Paramount's executives confer with one another and say: "These are times of death and bloodshed and legalized murder; these are times when, if an audience can stomach newsreels of atrocities, it can take any-thing. Therefore let's buy *Double Indemnity*." Or did someone simply say: "This is a fast-moving story. We can buy it cheap. Let's do it!"

Well, these are the facts on how *Double Indemnity* came to be made and started the cinema's cycle of crime.

One afternoon early in 1944 Joe Sistrom, a producer at Paramount, buzzed for his secretary, Miss Thelda Victor, an attractive brunette with blue eyes. He got no reply. He rang again. Still no answer. Mildly irritated, he rose from his desk, stalked out front and asked another secretary where Miss Victor was.

"She's been in the ladies' lounge for the past hour," the girl volunteered, "read-ing a script."

"On studio time, no doubt," Sistrom sputtered and stalked back to his office.

When he next saw Miss Victor, Sistrom demanded to know what story had kept her away from her desk for more than an hour. Miss Victor was all aglow.

Her eyes were rhapsodies in blue. She couldn't contain herself. Her voice shook like a taut rope. "The story is sensational," she began, "simply sensational. It's by James Cain, and it's called *Double Indemnity*, and it's a natural for Billy Wilder to direct. You said Wilder was looking for a story. This is it. It's hot. It's sexy. It's exciting. It's got everything."

And she forthwith launched into a resume of the novel which Cain had written in 1935 and the Hays office had banned for the movies on the ground that it was "a blueprint for a murder."

In Hollywood most opinions of women are considered as interesting as laundry lists and about as important, but Miss Victor's are usually valid. Because he knew this, Sistrom took *Double Indemnity* home with him that night. He read it, liked it and, after several conferences with Billy Wilder, bought it.

Skillfully adapted for the screen by Raymond Chandler and Wilder, the story was filmed last year with Fred MacMurray and Barbara Stanwyck in the leading roles. It was received with outstanding critical acclaim and considerable box-office enthusiasm.

Forever watchful of audience reactions, the rest of the industry almost immediately began searching its story files for properties like *Double Indemnity*. RKO suddenly discovered it had bought Chandler's novel, **Farewell, My Lovely**, on July 3, 1941. If *Double Indemnity* was so successful, why not make **Farewell, My Lovely**? And make it RKO did, under the title *Murder, My Sweet*. Twentieth Century-Fox followed with *Laura*. Warner's began working on Chandler's *The Big Sleep* for

Below, Dick Powell as Chandler's Marlowe with Mrs. Grayle (Claire Trevor) in *Murder, My Sweet*.

Humphrey Bogart and Lauren Bacall. MGM excavated from its vaults an all-but-forgotten copy of James Cain's *The Postman Always Rings Twice*. The trickle swelled into a torrent and a trend was born.

When will the trend stop? Probably not until the market has been glutted with poorly made pictures of the type. So long as producers turn out interesting and entertaining murder pictures, the public will flock to them. There is nothing new, however, about these tough, realistic homicide yarns, nothing new at all. You can take the word of James Cain for that.

Cain, at 53, has been writing them (*Mildred Pierce, Serenade, The Postman Always Rings Twice*) ever since the death in 1931 of *The New York World*, on which paper he served, and he has sold all but one of his works–*Love's Lovely Counterfeit*–to the movies.

"The reason Hollywood is making so many of these so-called hard-boiled crime pictures," he explains, "is simply that the producers are now belatedly realizing that these stories make good movies. It's got nothing to do with the war or how it's affected the public or any of that bunk. If Billy Wilder, for example, had made *Double Indemnity* back in 1935 the picture would have done just as well as it has now.

"It's just that producers have got hep to the fact that plenty of real crime takes place every day and that it makes a good movie. The public is fed up with the old-fashioned melodramatic type of hokum. You know, the whodunit at which the audience after the second reel starts shouting, 'We know the murderer. It's the butler. It's the butler. It's the butler.'

Below, Humphrey Bogart as Marlowe with Lauren Bacall as Vivian Sternwood in *The Big Sleep*.

"The novels I write are honest and plausible. A lot of people come up to me and say, 'I enjoyed your last murder mystery very much.' Now, I've never written a murder mystery in my life. Some of the characters in my novels commit murder, but there's no mystery involved in them. They do it for sex or money or both. Take **Double Indemnity**. There's nothing mysterious about that. As a matter of fact, it's so clear and lucid that the insurance companies are now using it as a text. They're having their agents read it and they're distributing copies of it to some of their clients, just to let them know how thorough their claims department is. I think *Double Indemnity* started the trend toward the production of fast-paced, hard-boiled, life-like pictures, and I think it will last as long as the story supply."

One of the chief sources of this story supply is Raymond Chandler, a reserved, quiet writer with an unusual talent for literary imagery, e.g., "Old men with faces like lost battles... The surf curled and creamed almost without sound... She looked as if she would have a hall-bedroom accent... Dry white hair clung to his scalp like wild flowers fighting for life on a bare rock."

At the moment Chandler is the darling of tough-guy detective story readers and reviewers. He has been called the foremost practitioner of the art since Dashiell Hammett.

An American raised in England who returned to the United States in 1919, Chandler has written four novels, **Farewell My Lovely, The High Window, The Big Sleep**, and **The Lady in the Lake**, all of which have been made into motion pictures. In addition, he has written an original screen play *The Blue Dahlia*, in which Paramount's Alan Ladd will soon star, and in between jobs has worked on the scripts of *Double Indemnity* and *The Unseen*. He is, therefore, well qualified to discuss Hollywood's recent predilection for the hard-boiled murder yarn.

"My own opinion," Chandler says, "is that the studios have gone in for these pictures because the Hays office has become more liberal." (The Hays office denies this.) "I think they're okaying treatments now which they would have turned down ten years ago, probably because they feel people can take the hard-boiled stuff nowadays. Of course, people have been reading about murderers, cutthroats and thieves in the newspapers for the past hundred years, but only recently has the Hays office permitted the movies to depict life as it really is. The Hays office has lost Warner Brothers and United Artists and may be little fearful of antagonizing the remaining studios which support it. Then again it's entirely possible that the studios have become smarter and have submitted story treatments which satisfy the production code.

"In any event, the public likes well-done crime films for the very same reason they like good detective stories. They're escapist and interesting."

So there you have them—the authoritative, expert explanations of the cinema's current cycle of crime. You pays your nickel and you takes your choice!

Above, "There is no mystery here, we know everything from the beginning..." Fred Mac-Murray as Walter Neff and his mentor Edward G. Robinson as Keyes in *Double Indemnity*.

A New Kind of Police Drama: the Criminal Adventure

Nino Frank (1946)

Here we are one year after a series of poor quality American movies made it seem that Hollywood was finished. Today another conclusion is needed, because the appearance of half a dozen fine works made in California compels us to write and affirm that American cinema is better than ever. Our filmmakers are decidedly manic depressive.

Seven new American films are particularly masterful: *Citizen Kane, The Little Foxes, How Green Was My Valley,* plus *Double Indemnity, Laura,* and, to a certain extent, *The Maltese Falcon* and *Murder, My Sweet.* The first three are exceptional; but we cannot consider them if we want to focus on typical Hollywood productions. Instead let's look at the other four.

They belong to a class that we used to call the crime film, but that would best be described from this point on by a term such as criminal adventures or, better yet, such as criminal psychology. This is a major class of films which has superseded the *Western*: and there are wry conclusions to be drawn from the displacement of an on-screen dynamic involving chases on horseback and idylls in coaches by the dynamic of violent death and dark mysteries, as well as the change in background from a vast and novelistic treatment of nature to a "fantastic" social order.

This sort of film has now notably changed in the U.S. following the course of popular literature where the preeminence of S.S. Van Dine has ceded to that of Dashiell Hammett. Since Poe, since Gaboriau, and since Conan Doyle, we've become familiar with the formula for detective stories: an unsolved crime, some suspects, and in the end the discovery of the guilty party through the diligence of an experienced observer. This formula had long been perfected: the detective novel (and film) have substituted for the Sunday crossword puzzle and become overshadowed by boring repetition. I don't know of any enlightened devotees of the genre who could not nowadays plumb the mystery from the first fifty pages or the first two reels...

In motion pictures this handicap was heavier. First problem: long explications coming at the end of the narrative, at the exact moment when a film, its action being over, no longer interests the viewer. Another problem: if most of the characters could be lively and imaginative, the hero—that is to say, the detective—was

15

merely a thinking machine and, even under the best of circumstances ([such as Simenon's,] Maigret), a thinking machine while sniffing and stuffing his pipe. One would consider the scenery, a moment of levity, other crimes, anything to spark one's interest.

We are witnessing the death of this formula. Of the four works cited earlier, only *Laura* belongs to this outdated genre; but Otto Preminger and his collaborators forced themselves to renew the formula by introducing a charming study of the furnishings and faces, a complicated narrative, a perverse writer who is prosaic but amusing, and foremost a detective with an emotional life. To sum up, the result is a film lacking in originality but perfectly distracting and, one can say, successful.

For the other three, the method is different. They are to the traditional crime drama what the novels of Dashiell Hammett are to those of Van Dine or Ellery Queen. They are as what one might call "true to life." The detective is not a mechanism but a protagonist, that is the character most important to us: accordingly the heroes of *Maltese Falcon* and *Murder, My Sweet* practice this strange profession of private detective, which (in the U.S.) has nothing to do with bureaucratic function but, by definition, puts them on the fringe of the law—the law as represented by the police and the codes of gangsters as well. The essential question is no longer "who-done-it?" but how does this protagonist act? It's not even required to comprehend all the twists and turns of the action in which he is caught up (I would never be able to sum up coherently the sequence of events of

Below, a classic practitioner of "this strange profession," Dick Powell as private detective Philip Marlowe in *Murder, My Sweet* with "good girl" Ann Riordan (Anne Shirley).

Above, a moment from the "quite exciting" *Maltese Falcon*: Sam Spade (Humphrey Bogart, left) and Bridgid O'Shaughnessy (Mary Astor) watch the police (Barton MacLane and Ward Bond, right) manhandle Joel Cairo (Peter Lorre).

which these two films are composed), only the uncertain psychology of one and the other, at once friend and foe. Still more significantly neither the punch in the face nor the gunshot play a major role until the end. And it cannot be by accident that the two films end in the same manner, the cruelest way in the world with the heroines paying full price. These final scenes are harsh and misogynistic, as is most of contemporary American literature.

I would not go so far as to say these films are completely successful. While *Maltese Falcon* is quite exciting (and is taken from a novel by Dashiell Hammett), *Murder, My Sweet* is very uneven and at times vacuous (despite the excellent reputation of the Raymond Chandler novel from which it is adapted).

We rediscover this hardness, this misogyny, in *Double Indemnity*. There is no mystery here, we know everything from the beginning, and we follow the preparation for the crime, its execution, and its aftermath (just as in *Suspicion* which Alfred Hitchcock adapted from a remarkable novel by Francis Iles with poor results). Consequently our interest is focused on the characters, and the narrative unfolds with a striking clarity that is sustained throughout. This is because the director, Billy Wilder, has done more than merely transpose the narrative structure offered by the James Cain novel from which the film is adapted. He started by creating, with Raymond Chandler, a peremptorily precise script which deftly details the motives and reactions of its characters. The direction is a faithful rendering of this script.

In this manner these "noir" films no longer have any common ground with run-of-the-mill police dramas. Markedly psychological plots, violent or emotional action, have less impact then facial expressions, gestures, utterances–rendering the truth of the characters, that "third dimension" of which I have already spoken. This is a significant improvement: after films such as these the figures in the usual cop movie seem like mannequins. There is nothing remarkable in the fact that today's viewers are more responsive to this stamp of verisimilitude, of "true to life," and, why not, to the kind of gross cruelties which actually exist and the past concealment of which has served no purpose: the struggle to survive is not a new story.

Concurrently with this internal development, there is another, purely formal, change in expository style, the intervention of a narrator or commentator permits a fragmentation of the narrative, to quickly gloss over the traditional plot elements and to accentuate the "true-to-life" side. It's clear that this method permits the story to be rapidly engaged, but it also permits the insertion of a dynamic element into an otherwise static, psychological portrait.

Sacha Guitry was the first to utilize this technique in *Le Roman d'un Tricheur*. The makers of the films which I have mentioned (except for *The Maltese Falcon*) utilized it also and revealed both its flexibility and the enhanced possibility of adding a deeper layer to the narrative style. I must note, however, that Preminger in *Laura* has the story explained in the beginning by a character who cannot know the succeeding events nor, reason dictates, their conclusion.

Has Hollywood definitively outclassed Paris?

It seems to me that we shouldn't rush precipitously to this conclusion. Doubtless after this sort of film, it won't be easy to construct police stories in the usual manner. Doubtless we'll have to work harder, assiduously refine our scripts, and give up beautiful images, camera tricks, and other technical razzle-dazzle which diminish that "third dimension" on screen by creating visual falsehood and "going Hollywood" (in the bad sense of the term). Certainly we've witnessed the emergence of a new class of authors, the Billy Wilders, the Premingers, the Chandlers, the John Hustons, who promise to leave behind the old guard and the old school, the John Fords, the Wylers, and even the Capras.

But from this, to conclude that French filmmakers should fold up their tents...

There is one point, however, that deserves to be underscored for our own filmmakers: the primacy of the script, and the fact that a film is first and foremost a sober story well constructed and presented in an original manner. I read exactly the opposite of what I've just said from my old friend Georges Charensol writing about *How Green was My Valley*. Charensol and other reviewers seemed to be nostalgic for the silent movie and to judge a film by the quantity of pretentious flourishes it displays. I'm afraid it would be useless to contradict them: the relentless evolution of motion pictures will settle their case–motion pictures, the creation of which are more and more a function of the screenplay and where today one can find more dramatic energy in a static shot than in a majestic panorama.

The proof? Admirable films such as *How Green Was My Valley* and *The Letter*, admirable and profoundly boring. On the one hand, production value written in capital letters, graphic beauty, paternalistic traveling shots, and dullness precisely distilled by the camera. On the other hand, filmed theater in all its splendor made possible by a special lens, a ballet going nowhere, magnificently rendered, prodigiously breathed to life, that one follows with a yawn. Both are devoid of life, of truth, of depth, of charm, of vitality, of real energy–of that "third dimension" that I prefer. Trompe-l'oeil and filmed theater, these two antiquated and antithetical formulas come together and compel us to assert, sadly, that such magnificent gentlemen as John Ford and William Wyler are already museum pieces. The meaningful glances in *Laura* or *Double Indemnity*–it's sad to say, but it must be said–are more moving than the eloquent compositions of the former or the skilled touch of the latter.

Above all, don't make me say that the future belongs to crime movies told in the first person...

Translated from the French by Alain Silver

Below, "meaningful glances" between Laura (Gene Tierney) and Shelby (Vincent Price) in *Laura*

Above, Claire Trevor as Mrs. Grayle calm and ready to pull the trigger because "as naturally as drawing breath" killing comes easily for her in *Murder, My Sweet*.

Americans Also Make *Noir* Films

Jean-Pierre Chartier (1946)

"She kisses him so that he'll kill for her." Emblazoned on the movie posters, over a blood stain, is that description of Billy Wilder's *Double Indemnity*. The same line would work just as well for Edward Dmytryk's *Murder, My Sweet*. It would hold true again for *The Postman Always Rings Twice* which is currently a big hit in the U.S. We understood why the Hays Office had previously forbidden film adaptations of James M. Cain's two novels from which *Double Indemnity* and *The Postman Rings Twice* are drawn. It is harder to understand, given this censor's moral posture, why this interdiction was lifted, as it's hard to imagine story lines with a more pessimistic or disgusted point of view regarding human behavior.

Doubtless the crime film has its genre conventions: one needs a dead victim, and no society condones murder. But with a detective as protagonist and a few innocent bystanders in support, human nature's tendency to do right can still be reaffirmed. In *Double Indemnity*, as in *Murder, My Sweet*, all the characters are more or less venal. And while there is a pure young girl in both films, which permits some hope about future generations, the females are particularly monstrous. Practically every scene reveals a new evil created by Barbara Stanwyck portraying Phyllis Dietrichson in *Double Indemnity*. As the film opens, she flirts with the young insurance salesman who has come to close a deal with her husband; two meetings later she asks him to kill her husband after insuring his life; she cold-bloodedly takes part in the murder; we then learn that she had previously poisoned Dietrichson's first wife; when things gets complicated, she tries to kill her insurance agent accomplice; and the film hasn't yet reached its climax before we further learn that, while all this was going on, she was having an affair with her stepdaughter's fiancé.

Claire Trevor in *Murder, My Sweet* has no less charming a role. Despite having married into respectability, she acts like a cheap hooker: after committing murder to cover up her sordid past, the least she can do, as naturally as drawing breath, is to offer her favors to a private detective in exchange for helping with a second killing.

We can see how significant sexual attraction is in the through line of these narratives. It's a sort of contradiction that, from convention, the film censors, insensitive to the pessimism and despair which radiates from these characters, forbids putting the real emphasis on the sexual drive that dooms them. The result is that

21

the actions of all these figures seems conditioned by an obsessive and fatal attraction to the crime itself. The sexual expropriation that Phyllis Dietrichson exercises over the free will of Walter Neff (Fred MacMurray), if it were underscored even more, would make his character even more hapless, as he actually is while under her spell, and this would be a sort of relief for the viewer.

As with many new films from the U.S., *Double Indemnity* and *Murder, My Sweet* are told in the first person. This choice of a specific point of view is used in both films but with very different results.

The narrator of *Murder, My Sweet* is a private detective. He is catapulted into a shadowy scheme without knowing either the principals nor their intentions. The confusion of the film, that the viewer is immersed in an imbroglio, these are the desired effects. *Murder, My Sweet* is no ordinary crime drama where from scene to scene more of the mystery is revealed: the script is not a whodunit designed to draw the viewer into guessing the outcome, it aims not to intrigue but to create an atmosphere of fright. Precisely because we don't understand them, we sense the menace of unknown dangers. *Murder, My Sweet* genuinely deserves the label of thriller, as the first person narrative is used to make the viewer shudder with the thrill of fear. This forced perspective is uncompromising. Several times in the

Below, another "sordid tale": Phyllis Dietrichson (Barbara Stanwyck) ignores company owner Norton (Richard Gaines, center) and her accomplice Walter Neff (Fred MacMurray) to fix her gaze on investigator Barton Keyes (Edward G. Robinson, seated right) in *Double Indemnity*.

course of the film, the detective is rendered unconscious, and each time the screen tries to render the experience of someone being knocked out: a play of twisted shapes, which makes us think of the experiments of "pure cinema," of the presentation of a nightmare and disturbed vision in the manner of the old school of avant-garde filmmakers. *Double Indemnity* used the narrative progression for psychological ends: as the guilty man is telling the story, there is no formal mystery; on the contrary, it is the psychological mechanism by which Walter Neff is dragged unrelentingly into the criminal action that unwinds before our eyes. The action doesn't spring from exterior causes: the seduction of law-abiding young man by a calculating bitch, the appeal of the perfect crime, the gauntlet thrown down to the friend in charge of investigating fraud have a verisimilitude that draws us personally into this sordid tale.

Raymond Chandler is the author of the source material for *Murder, My Sweet* and the co-screenwriter of *Double Indemnity*; and one can sense the same influence on both films. *Double Indemnity* doubtless owes its superiority to the source material of James Cain. But the hand of director Billy Wilder is clearly evident, particularly in the first person narrative which is used as well in his other *"noir"* film *The Lost Weekend*. In that film, the development of the story is extremely stylized and Wilder's success is even more telling: Ray Milland, who portrays the protagonist, is in every frame and often alone. It's almost a case study: as per its tag line, the film is "the diary of an alcoholic." The entire story is restricted to the memories of a pathological drunk. Usually in the care of his brother, Milland, left alone for a weekend takes a drink and starts to talk, takes another drink and resumes his monologue, sleeps for awhile and then drinks some more. The impressions of insanity, of a senseless void, left by the drama of a young man in the grip of singular addiction, makes *the Lost Weekend* one of the most depressing movies I have ever seen. Certainly a charming young lady helps our alcoholic hero sober up and permits the film to end with a kiss. But the impression of extreme despair persists despite this upbeat ending.

Women as insatiable as the Empress Messalina, animalistic or senile husbands, young guys ready to kill for the sexual favors of a femme fatale, unrepentant alcoholics, these are the charming types from the films we've discussed. There's been talk of a French school of *film noir*, but *Le Quai des Brumes* and *L'Hotel du Nord* contain some glimmer of resistance to the dark side, where love provides at least the mirage of a better world, where some re-vindication of society opens the door for hope, and even though the characters may despair they retain our pity and our sympathy. There is none of that in the films before us now: these are monsters, criminals and psychopaths without redemptive qualities who behave according to the preordained disposition to evil within themselves.

Translated from the French by Alain Silver

Above, "gratuitous use of subjective camera...in *Lady in the Lake*": cops and a dead blonde from Marlowe's point of view.

The Evolution of the Crime Film

- ## Claude Chabrol (1955)

I. In Memoriam

Success creates fashion, which defines genre. At the height of popularity for the crime novel between the two world wars there was a correspondent event in American films–poorly imitated by many others–the creation of a genre which quickly lapsed, as often happens, into mediocrity and low-budget versions. The earliest examples, taken from the successful fiction of S.S. Van Dine and Earl Derr Biggers, were a smattering of movies which were, if not admirable, at least compelling and well turned out like the celebrated *Canary Murder Case*, unforgettable for a reason not directly related to this discussion.[1] The immense success of these movies gave merchandisers the bright idea of an endless array of inexpensive knock-offs cheaply packaged by Smith, Jones...or Dupont, in which Charlie Chan, Perry Mason, Philo Vance and Ellery Queen returned periodically in new adventures, usually putting on the same face (that of Warner Oland, Warren Williams, or other character actors), all in order, it would seem, to give their not-terribly-demanding viewers an experience akin to following the Sunday funnies.

There was a similar occurrence with gangster films, which were born from the complex social, economic, and political alliances of the 1930s. Certainly the early examples were masterpieces; they were drawn from the exploits of the Prohibition era's celebrated Italian bootleggers and, as they say, "ripped from today's headlines." But those quickly became yesterday's headlines and were gone as a source of inspiration. The knock-offs, which are never embarrassed by their own low quality, then had the field to themselves.

Curiously, although they were already running out of steam in 1935, there are practically no examples of either genre before 1929. The attempts to adapt the novels of Dashiell Hammett had no results other that to bring the protagonists of *The Thin Man* to the screen in a series of films which persisted through increasingly fatigued, forlorn, and flat examples until near the end of the War. Accordingly the status of the crime genre–of all the crime genres–was hardly promising in 1940. The straight-forward mystery novel was stumbling and becoming untranslatable into movies. Prohibition had long since been repealed by the proponents of strong drink and the persistence of organized crime had not been

Above, giving "the hard-boiled genre acclaimed status," Roy Earle (Humphrey Bogart) menaces Babe (Alan Curtis) as Red (Arthur Kennedy) and Marie (Ida Lupino) look on in *High Sierra*.

generally perceived. The related movies were becoming sinister cop stories effectively restricted to small budgets and even smaller talent.

Then an abrupt rediscovery of Dashiell Hammett, the appearance of the first Chandlers and favorable social atmosphere suddenly gave the hard-boiled genre acclaimed status[2] and opened the doors of the studios to receive it. The popularity of these films from Raoul Walsh's *High Sierra* and Huston's *Maltese Falcon* continued to grow until 1948. The concept of the movement underwent important modifications: they were still mining a rich vein based on the preestablished plot lines, but the new works were nonetheless different from each other due, in the best instances, to their tone or style; and if the same character appeared in several movies, it was merely by chance or on account of similar literary sources: no one but a fool would mistake the Marlowe of *Murder, My Sweet* for the one in *Lady in the Lake*. Many of these releases were of exceptional quality, often much better than one would expect from their directors (I'm thinking of Dmytryk, Hathaway, and Daves). In this regard, there are two reasons: these films were drawn from the work of talented writers, specialists in the genre such as Chandler, Burnett, Jay Dratler or Leo Rosten;[3] and the filmmakers had perfected a standard style, extremely suitable and rich in visual effects, which was just right for a type of film in which refinement acted as a counterpoint.

As fate would have it, this movement carried within itself the seeds of its own destruction. Based on shocking and surprising the viewer, it could offer even the most imaginative of screenwriters and the most diligent directors, a limited number of dramatic situations, which, after a few repetitions, could no longer achieve either shock or surprise. If the *noir* crime films–and with them, the novels–held on for eight years, it was thanks to two qualities which began as external elements: suspense[4] and documentary reality. These elements were, once again, snares. Suspense introduced a new, extremely hazardous mood, the achievement of which was appropriate to only a few situations and which concealed the problem without resolving it. As for documentary reality, its multitude of possibilities were muzzled by the nature of the genre, which soon rendered it dull and monotonous. Thus trapped in a generic prison of its own construction, in searching for a way out, the crime film could do nothing but hit its head against a wall like a frenzied fool. The gratuitous use of subjective camera such as that of Robert Montgomery in *Lady in the Lake*, the inappropriate shift to period in Sam Wood's *Ivy*, the sophomoric and distorted surrealism of Robery Florey in his tale of an amnesiac [*The Crooked Way*], all this resounded like a knell. One day, Ben Hecht, to put an end to it, hacked out, from a very bad novel by Eleazar Lipsky, a remarkable script that included to the nth degree all the archetypes of the crime genre. And as if to underscore the strengths and the weaknesses of such an enterprise, *Kiss of Death* was directed by a capable technician with a trace of individuality, Henry Hathaway (who turned out of one of the finest examples of the genre in the first half of *Dark Corner*); and *Kiss of Death* was a swan song for a formula, for a recipe, for a mother lode which exploded in one's face with a few rich nuggets but soon played out.

2. Noblissima Visione

The crime film is no longer, nor by the way is there still a crime novel. The source is dried up, and renewing it is impossible. What's left, now that it has run its course? In the wake of all the other genres that made up the best of the American

Below, studio film directed "by a capable technician," Nick (Victor Mature) and Nettie (Coleen Gray) in *Kiss of Death*.

cinema of yesteryear, the crime film, while in itself gone, remains a marvelous concept.

Inside civilized society–of which Valéry took the measure–successes, popular styles, genres are all mortal. What remains are the works, which may be good or bad but are the sincere expression of the ideas and preoccupations of their authors. In the matter before us, another historical panorama reveals itself and offers for our review *Lady of the Pavements* [Griffith, 1929], *Underworld* [Von Sternberg, 1927], *Scarface* [Hawks, 1932], a wide, mournful, and protracted long shot, until at last a few films from today predict the crime film of tomorrow.

It is out of the question for these films to renew a genre by widening its scope or intellectualizing it in some manner. It is, effectively, out of the question to renew anything but simply to express oneself by mediating any misguided mythologizing. Are not the best criteria of a work's authenticity most often its complete ingenuousness and its perfect spontaneity? Is it forbidden after considering the ably constructed *Dark Passage* with its cunning use of the camera in the opening sequences and its wry, surrealistic ending, to prefer the barely decipherable plot, the freshness and wit of *Out of the Past* directed by Jacques Tourneur from an awkward but perfectly earnest script by Geoffrey Homes [Daniel Mainwaring]? By what virtue, one can ask, is this latter film more sincere than the other? By virtue of its very awkwardness! The perfect sublimation of a genre usually comes down to its complete submission to this: to make a crime film, what's required is that it be conceived as such and no more; or, otherwise stated, that it be made from the components of a crime film. The genre demands a certain inspiration, which it hems in with its strict rules. So what is needed, one must concede, is the uncommon talent to be true to one's self while in the embrace of this rather odd enter-

Below, "so simple and so subtle that its first expression is incomprehensible": Marlowe (Humphrey Bogart, right) rescues Vivian Sternwood (Lauren Bacall) from a mugger in *The Big Sleep*.

prise (that's the wonder of *The Big Sleep*); or at least an inspiration, an aspiration, a world view in communion with the rules of the genre (exemplified by another miracle, *Laura*; and as well, from a certain point of view, by the cases of Lang and Hitchcock).

Certainly the superiority of *The Big Sleep* proves the case of function over form for which writers and directors strive. The central intrigue of this film is a model of the crime film equation with three variables (the blackmailer, the killer, the avenger) so simple and so subtle that its first expression is incomprehensible. In truth, nothing could be easier to follow, in its second rendering, than this film's line of inquiry. The only difference between the viewer and Bogart as Marlowe is that the character understands and picks up clues from the first. It would seem that this film resembles others of its type only in the measure by which it dominates them but that its deepest roots and strongest ties relate back to the total output of director Howard Hawks. It's no accident that the private detective in this instance is more perceptive and more competent than we are, and, more palpably than elsewhere, is confronted by the brutal strength of his antagonists. *The Big Sleep* is closer to *Scarface,* to *The Thing*, and even to *Monkey Business* than to Robert Montgomery's *Lady in the Lake*. One must also admit that in this instance function subordinates creation–that it markedly displaces it once and for all, because the "Hawksian" model of the hard-boiled film could never be reconstructed without creating in its turn a sterile and flaccid knock-off.

Matters present themselves somewhat differently in the case of Otto Preminger's *Laura*: here the element of pure crime drama is completely subsumed by the preselected narrative style which markedly transmutes it. The novel of Vera Caspary, from which the film is taken, is a crime fiction of the classic sort, or more precisely neo-classic, that is to say based on a less stereotyped and realistic story. In any case, it's a perfect example of a formula worn down to the bone. It's on the character plane that the distinct features of the film take off, as the writers (Preminger and Jay Dratler) push them to their logical extremes and thus create personas intrinsically attractive to the viewer, so that the course of events in which they are caught up seems to be the *only* one possible. Here things happen as if these people had existed before the crime (given that the opposite is usually true), as if they themselves were creating the intrigue, were transposing it to a place where no one dreamed of being. To underscore this effect, Preminger devised an original narrative progression (which incidentally gives his film a significant historical importance): long sequences shot with a dolly that accompanies the movements of the key characters in various scenes, in such a way that these figures are *trapped* in the frame (usually a medium close shot or an American plan [medium shot from head to ankle]) and must watch their surroundings mutate and alter according to their actions. We have demonstrated here that a crime story, done well and with depth, can simultaneously be a matter of style and conviction. Vera Caspary wrote a crime novel, Preminger shot a character piece that

Above, "figures are *trapped* in the frame (usually a medium close shot or an American plan)": Waldo Lydecker (Clifton Webb) is confronted by Det. Mark McPherson (Dana Andrews) while Shelby Carpenter (Vincent Price) looks on in *Laura*.

remains nonetheless an atypical work, because its success relies on a pre-existing mystery that fits well enough with the director's style, or, more exactly, compels the director to integrate his vision into a given crime story. Here again the film-maker takes the first step and adapts himself to the genre. And is the result, which we find admirably done, worth infinitely more than the principal of self-expression, of which we get but a half measure?

Meanwhile we can easily understand how these films were decisive stages in the peaceful struggle for the liberation of the genre and the destruction of its formulas: if deficient as prototypes they were catalysts. Accordingly we can perceive a group of films that were daring, at times falling short, but mostly remarkable, and in all cases earnest and personal, for which the crime theme was but a pretext or a means but, in any case, not an objective, I would quickly cite Welles' *Lady from Shanghai*, Nick Ray's *On Dangerous Ground* and *In A Lonely Place*,[5] Joseph Losey's *The Prowler*, Preminger's *Where the Sidewalk Ends* and *Whirlpool*, and assorted other titles which made the crime film worthy of accolades, movies which would not adhere to absurd guidelines or arbitrary classifications. On the surface we can surely see little in common between *Lady from Shanghai* and *In a Lonely Place*. For what they have in common in their very difference, is the striking honesty, face to face with their own visions, of Welles and Nicholas Ray. Rewards don't come from mining a vein but from prospecting to find it.

I can see an objection here: all the films mentioned—and they were specifically selected—derive their most obvious merit from pulling the wings off the genre; they hang from it by the slenderest of threads, which has nothing to do with their best qualities. It is not a bit dishonest to fortell the future of the crime film from this, from the very diminution of the criminal elements in these films, because, to push this thing forward to its paradoxical conclusion, could one not easily conceive an ideal evolution in which this element is purely and simply eliminated?

In truth, what may seem a diminution is, in reality, development. All these filmmakers have one thing in common: they no longer consider the crime or all the other criminal appurtenances as dramatic situations leading to variations that are more or less adroit, but see them from an ontological (in the case of Ray, Losey, or Dassin) or metaphysical (in the case of Welles, Lang, and Hitchcock) point of view.

It may be a valid approach to focus on one theme, as Proust tried to do with time or [Marcel] Jouhandeau with homosexuality. In the realm of motion pictures, this can be accomplished through the actual direction of the film, as is the case with Preminger, or through the refinement of the script in anticipation of a certain direction (Hitchcock and Welles). It can also be accomplished, if I dare say, in an autonomous fashion, in the pure refinement of the script. And, as written description is the easiest, I will take my example from this last category.

Consider Robert Wise's *Born to Kill*, which came and went without much notice. Here is an instance of the script itself embodying the value and complete originality. The flaw in the armor is in fact the direction, technically beyond reproach and occasionally powerful but, alas, terribly ordinary and typical of the genre, which the aim of the film should have been precisely to avoid being, if not to grind the genre's remains under its heel. The script is a faithful adaptation—even if the times require it to be a bit simplistic—of a novelist named James Gunn. This

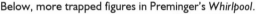

Below, more trapped figures in Preminger's *Whirlpool*.

young man wrote his book as "an exercise for a creative writing class." The curriculum gave him the initial impulse; but in the next moment he pared away the useless elements and then was exceptionally astute in selecting, as the framework of his narrative, two well-worn themes from a dying genre: a woman more monstrous than a male monster (*Deadlier than the Male* is the original title, *Tender Female* is the French title) and an old woman who becomes an amateur detective to avenge a murdered friend. These are stereotypes which he literally blows up in front of our eyes. By the mediation of a freely developed plot and an absolutely extraordinary tone, pushing each scene towards a violent, ironic, and macabre paroxysm, he succeeds in giving all these elements an unexpected dimension, a poetic depth, and, at the same, in validating his chosen themes, because they alone are capable of driving the characters to their own ends, they alone are capable of distilling their essences, they alone are capable of justifying the tone, the style, and the subject matter. Ignorant to a fault, Wise did not know how to–or simply could not–take the reins, and *Born to Kill* could not quite live up to its potential as either a complete masterpiece or as a manifesto.

Whatever it may be, spanning successes and failures, this evolution is undeniable; and no one, I think, would pine for *The Thin Man* or *Murder, My Sweet* of yesteryear while watching today's *In A Lonely Place* or *The Prowler*. For those who remain unconvinced by the strength of my argument, I've kept an ace up my sleeve. Here it is, the crime film of tomorrow, free from all restraints and its own roots, illuminating with its powerful vision the unspeakable abyss. To make it harder, they chose the worst material imaginable, the most pitiful and sickening product of a genre fallen into putrefaction: a novel by Mickey Spillane. From a crushed, discolored, and chewed-up sow's ear, Robert Aldrich and A.I. Bezzerides[6] have violently and sure-handedly fashioned a silk purse embellished with elaborate and fanciful patterns. In *Kiss Me Deadly* the usual aspects of the crime film aren't even on screen, but merely lurks in the undercurrent for the unenlightened. It's about something more profound and unveils alluring images of Death, Fear, Love, and Horror. Still all the elements are there: the tough detective with a familiar name, atomic age gangsters with glass jaws, cops, beauties in bathing suits, and a bleached blonde killer. Who would not recognize them, who would be embarassed not to recognize them, unmasked, their measure taken, these sinister acquaintances from the past?

Crisis in the genre, proclaims the straightforward observer! As if the genre was not what its authors made it!

Translated from the French by Alain Silver
and Christiane Silver

Notes

1. It's called Louise Brooks.

2. Although the genre had existed for some time, its recognized source was the pulp magazine *Black Mask* which published the first short stories of Chandler, Hammett, Cornell Woolrich, and Raoul Whitfield. Moreover, *The Maltese Falcon* and *the Glass Key* had already been made into very low budget movies around 1933.

3. Editors' Note: W.R. Burnett, novelist and screenwriter (*The Asphalt Jungle, Beast of the City, High Sierra, I Died A Thousand Times, Nobody Lives Forever, The Racket, This Gun for Hire*); Jay Dratler, screenwriter (*Call Northside 777, The Dark Corner, Laura, Pitfall*); Leo Rosten, screenwriter (*The Dark Corner, Sleep My Love, Where Danger Lives*).

4. It is very difficult to define clearly the boundaries of the "suspense" film and those of the "thriller." In a literary context, the former is closer to William Irish [Cornell Woolrich], and the latter to Chandler. In actuality they have always been intermingled.

5. It appears that Ray chose to adapt some of the most highly regarded writers in the genre. *On Dangerous Ground* is taken from a good novel by Gerald Butler, **Mad with Much Heart**. As for *In a Lonely Place*, it is very, very loosely drawn from an excellent work by Dorothy B. Hughes (to whom we owe the story for *Ride the Pink Horse*) also entitled **In a Lonely Place**.

6. Bezzerides is one current Hollywood's best screenwriters: breaking in with the adaptation of his novel **Thieves' Market** for Jules Dassin (*Thieves' Highway*). He has since been screenwriter and adapter on *Beneath the Twelve Mile Reef, On Dangerous Ground*, and other solidly crafted films rich in original ideas. The character of "Nick" in *Kiss Me Deadly* is a typical Bezzerides creation... One can get an idea of the physical aspect of this fascinating personality in the beginning of *On Dangerous Ground*: he's the second tempter of Robert Ryan (who wants to bribe him).

Below, "a bleached blonde killer" with a shiny gun, Lily Carver (Gaby Rodgers) in *Kiss Me Deadly*.

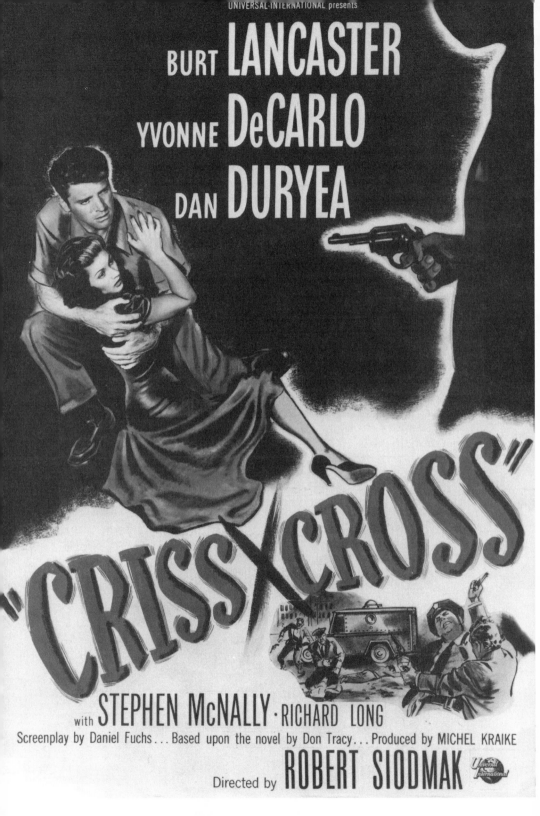

Above, one sheet for *Criss Cross*.

Three Faces of *Film Noir*

Tom Flinn (1972)

Rather than hazarding a definition of *film noir*, a thankless task which, hopefully, will be broached elsewhere in this magazine, this article contains a descriptive analysis of three films that the author paradoxically considers both typical and distinctive. Together they provide a sample of the *noir* output from the important years of 1940, 1944, and 1949. This in no way attempts to trace the limits of *film noir* since that style continued well into the Fifties and is still subject to periodic revivals. But *film noir*, like shoulder pads, wedgies, and zoot suits was an essential part of the Forties outlook, a cinematic style forged in the fires of war, exile, and disillusion, a melodramatic reflection for a world gone mad.

One of the earliest American examples of the *film noir* is *Stranger on the Third Floor*, an ambitious sixty-five minute "B" film made in 1940 at R.K.O. Although not entirely successful, it is extremely audacious in terms of what it seeks to say about American society, and particularly impressive in view of the way in which it pre-dicts the conventions of the *film noir*. *Stranger on the Third Floor* was directed by Boris Ingster and scripted by Frank Partos, who deserves full credit for the the-matic content of the film since he adapted it from his own story.

Like most *noir* films, *Stranger on the Third Floor* takes place in an urban milieu, in this case a studio-built New York of sleazy rooming houses and rundown restau-rants, populated by hostile strangers and prying neighbors. The protagonist, Mi-chael Ward, is a young journalist who discovers a murder at an all-night beanery. His exclusive story on the crime and the subsequent publicity get him the raise he needs to marry his girlfriend, but his testimony implicates a young ex-con (Elisha Cook Jr.) who is railroaded towards the chair by a conviction hungry D.A. The trial of the ex-con is a vicious rendering of the American legal system hard at work on an impoverished victim. The film displays a fine sense of caricature espe-cially apparent in the figure of the judge, who when roused from a judicial stupor reprimands a sleeping juror. A realistic assessment of the gullibility of the average jury and a cynical appraisal of the sinister role of the police and prosecutors in ob-taining confessions and convictions were hallmarks of the hard-boiled literature that paralleled and predicted what we call *film noir*. But even in Bay City, Ray-mond Chandler's outpost of corruption, trials were conducted with more deco-rum than is evidence in the legal proceedings in *Stranger on the Third Floor*. In the film the congenital cynicism of the genre is personified by Ward's elder colleague and mentor on the newspaper–the newspaper reporter being traditionally the most hardened of mortals (*Ace in the Hole*)–who spends most of his time mixing wisecracks and whiskey at the press club bar.

Moved by the sincerity of the ex-con's courtroom outbursts, Ward begins to feel pangs of guilt, since it was his testimony that completed the web of circumstantial evidence responsible for the conviction. Back in his grimy room, he suddenly realizes that his obnoxious next-door neighbor, Mr. Meng (Charles Halton at his slimiest) is not snoring as usual. When banging on the wall does not bring an answer from the normally sensitive neighbor, Ward flashes back to several "run-ins" he had with Meng involving threats he had made on Meng's life. At this point Ward's paranoia reaches epic proportions and is expressed in a marvelously apt expressionistic dream sequence that is the psychological center of the film. Unlike the neat, modish Freudian dream montages of the fashionable Forties films of psychoanalysis (*Spellbound*), the dream in *Stranger on the Third Floor* is alive with subconscious desires, seething with repressions, awash with pent-up hatred, and constructed from the nightmarish circumstances of the character's real situation.

Ward's paranoia links him to other denizens of the urban jungles of Hollywood's nightmare films of the Forties, where the dividing line between dream and reality can be merely the whim of a director, as in Fritz Lang's *Woman in the Window* (dream) and *Scarlet Street* (reality). In *Stranger on the Third Floor* Ward's paranoia fantasy works because the twin motivations of guilt (for participating in the sham trial) and fear (of being caught up in the system himself) are well established; while the climax of the dream in which the "victim," Meng, attends Ward's execution functions perfectly as dream logic expressing Ward's strong subconscious desire that Meng be alive.

The dream sequence itself is so completely expressionistic in style that it resembles an animation of one of Lynd Ward's woodcut novels (**God's Man, Madman's Drum**) with strong contrasts in lighting, angular shadow patterns, and distorted, emblematic architecture; in short, a kind of total stylization that manages to be both extremely evocative and somewhat theatrical. The use of a tilted camera destroys the normal play of horizontals and verticals, creating a forest of oblique angles recalling the unsettling effects of expressionist painting and cinema. This tilted camera was a favorite device of horror director James Whale (*Bride of Frankenstein*, 1935) and it later enjoyed a great vogue around 1950 (*The Third Man, Strangers on a Train*). In *Stranger on the Third Floor* the Germanic influence, so important in the creation of the *film noir* style, is quite obvious, and not confined to the dream sequence. Throughout the film the lighting by Nick Musuraca is very much in the baroque Forties manner with numerous shadow patterns on the walls.

Peter Lorre, who appears only briefly in Ward's dream, brings a full expressionistic approach to his brief role as an escaped lunatic, slithering through a door in a manner distinctly reminiscent of Conrad Veidt in *The Cabinet of Dr. Caligari*. In

1940 Lorre was quite thin and much more graceful than he had been in his debut as the pudgy child murderer in *M* made nine years earlier. Actually his role though even briefer than in *M* is quite similar, and in both films he manages to obtain the audience's sympathy in the final moments with just a few lines of dialogue.

Working in a more naturalistic style, Charles Halton portrays a particularly obnoxious specimen of hypocritical busybody, a vicious prude who is totally fascinated by sex; while Elisha Cook Jr. is suitably intense as the unjustly accused ex-con.

Unfortunately, John McGuire as Ward is stiff and reserved, though he does perform near the top of his limited range (compared with his disastrous role in John Ford's *Steamboat Round the Bend*). On the positive side McGuire handles a considerable amount of voice-story narration quite well, and his very vapidness is an aid to audience identification.

In comparison Margaret Tallichet (who later became Mrs. William Wyler) gives a remarkably honest and unaffected performance as Ward's fiancée. More sensitive than Ward, she is first to sense the disastrous effects of his involvement with the murder trial on their relationship. Later when Ward is being held for the murder of Meng, she searches for the man with a scarf (Lorre) who actually committed both murders. Thus in its last moments *Stranger on the Third Floor* becomes a girl-detective yarn. This segment of the film clearly prefigures *Phantom Lady* (1944) in which another working girl (both are secretaries) searches for the elusive witness that will save her man from the chair.

Thematically, *Phantom Lady*, based on a tepid thriller by Cornell Woolrich, is far less interesting than *Stranger on the Third Floor*; but Robert Siodmak's mise-en-scene is so exciting that other considerations pale in the face of his inventive direction. Like *Stranger on the Third Floor*, *Phantom Lady* concerns an innocent man convicted of murder, but Siodmak's work lacks the specific social criticism of the earlier film, though it retains the aura of menace in its portrait of the city, a quality that is absolutely de rigueur for any *film noir*. *Phantom Lady* was also filmed on studio sets, though in contrast to *Stranger on the Third Floor* the atmosphere of New York City sweltering in mid-summer heat is evoked with extreme veracity. With one or two exceptions the sets are near perfect in their simulation of reality, demonstrating a far greater interest in realism than is evident in pre-WW II films. The realistic atmosphere of the decor is aided by Siodmak's sparing use of background music, all the more remarkable in an era of "wall to wall" scoring. The suspense sequences, in particular, benefit from an adroit use of naturalistic sound.

With *Phantom Lady*, Siodmak, who had served a tough apprenticeship in America (directing five "A" pictures followed by "vehicles" for two of Universal's biggest attractions, Lon Chaney Jr. and Maria Montez), established himself as one of the foremost stylists of *film noir*, creating a sombre world of wet streets, dingy offices, low-ceilinged bars, crowded lunchcounters and deserted railway platforms, all unified by an atmosphere of heightened realism in which the expressive quality of the image is due entirely to lighting and composition. Siodmak arrived at this UFA-esque style naturally, since he directed in Germany from 1928-33. On *Phantom Lady* he enjoyed the services of legendary *noir* cameraman Elwood Bredell, who, according to George Amy, could "light a football stadium with a single match."

For a film of bravura visual style *Phantom Lady* opens rather unpromisingly on a closeup of Ann Terry (Fay Helm). Wearing one of those improbable creations that only Forties milliners could envisage, Miss Helm looks very much like a middle-aged neurotic left over from a Val Lewton film. Into Anselmo's Bar comes Scott Henderson, successful civil engineer on the brink of marital disaster. He suggests that they pool their loneliness ("no questions, no names") and take in a show, typically one of those Latin revues so popular in that era of Pan American solidarity. After the show he deposits his companion back at Anselmo's and returns to his wife's apartment. Here the nightmare begins. When he turns on the light he notices the room is already occupied by a formidable triumvirate of police officers (Thomas Gomez, Joseph Crehan, and Regis Toomey). Siodmak stages the confrontation with his usual flair; breaking the rules by deliberately crossing the axis during the interrogation to emphasize Henderson's isolation, framing him with a portrait of his murdered wife in the background, and tracking in slowly on the suspect (Henderson) while the cops deliver a snide, menacing third degree.

Like Ward in *Stranger on the Third Floor*, Scott Henderson is caught in an impenetrable web of circumstantial evidence, though his situation is further complicated, since a number of witnesses were bribed by the real murderer in an attempt to destroy Henderson's alibi (already very weak since he could not produce the "Phantom Lady" he took to the "Chica Boom Boom Revue").

In contrast to *Stranger on the Third Floor*, Siodmak handles Henderson's trial obliquely. The camera never shows the accused, the judge, the jury, or any of the lawyers. Only the voice of the prosecutor (Milburn Stone) relates the proceedings as the camera dwells on the spectators, singling out Henderson's secretary, Kansas (Ella Raines) and Inspector Burgess (Thomas Gomez). The trial sequence serves as a transition. Kansas and Inspector Burgess become, in effect, the new protagonists in the search to prove Henderson's innocence.

Kansas, like Ward's fiancée in *Stranger on the Third Floor*, is a determined innocent who contrasts sharply with the corrupt society she must search. This juxtaposition was a favorite device in Forties films, reaching its climax in *The Seventh Victim* (Val Lewton/Mark Robson, 1945) in which schoolgirl Kim Hunter ferrets out a colony of Satanists in Greenwich Village. Kansas (the name reeks of Midwestern grit and determination) begins her quest by dogging the night bartender at Anselmo's (Andrew Toombes). Seated at the end of the bar she watches and waits. On the third night of her vigil she follows the bartender through the wet streets to a deserted El station where Siodmak emphasizes the vulnerability of his protagonist with a quick turnaround, in which the hunter becomes the hunted. Undaunted, Kansas follows the bartender downtown through narrow streets where, long after midnight, the residents are still lounging on their front stoops and the atmosphere is charged with latent violence.

The high point of her search (and of the film) is her encounter with Cliff Milburn (Elisha Cook Jr.), the trap drummer in the orchestra at the "Chica Boom Boom Revue." Seated in the front row, dressed in a black satin sheath, and chewing at least three sticks of gum, Kansas is about as inconspicuous as Princess Grace on the Bowery. Naturally she has no trouble picking up the hapless musician and he takes her to a jam session which ranks as one of the most effective bits of cinema produced in the Forties. Siodmak gives full rein to his expressionistic propensities in a rhythmically cut riot of angles that "climaxes" in a drum solo that melds sex and music into a viable metaphor of tension and release.

Unfortunately, the last half of *Phantom Lady* is dominated by Jack Lombard (Franchot Tone), the real murderer, who is afflicted with delusions of grandeur, migraine headaches, and overly emphatic hand gestures. Van Gogh's "Self-portrait with a Bandaged Ear" on Lombard's studio wall neatly identifies him as the mad artist, but he comes off more like a re-fried Howard Roarke (*The Fountainhead*) than Van Gogh. Though he sounds vaguely Nietzschean, "When you've got my gifts you can't afford to let them get away," Lombard generated very little excitement.

Below, "*Phantom Lady* is primarily a work of style."

Phantom Lady is primarily a work of style, created by the interaction of considerable intelligence (on the part of the director, producer, and cameraman) with very bland pulp writing (Woolrich's novel). Some of the dialogue is, as James Agee has pointed out, depressingly banal, but the film is redeemed by the originality of its mise-en-scene and by its all-pervading style which represents a considerable advance over the more overtly expressionistic *Stranger on the Third Floor*.

In the pessimistic post-war years, the *noir* influence grew like an orchid in General Sternwood's overheated greenhouse. Rare indeed was the Hollywood melodrama that did not include some *noir* element or theme. The influence of Italian neo-realism combined with already existing domestic tendencies toward location shooting to produce an expressive, increasingly veristic style tinged with violence and sadism. At the same time plots of bewildering complexity proliferated as Hollywood's affair with the flashback reached the height of absurdity during the period from *Passage to Marseille* (1944) to *The Locket* (1948). The newsreel reporter of *Citizen Kane* reappeared as the insurance investigator in Siodmak's *The Killers* (1946), while the comedies of Preston Sturges, such as *The Miracle at Morgan's Creek* (1944) and *Mad Wednesday* (1947) have intricate plots worthy of the author of "narratage."

Siodmak's *Criss Cross* (1949) combines complexity of narrative, a realism born of location shooting, and Siodmak's expressive stylizations. The opening aerial shot of Los Angeles sets the tone for what proves to be a fascinating chronicle of lower and middle class life in the western metropolis. Much of the action in *Criss Cross* takes place in the shadow of the funicular railway (Angel's Flight) in the Bun-

Below, "Kansas" (Ella Raines) and Inspector Burgess (Thomas Gomez) in *Phantom Lady*.

none of the films made from his books or scripts can compare with *Criss Cross* in the evocation of this milieu):

> Bunker Hill is old town, lost town, shabby town, crook town. Once very long ago, it was the choice residential district of the city, and there are still standing a few of the jigsaw Gothic mansions with wide porches and walls covered with round-end shingles and full corner bay windows with spindle turrets. They are all rooming houses now, their parquetry floors are scratched and worn through the once glossy finish and the wide sweeping staircases are dark with time and with cheap varnish laid on over generations of dirt. In the tall rooms haggard landladies bicker with shifty tenants. On the wide cool front porches, reaching their cracked shoes into the sun, and staring at nothing, sit the old men with faces like lost battles...

Criss Cross attains a kind of formal excellence, due to the tautness of its complex narrative structure, the uncompromising nature of its resolution, and the inexorable character of its Germanic fatalism. The film opens *in medias res* with Steve Thompson (Burt Lancaster) and Anna (Yvonne de Carlo) sharing a furtive kiss in the parking lot of the Rondo Club. The reason for their secrecy soon becomes obvious. Anna is married to Slim Dundee (Dan Duryea), a local tough guy who is giving himself a farewell party in a private room at the club. Gradually the audience becomes aware that Steve and Slim, obvious rivals, are connected in a robbery scheme. The action continues the next day as Steve, driving an armored truck, picks up a huge cash payroll at the bank. During the forty-minute run to the plant at San Raphelo, Steve reviews the intricate chain of circumstances that brought him into the robbery. By opening in the middle, the audience is forced to accept the central situation (the robbery) as reality, and the contrived circumstances leading up to it are given additional credence.

The success of *Criss Cross*'s fatalistic mood depends to a large extent on the complex relationship between Steve and Anna. Anna is a creature of dazzling insincerity, another in the seemingly endless succession of Forties *femmes fatales*. The archetype is, of course, Mary Astor hiding her Machiavellian designs behind a mask of gentility in *The Maltese Falcon* (1941). Barbara Stanwyck in *Double Indemnity* (1943) was of a tougher, less bourgeois breed, that reappeared with subtle variations in Siodmak's *The Killers* (1946) (Ava Gardner) and Tourneur's *Out of the Past* (1948) (Jane Greer). Anna definitely belongs to this second class of fatal women, although her essential coldness and grasping ambition are accompanied by immaturity, a general ineffectualness, and vulnerability. Her hold on her ex-husband Steve depends on his feeling sorry for her. She is, in fact, persecuted by the police (at the instigation of Steve's mother), and tortured by Slim. But she finds it difficult to overcome the spectre of divorce, with its overtones of betrayal and failure, which divides her from Steve and reflects the film's central theme of treachery.

and failure, which divides her from Steve and reflects the film's central theme of treachery.

Anna is always seen from Steve's point of view for *Criss Cross*, like a Chandler novel, is set firmly in the first person. Steve narrates his flashbacks, supplying additional motivation and coloring events with his own fatalism. Siodmak complements the first person nature of the script (by Daniel Fuchs) with a number of subjective shots which make crucial thematic points. Steve's loneliness is expressed in a shot of his brother and future sister-in-law kissing in a corner of the dining room seen from Steve's point of view on the living room couch. A far more frightening example of the same technique occurs after the robbery goes haywire and Steve ends up in the hospital with his arm and shoulder in traction. Here Siodmak uses numerous subjective shots that force the audience to participate in Steve's nightmare situation. Lying helpless in the hospital bed he waits for Slim's vengeance, playing a cat and mouse game with a traveling salesman (Adam Williams), who turns out to be one of Slim's hirelings. The "salesman" snatches Steve from the hospital in a scene that can only be described as a paroxysm of pain. The ever-venal Williams is too easily bribed to take Steve to Anna instead of Slim, and the executioner is not far behind.

The role of Steve Thompson is so important to the film that those offended by Lancaster's mannerisms may not enjoy *Criss Cross*, in spite of a number of excellent character portrayals: Percy Helton, the rotund bartender with a voice like a

Below, Slim Dundee (Dan Duryea, left) catches up to Steve Thompson (Burt Lancaster) and the unfaithful Anna (Yvonne de Carlo) at the fatal conclusion of *Criss Cross*.

wood rasp; Dan Duryea, with or without an icepick, the ideal pimp and small-timer of the decade; Tom Pedi, Slim's henchman Vincent, who delivers his dialogue with a greedy verve ("That's the ticket"); John Doucette, another of the gang, with a dour voice to match his sombre personality; and Alan Napier, Finchley, the alcoholic mastermind of the big "heist."

The central importance of the robbery in *Criss Cross* demonstrates an increasing interest in criminal methods and mythology. *Criss Cross* is actually a "caper" film, a subgenre of the gangster film that can be traced back to *High Sierra* (1940) and further. The caper film concentrates all values and expectations on one last crime which, if successful, will put all the participants on easy street. The influence of *Criss Cross* can be seen in subsequent caper films including John Huston's *The Asphalt Jungle* (1950) where Sam Jaffe's Doc Riedenschneider resembles a Germanized Finchley, and Stanley Kubrick's *The Killing* (1956) which carries the temporal experimentation of *Criss Cross* to the point of absurdity.

Although *Criss Cross* has a more realistic, less decorative look than *Phantom Lady*, both films demonstrate similar photographic stylization. The sharp, fluid, high contrast photography and low key lighting in *Criss Cross* are the work of Franz Planer, another old UFA colleague of Siodmak's and another link between Weimar cinema and *film noir*. Siodmak himself never lost a taste for the "disguised" symbolism found in German silents. In one symbolic cut he juxtaposes his principals, appropriately clad in black and white, to form a visual pun on "criss cross".

As in *Phantom Lady*, Siodmak displays a real interest in American popular music, including a number by Esy Morales and his band which, unlike most Forties musical numbers, is an impressive musical performance, well integrated into the context of the film. Miklós Rózsa, who ranks as the chief composer for *film noir* (*Double Indemnity*, *The Killers*, ad infinitum) provided an effective score with garish harmonies that mirror the harsh conflicts of the narrative.

By 1949 the battle against that scourge of Hollywood known as the "happy ending" was largely won, and the essential pessimism of the *film noir* could be fulfilled. As a result, *Criss Cross* has a thematic completeness that *Stranger on the Third Floor* and *Phantom Lady* lack. Slim stalks into the doorway of the beachhouse hideout like an avenging angel, awakening memories of other destiny figures, Bernard Goetzke visiting the young couple in Lang's *Der Mude Tod* (1921), or Hitu hounding the lovers in Murnau's *Tabu* (1931). With its thematic pessimism, realistic mise-en-scene, and aura of ambient fatalism, *Criss Cross* reflects something of the mood of a country about to discover the apocalyptic nature of the coming decade of nuclear stalemate.

Above, Miildred Pierce (Joan Crawford, left) sacrifices everything for her daughter Veda (Ann Blyth) in *Mildred Pierce*.

Violence and the Bitch Goddess

Stephen Farber (1974)

There are essentially two types of violent heroes in American films, those who perform the violence sanctioned by their society (soldiers, Western sheriffs, police detectives, business tycoons) and those who direct their violence *against* society (criminals, delinquents, rebels, and outsiders). Of course the two characters overlap; they share some of the same qualities. But I do think some interesting distinctions can be drawn.

The respectable heroes of American films often pursue their enemies with a fierceness and intolerance harsher than their duties require. Propagandistic Second World War movies ruthlessly stereotyped the Germans and especially the Japanese, celebrated American boys for cheerfully and pitilessly eliminating the Yellow Peril. The last image of *Bataan*—Robert Taylor turning his machine gun on the Japanese, and letting go in a near orgasmic fury of "righteous" slaughter—summarizes the hideous brutality that American war movies have exalted in the name of freedom and democracy.

In a movie like *Bataan*, since the aims of the American soldiers are defined as noble, their violence must be applauded. In Westerns, which provide a mythic idealization of violence in America, the "good" hero is allowed to use any means—including murder—to eradicate the "evil" in his society. We are told that the Westerner acts only defensively, never offensively (indeed, that is generally a justification for violence in American films), but this distinction blurs very easily. The hero's right to kill is rarely brought under question. Violence in these films reflects the moralistic complacency of the figures of authority, and grows from a tendency to dehumanize those who threaten the status quo.

The same kinds of complacency and intolerance are characteristic of policemen heroes of American films. Until very recently cops have generally been secondary characters in American movies. But the phenomenally successful *Dirty Harry* and *The French Connection* have spawned a couple of dozen police movies that are often implicitly fascist in their celebration of vigilante justice and their respect for the "order" provided by a billy club.

A more popular genre over the years has been the detective story, and although the private eye has often been presented as more independent and iconoclastic than his uniformed counterpart, many of these movies also have

45

Above, "a particularly ugly version of the American detective," Mike Hammer (Ralph Meeker, left) grins at small-time gangster Carl Evello (Paul Stewart) in *Kiss Me Deadly*.

authoritarian overtones. A particularly ugly version of the American detective was created by Mickey Spillane in the early postwar years and became the hero of several American films of the middle Fifties—the only interesting one of which was Robert Aldrich's *Kiss Me Deadly*, because it subtly criticized its own hero. Spillane's Mike Hammer is the private eye as sadistic vigilante, on a personal crusade to save America from the scourge of Communists and degenerates. Hammer makes his own laws, carries out his own vendettas, all in the name of freedom and the American Way. Brutal, merciless, anti-intellectual, Hammer flourished during the McCarthy era and carried to an ugly extreme the deep-rooted American belief that the ends justify the means.

In these genre films violence is intuitively celebrated as being consistent with the highest American ideals; violence almost seems to be the most appropriate expression of American aspirations. The drive for success is by nature violent. America exalts the *rugged* individualist, the self-made man who wins a place in the sun on his own initiative, regardless of the means that he uses in his struggle to the top. We reward the ruthless businessman, the robber baron, the man with a gun.

Seen in one way, the gangster film is only a dark parody of a national myth. The gangster can be understood as a mutant variation on the American rugged individualist, living a perverted version of the American Dream; he acts out the wishes and values of the successful businessman, but with the high-sounding moral rationalizations stripped away. *Scarface* contains a burlesque of the traditional entrepreneur. And Howard Hawks' film often plays as a weird black comedy. Tony seeks the same trappings of success that respectable Americans are taught to pursue. On the way to the top he acquires a fancy apartment, an elegant lounging robe, even a secretary, in imitation of the aristocratic gangster whom he admires; in one witty scene he shows off his bullet-proof shutters to his girlfriend as if he were demonstrating gold lamé curtains. His credo is one that most Americans would respond to: "Do it first, do it yourself, and keep on doing it." The only difference is that Scarface does it with a machine gun.

In the late Forties, prizefight movies like *Champion* and *Body and Soul* were more self-conscious attempts to comment on the violence that the success drive stimulates. The heroes of those two movies become prizefighters because they have been rejected by American society, and they express their resentment by fighting in the ring. Yet in releasing their aggressiveness, the fighters, like the gangsters, are enacting a bizarre parody of the prototypical American success story. These movies take the form of poor boy making good, and they even include the standard Hollywood montage sequences for success stories (whether backstage musicals or prestige biographies or gangster films) in which brief shots of the hero's rise to fame are cut together in crescendo rhythm to create the sense of exhilaration that attends "making it" America-style. But for the prizefighter, as for the gangster, success leads finally to corruption and death, for the fighter has once again made the violence implicit in the American success story too *explicit*. In *Champion*, when Arthur Kennedy, the goody-goody brother of the heel-hero, Kirk Douglas, criticized him for his heartlessness after he fires his first manager, Douglas replies that the prizefight business is no different from any other business in America except that it brings the blood out into the open.

Below, "a poor boy making good," Charlie Davis (John Garfield) abandons Peg (Lilli Palmer), the girl from his old neighborhood, in *Body and Soul*.

In *Body and Soul* too, the fight business seems to heighten the violence that is usually more subtly manifested in America. As the evil promoter Roberts says, "It's a free country. Everything's for sale." Friends are betrayed, good women left behind, honor smothered during the fighter's ascent, and he is eventually at the mercy of the syndicate to which he has sold himself. The brutality of the prizefight racket is intended as a metaphor for the corruption of the spirit in a belligerent capitalist society; Charlie's success as a fighter turns him into a "money machine." And it is interesting that in both of these films, when the hero finally decides to take a stand against the system that has victimized him, he does it by deciding to win that fight that he has been told to lose. The only alternative to his acquiescence in the ruthless spiral of success is another act of violence; he seems hopelessly trapped.[1]

Norman Podhoretz has written about success in an autobiographical study of his own career, *Making It* (1967): "My second purpose in telling the story of my own career is to provide a concrete setting for a diagnosis of the curiously contradictory feelings our culture instills in us toward the ambition for success, and toward each of its various goals: money, power, fame, and social position . . . On the one hand, 'the exclusive worship of the bitch-goddess SUCCESS,' as William James put it in a famous remark, 'is our national disease'; on the other hand, a contempt for success is the consensus of the national literature for the past hundred years or more. On the one hand, our culture teaches us to shape our lives in accordance with the hunger for worldly things; on the other hand, it spitefully contrives to make us ashamed of the presence of those hungers in ourselves and to deprive us as far as possible of any pleasure in their satisfaction."

These comments about the ambivalence toward success in American culture generally are closely echoed in Robert J. Warshow's provocative remarks about the gangster film, in his famous essay on "The Gangster as Tragic Hero": "At bottom, the gangster is doomed because he is under the obligation to succeed, not because the means he employs are unlawful. In the deeper layers of the modern consciousness, *all* means are unlawful, every attempt to succeed is an act of aggression, leaving one alone and guilty and defenseless among enemies: one is *punished* for success. This is our intolerable dilemma: that failure is a kind of death and success is evil and dangerous, is–ultimately–impossible."

The dream of success is pursued fiercely, but it is also haunted by intense feelings of guilt and fear, and in the imaginations of the people who dramatize American success stories, these feelings of guilt and fear find expression in images of terror and violence. The success story is most often told as a story of destruction and betrayal. The crucial American drama of "Making It" slips again and again into dark, lurid melodrama.

During the Forties particularly, many success stories were also murder stories. One interesting genre was the woman's picture. During the war years and immediately afterward, strong women flourished in American films, and were often presented as monsters and harpies, hardened by greed and lust, completely without feeling for the suffering they caused. These films undoubtedly reflected the fantasies and fears of a wartime society, in which women had taken control of many of the positions customarily held by men. Fear of the violence that may attend success is a recurring anxiety in American films, but during the war years another psychological dimension was added to this anxiety—fear of the evil, overpowering woman with a shocking ability to humiliate and emasculate her men.[2]

The Postman Always Rings Twice, for example, concerns a woman who marries an older man for the money and security he can provide, and is eventually led to murder him because he is not ambitious enough to satisfy her greed. After she and her lover murder her husband, they fix up his roadside café as a stylish garden restaurant and turn it into a flourishing business enterprise.

The same type of scheming materialistic woman is the heroine of *The Strange Love of Martha Ivers*. As a child Martha has been perverted by her aunt's greed. In a moment of rebellion, she murders her aunt and then is trapped by the deed—and by her own irrepressible love of luxury—into living out the rest of her life in an ironic tribute to her aunt's values. She becomes a hard, ruthless businesswoman who controls her weakling husband by depriving him of sex; eventually she tries to convince an old childhood flame to murder her husband. In both of these movies money and the success drive are blamed for the heroine's viciousness. Violence is the inevitable result of the evil woman's ambition.

Below, Sam Masterson (Van Heflin) is almost enmeshed by the "heroine's viciousness" as Martha (Barbara Stanwyck) watches in *The Strange Love of Martha Ivers*.

Billy Wilder's *Double Indemnity* (1944), remarkably similar in theme, chronicles a murder plot growing from a pervasive American fantasy of outsmarting the insurance company. Walter Neff (Fred MacMurray) is a cynical insurance agent who has always toyed with the idea of cheating his company with the perfect scheme. And Phyllis Dietrichson (Barbara Stanwyck), the married woman with whom he falls in love, plays on his vanity. She lets him feel that he is making the plans and triumphing over his corporation, while all the while she is manipulating *him* in her own scheme to win her elderly husband's money. Her avarice is completely cold-blooded, while Walter at least acts out of passion–admittedly of a sleazy variety– as well as greed. Phyllis shows no emotion at all after the murder of her husband; her mind is racing ahead to how she will get rid of Walter so that she can have the insurance money all to herself. The diabolical woman whose only lust is greed has rarely been more chillingly rendered.

A few years later, in Anatole Litvak's *Sorry Wrong Number* (1948), Barbara Stanwyck created another memorable portrait of the domineering American wife. Leona Stevenson meets her husband Henry (Burt Lancaster) at a college dance when she cuts in on a friend who is dancing with him; she then begins to chase him quite furiously, in a complete reversal of conventional courting procedures. Leona's father is a business tycoon, the head of a major drug company, and Leona dangles the prospect of success before the working-class Henry. When she first meets him at the dance, she asks him to come for a ride in her expensive Euro-

Below, Leona Stevenson (Barbara Stanwyck) is stalked in *Sorry, Wrong Number*. Opposite, anxious conspirators to murder, Cora (Lana Turner) and Frank (John Garfield) in *The Postman Always Rings Twice*.

pean car, and offers him a cigarette from her gold case; she seals their courtship by offering him a lucrative job with her father's company. It is at this point that he grabs her for the first time and kisses her. The "love-match" seems indistinguishable from a business match; Leona has no qualms about buying love with her wealth and position. At the marriage ceremony she recites the wedding vow with implacable determination. When she says fiercely, "I Leona take thee, Henry," it is a declaration not of love but of brutal possession. Leona claims to love Henry, but her only way of showing it is by offering riches. The film draws an interesting connection between Leona's sexual aggressiveness and her materialism—a connection that most of the Forties 'black-widow' pictures imply consciously or unconsciously.

Once they are married, Leona asserts her domination over Henry with complete pitilessness. She refuses to let him leave her father's business or even her father's house (her Oedipal fixation is a fairly ludicrous example of the pop Freudianism so prevalent in Forties movies) and constantly reminds him of his dependence on her. When he tries to fight her, she develops a phony psychosomatic heart condition to keep him at her mercy. In some measure we understand and share her husband's frustration and resentment of her domination, and we feel she almost deserves the brutal murder that he plots for her at the end of the film. It is her own ruthless possessiveness that leads to her violent death.

At the same time, Henry's ambition makes him a willing victim. He is attracted to Leona for the very qualities that later stifle him—her success, her confidence, her toughness; he clearly loves her gilt life too much to give it up, even when his dignity is smothered by her power. Recalling his humble past, Henry tells Leona's father, "I couldn't go back to Grassville." He relishes his position in her father's business—as we can see in the brief scenes that show him ordering people around in his office and in the restaurant where he has lunch. Henry is just as ambitious and ruthless as Leona; his only complaint is that he wants to make it on his own, without having to depend on her patronizing favors. He wants *more* than what she gives him. Both Henry and Leona are familiar American characters—the ambitious businessman on the make, the heiress of the *nouveaux riches*—portrayed very harshly; their values contain the seeds of violence.

Mildred Pierce (Michael Curtiz, 1945) also concerns the terrible price a woman must pay for power, wealth, and success. In this film the domineering woman is split in two: the good Mildred Pierce (Joan Crawford), the bad daughter Veda (Ann Blyth). Mildred's ambition appears to be essentially generous—she only wants the good things in life for her two daughters. But all of the horror connected with ambition is projected onto Veda; she has absorbed the poison from her mother's success drive, and she grows up a greedy, heartless monster, who eventually becomes a remorseless killer. Mildred's values have nourished murder.

Mildred makes innumerable mistakes in her struggle to provide her daughters with the material possessions that she never had. When her husband Bert loses his job, she nags him incessantly about getting a high-paying job so that she can bring up her girls in style. She wants more than anything for the girls "to amount to something." So she buys expensive piano lessons for Veda, expensive ballet lessons for Kay. As she tells Bert coldly, "Those kids come first in this house. I'm determined to do the best I can for them."

Before long she loses Bert. To keep providing for her girls, she gets a job as a waitress, but she isn't doing well enough, and she arranges to buy property to open her own restaurant. Soon she is running a chain of restaurants and is a successful Los Angeles tycoon. And she has clearly been tainted by her success; in true Hollywood fashion, the change in her appearance defines her moral transformation. Her hair is now piled on top of her head, and her clothes become more severe and more mannish, her face haughtier and colder. In the opening scenes Mildred looks soft and womanly; at the height of her success, she has the harsh glint of a frigid career woman. She treats the decadent aristocrat Monte Barrigan (Zachary Scott), from whom she bought her first piece of land, with emasculating contemptuousness. Yet when her daughter pleads for the fancy life that Monte represents, Mildred humbles herself and goes to him to propose marriage, offering him a one-third share in the business as payment. As he bends to kiss her to seal the bargain, she mutters coldly, "Sold. One Barrigan." Mildred has sold everything—her husband, her feminine warmth, even her self-respect—to give her girls the rich material life that she thinks they must have. She is clearly an accomplice in Veda's growing corruption.

Below, Mildred (Joan Crawford) and her "decadent aristocrat" Monty Barrigan (Zachary Scott) in *Mildred Pierce*.

Mildred Pierce warns of the punishment that shadows success. At every turn Mildred suffers for her ambition. Her younger daughter Kay dies of pneumonia. And she loses her older daughter Veda too–to the gas chamber. She complains, "I've worked long and hard, trying to give Veda the things I never had," and her only rewards are hatred, abandonment, death. When she buys Veda a dress, Veda scorns its cheap material. After her father leaves them, Veda begs her mother to marry his crude, lecherous partner so that she will have a new house, a maid, a limousine. On learning that Mildred is a waitress, Veda cries, "How could you degrade us, Mother?" Yet Mildred persists in making sacrifices for Veda. At the end she is even willing to be executed for her daughter's crime; but the irony is that she has never won Veda's love. Veda takes everything from Mildred–even, at the end, her mother's husband–and gives nothing. The film as a whole seems almost a vulgar, unconscious Americanization of *King Lear*–the story of a woman who *buys* her daughter everything imaginable, only to be repaid with a withering ingratitude.

There is a furtively ambivalent attitude toward success even in this film. The most evil character in the film, aside from Veda, is slimy Monte, and his greatest sin is that he has never worked for a living. Languorous, arrogant, devious, he embodies all of the American prejudices against the man of leisure. Mildred's robustness and energy are deliberately contrasted to his indolence. In the scene in which she belittles him for his dependence on her, the film's attitude is unclear. Mildred may look preemptory and cruel to us, yet the filmmakers cannot help preferring her sturdy, homely aggressiveness to Monte's ruffled-shirt decadence.

But in the characterization of Veda the filmmakers have considered the other side of the coin; she represents all their fears about success. Ambitious Americans often justify their avarice and their aggressiveness by saying that they are doing everything for their children; and they may well be trying to escape the humiliation of their own past by giving their children the luxuries that they had imagined for themselves while growing up in poverty. In the deepest sense, Mildred *is* selfish–living out her own dreams of material glory vicariously, through her pampered daughters. *Mildred Pierce* makes a shrill, melodramatic, but still pertinent criticism of this American compulsion by showing that the spoiled child is a moral monster, deadened by greed and unaffected by murder. What the film seems to say–with all its contrived plot machinations it's difficult to be sure–is that the obsessions of materialistic, success-oriented parents lead to violence and corruption; the fruit of ambition is murder.

The same themes are central to the more pretentious success stories of the next few years–movies like *All The King's Men* (Robert Rossen, 1949), and *A Place in the Sun* (George Stevens, 1951). In these movies violent resolutions attest to the same fears about ambition and success as in the black widow melodramas. In *All The King's Men* both the grassroots politician Willie Stark and the intellectual newspaperman Jack Burden start small and pure, but grow increasingly corrupt on their way to the top. As is usually the case in these success stories, the transformation in Willie is not really convincingly motivated. We simply have to accept the film's assumption that, as a person becomes more famous and more powerful, he also becomes more venal and more vicious; Willie's success involves such devious and macabre betrayals that it can only result in violence. He is murdered at the height of his success by a brother of the aristocratic girl who has soiled herself by becoming Willie's mistress.

The ambivalence of *All The King's Men* toward the American success ethic can be seen in the fact that, like *Mildred Pierce*, it condemns both the ambitious common man and the decadent aristocracy. Jack Burden's family is indifferent to social problems, lazy and complacent. And although his girlfriend's family is far nobler, they too are tainted by their detachment from the crude energy of working class America. Jack sells his soul to Willie Stark, his girlfriend sells her body, her father is disgraced, her brother becomes a murderer. The aristocrats who have never worked for a living are doomed to humiliation and death. (In this film, though, there is also a very confused current of admiration for the aristocracy.) Yet the working man who rises through his own initiative is also doomed. He becomes a ruthless egomaniac; he must be destroyed. The self-made man and the rich idler are both guilty, and the world crashes down around them in violence.

I would not suggest that all of these films can be reduced to one simple theme. Three of the films I have discussed—*Double Indemnity, Mildred Pierce, The Postman Always Rings Twice*—are based upon novels by James M. Cain, and their concern with destructive materialistic women cannot be explained simply in terms of a cultural obsession. Similarly, Robert Rossen directed three films about young men on the make whose ambition leads to murder and suicide—*Body and Soul, All The King's Men, The Hustler*—and it would be naive to ignore the qualities unique to Rossen in these films. Still, there are enough American films linking success and violence to suggest that the theme is an important one to our writers and directors.

Notes

1. The picture had changed by the middle of the optimistic Fifties, when *Somebody Up There Likes Me* celebrated Rocky Graziano as a true American hero; a juvenile delinquent, army deserter, and ex-convict, antisocial Rocky "makes good" when he becomes a champion. In this film, violence is seen as perfectly consistent with moral reformation and social accommodation. In fact, socially channeled violence seems *necessary* to Rocky's adjustment. The irony and bitterness of the Forties fight movies toward this same phenomenon have completely disappeared.

2. In ***Movies: A Psychological Study***, Martha Wolfenstein and Nathan Leites discussed the dominating woman as one of the central obsessions of American films of the late Forties.

Above, Jeff Bailey (Robert Mitchum) and Kathie Moffett (Jane Greer) *Out of the Past*.

The Filmic Transaction:
On the Openings of *Films Noirs*

Marc Vernet (1983)

Translator's Introduction

In "The Filmic Transaction,"* Marc Vernet is concerned less with a generic definition of *film noir* than with the elaboration of the general conditions of hermeneutic development and narrative suspense in the classic American film, of which the *noir* is an extreme example. As a form of textual analysis, Vernet's method is interesting because he assumes the point of view of the spectator before the film in movement rather than that of an analyst at the editing table. Neither purely phenomenological nor impressionistic, Vernet's approach–a rigorous combination of Propp, Freud, and Levi-Strauss–is aimed at a reconstruction of the *processes of reading* and narrative competence which the American studio film presupposes.[1]

Vernet's particular fascination then is with the system of exchange whereby the ordering of discrete narrative elements conditions possible readings on the part of the spectator, readings which are in fact alternately buttressed, undercut, reassessed, or reversed through the viewer's interaction with the text of the film. In this essay, the Proppian contract which binds victims and heroes in the deployment of narrative actions also describes the negotiation of a narrative contract between film and spectator. Vernet's precise concern is therefore not with the exact description of the narrative order of particular films. Rather, it is with the generic distribution of elements in the form of a pattern which doubled that of the interpretive activity of the spectator as the perception, rememoration, anticipation of narrative actions. In Vernet's analysis, the juxtaposition of elements in a structure of contradiction and reversal, disjunction and contiguity (of which the asyndeton is the principal trope and the opposition of the "set-up" to the "enigma" is the overdetermining instance) relies not so much on the physical ordering of the narratives as much as the material reading they offer as the result of

* First published as "La transaction filmique" in *Le cinéma américain: analyses de films, II*, eds. Raymond Bellour and Patrick Brion (Paris: Flammarion, 1980), pp. 122-43. Reprinted with permission.

the common structure which subtends them. This is why, for example, it does not matter to Vernet which comes first, the set-up (*mise en place*), or the enigma (*pot au noir*), in the opening movements of the *film noir*; for *it is the relationship between them*, the juxtaposition of their constituent elements, which is the basis of his theory of reading.

In this regard, Vernet's essay may finally be understood as a contribution to the metapsychology of spectatorship similar to that of Metz, Kuntzel, Bellour, and others. For what Vernet designates as the "filmic transaction" between narrative structuring and the physical conditions of spectatorship is an unconscious process comparable to Freud's notion of the "dream-work," or similarly, the structure of fetishism which allows the simultaneous belief in contradictory propositions. Here once again the *noir* is considered to be a limit-text in which the structure of fear and suspense, the sudden contrasts and contradictions of story development, and the relations of intrigue and betrayal among the characters, are considered to replay the conditions of fantasy and desire discovered by Freud, which are the constitutive elements of every narrative.

David Rodowick

To begin this interrogation, we might ask why the genre of films often called *noirs* begins with an air of quietude. Why multiply, in the very first minutes, the signs of tranquility? Ordinarily, *film noirs* are characterized by their singular brutality and surfeit of violence. What paradoxical necessity, then, requires that their opening moves should take place so quietly? Without doubt, this air of safety is more or less relative since one may identify the distinctive traits of the *film noir* in its very first images. However, when these traits appear they are often nestled within a reassuring tableau. Nothing in these first scenes can compare with those which will soon follow. How could the spectator comprehend the sound and the fury which will soon engulf this initial quiescence?

This structure of sudden contrasts reflects more than an interest in dramatic forms. Something else is taking place here which may shed some light on the problem of suspense and the place of the spectator in the narrative film.

1. The Set Up [Mise en place]: "Everything in its place..."

Here we will consider six films[2]: *The Maltese Falcon* (John Huston, 1941); *Double Indemnity* (Billy Wilder, 1944); *The Big Sleep* (Howard Hawks 1946); *The Lady from Shanghai* (Orson Welles, 1947); *Out of the Past* (Jacques Tourneur, 1947); and *The Enforcer* (Raoul Walsh, 1950).[3]

The opening movements of each one will display a network of signs denoting tranquility and thus constitute by degrees a *tableau* which is comforting to the spectator and coherent from the point of view of the narration. In *The Maltese Falcon*, for example, Sam Spade is rolling a cigarette when in walks Miss Won-

derly, an attractive and apparently proper young woman whose parents are trav-
elling in Hawaii. In *The Lady from Shanghai*, O'Hara is taking a leisurely stroll when
he meets a mysterious young woman riding in a horse-drawn carriage. On a
beautiful, summer afternoon, Neff knocks at the door of a luxurious villa, inter-
rupting the sun bath of the young Mrs. Dietrichson (*Double Indemnity*). In a little
country town, the hero of *Out of the Past* abandons his gas station for a pastoral
meeting with his fiancée. The venerable General Sternwood (*The Big Sleep*) assures a pampered and sheltered existence for his two young daughters. The beginning of *The Enforcer* is not quite identical to those above. However, the action
does unfold inside police headquarters, confirming that the initial dramatic movement will take place on the side of law and order.

On this pleasant foundation, the initial relations between characters will be
woven and the elements necessary for beginning the intrigue will appear. This
schema, which is not really new and permits many variations, resembles a situation described by Vladimir Propp in his analyses of Russian folk tales.[4] It is the establishment of a *contract* in which someone requests the aid of the hero and
promises him repayment for his efforts.

According to Propp, the primary function of the contract is to describe precisely the responsibilities of each of the characters and to regulate the relations
which bind them together. In much the same manner, the opening scenes of
many *film noirs* designate and clarify the roles and attributions of each character.
The vulnerability of the victim and of the dispatcher [*destinateur*] is thus emphasized through factors of age, sexual difference, dress, and irresponsibility.[5] General Sternwood, for example, is powerless: one of his daughters seems without
any sense of discretion and the other spends her time combating boredom with
alcohol. With her superficial elegance and air of discomfort, Miss Wonderly appears lost in San Francisco where she has come to rescue her sister from the
clutches of a sinister individual. The young woman in *The Lady from Shanghai*
seems at first to be innocent of the gang who menaces her and the surprised Mrs.
Dietrichson has trouble hiding her exposed body. And in *The Enforcer*, even
though Rico is distraught with fear, it is represented as being an unreasonable and
unwarranted fear.

On the other hand, the strength and appearance of the heroes inspires no
doubts in their abilities. With past experience in the police force, Marlowe (*The
Big Sleep*) is able to handle dangerous *affairs* without difficulty. The blasé Spade
sees Miss Wonderly's problems as little more than routine. O'Hara has travelled
the world over. He knows how to use his fists, and when necessary, a gun. The
experience of the police inspector in *The Enforcer* finds itself redoubled by the ef-
ficacity of the organization which supports him.

But beyond delimiting these positions, the encounters between heroes and victims inaugurate a precise series of exchanges. First, the heroes deplore their initial idleness: Neff and Spade are happy to escape the grey walls of their offices,

Marlowe is looking for work, and O'Hara a new form of distraction. The inspector in *The Enforcer* becomes impatient when he sees the investigation brought to a premature conclusion, and it is not at all certain that the hero of *Out of the Past* will be satisfied with the life of petty bourgeois domesticity which awaits him. For their part, the victims only wish to gain their lost tranquility as rapidly as possible. Miss Wonderly wishes the reestablishment of order before her parents arrive home, General Sternwood wants to rid himself of a petty blackmailer, and Rico seeks some form of secure shelter. At the beginning of these films, heroes and victims are both idlers but in different ways: the former wish to leave their idleness behind, the latter to regain it. The heroes restore peace to the victims in order to gain excitement for themselves.

A second form of exchange involves money: the heroes have little, the victims are wealthy, Mrs. Dietrichson and Mrs. Bannister (*Double Indemnity* and *The Lady from Shanghai*) both have very rich spouses, and in *The Maltese Falcon* and *The Big Sleep*, the comfort of the daughters is guaranteed by the wealth of the parents. The heroes have small salaries and less hope of enriching themselves; thus the opportunities afforded by the victims are initially welcomed.

A third variety of exchange is suggested by the idleness of the female characters—the fact that they are single or that their husbands are absent—which affords the possibility of a romantic liaison with the lonely heroes. (Three films do not have a feminine victim or dispatcher: *The Big Sleep*, *Out of the Past* and *The Enforcer*. However, all three place the virility of the victims in question: General Sternwood because of his age, the old boss of the mechanic because a woman has cheated and left him, Rico because of his debilitating fear.)

In its opening scenes, the *film noir* thus begins by distributing a restricted set of corresponding elements which, in their turn, regulate a series of multiple exchanges between the victim/dispatchers, on the one hand, and the heroes on the other:

	Victim/Dispatchers	Heroes
StrengthExperience	-	+
Trouble	+	-
Money	+	-
Gender	feminine	masculine
Sexual availability	+	+

The contract also determines the task which the heroes must accomplish. At first these tasks seem inconsequential when compared to the usual work of the film detective: locate and return home a man or a woman (*Out of the Past, The Maltese Falcon, The Big Sleep*), silence a petty blackmailer (*The Big Sleep*), chase off some hoods (*The Lady from Shanghai*), or guard a prisoner until morning (*The Enforcer*). Moreover, these tasks appear to be somewhat beneath the training and ability of the heroes. They have all the qualities required to accomplish the work before them, and even if they are not always able to complete their mission, as in *The Lady from Shanghai*, they have knowledge of the necessary clues such as the names, addresses, and activities of the malefactors. Therefore, what takes form in the accomplishment of the task appears to be more a rapid restoration of normality than the beginning of a long and dangerous adventure. The "contract" is a guarantee, then, insurance that things will not get out of hand. The impossible is not considered therein. The detective or his like have one job to do. Its requirements are precise and remuneration has been fixed beforehand. In itself, this reinforces the sense of calm, order, and propriety which marks the beginning of the *film noir*. Spade acts paternally with Miss Wonderly, O'Hara and Mrs. Bannister exchange plesantries, Marlowe and General Sternwood tell stories, Neff and Mrs. Dietrichson flirt without really exceeding the bounds of decency. So far, society is peaceful and orderly.

Finally, this contract appears to be short-term, both for the heroes and the spectator. According to certain conditions, it is going to "make something happen." It frames and directs the events to come, channeling the fiction, giving it sense and signification. The text must lead without fail to a truth, the terms of which are already (or nearly) constituted. From the very beginning, the *film noir* insists on the transparency of the disguise: it will suffice to merely uncover the mystery. In the opening sequence of *The Enforcer*, for example, the culprit is already under lock and key. The police arrive in the middle of the night to place an indispensable witness under protective custody and only a few hours separate us from the beginning of the trial.

Both the titles and opening credits of *film noirs* seem to participate in the structuring of this type of fiction. They offer, in effect, a foretaste of what will be the truth: the final pleasure, the solution of the intrigue. The two abandoned cigarettes, side by side, at the end of the credits to *The Big Sleep* suggest that the hands and lips of the couple are otherwise occupied. The credits of *The Maltese Falcon* present a "historical" discourse ("1539, Charles V..." etc.) at the same time as the "actual" image of the fabulous statue, thus confirming its existence. The very title of *The Enforcer* places the hero in a position where he is required to protect the letter of the law no matter what the cost. Finally, the slow but inexorable advance of the man on crutches, which illustrates the title sequence of *Double Indemnity*, recalls the determinedness of *The Enforcer* and provides a preview of the character who will avenge himself without pity.

Titles and credits thus consolidate an *a priori* impression in which the final sequence prevails over the first: the story *will* advance in a rectilinear fashion. They establish what Freud would call a "purposive idea," working beneath the development of the fiction as a structuring absence.[6] And even though the enigma will detail this force and dispatch it from the scenic space, when uncovered, it stands revealed as the fundamental interest of the fiction. Although it may be diverted and slowed down, like the central characters of the films, nothing will prevent it from finally attaining its ends. There is another aspect of the *film noir* which supports this idea: the flashbacks which often organize the global structure of the narrative. Here the final truth preexists the actual telling of the story; the hero will evidently survive his adventure without too much damage.

When the *film noir* takes off, and when the intrigue begins to take form, everything seems destined to go well. This is the "set-up" [*mise en place*]: where the setting into play of the narrative seems to correspond to a satisfactory arrangement of the elements of the fiction. It is also a time of stability and certainty in which the spectator persuades himself that knowledge of what is important, and pleasurable, is at hand: adventure, love, wealth, and easy living, along with the resolution of the intrigue, as eventualities which no one doubts. The first movement of the *film noir* sets in motion a narrative machine whose every part is well-oiled and in gear: the characters are fully drawn and their functions clearly established (hero/victim/aggressor); a problem has been carefully and completely laid out with the conditions of its solution clearly stated (this task to accomplish, these actions foreseen).

Although the set-up is logically speaking the first step in the development of the narrative, chronologically speaking it does not have to be the first sequence of the film. In *Double Indemnity*, for example, the set-up takes place in the second sequence while the first sequence functions as what I will identify as the usual *second* movement of the *film noir*. Here it is a question of the inversion of a model which is typical of the other films, but whose final result is, as we shall see, identical to them. In addition, the set-up does not necessarily take place within the confines of an autonomous segment. Its constituent elements may be distributed across several scenes in conjunction with other elements which cannot be integrated into the systematic functioning of the movement [*mise en place*] such as an especially strong menace or a character whose role is ambiguous. This is the case in *Double Indemnity*, but it is also true for *The Enforcer* and for *The Big Sleep*, whose intrigue is much more complicated.

2. The Enigma [Pot au noir]: The "black hole"[7]

Perhaps you are waiting for romance, but in the *film noir*, it's revolvers that count. The nearly perfect accord of the first movement now falls into chaos. Having barely taken the second step, you are already on a collision course with violence. The smile on the face of the spectator vanishes as brusquely as Archer's when the barrel of a gun rises into the frame. One shot: Archer and Geiger are dead (*The Maltese Falcon, The Big Sleep*). Rico misses a step and falls to his death on the concrete below (*The Enforcer*). Two surly types shadow Rita Hayworth in *The Lady from Shanghai*; a killer orders the young fiancée to follow him in *Out of the*

Past. Only moments ago foreknowledge of the truth was certain, but now the expected disappears from the film with a brutal and unpredictable force.

The principal function and effect of this second movement in the *film noir* is to detail the fiction, to slow down and divert its development. Murder eliminates the first witnesses and thus the first indices of the truth. Only Rico can testify against Mendoza, only Archer can identify his murderer, and only Geiger can explain the nature of the affairs he was involved in. The narrative thread is broken: the hero, and the spectator, are suddenly engulfed by a black hole [*le pot au noir*]. The truth which seemed so close dissolves and scatters to the four winds. The intrigue has hardly been unmasked when a flashback carries us back either to the first movement or into a time where all certainty fades.

In the *film noir*, there are several possibilities for linking the first and second movements in order to maintain the progression of the fiction: unexpected murder–murderer unknown (*The Maltese Falcon, The Big Sleep*); death (whether expected or unexpected) already accomplished–murderer known–flashback (*The Enforcer*,[8] *Double Indemnity*). Neither *The Lady from Shanghai* nor *Out of the Past* assumes these routes, but even so, one may note that in the former the film opens with a flashback sketched in by the voice-off narration of the hero, and in the latter, even if it is not a question of a return to the past, there is a return *of* the past as Bailey is forced to resume his criminal activities. In addition, death's brutal intervention is signified in *The Lady from Shanghai* by Rita Hayworth's gun, the theme of her conversation with O'Hara, and by the two hoods lurking in the shadows. In *Out of the Past*, it is marked by the sudden appearance of the killer. In

Below, "Perhaps you are waiting for romance, but in the *film noir*, it's revolvers that count.": Marlowe (Humphrey Bogart) and Vivian (Lauren Bacall) in *The Big Sleep*.

fact, these last two films belong to an intermediate category which borrows elements from the two, more general categories.

These three varieties of linkage respond to the same necessity: they interrupt and disconnect the narrative, hollowing out the fiction and shooting it full of holes. The second movement of the *film noir* is a black hole. As a generalized inversion of signs, it demonstrates the structure of an enigma, a lacuna in which all certainty suddenly fails, as well as a force which turns the space of the fiction inside out with an unexpected violence. He who must talk is silenced (*The Maltese Falcon, The Big Sleep, The Enforcer*), an honest man is discovered to be a former criminal (*Out of the Past*), an insurance agent is revealed as a murderer (*Double Indemnity*), an innocent young woman, apparently without protection, is found to be a liar, married, and never without the protection of a pistol and two bodyguards (*The Lady from Shanghai*). In *The Big Sleep* and *The Lady from Shanghai*, the victim turns out to be a consenting one, and in *The Maltese Falcon* and *The Big Sleep*, the dispatcher, whose good faith was never in doubt, is found to be lying, or at the very least, not telling the whole truth. The confident and experienced detective commits a gross error overturning the investigation (*The Big Sleep, The Maltese Falcon, The Enforcer*); the sailor who has known every danger is led onto a boat by a woman (*The Lady from Shanghai*).

This generalized inversion of signs may take several other forms: passage from day to night, or night to day (*The Maltese Falcon, Double Indemnity, The Lady from Shanghai, The Big Sleep, Out of the Past*); from interior space to exterior space (*The Maltese Falcon, Double Indemnity, The Big Sleep*), or from exterior to interior (*Out of the Past, The Lady from Shanghai*); from country to city (*Out of the Past, The Lady from Shanghai*), or from city to gardened suburbs (*Double Indemnity, The Big Sleep*); and from sunshine to storm (*The Big Sleep*) or vice versa (*Double Indemnity*). In certain films, these shifting oppositions can be extremely vigorous and forceful. In Welles's film, for example, O'Hara makes off with the mystery woman in an open carriage, continuing his journey through the park. Consider then, this ensemble of signs: nature–horse-drawn carriage–darkness–male driver–a woman pedestrian is given a lift–confidence. A few moments later, after the mystery of Mrs. Bannister is revealed, all this is left behind in the interior of a parking lot. O'Hara is chilled, then: concrete–automobile–light–a woman driver–a male pedestrian left behind–caution. During the scene of Archer's murder in *The Maltese Falcon*, it is the spatial axes themselves which are turned around and subverted. Archer looks off-screen high and to the right while lunging toward the right hand side of the frame. From below, a revolver is raised into the frame along its right side, held to the right hand of the assassin–one must then conclude that the camera is situated in the place of the murderer. But it is not there that Archer glances; it is rather more to the right as if the assassin were left handed. Nothing is in its proper place. What is expected from above comes from below, and what must come from the left seems to come from the right. All sense of continuity is lost.

This sense of disorder and reversal, however, is in every case relative. What the spectator witnesses is incontrovertible: there is never a moment where he doubts what he sees. The *sense* of the action may be difficult to comprehend, but the *representation* of the event is always produced as a clear and coherent picture. Even if it shrouds the scene in mystery, the black hole never places in doubt the reality of the event it portrays. It requires for itself a minimum of coherence even if I raised more questions than it answers.

3. Disjunction and contiguity

The oppositions internal to the first movements [*mise en place*] of *film noirs* are complementary, and in fact, they cancel out one another within their own system of exchange. The lacunae of the second movements [*pot au noir*] do not prevent the comprehension of the represented actions. However, the oppositions which take place *between* the first and second movement are mutually exclusive, setting up a system of irresolvable antinomies: the hero cannot be both strong and vulnerable, the woman good and evil, the dispatcher frank and deceitful. For the spectator, each term and each element is not necessarily less "true" than its contrary, for each functions perfectly within the context of its own system. It is not their existence which the subsequent interrogation must support and explain (separating truth from falsehood, the judgment of one condemning the other), but rather the fact of their coexistence.

The spectator can only try to accept and understand the distance which separates the two ensembles, for this disjunction is the result of powerful oppositions which threaten the collapse of the narrative. The fiction passes from a minor familial squabble to an unexpected slaughterhouse, from pastoral romance to cataclysm, or from a commonplace inquiry to an inexplicable mystery. The gap between the two movements is an asyndeton: a rupture in the chain of significations where the spectator feels as if he has somehow skipped a necessary logical step. The bridge between the two movements has escaped him; the second [*pot au noir*] does not appear to be logically derived from the first [*mise en place*]. There is instead a disconnection, a gap, where the spectator feels the absence of a necessary structural relation. Without this, the film would lapse into prattle without value or meaning; it would no longer be a classical narrative. Only the restitution of a logic not yet apprehended can maintain this structural relation and evade a collapse of the fiction. In this, the openings of *film noirs* reprise an essential feature of the dream-work as described by Freud who explains that if two contiguous images appear without any apparent logical relation between them, their simple succession will nevertheless indicate that a causal relation exists between them.[9] The very fact that the "black hole" immediately follows the "set-up" suggests that even if the rapport between them is not yet visible, it is nonetheless *necessary*.

Although generally felt as unpleasurable (sudden death, sinister decors, confusion) the black hole will manifest the force of its relation with the set-up by revealing the gaps and marking out the absences contained within its own
movement (who is the killer? what is the connection? what is going to happen
now?). In other words, the possibility of this enigma [*pot au noir*] must be conditioned by a relation which precedes it in the set-up [*mise en place*]. The logic of
this relation is missing, of course, but the spectator believes in it all the same, bet-
ting on its existence in order to maintain the film's "sanity." To appear realistic,
the second movement must somehow anchor itself, or derive a portion of itself,
from the interior relations of the first movement. Thus considered, the first
movement is placed into doubt as having decoyed and deceived the spectator.
The fiction it proposed now seems flawed, corroded, blown apart, the pleasures
it promised are now impossible. Having stopped dead in its tracks, the well-oiled
machine which produced such an agreeable, straightforward, and seamless story,
has now fallen into pieces. Its discretion and meaning have been suddenly ex-
hausted through its collision with the black hole.

Now, the first function which we can attribute to the openings of *film noirs* in
the form "set-up–black hole" would be to create and delimit a certain kind of fictional space. Thus, in uncovering a gap, we have already begun to fill it in, and in
destroying one line of logic, we have already begun to construct another. It is a
question, then, of bridging the two movements, reducing and explaining the dis-

Below and opposite, *Lady from Shanghai*: Michael O'Hara (Orson Welles) misperceives Elsa
Bannister (Rita Hayworth).

tance which separates them, and filling in the holes which the enigma has bored into the text.

What can be made of this situation? We know that Levi-Strauss has defined the enigma as a question without an answer or an answer without a question; or more precisely, for him it is the impossibility of each answer connecting up with its question and vice versa.[10] The ensemble "set-up–black hole" seems to contain these two models within itself. The first movement proposes an answer which suddenly fades away and the abrupt appearance of the second movement seems to provide the answer to a question which has not yet been asked. The mystery of the *film noir* is particularly intense when the set-up and the black hole cross paths without appearing to have met one another. In this manner, the first movement projects onto the second an answer which it cannot find and the second movement reverts back on the first as a question which it cannot ask.

Question II <————————> (Answer I)

(Question II) <————————> Answer II

It is only with the resolution of the intrigue at the film's conclusion that the answer will finally rejoin its question.

Levi-Strauss also notes that in the myth of Oedipus it is not surprising that the resolution of the riddle of the Sphinx precedes the act of incest. For him the two are equivalencies: the impossible intercourse supposed by the form "question–answer" is homologous with that of "mother–son." In like manner, the structure of the *film noir* seems to join together that which is impossible; to cancel the distance which forbids the union of its two movements. As the spectator wishes to see the

film re-composed by transgressing the barriers which have been thrown up be-fore him, he appears to participate in the incestuous wish which is the impossible conjunction of the set-up and the black hole.

But does this explain why the openings of *film noirs* should place two disjunct movements side by side in apparent continuity? The two movements contradict and exclude one another from the point of view of both expression and content. However, they are presented together, and for the spectator who believes equally in both, it is not a question of understanding the first *or* the second move-ment, but rather set-up *and* black hole. This abusive relation between two con-tradictory movements is also a form of "incest": an impossible intercourse which is nevertheless realized.

In sum, the *film noir* functions according to an incestuous exchange: the first act ("set-up–black-hole") is exchanged for the final act ("question–answer").[11] The former unravels itself as the latter is accomplished. The two beginning move-ments are continuous when question and answer are discontinuous (see schema above). At the end of the story, this continuity will be broken down when ques-tion and answer will finally rejoin one another:

$$Q\ I <————————> A\ I$$

$$Q\ II <————————> A\ II$$

In effect, the final solution presents the victory of one form over the other: the heroes reestablish, for themselves or for others, the initial situation by defeating the antagonists. In this sense, the solution of the intrigue is a re-placing of the first movement which reestablishes a belief in the power of the heroes and the truth of the fiction. The unravelling of the film thus permits a mediation of the first and second movements which explains the reasons and motivations underpinning their relationship. This mediation is itself a disjunction, though, in that it reestablishes the oppositions by eliminating the "and" of the logical connections and by reinstating the function of difference: one term *or* the other. The endings of *Double Indemnity*, *The Lady from Shanghai*, and particularly *The Maltese Falcon* are exemplary in this respect. Here the woman is condemned–which is to say rendered evil and pushed aside–for having confused the difference between good and evil or between love and the desire for power; in short, for having transgressed the categories of the heroes' personal code.[12] And here we can note that the "incest form" which we examined does not exhaust the forms of exchange in the *film noir*. The "triangle" has often been pointed out as a principal form of relation among the characters: the young hero desires and conquers a rich woman who is quite often tied to an older man or some other representative of patriarchal authority (*Double Indemnity*, *The Lady from Shanghai*, *Out of the Past*, *The Big Sleep*, *The Maltese Falcon*)[13] However, in most of these films the woman is made guilty and despite her protestations she is either abandoned or killed by the hero. In this manner, the resolution of the intrigue is guaranteed by the annulment of the incestuous relations. The only film which does not conform to this trajectory (*The Big Sleep*, where the hero and the woman are happily united even though only minutes before she was believed complicit with the gangsters) is one where the intrigue is so confused that its resolution is not clearly apparent to the spectator.[14]

To commit or not to commit incest: this is the fundamental problem of the *film noir*. It is important that at least for a moment, this question was possible before becoming impossible, and that even though it was forbidden on one level, it was realised on another. The *film noir* thus accomplishes what Freud recognized as the primary function of the art work: to overturn and reinforce defensive structures at one and the same time. We might call this operation a filmic transaction: "I know that incest is impossible, but even so, I see it accomplished." In the same way, the filmic transaction resembles the structure of fetishism, permitting us to maintain a pleasant and comforting belief against the contradictions of reality.[15]

The first movement of the *film noir* guarantees this function by assuring, in its own right, a comforting belief: the heroes dominate a situation where all the elements of the ensemble work together without gaps or discord to form a stable and balanced fiction. This belief is only a happy illusion, however. It is overturned by the eruption of the enigma [*pot au noir*] which, on the one hand, uncovers an anomaly (the black hole: that which one has expected has not come to be), and on the other exposes the illusion of the set-up, destroying the belief which it permits. The black hole thus threatens to destroy the possibility of pleasure promised by the set-up. From this point of view, the element of suspense promised by the intrigue (that is, the knowledge that something is wrong or that some fact is missing) does not seem to rely on the spectator not knowing what will happen. The set-up has previewed for him the pleasures which the text promises, but the black hole has confirmed the risk of un-pleasure in the continuation of the narrative. In this structure of suspense, the spectator only knows what *cannot* happen. There are only two possible solutions to the intrigue, he *thinks*, the good and the bad. But what he *believes* is the disappointment of his first pleasure, that is, the eruption of evil in place of good. In the *film noir*, suspense is always a balanced mixture of belief and hope, but this belief is only possible because a disturbance has brutally and unexpectedly disrupted the text: the black hole which consumes the sense of narrative. However, the structure of suspense may not maintain any indecisiveness which will threaten its already established trajectory: a satisfactory solution corresponding to the situation of the set-up. For the fiction, all solutions are happy ones provided that they are believable. A resolution is disappointing only when the spectator has foreseen another one, that is, when he has invested his belief in another end to the story.

Even if they are not in themselves suspenseful, the beginnings of *film noirs* are of necessity a time of suspense in that they condition the possible positions of the spectator with respect to the text: quiet expectation or unpleasant surprise. The desire of the spectator is always to recover what has been lost, to find once again his initial, happy belief.

Hoping to maintain a first impression, afraid of having recognized what is missing in place of what one desired to see: in the structure of suspense which typifies the *film noir*, it is possible to recognize a configuration characteristic of the fear of castration and its fetishistic elision. The air of suspense. Doesn't this celebrated apprehension of the spectator in the *film noir* correspond to the fetishist's stare, fixed on a shoe or a piece of feminine lingerie, which marks the last moments of his belief in the phallic woman and the problem of castration she poses? The black hole thus comprises a movement where the hero is deprived of his strength and his power; hereafter, the film must work to restore his stature. It is this initial belief in the hero which is first in the film and first as well in the cinema where, in the best fictions, good must overcome evil. The *film noir* acts out the destruction of this fiction, this collapse of the narrative-representational cinema. In this it constitutes a passage to the limit where the cinematic signifier would no longer be weak because it could welcome any signified, where this signifier could no longer lure the spectator since its contrary would have equal force, and where its value would be diluted in an infinite play of signification. But this fictional destruction is only momentary. The *film noir* hastens to reestablish its structuring oppositions, to straighten out its situations, to reinstate, as it were, the cinematic institution which it threatens.

NOTES

1. Translator's note: It is interesting to note in this respect that Vernet was a student of Barthes and began his work on the *film noir* under Barthes' tutelage. His assimilation of analytic procedures from Russian Formalism, psychoanalysis, and anthropology all compare favorably then to similar concerns in Barthes from the period of "Introduction to the Structural Analysis of Narratives," in *Image-Music-Text*, tr. and ed. Stephen Heath (New York: Hill and Wang, 1977), pp. 79-124, to *S/Z*, tr. Richard Howard (New York: Hill and Wang, 1974).

2. This choice has not only been determined by membership in the subgenre of *film noir*, but also by the frequency with which these films are shown and by the pleasure which they give me. Each film is representative of this subgenre, I think, so I will designate them globally, according to my hypothesis, as *"film noirs."*

3. The title credits Bretaigne Windust but it is generally known that Raoul Walsh is the actual director of the film.

4. *The Morphology of the Folktale*, tr. Laurence Scott (Austin and London: Univ. of Texas Press, 1968). [Tr. note: Although Vernet footnotes Propp at this point, in his discussion of the function of the contract, he is undoubtedly referring to subsequent interpretations of Propp by Claude Bremond, Roland Barthes, and others. See for example Barthes' discussion in "Introduction to the Structural Analysis of Narratives," pp. 101-4.]

5. [Tr. note: These terms are used in Propp's sense to designate functions which are attributable to, and shared by, individual characters. A "dispatcher" is a character who sends the hero on his or her quest, often promising remuneration in exchange for aid. A "victim" suffers injury as the result of the actions of the villain. Heroes, dispatchers, and other characters may thus function alternately as victims.]

6. Tr. note: ct. Sigmund Freud's *The Interpretation of Dreams*, tr. James Strachey (New York: Avon Books, 1965), pp. 567-70.

7. Tr. note: In the original, *pot au noir*, a French expression whose only near English equivalent is "pitch-pot," that is, a mysterious fog bank which legendarily lures and entraps vessels.

8. This is taking into consideration that Rico is himself his own killer.

9. Tr. note: See for example, the section of *The Interpretation of Dreams* entitled "The Means of Representation," p. 349 et. passim.

10. Cf. "The Scope of Anthropology" in *Structural Anthropology, Vol. 2*, tr. M. Layton (New York: Basic Books, 1971), p. 22.

11. When I speak of "incestuous forms," it should be clear that I am using Levi-Strauss' sense where the relation between incest and the solution of the enigma is a *homology* ("The Scope of Anthropology," op. cit., pp. 23-24). This formula should then be understood in the context of remarks made by Roland Barthes ("As, fiction, Oedipus was at least good for something: to make good novels, to tell good stories..." *Pleasure of the Text*, tr. Richard Miller (New York: Hill and Wang, 1975), p. 47), by Christian Metz (cf. "The Imaginary Signifier," tr. Ben Brewster, *Screen*, 16, No. 2 (Summer 1975), pp. 14-76), and by Raymond Bellour (cf. "Alternation, Segmentation, Hypnosis," *Camera Obscura*, Nos. 3-4 (Summer 1979), pp. 71-101). There is no question of referring to the notion of incest, or of Oedipal relations, as "objects" in the film. Rather, they are understood to inform the structure of the text through a homologous relation.

12. On the function of ambivalence in the figure of Woman as double, see Julia Kristeva's "The Bounded Text" in *Desire in Language*, tr. Thomas Gora, Alice Jardine, and Leon S. Roudiez (New York: Columbia Univ. Press, 1980), pp. 36-63.

13. Note here that wealth functions as a sign which establishes an opposition with the hero, since the factor of age does not.

14. Raymond Bellour suggests to me that even if this resolution is not clearly understood, it is readily comprehended because the film privileges the constitution of a mythic couple (Bogart and Bacall) which overshadows the problems of the narrative.

15. Cf. Victor N. Smirnoff's "La transaction fetichique," *Nouvelle Revue de psychanlyse*, No. 2 (Fall 1970), pp. 41-63. [Tr. note: The relation between fetishism and belief in the spectatorial relations offered by film has been argued by Christian Metz, among others. See his "The Imaginary Signifier."]

Above and below, *Fallen Angel* "centers on the waitress, Stella, as the object of the male gaze." Stella (Linda Darnell) gets involved in a scheme with an admiring drifter, Eric Stanton (Dana Andrews, center above). Retired Det. Mark Judd (Charles Bickford, below) is also taken with her.

Film Noir: Style and Content

Dale E. Ewing, Jr. (1988)

The idea of an American *film noir* affords the analyst of ideology and culture an interesting definitional problem. The term itself is the invention of movie critics who hold the opinion that style is the sole vicinity in which meaning can be found in the cinema. And although these critics have done well in defining a consistent "*film noir* spirit," their work has been less than satisfactory in identifying precisely which movies this spirit fits. It is the argument of this study that the term *film noir* has been applied too loosely to give us an accurate definition of the subject. In the first section, an attempt will be made to prove this contention by reviewing the style-is-content literature on *noir* and then undertaking a metacritique of it. In the second section, a new interpretive method for looking at *film noir* will be proposed that uses style and content as interrelated principles that work in the films to create a totality of meaning. In this sense, a particular film cannot be defined as a *film noir* because it reflects one aspect or several aspects of the *film noir* spirit; it has to reflect every aspect of the *film noir* spirit or it is something other than *noir*.

The viewpoint projected here is that, although *films noirs* were supposed to be more nihilistic than the usual Hollywood films, they were still Hollywood films. In other words, a *film noir* cannot be defined adequately until the movie in question is evaluated as a complete work in which the themes develop from a plot that has the conventional beginning, middle, and end characteristic of Hollywood movies during the *noir* period.

Film noir means "black film," and it was a French appellation given to an unusually despairing group of Hollywood crime thrillers that began showing in France after World War II. These films had a dark style of visual presentation that combined gothic chiaroscuro lighting effects with an ambiguous and dislocated sense of space borrowed from the technical achievements of German Expressionism. Although the subject matter of *film noir* varied–it seemed to overlap into several previously established crime genres–the French saw in it strong affinities with a literary genre popular in their country called "*série noire*."[1] *Série noire* literature included French translations of Gothic novels and what in America are called "hardboiled" mystery novels. The world projected in *film noir* corresponded most closely to these latter works.

The American hardboiled mystery was an attempt to create a grittily realistic world of criminals and detectives, but its chief emphasis was on urban sordidness and melodrama. The hardboiled mystery novel fell into two categories. The stories of Dashiell Hammett and Raymond Chandler were about tough, outspoken private detectives. Heroes such as Phillip Marlowe and Sam Spade were interesting figures primarily because their creators gave them a sense of social justice and a certain amount of stoic virtue underneath their cynicism. The other category of hardboiled fiction–exemplified by the novels of James M. Cain and Cornell Woolrich–depended on a more *faux naif* approach in which the writers delighted in showing ordinary people becoming embroiled in crime due to some unlucky accident or character fault. In Cain's *Double Indemnity*, for example, an insurance salesman, Walter Neff, falls in love with one of his clients, an attractive housewife. The housewife, it turns out, is thoroughly despicable. She persuades Neff to kill her husband so they can cash in on his life insurance policy. In Woolrich's *The Window*, a small boy who lives in a tenement sees his neighbors rob and murder a sailor. The boy has a reputation for lying, and no one believes his story except the killers themselves. Even after they make an attempt on his life, no one believes him. The killers are eventually caught, but it is by accident rather than human design.

In his 1970 article, "The Family Tree of *Film Noir*," Raymond Durgnat suggests that an American *film noir* was usually preceded by a French version–*La Chienne* became *Scarlet Street*, *La Bête Humaine* became *Human Desire*.[2] But one of the earliest critics to write about *film noir,* Jean-Pierre Chartier, viewed the American strain as far more nihilistic:

> One speaks of a French school of black films, but at least *Le Quai des brumes* or *Hotel du Nord* had touches of revolt, love entered in the mirage of a better world. In these films, there was hope and even if characters were in despair they solicited our pity or sympathy. But here they are monsters, criminals, or sick people without excuse, who act as they do because of the fatality of evil within them.[3]

Chartier does not, however, attempt to account for the pessimism of American *film noir*. The first critics to analyse motive in these productions were Raymond Borde and Étienne Chaumeton. When their book-length **study Panorama du Film Noir Américain** appeared in 1955, the authors argued that *film noir* was a synthesis of three of Hollywood's most popular genres, the gangster movie, horror films–such as Val Lewton's style-conscious *Cat People*–and the private detective film. Borde and Chaumeton explained that these earlier genres contained the seeds of alienation and revolt that *film noir* was to later more sharply define. From the detective movie, *film noir* got its powers of observation and atmospheric detachment. From horror films, such as *I Walked with a Zombie* and *Cat People*, *film noir* gained a mise-en-scene of repulsion and dread. The gangster film bequeathed to *film noir* its rebellious, gun-toting antiheroes. Borde and Chaumeton concluded that *film noir*, in its eclectic borrowing of generic influences, developed into a distinctive genre of social commentary. *Film noir*, according to Borde and Chaumeton, was expressing deeply pessimistic themes that were related to the aftershock of the Depression and the 1930s gangster era, America's involvement in World War II, and the social upheaval caused by the post-war readjustment to civilian life. The authors also suggested that the arrival in Hollywood of a large number of German directors–among them Fritz Lang, Robert Siodmak, Curtis Bernhardt–all of whom were refugees from Hitler, were the dominating force behind its gloomy expressionistic style.[4]

At this point, it should be pointed out that French film analysts were of the school of thought that "style is content" in the movies. This approach was not accepted in America in the 1950s–which makes American and French ways of reading films diametrically opposite during this period. For example, when the French critic Chartier saw *Murder, My Sweet*, he saw the private detective hero, Marlowe–as he searches for the missing girlfriend of the gangster Moose Malloy–getting repeatedly drugged and beaten against a dark, stylistic background of corrupt police and semmingly honest citizens deceiving one another.[5] At the same time, in the United States, the American critic Clayton Henry, Jr., went to a screening of *Murder, My Sweet*, and, although he saw the same negative qualities Chartier saw, he realized that the plot tied together all these loose ends when Marlower saved the day and married the pretty heroine, Ann. Such factors led Henry to write, in the American publication *Film in Review*, that *Murder, My Sweet* was a film that "supported positive values."[6]

By the late 1960s, however, American film analysts had begun to come over to the French style method. It is beyond the scope of this study to account for this change, but the critics Charles Higham and Joel Greenburg laid the foundations for the American version of the style argument in their 1968 book *Hollywood in the Forties*. In their chapter "Black Cinema," concentrating on *film noir*'s most provocative visual components, they provided a melodramatic description of its basic intention: to create a world without "a single trace of pity or love."[7] For Higham and Greenberg, this pessimistic world view was defined by sensational visual imagery:

> A dark street in the early morning hours, splashed with a sudden downpour. Lamps form haloes in the murk. In the walk-up room, filled with intermittent flashing of a neon sign from across the street, a man is waiting to murder or be murdered....[8]

These kinds of images, Higham and Greenberg explain, are what gives *film noir* its "specific ambience." In a remarkably colorful passage, they describe some of the ways *film noir* develops this ambience through the use of trains speeding through the night:

> These trains, transporting their passengers on sinister errands, clank and sway through storm-swept darkness, their arrival at remote stations signalled by the presence of mysterious raincoated figures, while in the narrow corridors, the antiseptic, cramped compartments, assignations are made, and more often than not, a murder is planned.[9]

The authors suggest that such images have no other purpose than to employ romantic pessimism as a kind of slap in the face of American naivete and innocence. Higham and Greenberg state that *film noir* shows viewers "a world waiting to pounce in at the gates of the respectable, the jungle is already thrusting upwards."[10]

It might be argued that American film critics were adding to their analysis of the *film noir* their own impressions of living through the calamitous 1960s and early 1970s. They were casting a cynical look back on the middle-class innocence of their post-World War II generation. The stylistic gloom of *film noir* afforded an appealing paradigm of disorder. At the surface of life, America reflected an innocent appearance, but this was only repression, which is a breeding ground for all sorts of irrationalities and fears. Higham and Greenberg's metaphor of a "jungle thrusting upward" corresponds to Jung's idea that when a man represses his evil side, it causes a shadow to be cast on his unconscious. If the individual fails to acknowledge his evil side, his repressive mechanisms cause the "shadow" to grow to the point where it will burst out into his conscious mind and overwhelm him.[11]

After 1970, all *film noir* criticism seemed to spring from this central idea. In an influential article written in 1972, the critic and screenwriter Paul Schrader suggested that the style of *film noir* consistently undermined traditional plot resolutions in which the hero triumphs over the forces of evil:

> American film critics have always been sociologists first and scientists second: film is important as it relates to large masses, and if a film goes awry it is often because the theme has been somehow "violated" by the style. *Film noir* operates on opposite principles: the theme is hidden in the style, and bogus themes are often flaunted ("middle class values are best") which contradict the style.[12]

Schrader believed that the *film noir* style was representative of a struggle for freedom within an otherwise repressive film form. Hollywood films had a classical or "Aristotelian" approach to art that attempted to imitate nature in such a way as to convince spectators that their religious and secular institutions corresponded to a universal order. In the final analysis, this universal order was regulated by principles of cosmic harmony–forcing the classical drama into a position where it was necessary for it to illustrate this concept by following a prosaic chain of causation from beginning, middle, to end.[13] In *Romeo and Juliet*, for example, the plot unfolds in a step-by-step fashion, like a series of carefully choreographed ballet routines designed to illustrate disorder and eventual reconciliation. For Schrader, the *film noir* style radically deconstructed the idealism of this formula by adding to it an underlying mood of tension and cynicism.

In their cumulative reference guide, **Film Noir: An Encyclopedic Reference to the American Style**, Alain Silver and Elizabeth Ward agree wholeheartedly with Schrader:

> [These films] reflect a common ethos: they consistently evoke the dark side of the American *persona*. The central figures in these films, caught in their double binds, filled with existential bitterness, drowning outside the social mainstream, are America's stylized vision of itself, a true cultural reflection of the mental dysfunction of a nation in uncertain transition.[14]

The "existential bitterness" Silver and Ward refer to has been described by Robert Porfirio as "undercutting any attempted happy endings and prevents the films from being the typical Hollywood escapist fare."[15] From Porfirio's point of view, *film noir* epitomizes a black vision of American life in which the only shared responses are fears and repressed impulses:

> What keeps *film noir* alive for us today is something more than a spurious nostalgia. It is the underlying mood of pessimism.... This...is nothing less than an existential attitude towards life. It places its emphasis on man's contingency in a world where there are no transcendental values or moral absolutes.[16]

By now, it should be clear that the spirit of *film noir*–as identified in the literature discussed above–was one of relentless pessimism and alienation. In an excellent series of articles that developed out of the British Film Institute Summer School in 1975–which was published in a short book, **Women in Film Noir**, edited by E. Ann Kaplan–this textual pessimism and alienation was viewed as a purveyor of dominant and repressed ideologies concerning the place of women in society:

> *Film noir* is particularly notable for its specific treatment of women. In the films of another genre, the Western, women, in their fixed roles as wives, mothers, daughters, lovers, mistresses, whores, simply provide the background for the ideological work of the film which is carried out through men. Since the placement of women in this way is so necessary to *patriarchy* as we know it, it follows that the displacement of women would disturb the patriarchal system, and provide a challenge to the world view. The *film noir world* is one in which women are central to the intrigue of the films and are furthermore usually not placed safely in any of the familiar roles mentioned above. Defined by their sexuality, which is presented as desirable but dangerous to men, the women function as the obstacle to the male quest. It is largely because of this

interplay of the notion of independent women *vis-a-vis* patriarchy
that these films are of interest to feminist film theory.[17]

The authors in **Women in Film Noir** talk more about story than analysts such as
Silver and Porfirio. However, their discussions are necessarily subordinated to the
question of domination and emancipation from the male gaze. The male gaze
denotes a specific style of visual presentation in which the male is the subject and
the women is the object.[18] All of the authors in the study agree that the *noir*
world is defined in male terms. Women in *film noir* are viewed through the eyes
of men who measure their worth according to sexist and oppressive standards.
The contradiction rests in threatening women's roles that victimize the male
heroes and undermine the patriarchal order. The extent to which the hero
becomes disenchanted with these roles and attempts to combat them illustrates
the dialectical relationship between the oppression and empowerment of women
as a group.

In respect to defining a general spirit of textual alienation and oppression, the
style-is-content literature reflects a remarkable consistency. But how is this spirit
applied to specific films and how does it operate? This question raises a fundamental problem with the style-is-content literature. None of the analysts mentioned—from Higham and Greenberg to Sylvia Harvey—ever explain in their studies
how a particular film that supposedly reflects the *noir* spirit does so in terms of
overall closure. At this point, some perspective is needed on what the critics have
said and whether or not it affords an adequate definition of the subject. To be fair,
their assessment of *film noir* is not altogether inaccurate. However, their tendency
to construct generalizations based on the style of the films has caused them to
overlook the way content is expressed. The critics, for example, never pinpoint
specific points of view in the films. They never examine one film and then elaborate on the implications of its actual conclusion. This is because literal conclusions
are wholly suspect in modern film criticism. They usually represent "bogus
themes" that contradict the spontaneous purity of the style.

When critics make such artistic preferences, it is generally with good intentions: they desire to broaden the horizons of art. But problems develop when a
certain perference becomes a mono-causal theory of reality. Its terms become
"reified," to use Max Weber's expression; the theory seems to acquire a life of its
own, and many people will follow its lead without questioning it. Because style
has become something of a mono-causal theory in *film noir* criticism, it seems important to analyze the value of its approach.

The style-is-content argument in *film noir* studies touches upon the problem of
values clarification in art criticism and scholarship. In America especially, movies
were not considered an object of serious study until the late 1960s, when film
courses began to be taught in community and four-year colleges. The teaching
method in these courses was primarily descriptive. How was a film made? What

distinguished the cinema from other representational art forms such as painting and theatre? What were a film's textures, structures, and symbols? On campuses, key movements in film were discussed such as *Nouvelle Vague*, and individual movies were dissected–as if under a microscope–then relegated to the latest genre or subgenre the critics and analysts had discovered.

This emphasis on formal achievements was not as cold and reductionist as it might sound. It had an antecedent in the longing for freedom expressed in modern art theory in the 1930s and 1940s. Believing that fascism and Stalinist Realism were debasing art and culture, critics such as Alfred Barr and Clement Greenburg came to view style as the principal liberating factor in art. Content was dismissed because it implied a certain amount of reflection upon already existing norms, values, and beliefs. The purpose of art was not to reproduce old values–political, religious, ethical–because these values had become trivialized by mass culture. The fundamental purpose of art was to produce new forms in acts of spontaneous creation.[19]

During the same period that Barr and Greenburg were writing, Alexander Astruc was developing, in France, a similar line of reasoning that he applied to film: his important theory of *camera-stylo* (camera-pen). This approach argues that the theme of a movie is implicit in its visual style and that visual composition is more important than the meanings found in spoken dialogue. In the past, filmmaking had imitated literature and the play; this had been one of its biggest mistakes. Astruc stated that "the cinema will gradually break free from the tyranny of what is visual, the image for its own sake, from the immediate and concrete demands of the narrative, to become a means of writing just as flexible and subtle as written language."[20]

According to Astruc, the cinema was just as much an art as writing or painting, and one of its central aims was liberation from content. By the 1960s, Susan Sontag, in her essay "On Style," was calling for the limitation of the human content in art. One of the central purposes of art, she explained, was to "fend off tired ideologies like humanism or socialist realism which put art in the service of some moral or social idea."[31] Sontag went on to formulate a philosophy of art as "dehumanized representation":

> All works of art are founded on a certain distance from the lived reality which is represented. This "distance" is, by definition, inhuman or impersonal to a certain degree; for in order to appear to us as art, the work must restrict sentimental intervention and emotional participation, which are functions of "closeness." It is the degree and manipulating of this distance...which constitute the style of the work. In the final analysis, "style" is art. And art is nothing more or less than various modes of stylized, dehumanized representation.[22]

Sontag concluded that this act of distancing encompassed a language of possibility and liberation because it represented "movement...not just away from but toward the world."[23] This point is restated in somewhat clearer fashion by Ernst Fischer in his 1967 book **Art Against Ideology**:

> Art is now obliged to reveal the real world behind the apparent one, to drive men who are escaping into irresponsibility back into reality.... The fetishes of our time are objects of external life: mechanisms, institutions, clichés, "facts," phrases. To get rid of fetishes means to break through this *substitute reality of connivance* and to reveal the latent reality. But the fetish formations in a highly developed industrial society are so dense and strong that without the help of shock the imagination can scarcely hope to break through them into reality. How can art, using old methods, challenge if not defeat the barbarism which is establishing itself in the midst of our civilization? If art is determined to fight against the fetishes, it must adapt itself to the conditions of that struggle and risk breaking with the old categories of aesthetics.[24]

Critics such as Barr and Greenburg, Sontag and Fischer, were using style as the basis for a heuristic theory of art in which the artist was supposed to make a clean break with traditional values. In 1970, in his book **Expanded Cinema**, Gene Youngblood explained how this metacritical conception of art could be applied to film. According to Youngblood, the purpose of film is to broaden our spiritual horizons by extending the technical and aesthetic possibilities of the medium into new, exciting frontiers. But Youngblood insists that before this can happen, the cinema must first do away with the traditional idea of the film as escapist entertainment:

> Commercial entertainment works against art, exploits the alienation and boredom of the public, by perpetuating a system of conditioned response to formulas. Commercial entertainment not only isn't creative, it actually destroys the audience's ability to appreciate and participate in the creative process. To satisfy the profit motive, the commercial entertainer must give the audience what it expects, which is conditional on what it has been getting which is conditional on what it previously received, ad infinitum.[25]

Art and film theories such as Greenburg, Barr, and Youngblood, in their conviction that representational art created a trivialized and debased mass culture, came to regard style as the aesthetic platform upon which to uplift society by making a break with popular forms of artistic expression and creating new ones. But as Stanley Aronowitz has observed, in **The Crisis in Historical Materialism**, their ideals backfired and created an elitist art criticism that "served to legitimate the production of an academic canon of high culture."[26] This would have been less of a problem had the modernist and realist categories remained mutually exclusive. However, inevitably, modernist standards of value descended into critical interpretations of so-called popular art as well. All of this discussion of movies as art and art as a tremendous liberating force had a definite impact on film and cultural analysts who came across the French work on *film noir*. When these analysts began to "discover" *film noir*, they were delighted that its modernist style seemed to propose a counter-cinema within the traditional narratives to which it was applied. Unfortunately, their use of an interpretive values model that worked independently from the specific historical contexts and values contexts, which made up the overall narration of *film noir*, made their assessments only half true.

At this point in our study, it is necessary to propose a new interpretation of the use of style and content in *film noir*. Where modern style-is-content analysts have been concerned with the cataloging of paranoid figurations, lighting techniques, and camera angles, they have used the elliptical language of style to support a normative criticism. If merely silent and disjointed sound fragments of the films existed, the logic behind drawing historical observations from incomplete evidence would be understandable enough. But *film noir* is not like a series of hieroglyphs in which only a few symbols have been translated. The films themselves are intelligible, complete works, that contain elements of plot, theme, and the conventional beginning, middle, end, common to traditional American films, novels, plays, and short stories. In believing they have discovered a Rosetta stone in the *film noir* style, modern critics have become stuck on form and neglected content. The Hungarian critic, Georg Lukács, sees an inherent fallacy in this—a kind of theoretical imbalance:

> Content determines form.... The distinctions that concern us are not those between stylistic "techniques" in the formalistic sense. It is the view of the world, the ideology of *weltanschauug*...that counts. It is the...attempt to reproduce this view of the world which constitutes "intention" and is the formative principle underlying the style.... Looked at in this way, style ceases to be a formalistic category. Rather, it is rooted in content; it is the specific form of a specific content.[27]

Lukács' argument offers extremely important insights into the nature of *film noir*. The fact that analysts have made generalizations about *film noir* from its stylistic qualities does not necessarily invalidate their conclusions; it only forces them to take into account basic objections to their method. Bill Nichols, in his article "Style, Grammar, and the Movies," suggests that it is not as important to value content over style as it is to fuse them both into an integrated critical theory.[28]

If style and content are viewed as working together in *film noir* as a kind of monad, it becomes possible to use this perspective as a way of qualifying some of the generalizations made by the style-is-content analysts. For these analysts, the idea of an American *film noir* is the idea that certain Hollywood films reflect a spirit of alienation, nihilism, despair, loneliness, and dread. But these negative terms have been applied so loosely as to have lost all meaning. If we are to inquire into the precise nature of these terms, we must begin our inquiry with the film story itself. If the principal characters in a given film are unhappy and alienated, what are their reasons? If the protagonist is despairing and nihilistic, what does he do about it? If we follow the style-and-content approach, the "story" will tell us what he does. If the hero is able to reconcile these negative terms—learn something positive from his alienation and despair—then we are not dealing with a black film. If the hero suffers continually and never learns anything, then we are looking at a genuine *film noir* in the light of what James Agee called "the cruel radiance of what is."

NOTES

1. Alain Silver and Elizabeth Ward, eds., **Film Noir: An Encyclopedic Reference to the American Style** (Woodstock, NY: Overlook Press, 1979), p. 1.

2. Raymond Durgnat, "The Family Tree of *Film Noir*," *Cinema* (UK), 6/7 (1970), p. 49.

3. Jean-Pierre Chartier, "Les Américains aussi font des films 'noirs'." *Revue du Cinéma*, No. 2 (1946), p. 70. (Translation mine).

4. Raymond Borde and Etienne Chaumeton, **Panorama du Film Noir Américain** (Paris: Les Éditions de Minuit, 1955), pp. 29-37.

5. Chartier, "Films 'noirs'," p. 68.

6. Clayton Henry, Jr., "Crime Films and Social Criticism," *Films in Review*, 2, No. 5 (1951), p. 33.

7. Charles Higham and Joel Greenberg, **Hollywood in the Forties** (Cranbury, NJ: A. S. Barnes, 1968), p. 21.

8. Higham and Greenberg, p. 33.

9. Higham and Greenberg, p. 34.

10. Higham and Greenberg, p. 36.

11. Jeffrey Burton Russell, **The Devil: Perceptions of Evil from Antiquity to Early Christianity** (Ithaca, NY: Cornell University Press, 1979), p. 31.

12. Paul Schrader, "Notes on the Film Noir," *Film Comment*, 8, No. 1 (1972), p. 13.

13. William Charles Siska, **Modernism in the Narrative Cinema: The Art Film as Genre** (New York: Arno Press, 1980), pp. 23-24.

14. Silver and Ward, **Film Noir**, p. 6.

15. Robert G. Porfirio, "No Way Out: Existential Motifs in the *Film Noir*," *Sight and Sound*, 45, No. 4 (1976), p. 213.

16. Porfirio, p. 213.

17. E. Ann Kaplan, ed., **Women in Film Noir** (London: BFI Publishing, 1980), pp. 2-3.

18. Christine Gledhill, in Kaplan, **Women in Film Noir**, p. 11; cf., Sylvia Harvey, in Kaplan, **Women in Film Noir**, p. 33.

19. See Alfred Barr, **Cubism and Abstract Art** (New York: Museum of Modern Art, 1936); and Clement Greenburg, **Art and Culture** (New York: Beacon, 1961).

20. Alexander Astruc, quoted in David Thomson, **Overexposures: The Crisis in American Filmmaking** (New York: Oxford University Press, 1981), p. 70.

21. Susan Sontag, **Against Interpretation** (New York: Farrar, Straus & Giroux, 1967), p. 31.

22. Sontag, p. 30.

23. Sontag, p. 31.

24. Ernst Fischer, **Art Against Ideology** (New York: Braziller, 1969), pp. 168-169.

25. Gene Youngblood, "Art, Entertainment, Entropy," in Gerald Mast and Marshall Cohen, eds., **Film Theory and Criticism** (New York: Oxford University Press, 1979) pp. 754-760.

26. Stanley Aronowitz, **The Crisis in Historical Materialism** (South Hadley, MA: Praeger, 1981), p. 275.

27. Georg Lukács, **The Meaning of Contemporary Realism**, trs. John and Necke Mander (London: Merlin Press, 1979), p. 19.

28. Bill Nichols, "Style, Grammar, and the Movies," *Film Quarterly*, 28, No. 3 (Spring 1975), pp. 34, 44.

Whatever Happened to the *Film Noir*?
The Postman Always Rings Twice (1946-1981)

Robert G. Porfirio

Now that some of the smoke surrounding the release of Hollywood's new version of *The Postman Always Rings Twice* has finally cleared, we are in a better position to assess its relationship to the Cain original and to determine its status within the larger canon of the American *film noir*. Those of us who still insist that toughness is a virtue bred by hard-boiled fiction and the *film noir* were never very satisfied with Hollywood's first attempt, for it gutted the novel of much of the sex and violence whose interaction is a hallmark of James M. Cain, and the glossy production values that then prevailed at MGM seemed to run counter to the dark, gritty ambiance of the *film noir*. That version, directed by Tay Garnett and released by MGM in 1946, was commercially successful though it never made the impact of Paramount's *Double Indemnity* (adapted from Cain's magazine story by Billy Wilder and Raymond Chandler in 1944), a film which mitigated the constraints of Hollywood's Production Code just enough for the *film noir* cycle to develop in earnest.

The prospect for this latest production of *The Postman* (1981), therefore, were quite encouraging. For one thing it was being directed by Bob Rafelson, an uncompromising young talent with a special affinity for alienated Americans (*Five Easy Pieces*; *The King of Marvin Gardens*; *Stay Hungry*) and Rafelson was working once again with Jack Nicholson, the star whose rebel image he had helped to fashion. For another, Rafelson had chosen the ingeniously atmospheric Sven Nykvist as his cinematographer and David Mamet, a young playwright with a recognized gift for dialogue, as his screenwriter on this project. With the constraints of the old Production Code no longer in contention, it appeared as if the time had finally arrived for a film to acknowledge an older Hollywood tradition with a modernity that would be fully consistent with its literary source. [1]

Yet the 1981 *Postman*, as well-crafted a film as it is, fails to meet this sort of expectation. It does indeed deliver on the sex and violence as promised in the ads, but I found it to be less compelling even than the earlier version and, what's more surprising, less effective in capturing the mood of the book. The whole of this newer production is something less than the sum of its parts and I suspect that

Opposite, Cora Smith (Lana Turner) and Frank Chambers (John Garfield) in the 1946 adaptation of *The Postman Always Rings Twice*.

85

The Postman Always Rings Twice has run slightly afoul of its creators' best intentions.

Rafelson, for instance, sincerely believed that Cain's novel demanded the pictorial integrity of a Hopper painting rather than a modish preoccupation with Art Deco,[2] so he and his production designer, George Jenkins, have been meticulous in their evocation of a Depression America. But in providing the "proper" setting for their story, the filmmakers have also distanced the spectator from the lives of its characters and one is quite easily distracted by each period icon. Such is not the case with the 1946 version because, like *Double Indemnity*, it was able to remain completely indifferent to a Depression setting, relying instead on the nondescript look of the early forties whose inconspicuousness provides a neutral ground for the story, although its modern, white "Twin Oaks" is definitely not the run-of-the-mill "joint" alluded to by Cain.

Bob Rafelson, on the other hand, has created a Twin Oaks that bears all the traces of being a "joint," and his observance of its staircase as "the predominant symbol of the film" harks back to the *film noir* where it is so often the nexus of domestic intrigue; however, he resists using it in the same telling fashion. (See, for instance, *Double Indemnity*.) While Rafelson prefers a fluid visual style that does not call attention to itself, there is something a bit too calculated about *The Postman's* images. The interiors are so unnaturally dark that even the sunlight, dissipated as it is to form shadow patterns on the walls, can do little to dispel a gloom that seems to have been painted on (it was); the living quarters are either so bereft of humane qualities that there appears little beyond the bare bulb hanging from the ceiling or so cluttered that the walls appear to be closing in! After a time one even begins to anticipate the appearance of appropriate motifs–a tell-tale rain, say–instead of being carried along by them.

Moving the action away from Twin Oaks–here *clearly* Cora Papdakis' personal prison–does not really improve matters. When Frank and Cora run off together, for example, the futility of their gesture is lost to a period Los Angeles with its pathetic breadlines, its grim bus depot, and the sleazy back alley where Frank shoots craps while Cora sneaks back to Nick. Obviously Rafelson felt that the Depression setting was necessary to motivate behavior ("It was more difficult in 1934 for a woman to leave a man than it is today"), yet his characteristic ellipsis here undermines the historical background by masking a crucial discernment: despite her passion for Frank, Cora is unable to walk away from the economic security represented by Twin Oaks. Later, in rationalizing her murderous suggestion to Frank, she is allowed no more than an expression of some vague fear that her husband will pursue them if they run away together. In both the novel and the earlier film, this economic motivation is made manifest, though that film needs little more justification than the sight of an immaculately clad Lana Turner becoming progressively disheveled as Frank and Cora attempt to hitchhike their way out.[3] And

MGM's prim and sanitized Twin Oaks seems to make its appeal all the more cogent.

Even the care Rafelson exercised in selecting a ranch near Santa Barbara as the primary site for his exteriors misfires. Cain's location somewhere "near Glendale" is out of the question today, but now the countryside surrounding Twin Oaks is too bucolic, with a "highway" that winds through meadowland and "mountains" that are soft, green, and bathed in mist. Yet even this setting might have sufficed had Rafelson not staged the final sequence there, ending his film with the auto accident that kills Cora so that this scene is then tempered by the warm, golden hues of the afternoon sun. Cain's bloody details are eliminated, but so is the scene where Cora swims out too far to "test" Frank's love, thereby precipitating the fatal crash that ironically recalls the earlier "accident." The MGM version retained this beach scene and staged it at night so that its disquieting stillness could be counter-pointed by the accident, occurring appropriately enough *at night on the coast highway* and centered emotionally on the lipstick that rolls out of the dead Cora's hand, a fetish which brings together Cora's feminine mystique and Frank's fatal obsession.

Rafelson ends *Postman* with a shot of Frank weeping over the roadside body of Cora. Such sentimentality is surprising because it is so at odds with the mood of Cain's novel and even with the rest of this film which engages us more through its sombre visuals than through the lives of its characters. The MGM version, on the other hand, distances its audience less and is far stingier with its mannered visuals. Yet the visual style of that film is better able to advance its mood and this is due precisely to its adherence to the codes of lighting which then prevailed (as described, for example, in John Alton's *Painting With Light*): most of its shots are well-lit but those involving Frank and Cora's illicit relationship, their intrigues against Nick, and the chain of events leading to Cora's death are progressively darker and more mannered so that the film seems to move from light to darkness (except for the last scene on death row which in any case fades to black at "The End"). The new *Postman* carries one in the opposite direction, from the startling blackness of its opening title shot (Frank hitchhiking at night) to the amber brilliance of its plein-air conclusion.

The visual disparities we have been describing are troubling, but major defects begin to emerge once we enter the domain of iconology, for then we must confront one of the film's chief problems—Jack Nicholson. It is not that something is "wrong" with this actor's performance here; in fact it is remarkably subdued. The trouble lies rather in the economy of means which casts Nicholson in a role that draws upon only a portion of his pre-established "star" qualities too devious and cunning for Frank Chambers. The Frank of Cain's novel is hardly "cool" by traditional hard-boiled standards. He is more the passionate man whose emotions sometimes betray him and whose toughness is defined by the immediacy of his actions and his resignation to their consequences. When Rafelson initially brought

Above, John Garfield's Frank Chambers prepares to assault Nick Smith (Cecil Kellaway) while Lana Turner's Nora cringes. Below, a romantic moment between Jack Nicholson as Frank and Jessica Lange as Cora Papadakis in the 1981 version.

this story to Jack Nicholson's attention, he rightly perceived a kinship between Nicholson and the late John Garfield based on their mutual affinity for alienated characters. But the Garfield persona, street-wise as it may have been, carries with it a certain boyish charm and vulnerability: witness how convincingly he begins to lose his nerve during the first attempt on Nick's life in the MGM film. John Garfield's Frank leaves little doubt that he could vacillate between passionate devotion and nervous betrayal.

In the novel Frank is more confident seducing Cora once he realizes that she is defensive about her dark features and feels less "white" for having married a Greek. Obviously something more than Frank's youthful brashness appeals to Cora and that something has to do with his looks: when Nick suggests she become pregnant, Cora contemplates suicide, insisting that only Frank can father her child! The new *Postman* heightens Nick's ethnicity as a basis for Cora's antipathy, compensating perhaps, for the suppression of the economic motivation for his death. Yet it also relies upon Nicholson's willingness to appear unkempt and slovenly, and he fails to provide the requisite visual contrast to John Colicos' Nick. At the same time Nicholson's physical encounters with Jessica Lange's Cora, though graphic enough by the novel's standards, are hardly an improvement over the debasement she suffers at Nick's hands since Frank's violence here is never clearly motivated by Cora as it is in Cain's: compare with the corresponding scene in the book, for instance, the rape-like force he exerts on their first encounter.

Consistent with Hollywood's war-induced conservation, the 1946 film version expunged virtually all of the novel's ethnic connotations (Papadakis becomes Smith, Katz becomes Sackett). Nick is transformed into an older, slightly alcoholic man (amiably played by Cecil Kellaway) whose marriage to the young and glamorous Cora (Lana Turner) is rationalized as one born of economic necessity: he was lonely and she attracted only the wrong kind of male attention. Little wonder that Nick is unable to satisfy Cora, and her fear at the prospect of bearing his child is displaced by her reaction to Nick's preemptory decision to move them to Canada where she can help take care of his invalid sister! Such glossing extends to Frank also, and now we have a well-groomed John Garfield to identify with, a man who looks so much a part of the middle class that constant reference must be made to his "itchy feet" to remind us of what a "bum" he really is. Despite such alterations of character, however, Garfield captures more of Cain's Frank than Nicholson does because he can convey a sensibility that might well say: "I kissed her. Her eyes were shining up at me like two blue stars. It was like being in church." Such words voiced by Jack Nicholson could only sound disingenuous.

Such words, of course, are better read than spoken and were wisely omitted from the voice-over narration that structures the 1946 *Postman*. Nonetheless, Cain's successful experiments with first person voice served to wed it more closely to the hard-boiled style, although unlike two other influential innovators,

Hammett and Chandler, Cain was little interested in writing detective fiction or in creating a character whose "toughness" is measured by the way he controls his emotions, preferring instead a protagonist whose emotions might lead him to crime. Cain's fiction is more psychological in tone than either Hammett's or Chandler's, and his hard-boiled style (much as he disliked the term) resides mainly in his unsentimental approach to sex and violence. Despite widely varying styles, Cain shared with Cornell Woolrich the knack of imbuing middle class crime with an aura of doom, and the breed of crime fiction they helped to fashion became a major influence on the *film noir* (its psychological dimension is certainly consistent enough with the *film noir's* expressionistic proclivities). And though Cain wrote "to the eye" and not "to the ear" (as Cain himself acknowledged to Billy Wilder, confirming Chandler's judgment), this did not prevent his first person voice from being revised and used as voice-over in both *Double Indemnity* and *The Postman Always Rings Twice*. Such voice-overs, in fact, soon became a staple of the *film noir*.

In spite of his admiration for the job Chandler did with Cain's dialogue in *Double Indemnity*, David Mamet convinced Rafelson to dispense with any such narration in the 1981 *Postman* on the grounds that it is cinematically redundant and tends to disengage the audience by doing part of their job for them.[4] Now it seems this decision was responsible for another of the film's problematic areas: in forcing the audience to perceive the story straightforwardly, as indicated by Rafelson's expository style, Frank is repudiated as its psychological center, thereby denying all access to the workings of his mind and the fatalism of this perspective.

Though the novel achieves these effects through literary means, the cinema does have at its disposal *both* sound and image to approximate this psychological function. Mamet appears to overlook this when he discredits the use of narration in older films forgetting how well *Double Indemnity* "frames" the movie and even telegraphs its ending ("I didn't get the money and I didn't get the girl," says Neff in one of the opening scenes). Still, such an oversight is understandable given the dominant role of visuals in today's Hollywood.

If I am correct in contending that the mood of the novel is better expressed by the earlier film than the later one (despite the liberties the former took with the content of its story), then we should look more closely at these differences in narrative structure and the effect each has on its audience. Such a comparison is difficult because we are dealing with two different types of narrative as well as the process by which each engages the individual reader or spectator. This, unfortunately, carries us into dangerous theoretical waters where we are exposed to questions of "identification," "enunciation," "positionality," "subject inscription"–to almost anything, that is, which is currently under debate among a variety of critical factions. It is not my intention to open up a theoretical discourse here nor to ally myself with any faction. I would rather waive all such thorny issues now, subsuming them as best as possible under an imprecise notion of point of view (POV) so that we may proceed with the critique at hand.[5]

Without any further explication then, let us simply observe that in making Frank Chambers the ostensible enunciator of his story, Cain forces us to accept it from Frank's point of view and thus enhances the capacity of a potentially unpleasant character to engage our emotions. Recall now how the iconographic elements associated with Jack Nicholson mitigate against provoking sympathy for his character. The newer *Postman* compounds this distancing effect with an expository narrative that favors an objective visual style. After all, it contains few purely subjective POV's, and while its visual field for the most part tends to be associated with Frank (the so-called "view-along-with" or semi-subjective POV), there are some significant exceptions, namely the domestic scenes between Nick and Cora, which are really less questionable (from Frank's standpoint) than the intercutting during the first murder attempt that shifts perspectives from Frank's outside the Twin Oaks to Cora's within. A less expository structure in the MGM *Postman* allows for a good deal of fluctuation between objective and subjective viewpoints, and while voice-overs hardly prevented the camera from assuming privileged positions in the classic Hollywood film, here the visual field does not stray far from Frank's purview, as if compelled there by Garfield's narration: for example, during the corresponding murder attempt sequence, note how the visuals stay with Frank, leaving his presence only long enough for Cora to telephone for help (while Frank, presumably, is pulling Nick's body from the tub).

But whether or not such narration dictates visual style, there is a significant relationship between it and the spectator's perception of the diegesis. For surely Garfield's narration in the MGM film shades our apprehension of the story, providing a running commentary on the action, explaining emotions, even reinforcing its subjective POV's in a manner that is missing from the later version. Of equal importance, it fosters a sympathetic response by deepening our involvement with his character. Unfortunately, most recent speculation around the general area of spectator involvement has paid scant attention to the soundtrack, though it seems to me that aural perspectives also have something to do with the whole mechanism of "identification."

To illustrate, let us consider briefly *Lady In the Lake*, another *film noir* released by MGM (1947, directed by Robert Montgomery). This film, of course, is used most often to demonstrate that a purely subjective POV does not always further spectator identification with a specific character, particularly in this instance where it is deployed consistently throughout the film. Yet if the film as a whole is troubled by its subjective viewpoint, some portions of it are not, and one sequence holds up quite well in its use of subjectivity: after being "set up" in a remote area, a soporific Marlowe must drag himself some little distance along a highway to reach a telephone booth. And if it is easier here to accept "Marlowe's" field of vision than elsewhere, it is because the scopic field here is so heavily reinforced by the naturalistic sounds we would normally associate with it (groans, heavy breathing, gravel crunching, etc.).

It is yet to be demonstrated that there are aural POV's exactly commensurate with optical POV's, but I think we are safe in assuming that the soundtrack creates its own perspectives (through speech, music, and sound effects) and has a good deal to do with binding the spectator to the diegesis. If so, then the soundtrack of the 1981 *Postman*, with its conservative use of music and lack of narration, does little to compensate for its visual problems and its individual scenes follow one another like a series of tableaus, resisting a smooth narrative flow. In the *film noir*, narration is frequently used to counteract the effects of a somewhat aberrant structure (by the standards of the classic film of the thirties, of course) though the modernist authenticated one, commonly found in semi-documentaries like *T-Men*.

In the MGM *Postman* Garfield's narration *appears* to be aimed directly at the audience to approximate the first person voice of Cain's novel. Now if we consider this narrative voice more carefully in terms of its mode of enunciation,[6] we shall discover a significant source of kinship between the *film noir* and the hard-boiled tradition. For as a cinematic device, narration is by nature redundant and this very redundancy calls attention to its enunciative function, regardless of whether it is present through virtually the whole of the film (e.g., *Double Indemnity*; *Murder, My Sweet*; *The Postman Always Rings Twice*) or only a portion thereof (e.g., *Laura*; *Out Of the Past*; *Criss Cross*). It may be regarded then as "heavily marked enunciation" and its role as enunciator (i.e., ostensible "author" of the story) becomes even more apparent whenever the narrative voice addresses itself to the audience (e.g., *Raw Deal*; *Lady From Shanghai*; *Force Of Evil*). And insofar as the hard-boiled tradition adopts a mode of enunciation that is marked, it contributes to the fatalism inherent in much of that literature. Such fatalism is also a part of the dark ambiance that defines the *film noir*, an ambiance that is more the result of a multi-channeled redundancy of sound and image than of mannered visuals.[7] And wherever a diegetic narrative voice is involved, there is an implicit acceptance of these fatal connotations.

True, a stoic resignation to life is frequently suggested by the iconography of actors like Garfield, Mitchum, or Lancaster, but it is conveyed as well by tonality of voice and rhythm of delivery (here the interaction of literature, radio, and film is clearly at work). The framing flashbacks then enhance this atmosphere by imparting to the film a sense that its story has already been played out and, often as not, the future of its narrator too (or as Keyes tells the narrator of *Double Indemnity*: "Walter, you're all washed up!").

As David Mamet would have it, the 1981 *Postman* attempts to establish such a mood implicitly through the steady exposition of its action:

> I tried to get the audience in the same position as the protagonists: led forth by events, by the inevitability of the previous actions. They don't know what they're going to do next either. They find out after they've done it.

But Mamet seeks a solution that is probably too dramaturgic for the film and a sense of fatality of Frank and Cora's actions is simply missing. Curiously, the very redundancy that led Mamet to reject narration as outmoded could have served to draw the audience into the film while heightening its mood with a sense of irony akin to the novel's. In the MGM film the action progresses Frank's relationship with Cora but we are aware of it as a dangerous obsession even before the first attempt on Nick's life since the narrator tells us: "Right then I should have walked out of the place, but I couldn't make myself do it. She had me licked!" And though the music punctuating his remarks becomes more ominous as the film moves towards its conclusion, his narrative voice sounds resigned until the final scene that converts all the rest of the film into a flashback related by Frank to a priest during his last moments on death row. Then and only then does it briefly lose its composure as its status changes from a disembodied voice directed at us to a diegetically motivated one directed at the priest (and later at the district attorney, Sackett). This, in turn, rationalizes Frank's concern over the possibility of a stay of execution, his desire that Cora realize that he did not intend to kill her, and his final plea (directed at us in the book): ". . . send up a prayer for me, and Cora, and make it that we're together, wherever it is."

In streamlining the story Bob Rafelson has eliminated the novel's last chapter, with its references to Frank's trial and forthcoming execution, and ends his film with Cora's death (perhaps we are to fill in this ending since here Sackett vows to "get" Frank after the first trial). The MGM version also elides the trial (covering it with a montage sequence typical of that era), but it retains the perspective of the novel by placing its story in the past as the confession of a condemned man. And in a significant departure from both the novel and the more recent film, which do not even introduce Sackett until the first trial, this version enlarges his character so much it tests the canons of realism established by the hard-boiled tradition. Sackett ventures far from the courtroom to make his presence felt at almost every crucial moment: he is the one who gives Frank a lift to the Twin Oaks in the opening scene; he is in the hospital room with Frank and Cora when Nick regains consciousness after the failed attempt at Nick's life; he is there for the discovery of the dead cat that seems to corroborate Cora's story; he is outside the Twin Oaks the night Cora and Frank set up Nick for the auto "accident"; he is first on the scene after the "accident" to confront a distraught Cora; he even comes to Frank's cell at the end to tell him that no stay has been granted. The figure of Sackett lapses into an obvious portent of doom, certainly, yet he illustrates our contention about the function of redundancy in the *film noir.*

The way the MGM film has restructured his character also illustrates something of the special psychodynamics of the *film noir.* Sackett's authority here is not simply a matter of his position as representative of the law, for he takes on all the attributes of the father as well, beginning with the established paternal connotations of actor Leon Ames. His fatherly affection for Frank is indicated immediately by his use of the familiar term "laddie" and it pervades his most intense efforts to prove Frank's guilt. But Sackett's presence becomes most telling with the death of Nick, and it haunts the lovers long after the close of the trial by posing a threat to their happiness together. And this is appropriate too because Sackett must replace the departed Nick as the father (more the case here where the elderly Kellaway plays Nick) in order to end the transgressive affair and punish the errant son, following an Oedipal trajectory peculiar to so many *films noirs*. It is not surprising to find him in Frank's cell at the end, acting as his emissary before the law (else why Sackett's interest in the stay of execution?), sharing the secret of his guilt, and reassuring him that his punishment is for Nick's death and not Cora's. As a symbol of Father/Law, Sackett recalls the figure of Keyes in *Double Indemnity*, hardly a coincidence since each film is structured through a perilous breakdown of the family order–familiar enough terrain for both Cain and the *film noir*.[8]

In the interests of realism the 1981 *Postman* has pared away all such Freudian overtones and has made a praiseworthy attempt to eliminate the misogynistic bias of the novel and the earlier film by giving us a contemporary Cora who is more human and more clearly victimized than any of her predecessors. Rafelson benefitted smartly here from the sensitive performance of Jessica Lange, one of the major assets of his film and well deserving of the acclaim it has been given. Free of the glamour treatment accorded Lana Turner, Miss Lange imparts a sense of quiet desperation to this Cora who only comes alive during sexual encounters, although she still retains a bit too much class for the voluptuous "hellcat" described by Cain. Mamet and Rafelson have also taken advantage of Hollywood's new permissiveness to give free rein to a sexuality that had previously been shrouded in the mystique of Lana Turner's image. But here it stands demystified, an object of Cora's pleasure too as she guides Frank's hand to its source with both of hers–so equal a partner to the act that she finishes on top during their first encounter. It is revealed once again on the occasion of Nick's murder, Cora's hand suggestively pointing the way for a union of blood lust and carnal desire (Frank and Cora have just bloodied each other trying to make the "accident" look real) in a scene quite worthy of Cain.

Of course Hollywood filmmakers in the forties did not have the freedom to be so explicit and that era's *Postman* is quite typical of the *film noir*'s subtle and sometimes ingenious way of circumventing the Production Code. For *film noir* is itself the embodiment of a clash between the sensationalism of the hard-boiled style and the constraints imposed by both the Code and the personal inhibitions of the filmmakers themselves. Viewed thus as the product of a mechanism akin to the Freudian conception of censorship, the *film noir*'s characteristic over-determination developed as a variety of controversial elements were condensed, displaced, or otherwise altered until the time when Hollywood's "official" morality changed. With such a heritage, it is apparent why critics of certain persuasions find its multiple meanings so appealing today.

Above, Leon Ames as lawyer Kyle Sackett in the 1946 adaptation. Below, a more rumpled and physical presence, Michael Lerner as attorney Katz defending Cora in the 1981 version.

As far as the earlier *Postman* is concerned, its producers were quite sensitive to the controversial aspects of Frank and Cora's affair and finally decided to keep their relationship discretely ambiguous, dressing Lana Turner in white to suggest that Cora remained chaste (thereby obfuscating how Cora could announce her pregnancy shortly *after* her marriage to Frank).[9] But Miss Turner is also dressed in black on at least three occasions, making Cora literally *both* light and dark lady, apt symbol for the *femme noire* where cultural pressures so often produced glaring inconsistencies of character. Her Cora, for instance, is by turns passionate in her love for Frank, treacherous in her manipulation of him, desperate at the thought of losing the Twin Oaks, honest in her outrage at his betrayal, and joyful at the prospect of motherhood.[10] Even Lana Turner's carefully molded beauty works towards an ambivalence here: the severity of her platinum hair and dark eyebrows as artifices suggests some hidden threat, a danger reinforced by a certain cunning in Turner's performance (she is surely at her languorous best in this film).

Not that Miss Turner was called upon to act, for she is little more than an icon of desire, her sexuality hidden somewhere beyond those legs that first captured Frank's imagination. In this wise, even incongruities of character are justified, since Cora is "seen" through Frank's eyes as the locus of male desire and fear. It is Frank's viewpoint, after all, that prevails so that over the shot of her hand releasing the lipstick in death we hear *his* voice gasping "Cora," as *his* eyes along with ours are caught and held by the fetish that once served to introduce her. No wonder Frank cannot rest until Sackett "forgives" him for Cora's death. For here, as in the novel, Frank is tortured with the thought that Cora might have believed he intended to kill her, or that he might even have desired it himself subconsciously. Rafelson's *Postman* has gone far to correct for these distortions of the male ego, removing Frank as its perceptual center and making Cora its most sentient character.[11] But once Cora is dead, the film has nowhere to go. Perhaps Rafelson sensed this when he decided to conclude the film with her death. And as humanistically praiseworthy as such alterations may be, they have served to skew Rafelson's film away from its hard-boiled center—a center which can still remain at the heart of a contemporary film like *Thief* despite its anachronistic flavor.

NOTES

1. Dan Yakir's "'The Postman' Rings Six Times," *Film Comment*, March-April, 1981, pp. 18-20, contains an overview of the many foreign and domestic film versions of Cain's story.

2. See David Thomson's interview with Bob Rafelson in *Film Comment*, March-April, 1981, pp. 28, 32.

3. Cain's novel also contains the hitchhiking scene but there it occurs after three unsuccessful attempts on Nick's life. In both American film versions, Frank and Cora first try to run off before embarking on a plan to kill Nick—an obvious ploy to provoke audience

sympathy. Significantly, it is Frank who devises the plan in the novel and Cora in the MGM film.

4. See David Mamet's comments in Dan Yakir's "The Postman's Words," in *Film Comment*, (Note 1 above), p. 14.

5. While I am sympathetic to much of the criticism that proceeds from a modernist synthesis of Freud and Marx along a broadly based semiotic axis, I am troubled by some of its theoretical underpinnings, especially those allied to the Lacanian notion of the "suture." Anyone interested in my own appreciation of them and their application to the *film noir* may consult my doctoral dissertation, "The Dark Age of American Film: A Study of the American *Film Noir* (1940-1960)," available from University Microfilms International, Ann Arbor, Michigan.

6. Perhaps unwisely, I am assuming here some familiarity with the notion of enunciation and its applications to film. To save time, the uninitiated can consult Brian Henderson's "Romantic Comedy Today: Semi-Tough or Impossible?" (*Film Quarterly*, Summer, 1978, pp. 11-23) for a brief explication and rather coherent application of the concept. See, in particular, pp. 20-21 which also contains a humorous reference to *film noir* that I found quite provocative.

7. For a more extended treatment of the fatalistic link between hard-boiled literature and the *film noir* and its origins within an existential sensibility, see my article "No Way Out: Existential Motifs in the *Film Noir*," in *Sight and Sound*, Autumn, 1976, pp. 212-17.

8. This is not the place to probe the tangled skein of family affairs in the *film noir* since it has been given a good deal of critical scrutiny lately. Out of the ever-growing mass of such criticism I would, however, refer the reader to two essays which take up some of the specific issues raised here: Sylvia Harvey's "Women's Place: The Absent Family of *Film Noir*" and Claire Johnston's "Double Indemnity," both in E. Ann Kaplan, ed., **Women in Film Noir**, BFI Pamphlet, 1978.

9. For more insights into Hollywood's manner of handling the controversial aspects of Cain's fiction, see the Cain interview published in *Film Comment*, May-June, 1976, especially pp. 56-57.

10. A more detailed analysis of these character reversals can be found in Richard Dyer's "Four Films of Lana Turner," in *Movie*, No. 25, Winter 1977-78.

11. An observation I share with David Thomson. See his remarks preceding the interview with Bob Rafelson in *Film Comment*, (Note 2 above).

Different concepts of domesticity: above, in *Kiss Me Deadly* the vulgar divorce dick Mike Hammer (Ralph Meeker) watches his girlfiriend Velda (Maxine Cooper) stay in shape to help incriminate errant husbands in divorce cases. Below, the idealist police detective Bannion (Glenn Ford) with his wife (Jocelyn Brando) and daughter in *The Big Heat*.

Creativity and Evaluation:
Two *Film Noirs* of the Fifties

Robin Wood

In a course during which I screened two films, we discussed at great length the historical antecedents and development of *film noir*; the somewhat tedious and "academic" question of whether it was a genre or a style; its relation to American (and, more widely, patriarchal capitalist) ideology; its relation to other genres, either precedent or contemporary (screwball comedy, the musical, the horror film, the World War II movie, the woman's melodrama)–the areas of difference and overlap ... All of this proved profitable and important of course, but I found myself, increasingly, wanting to argue for the importance of discrimination between different works on quite traditional grounds that always came back, in the end, to the question of personal authorship: discriminations that drew necessarily on terms like "intelligence," "sensitivity," "complexity"... I have mentioned the vague sense of guilt and uneasiness that this induced. It can be traced, I think, especially, to a fashionably dominant trend in film theory/criticism, the notion that what one should attempt to "read" (or initiate a reading of, the process being by definition interminable) is the entire text in all its endless determinations. (John McCullough's article on *The Big Sleep*–"Pedagogy in the Perverse Text"–in the last issue of *CineAction!*, than which you cannot get more fashionable, is a useful example.) I think the attempt to decipher texts as cultural products without boundaries, interweaving infinitely with other texts both cinematic and non-cinematic, is very interesting and potentially very profitable; it is not what I personally wish to undertake, but I am certainly not "against" it, on principle. What angers me is the arrogance of the assumption that this is now the "only" way in which we "must" read texts. McCullough's tone, in the article cited, clearly tells us that it was very reprehensible of Michael Walker to offer an "auteurist" reading of *The Big Sleep*: "we" know better now (and, whatever he might have intended, McCullough's "we" sounds suspiciously like the "Royal We" to me.) Why an attempt to read a film in one way for one purpose should invalidate attempts to read it another way for a completely different purpose is a logic that escapes me. We are back with the "either/or" syndrome, or, to take up my earlier comparison, with the desire to replace a lawn-mower with a hair-dryer: if I possess both hair and a lawn I can use both. There remains, of course, the question of what is most important within a given text. I can only repeat that, if a text is alive, it is animated by personal creativity, and it is the text's aliveness that interests me.

One evaluative comparison that arose on the course was between Altman's *The Long Goodbye* and Penn's *Night Moves*; but I have already made what seem to me the necessary points in the essay on Altman reprinted in *Hollywood from Vietnam to Reagan*, and (although it was written 15 years ago) seeing the two films again in close juxtaposition fully reconfirms my judgment then. I turn instead to *The Big Heat* and *Kiss Me Deadly*.

The outcome of the comparison (to avoid any suspense)–that Aldrich at his best was a very interesting director, Lang, when working with congenial material, a great one–will cause little surprise (and will presumably, to semioticians, amount to more than a boring irrelevancy, if indeed it is allowed even to carry any meaning). What seems to me important is the grounds on which it can be based: especially in view of the fact that Aldrich's film is clearly the more "satisfying" (i.e. coherent) of the two.

The comparison rests on the fairly close parallels between the two films. Both belong to the '50s, and are characterized by that period's mounting paranoia and potential hysteria, with the threats of nuclear power and the Cold War in the background (with *Kiss Me Deadly* one might rather say the foreground). They consequently belong to what one might see as the first (partially) revisionist period of *film noir*, wherein the figure of the investigator (clearly the moral centre of the '40s Hammett/Chandler adaptations) is subjected to scrutiny and criticism. (The second far more drastic, revisionist period is the '70s, with *Night Moves* and *The Long Goodbye* as prime instances). The threat in both films is the greed for power: Lagana in *The Big Heat* wants to control the city; virtually all the characters of *Kiss Me Deadly* are trying to gain possession of "the Great Whatsit," which turns out to be nuclear energy itself, no less. In both, the hero's integrity/moral stature is called into question (ambiguously in Lang, unambiguously in Aldrich), and the criticism of the hero is articulated primarily through the women's roles. The dénouement, in each case, involves the downfall of the film's most prominent villain through a woman's violent actions (Debbie/Gloria Grahame revenges herself on Vince/Lee Marvin; "Lily Carver"/Gaby Rodgers shoots Dr. Soberin/Albert Dekker) before the hero intervenes. A crucial step in the early stages of each narrative involves the murder of a woman (Lucy, Christina) precipitated by the fact that she has given the hero information, and made possible by the fact that, because of his contemptuous attitude toward her, he offers her insufficient protection.

One of the most impressive things about Aldrich's film is its relationship to Mickey Spillane's thoroughly obnoxious novel, of which the film constitutes a drastic critique. Spillane's totally unreflecting fantasy-identification with Mike Hammer–there seems no critical distance whatever between author and character–is unambiguously rejected in favour of what amounts to a systematic discrediting of him.

The critique of the hero is clearly central to the progress of both films. In Aldrich this is far more devastating and uncompromised–but only because the overall vision is altogether simpler and cruder. Lang plainly dislikes Bannion/Glenn Ford, but cannot simply *denounce* him, as Aldrich can Hammer, because (a) he sees him as necessary to a culture that may not be entirely unredeemable (Hammer/Ralph Meeker is as necessary as a pain in the ass) and (b) he realizes that Bannion's virtues and flaws are inseparable from each other (Hammer *has* no virtues, he is all flaw). Bannion's virtues and flaws can be summed up in a single word: he is an idealist, always a problem for a pragmatic materialist like Lang. Hammer, on the contrary, is a mere *vulgar* materialist, like virtually everyone else in the film: the case is as simple as that. He is motivated by a greed that makes him indistinguishable from the nominal villains, and the means he employs are as callous and devoid of human caring as those of the FBI. The extraordinary, irresistible force of Aldrich's film is achieved at a certain cost: the elimination of all complexity of attitude.

In both films the critique of the "hero" is effected primarily through the female characters. It is characteristic of *Kiss Me Deadly* that there this is achieved by direct and explicit denunciation: Christina/Cloris Leachman near the beginning and Velda/Maxine Cooper towards the climax, are both given speeches whose function is in effect to tell the audience what they are to think of Mike Hammer. Neither speech seems very clearly motivated in terms of the characterization and situation of the speaker: Christina has only just made Hammer's acquaintance, so that her insights into his character, while certainly valid, seem somewhat abrupt and rhetorical; Velda has been thoroughly complicit with him (to the point of prostituting herself at his instigation to incriminate errant husbands in divorce cases), bolstering his egoism, and her only reason for turning on him appears to be her recognition that this time he is involved in something much more dangerous than usual. At least the film never applauds her for "devotion to her man," but it is also clear that the women in the film, although they suffer in various ways and degrees, carry absolutely no moral weight. Both Christina and the false Lily Carver die because, like everyone else, they are pursuing "the Great Whatsit'; as for Velda, what moral substance can we grant a character who devotes herself singlemindedly to the "hero" the film despises and condemns?

The case is very different when we turn to *The Big Heat*. Here, the critique of the hero–itself a far more complex matter: Bannion, unlike Hammer, is a moral crusader from the outset and subsequently motivated by his outrage at Katie's death–is dramatically enacted, not explicitly stated in somewhat arbitrary speeches: the evidence, I would claim, of Lang's far surer, finer, more complex grasp of his theme, the token of a finer mind and sensibility. Consider how our attitude to Bannion is defined (or more precisely redefined: hitherto we have seen only the idealism) in the scene in "The Retreat" with Lucy Chapman early in the film. In retrospect from it, Bannion's automatic readiness to take Bertha Duncan on trust develops a fresh significance (we saw it earlier, I think, simply as an aspect of his moral goodness). With the confrontation with Lucy (for whose death Bannion is clearly responsible—he offers her no protection despite the fact that she has given him "dangerous" information, and treats her with undisguised contempt because she doesn't measure up to his standards of bourgeois respectability) Lang shows us the other side of the idealism, a type of idealism that is usually a "given," an unquestioned positive, but is here subjected to astringent analysis: a self-righteous priggishness, class-based, that judges people purely in terms of their social position, and which blocks Bannion from any finer insights into character. (One might comment here, as an aside, on the perfect casting of Glenn Ford.)

Lucy, shortly after she gives our idealist hero the crucial information he needs to start him on the track, and is summarily dismissed for her pains, is tortured to death. Her fate seals what is already clearly there in the scene in "The Retreat," our detachment from Bannion as an identification-figure: for Lang ensures that *we* see Lucy very differently from the way in which *he* sees Lucy. The critique of Bannion is developed through his dealings with and attitude to Debbie Marsh/Gloria Grahame (another instance of perfect casting!). I discussed this at some length in an article mainly on *Rancho Notorious* in the *Film Noir* issue of *CineAction!* (No. 13/14), and shall try not to repeat myself more than is necessary for my argument. Consider, however, Debbie's death scene near the end of the film. Earlier, Debbie, in love with Bannion (or, more precisely, in love with his perceived idealism, his moral integrity) has asked him to talk to her about his dead wife Katie/Jocelyn Brando, and Bannion, seeing her as a "fallen woman" contaminated by her involvement with gangsters, in contrast to Katie's flawless, if somewhat artificially constructed, bourgeois purity, has shrunk in revulsion from doing so. At the end, he is able at last to grant Debbie's wish for three reasons: (a) Debbie has murdered Bertha Duncan for him, with the gun he somewhat pointedly left with her, thereby exposing and destroying Lagana; (b) she has been instrumental in the arrest of Vince Stone; and, most important (c) he perceives that she is dying: she can be safely sentimentalized, without the consequences of any awkward involvement or responsibility.

Between the death of Lucy Chapman and the death of Debbie Marsh (for both of which Bannion has a responsibility he never, in his smugness, allows himself to fully recognize, permitting the former by his negligence—Lucy is, after all, just a "B-girl," not a policeman's wife like Katie or Bertha Duncan—and precipitating the latter by insinuating Debbie into performing for him an action he is too "moral" to perform himself) comes the brief but crucial appearance in the film of another female character, Selma Parker/Edith Evanson, the crippled woman who works for Dan Seymour's car-wrecking company. Her one scene (apart from a very brief reappearance when she identifies Lagana's henchman Larry for Bannion) occurs around the midpoint of the film, and provides the narrative with its turning-point. Without the slightest ostentation or underlining of "significance," Lang privileges

Different concepts of honor: above, Bannion beats Vince Stone (Lee Marvin) whom he knows is responsible for the torture of his informant, Debbie in *The Big Heat*. Below, in *Kiss Me Deadly* Hammer's looks betray his intention to torture the avaricious morgue attendant (Percy Helton) while the sinister Lily Carver (Gaby Rodgers) looks on.

Selma's intervention. Although she appears briefly in the background of the scene in her boss's office–the image I think everyone retains is of her hobbling on her stick between the rows of wrecked cars toward Bannion, who is on the other side of a chainmail fence. She defends her boss (who, out of fear, has refused to give Bannion information)–he "isn't a *bad* man," and after all, who else would employ a woman like herself?–before risking her own life (we know that she could easily join Lucy Chapman in the morgue) by telling Bannion what he needs to know. It's an extraordinary little scene–understated, almost thrown away: Selma is the one character in the film whose motives are absolutely pure. Lucy talks to Bannion because she was in love with Tom Duncan; Debbie acts because she is in love with Bannion. Selma has everything to lose and nothing whatever to gain, except self-respect. While Lang admires the other women, I think he invites us to put Selma (and what a little gem of a performance!) in a special category. *The Big Heat*, consistently, reveals a sensitive awareness of the social position of women, and offers a moving, unobtrusive tribute to their resilience, courage and tenacity, that *Kiss Me Deadly* needs, but entirely lacks.

The three female victims of Dave Bannion (if Selma survives, it is not *his* doing) are roughly paralleled by the three female characters of *Kiss Me Deadly*. If Aldrich's film offers an equivalent for the death of Katie Bannion, it is the death of Nick, Hammer's devoted "best buddy." This points to what is surely the film's most interesting aspect, a dimension lacking from *The Big Heat* and from Lang's work in general: its pervasive suggestion that the American construction of "masculinity" (together with its accompanying paranoia) is built upon the repression not only of the male's "femininity" (which would account for Hammer's hatred of/contempt for women, the film's major debt to Mickey Spillane), but his innate homosexuality. It is a theme that Scorsese was to "realize" fully and magnificently a quarter of a century later in *Raging Bull*; in Aldrich it remains a flickering, tantalizing implication, a "subtext" in the strict sense, yet it is worth recalling that an interest in the ambiguities of gender and sexuality recurs spasmodically throughout Aldrich's work (and never in Lang's; the one apparent exception–the suggestion of homosexuality in the psychopath of *While the City Sleeps*–is treated entirely negatively, as no more than pathological symptom). *The Legend of Lylah Clare*, *The Killing of Sister George*, *The Choirboys*, are overt examples, but even a film like *All the Marbles*, with its "tag team" of female athletes under an "apathetic and nonathletic" manager, is relevant here. Aldrich's treatment of this theme is not notable for much complexity or sensitivity (the sledgehammer sensibility that is both the strength and limitation of *Kiss Me Deadly* prohibits any nuance), but its presence (which is perhaps, in subterranean forms, more pervasive than the few examples cited suggest) is partly responsible for the distinctive quality of his work.

It can certainly be argued (and I shall not dispute it) that *Kiss Me Deadly* is much the more striking of the two films. It has a force, directness and impact that one is never likely to forget, and isn't this the outward manifestation of an intense creative energy? Fair enough: such a description acknowledges the film's undoubted distinction and testifies to its authenticity as a response to the contemporary cultural climate. With it must be considered the film's stylistic progressiveness (beside which *The Big Heat* appears decidedly conservative): "Years ahead of its time, a major influence on French New Wave directors," as Leonard Maltin's **TV Movies** guide (and indispensable barometer of contemporary taste) succinctly puts it. The influence seems to me unproven: the *Cahiers* critics adored the film, because it demonstrated again what could be achieved within a generally disreputable Hollywood genre, but I can't see that, when they made their films, they learnt much from it directly. It is one of the those films that *appears* stylistically innovative, because it employs devices that one was not then accustomed to meeting within the general run of "private eye" thrillers. In fact, its pervasive "baroque" rhetoric (deep focus, strikingly extreme low and high camera angles) derives entirely from Welles and Toland: the "innovation" lies in applying it to *film noir* (from whose world it was never entirely alien). It is certainly an audacious film; I don't think this is a valid reason for preferring it to a movie that is content to utilize (with great intelligence) the shooting/editing codes dominant in the Hollywood cinema. *The Big Heat* proves yet again (how many demonstrations does one need?) that those codes can be put in the service of subversive and radical purposes. Lang at his best (as he is in *The Big Heat*) is among the cinema's subtlest and most subversive moralists; Aldrich's moral sense does not lend itself to the finer discriminations—which, it is worth insisting once again, are as much political as moral.

If both films depict a culture in which corruption is virtually all-pervasive, the world of *Kiss Me Deadly* is *just* corrupt, and there is little more to be said about it. Hammer is allowed one moment of grace; his grief over Nick's death, as he gets drunk in a bar: a moment that eloquently confirms one's sense that the emotional centre of the film is homoerotic (Hammer nowhere evinces this concern over women). Otherwise, the simplicity—the lack of complexity, of delicate exploration—of Aldrich's vision actually makes it much easier to enjoy *Kiss Me Deadly* on the superficial level on which genre movies are generally offered, the level that we call "entertainment." The to-hell-with-all-this, blow-it-all-up attitude to American civilisation actually provides a relatively easy excitement, satisfaction, exhilaration. (The studio, which added a final shot [Ed. Note: nothing was added. Several of Aldrich's shots were inadvertently excised in later prints] still there is some prints showing Hammer and Velda standing amid the waves, apparently safe, need not have worried: audiences generally seem to derive a lot of pleasure from the fact that Aldrich blows up *everybody*). Lang's cautious, probing attitude that qualifies every judgment makes an easy satisfaction impossible (we would get no satisfaction from blowing up a civilisation that contains Lucy Chapmans, Selma Parkers and Debbie Marshes). One is left with a sense of discord and disturbance—with the sense of a culture to whose problems there will be no easy solutions: a disturbance crystallized in the film's last line: "Keep the coffee hot."

Fragments of the Mirror: Hitchcock's *Noir* Landscape

Alain Silver

I. Introduction

The aim of this brief study is not an exhaustive theoretical analysis of landscape, *noir* or otherwise, but the examination of its use in a limited number of Hitchcock's late films. However, some parameters should be set. Filmed landscape delineates a fluid dramatic ground that is neither a representation nor a recreation of reality. Rather, it is a space that defines and intends its own reality of immediate visual experience while maintaining a relationship with the physical and potentially experiential reality from which it is drawn. Although the sources of filmed landscapes are often composites of real places, studio sets, and/or miniatures stitched together through editing and visual effects, the "film landscape" is that composite. In other words, the film landscape is posed as a synthesis of the immediate, particularized, and textural reality seen on the screen and a potential, generalized, structural reality which may be extrapolated from it.

The traditional (pre-cinematic) dramatic possibilities of landscape have usually operated and been defined in literary, theatrical, or painterly terms. Even in its broadest meaning, where landscape can be taken to include what might otherwise be labeled cityscape, seascape, or even skyscape, the concept of dramatic landscape implies that it is thrust forward from its more typical rear ground. The prose heaths of **Wuthering Heights**, a stage set for Macbeth's Birnham Wood, even the painterly impressions of Monet or Turner have relatively little specific geography. They exist irrespective of style as abstractions. It is conceivable for a film adaptation of the Brontë novel or Shakespease play to be translated into precisely the same images and for those images to be shot either in genuine exteriors or on the set of a soundstage. Given the nature of film production, it is also extremely unlikely. Witness the range of difference between William Wyler's *Wuthering Heights* or Orson Welles' *Macbeth* and the 1970s adaptations directed by Robert Fuest and Roman Polanski respectively. It is apparent that a specific visualization of a particular described landscape can draw from an almost infinite range of possibilities. This is not to say that, once set, the photographed geography has an absolute specificity. All images no matter how wide the angle are excerpted from the full natural environment. There is always something above or below, to

Opposite, constructed landscapes: top, on the backlot: Norman Bates (Anthony Perkins) poses by his mother's house in *Psycho*. Bottom, the stage set for *Rear Window*.

107

left or right, that is cut off by the frame line. But the ambiguities of a photographed landscape are different from other verbal or visual counterparts.

A shot of a cliff, once inserted into a motion picture, becomes the irrefutable topography of the moment but does not cease to contain a topography—landfall, brink, receding plateau—as well. The shot is further informed in both instants by any and all actual experience of "cliff" on the viewer's parts, that is the remembrance of dizzying heights, peril while standing on the edge, etc. A shot of an artificial element of topography such as a bridge, similarly contains not just the immediate associations of architectural span over water or chasm but all the experiential links with "bridgeness" provided by the viewer. This also includes the abstraction of "bridging" and all the connotations and figurative possibilities of the term. In short, everything in the viewer's consciousness which relates to any concept manifest in the image.

The use of a "monumental" landscape alters both these immediate and potential elements. In a kind of visual synecdoche, well known edifices such as the Eiffel Tower, Big Ben, or the Empire State Building identify not only themselves but also act as a convenient shorthand for the entire cities which encompass them. There is an analogous interaction between the Grand Canyon, the White Cliffs of Dover, or Victoria Falls and the surrounding countrysides. But the use of monuments does not necessarily expand the range of audience associations. Instead, if the Golden Gate Bridge is substituted for "a" bridge in the earlier illustration, the mental extrapolations of the viewer may be restricted or redirected depending upon the individual and whether the monument or the idea of bridge itself takes precedence in his or her mind. All of these factors are thus variably absorbed into the basic synthesis of image and spectator which triggers and delimits emotional and intellectual responses.

Narrative Values. Suspense.

The audiences of the classic period of *film noir* understood film landscape from the conventions of the previous decades. The use of process photography (that is, a background projected onto a screen before which actors stand) to permit shooting outdoor scenes on a soundstage, created a wholly "artificial" environment as it combined two very different actualities into one film geography. The cityscapes of *film noir*, the glistening streets and shadowy sidewalks of the urban night, could be created from "practicals" (actual locations), back lot structures, or even stage sets with or without process, and could easily combine two or all three methods in a given movie. Hitchcock's relationship to the *noir* cycle has always been ill-defined. Many of the films which he directed during the course of the classic period are ambiguously *noir*. Certainly *Shadow of a Doubt* (1943), *Notorious* (1946), *Strangers on a Train* (1951), and *the Wrong Man* (1957) are *noir* from their titles to their obsessive, anguished, and disturbed protagonists. But what of *The Paradine Case* or *Spellbound*? Or the wife who comes to fear her husband in *Rebecca* or *Suspicion*? Perhaps the most significant omission from the consensus list of classic period titles is *I Confess*, whose narrative and protagonists are mainstream *noir*. More recent commentators have argued late *noir* credentials for *Vertigo*'s obsessed detective, which was released after all in the same year as *Touch of Evil* (1958); for the "wrong man" in *North by Northwest* the following year; and for *Psycho*'s dark vision the year after that. Finally, there are *noir* pre-cursors in such late British films as *The 39 Steps* and *Jamaica Inn*.

The 39 Steps (1935), for instance, contains several sequences in which suspense and/or narrative development are contingent on the physical attributes of terrain. The escape of Hannay and Pamela late in the picture depends on the fact that they are in open country and there is a dense night fog. The landscape and weather function simply as a plot convenience. Hannay's earlier escape from the train, which takes place on a railway bridge, is more complexly fabricated. The setting immediately communicates to the viewer that–if he has left the train which is not certain–his avenues of escape are severely limited, either forward or backward along the track (in plain view and extremely vulnerable) or, an even more fatal alternative, downward. The spectator's appreciation of this situation creates an initial suspense over whether he will be able to evade capture or not; and this sensation is momentarily intensified when the viewer, sharing the point-of-view of the pursuing police for a few seconds, does not see him. A possible conclusion, given the viewer's "real" knowledge of railroad bridges, is that Hannay has leaped from it probably to his death. Working counter to that is the genre expectation which stipulates that Hannay, the hero cannot perish at this point in the film. The operation is simple if bifocal. The specific topography restricts the character's escape, yet he cannot be seen. The viewer's disquiet stems not so much from a fear that he has plunged off the bridge–the structure of the genre makes his death all but impossible–but from the inability to logically reconcile two narrative "facts." The détente merely requires a side-traveling which reveals Hannay standing behind a support column.

The final scene in *Suspicion* (1942) differs slightly in that it depends substantially on sharing a character point-of-view for its suspense. The extra long shots of Aysgarth's car driving along a cliff road do not give a present sense of perils. The car does not appear to be hazardously close to the edge. Only by assuming Lina Aysgarth's perspective–both the cumulative narrative point-of-view that centers on her suspicion that her husband is a murderer and the actual shots from her viewpoints looking down as the car veers near the brink and her door swings open–is the notion of imminent danger really conveyed and sustained through the "objective" long shots, so that the potential threat of the landscape is actualized throughout the sequence in the spectator's mind.

Suspense, in itself, is not a fixed value of landscape. It derives from narrative context–in these instances it is colored by point-of-view, either subjective or objective-being actualized, defined, and directed by it. Although a given scene may not significantly advance the plot lines, there is a functional relationship between such constructs as the escape in the fog in *The 39 Steps* or the tracks in the snow in *Spellbound* (plot revelation) and the cliffs at the end of *Suspicion* (suspense). Both uses are primarily narrative.

Figurative Values.

Suspense depends also on a fairly literal reading of landscape. For the spectator to share the experience—the anxiety, the tension—requires that the audience's sense of reality be engaged and that they possess sufficient information. This is not necessarily the case for figurative or non-literal (i.e. non-narrative) values.

The opening of *I Confess* (1952) is a slow traveling over water towards the hazy shoreline of a city (Quebec) at dawn. Under the main credits, the shot makes no literal statement. Figuratively, by moving forward as if under the power of a pre-destined *noir* pull, it sets up a pattern that imbues the cityscape with a deterministic faculty. It might be argued that this reading of the traveling shot is only one of many equally plausible interpretations; but this reading is not a generalization about the "deterministic" nature of all moving cameras. Rather, given the fact that the ideal viewer appreciates from past experience that a traveling-in does have a meaning (moving in to close-up for a reaction; revealing detail; simulating the point-of-view of someone walking) and given the particular circumstances of this camera movement—obviously it neither simulates POV nor moves in for a reaction shot, and it discloses no detail not visible from the wider angle—which communicates none of the usual meanings, the notion of a deterministic force stems from the viewer's objective response, from the unconscious sensation or conscious reasoning that something unseen and unknown, in short something fateful impels the camera inward. Accordingly, the initial value of landscape is a figurative one connoting exterior forces.

The succeeding sequence of shots develops and reinforces this value. Intercut with medium long shots angled up from the narrow streets of the city proper are inserts of one-way signs (marked "Direction" in the French and underscored with minor notes on Dimitri Tiomkin's lachrymose soundtrack). There is a clear sense

The opening of *I, Confess*: From **Frame I** (below left) which moves across the St. Lawrence river the "Direction" placards and other signs ("Quebec," "Canadian Pacific") quickly establish the specific geography. From the last sign (**Frame 9**, opposite left, fourth from top), a pan to a window (**Frame 10**), from whence a cut inside reveals a body.

of something momentous or dramatic, of something impending signaled by this "associational" montage. The selection of narrow, shadowy streets, in itself, visually limits perspective, is vaguely claustrophobic. The addition of the signs completes a metaphoric negation of the notion of choice or free will–the "direction" is fixed. The use of close shots (slightly distorted by wide angle lenses that hold depth of field on the buildings in the background) creates a dynamic line or vector that draws the viewer in much as the first traveling shot but focuses attention on an area outside the limits of the frame anticipates in a deterministic way something yet to be seen. The effect is analogous to hearing a noise around the corner of a building. Apprehension is directed both towards a locus and, although the audience does not yet realize it, towards an event. The latter is disclosed when the fourth close shot of a sign cedes through a pan (it follows or "is aimed" by the arrow of the sign itself) to a view of an open window and dollies in through it to discover a body lying on the floor. A second pan back to the street reveals a figure in a cassock hurrying away.

Figurative meaning in Hitchcock, particularly when linked to landscape, is not always as precise as this. As often as not, the values which supplement the literal reading of a shot may be discoverable only in the nuances of lighting (sunny exterior versus overcast; cramped, shadowy streets versus open, tree-lined squares) or angle (from eye-level to ground level to forty stories overhead with various degrees of tilting). Inversion of the usual, generic constructs must also be considered. The titles which provide minute details of time and place over the first shots of Notorious (1946) and Psycho (1960) and which imply conversely that it could be any time and place. Like the seemingly secure, rural bus stop in North by Northwest (1959), these are frequently cited examples of such a formula.

How then is one to read the silhouetted extra long (in time–20 seconds–as well as aspect) shot of the Forth Bridge in The 39 Steps? The geometry of the structure, the intricate steel frame rising in a high arch of slender girders in the centers could represent anything from the alteration of nature by man and the artificial strictures of society to a rough analog of a scaffold waiting for Hannay's footfall (a scaffold from which he has escaped in the previous scene). The voice-overs of police calls might be directing the viewer towards interpreting the shot as a classic landscape (rolling, wooded hills bisected by a shallow river) overlaid by the iron grillwork of a prison; but then what are the connotations of the dissolve to open country which follows? Escape? The fact that those artificial strictures, scaffolds, or jails are suspended visually over the succeeding shot or, by extension, over the whole of the film? The fugitive is a common figure in film noir, and Hitchcock's use of landscape to create a tone of uncertainty or menace in The 39 Steps anticipates similar interactions in many classic period noir films.

The flashbacks in I, Confess contain idyllic moments between two young lovers. From the viewpoint of present narrative time, the viewer knows that this idyll did not result in a permanent liaison between the lovers. Nonetheless, the conventional associations of the scene–rolling hills promising unlimited vistas, underlying fecundity, etc.–work both as a traditional landscape trope and in character context (the warm memories of the person recalling events). When it starts to rain, the lovers seek shelter. But neither a nearby house nor a barn are open. They end up under the roof or a small "summer house" or gazebo. Here Hitchcock uses landscape for irony: this tiny structure epitomizes their brief and constricted affair.

In actuality, this kind of manipulation of landscape elicits a complex response colored by those associations mentioned in the first few paragraphs of this study. The rear process shots of Sugarloaf and Rio de Janeiro in *Notorious* is a direct perceptual distortion. The spectator can "see" that they are not real–not normal screen reality but acceptable conventions for it–and can in a limited way coexperience the sense of detachment from reality which the characters in these scenes are feeling emotionally. These last are fairly straightforward, basically sensory reactions to images but pinning down the non-literal values of an element such as the lighthouse in the background of the balcony scene in *Notorious* with its cold white beam slicing the night sky like a blade while Alicia and Devlin move from love to estrangement is at best a matter of finding the "most probable" reading. And, usually, the context–here, the narrative fact that Devlin and Alicia are testing each other's sentiments, are wary of trusting anyone, so that the lighthouse may

Below, *Notorious*: Devlin (Cary Grant) and Alicia (Ingrid Bergman) kiss on a balcony in "Rio."

become a "tropological" emblem of their alienation, reaching out in a hostile environment—is a key to that most probable meaning.

2. The Monumental Landscape: *North by Northwest*

Claiming that *North by Northwest* is a picture which employs "monumental" landscape might seem to be a rather arbitrary stressing of sequences at the United Nations or Mount Rushmore at the expense of more innocuous locales such as the Indiana cross-roads or the Townsend country house. But the use of monumental here is meant to emphasize the notion of the man-made, of the artificial construct over the natural one. The titles of *North by Northwest* are formed from lines that intersect and separate into shifting patterns and shapes, varying in fineness and density so as to distort perspective and imposing a visual scheme over the frame that is texturally reminiscent of the Forth Bridge in *The 39 Steps*. From this geometric ballet Hitchcock derives, by means of a dissolve and gradually bleeding off the animated lines, the facade of a skyscraper. The bond between this man-made structure and the abstract vectors is unmistakable as one is literally formed from the other. What follows is the revelation of the hero, Roger Thornhill, on the street below. As he moves with the flow of the crowd and attends to some final business before lunch, the whole concept of artifice "hangs over" the scene, remains present above it just as by extrapolation the tops

Below, a restaurant terrace on a soundstage in front of a process screen in *Notorious*.

of the buildings which are not visible may be assumed to exist beyond the top edge of the frame. By moving from abstraction to monumental structure to human being, Hitchcock suggests several things about his hero. (1) He is at this point little more than an abstraction himself, a genre type or bundle of character clichés that should not be read as anything else as yet. (2) His life or his pattern of existence which has been isolated at random is like the pattern of the titles, an artificial construct. (3) That pattern itself is randomly generated or a product of chance. This doesn't mean that Thornhill is being somehow reduced to a monad in some vague metaphysical system. Rather Hitchcock is injecting added value, adding a preface to Thornhill's appearance which the viewer may use to supplement his generic expectations of Thornhill as the hero.

The function of monument in *North by Northwest* is initially at least, an alienating one. Thornhill is part of the cityscape like a line in the title patterns or a thread in fabric. The introductory movement is a dislocating one, towards the cameras, out of the crowds, off the streets. But on a larger scale, it can be argued that Thornhill never breaks out of his pattern. The shot of him escaping from the U.N. building admits both possibilities. The image itself–an extreme long shot from directly overhead which foreshortens and takes in the entire front face of the U.N. on its right–reduces him, on the one hand, to the status of indistinguishable dot, charts his movement as if it were a series of intersects on an infinite grid. On the other hand, while the shot may temporarily destroy Thornhill's identity by making him a minuscule, featureless object, it does not disrupt the audience's empathetic tie with the character. Moreover, either the "impossibility" of the angle or the direct realization that the building and grounds are matted-in miniatures, place Thornhill within the immediate reality of the image outside of the exteriorly real or structured world, make him a manifestation of natural (inexplicable or of different substance than the other material in the frame) phenomena maintaining a vector which is at odds with that world.

The notion of a character being "really" in the landscape is a difficult one, principally because Hitchcock situates his figures inconsistently. Thornhill/Cary Grant is really in Grand Central, not merely standing in front of a process screen; but he is not really in the station at Chicago. The U.N. sequence shifts from the genuine exterior of Thornhill's arrival to the matte shot as he hastily departs, an intricate but essentially "false', image. Yet the latter more aptly underscores the movement of the film as whole in terms of true or false, artificial or natural grounds. Mount Rushmore might represent the ultimate dichotomy: a massive, man-made edifice laboriously imposed onto a pre-historic topography. Thornhill's "death" takes place in an artificial locale (the restaurant), his "resurrection" in a natural one, so the location of the climactic ordeal becomes a synthesis of not only narrative (the choice of the monument itself) but also expressive (the matte work and other optical processes) components. As a genre hero, Thornhill is not really in peril–the audience fully expects that he will survive. Nor is Cary Grant actually clinging to

George Washington's forehead by his fingertips. The two "facts" reconcile themselves into a kind of ritual. The monument is both debunked (seen in close up so that its terracing and smooth surfaces tend to lose their monumental identity) and displaced by being relegated to the process screen which is a reality external to the characters (actors). This last is in marked contrast to the sequence at the crossroads, where the use of a day-lit, exterior extra long shot of Thornhill, of a dark, dwarfed vertical posed against an expansive, white horizontal trapped him, as it were, in a genuine landscape and alienated him both metaphorically and in real distance from the viewer (camera). When Mount Rushmore becomes the ground for a re-integrating ritual, it culminates in the dissolve out of landscape entirely to the train compartment and back, figuratively, into society.

3. The Romantic Landscape

If Robin Wood's postulation of worlds or spheres of influence in Hitchcock–organized along a fairly Manichaean principle of eternally contending forces of chaos and order and based primarily on a narrative analysis of the late films [see the chart on page 126]–is accepted as a thematic constant, does that imply a symbolic or iconographic dualism running parallel to it? Wood makes no significant attempt at deriving a consistent, purely imagistic pattern; and yet every

Below, the "artificial/natural" in *North by Northwest*: painted on the hotel room wall behind Thornhill (Cary Grant) and Eve (Eva Marie Saint) are a tree branch and flowers.

shot can fulfill a dualistic function either stated or implied. In the case of landscape, there is not just the film's ostensible terrain—i.e. the topography which Hitchcock allows into the frame—but also the real or intrinsic landscape that which actually exists beyond the distortions and/or omissions practiced on it during filming. Beyond all those values and qualifications mentioned earlier, landscape has a quality of duration. A mountain or monument, particularly an easily identifiable one, exists before and after the motion picture itself and possesses a substantial reality detached from that of the film.

Monument as an informing value in *North by Northwest* has a non-Romantic role—it is either an oppressive or neutral structure but never a truly liberating or transcendent one. A cynical interpretation of the film's ending might well conclude that when he is re-integrated into society Thornhill loses the vitality he has ac- quired and returns to the mannered existence of the film's first scene. Certainly nothing in *North by Northwest*'s landscapes runs counter to such a conclusion. Even the most Romantic of them, the scene in the woods after the shooting where Thornhill and Eve are flanked by the thick stand of trees and momentarily insulated from their problems and responsibilities, is after all, a studio forest.

There is a sardonic undertone in *North by Northwest* that encom- passes the interaction of the artifi- cial/natural dichotomy with other metaphors. For instance, in the Chicago hotel room the tree painted on the wall suggests that Thornhill and his Eve are in an ar- tificial Eden. And shortly thereaf- ter she betrays him.

Unlike *North by Northwest*, the various landscapes of *Vertigo* (1958), *The Birds* (1961), and *Marnie* (1964) interact consistently with their thematic constants. In the former, the wandering motif, the landmarking effect of the two prolonged drives through the streets of San Francisco, the ex- cursions to the redwoods, the coast, and the mission—all the indi- vidual usages of these locations, while eminently justifiable in themselves, only superficially aid the plot development and concen-

Below, Ferguson (James Stewart) rescues Madeleine (Kim Novak) from San Francisco bay

trate on figurative or more broadly thematic aspects.

The redwood forest, for example, acquires additional meaning from being un-established geographically in relation to the city. It lacks any of the precision given to the location of Bodega Bay in *The Birds* and is not even, like San Juan Batista, a stated number of miles south. This want of any specific geography, taken in con-junction with Madeleine's remarks ("Here I was born... and here I died") and ges-tures (tracing the span of her life in terms of the rings on the cross-section of a tree) establishes a method for escaping from the oppressive, ordered, and tem-poral constructs of society. The landscape becomes the ground for active com-munication with the past, like the Romantic concept of the ruined garden. It fulfills organically as well the archetypal notion of a timeless, Edenic existence, for the redwoods <u>are</u> preternatural within the filmic reality of place (they have no locus) and action (Madeleine's momentary disappearance). The camera movements are set so that both figures and trees seem fixed to the same axes. Exteriorly, as they walk aimlessly among them, for both Madeleine, Scottie, and, by extension, any-one the stand of trees are "in the past." They look and feel as they did hundreds

Below, framed images of monuments and landscapes look down on Madeleine in Fer-guson's bedroom after the rescue in *Vertigo*. Opposite, actual structures: the Palace of Legion of Honor Art Museum and the Portals of the Past.

of years before. Interiorly, for her alone, they become misty portals through which she may pass to leave the present, in mind (her distracted, somnambulant manner; the frightened recitation of her chain of thoughts, while she leans back against one of the trees) and body (when Scottie loses sight of her among them).

This last trope is clarified and expanded upon sometime later in the film by the monumental image of the "Portals of the Past." Gavin Elster originally mentions these portals as a place where Madeleine goes and "just sits and stares out across the water for hours at a time" in a state of mental distraction which the viewer may assume resembles that of the redwoods sequence. The portals do not actually appear until after Madeleine's "death" when Scottie, with Judy, is trying to find his own passageway into the past. They stroll past them silently while the camera, traveling in the opposite direction, traces an arc around the couple and the structure in the background, aligning their axes and linking them dynamically to the movements in the forest

Figurative Values.

The portals themselves—tall, fluted columns supporting a dome—resemble the trees both physically and metaphorically. Their principal value, like those of the redwoods may be a figurative one (unlocking the past); yet even in this capacity the nature of *Vertigo*'s narrative is such that they are critically involved in it.

Hitchcock's placement of his characters in this schema forms a thematic cycle—exteriorly with reference to reconstituted archetypes and interiorly through geography and action—which is itself a reflection of and reflected in the particulars of landscape. Scottie, Madeleine, and Judy are situated in and relate to their environment in a way that adds dimension to their functional existence as characters in a motion picture. This interaction may be conscious or unconscious, subjective or objective.

In *The Birds*, the pastel long shots as Melanie Daniels drives to Bodega Bay, with their subdued blues, greens, and browns under an overcast sky forming a terrain bare of shadows and unnaturally low in contrast, stylize the landscape and render it somewhat unreal. The sequence itself is rather overextended, if it is merely making the narrative point that "Melanie is driving north." By stretching out her passage through this unusual topography and sustaining the shots in which she moves from background to foreground or vice versa in the s-shaped curves of the

More actual locations from *Vertigo*: opposite Mission Dolores and its cemetery. Next page, top, "Here I was born, here I died": the display in Big Basin Redwoods State Park. Next page, bottom, the one way signs at the base of the corkscrew section of Lombard Street and, following page, Ferguson's apartment at Lombard and Jones (top) and the view of Coit Tower on Telegraph Hill from outside his front door.

highways Hitchcock <u>objectively</u> delineates the notion of passage from one distinct world (city/ artifice) to another (country/nature).

In *Marnie*, the Rutland Building–first seen in a long shot backed by a sky full of dark clouds, dissolving in from the want-ad section of a newspaper–is keyed directly to Marnie's point-of-view. It appears, as if out of her imagination over the page of newsprint and is textured so that it actually seems the representation of an oppressive (severe architecture; large sign in bold face) threatening (overcast) society which Marnie's disturbed mind believes it to be. There are, in fact, no unrestricted or "unforeboding" landscapes in *Marnie* until she goes riding at the Red Fox Stables (with an accompanying surge on the soundtrack), for only at such moments does she feel truly free or detached from those oppressive structures. Less subjective are instances such as the cross-cut side-views in the car trip after Rutland has caught Marnie, where the processed backgrounds in shots of her emphasize woodlands and open country while on Rutland's side of the road gas stations restaurants, and clusters of houses are seen. In *The Birds* there are intercut medium close-ups of Melanie and Mitch Brenner while they stand on a sandy hill,

Below, the "artificial/natural" in *Marnie*: Mark Rutland (Sean Connery) comforts a frightened Marnie (TIppi Hedren) during a thurnderstorm. Moments later a tree branch crashes through the side window splintering the artifact cabinet and bringing rain and wind directly into the room.

which alternately frame them against a cliff (Melanie) and the sky (Mitch). In both scenes, character traits–Melanie's inherent strength and Mitch's initial vacillation; Marnie's emotional (natural) aberration and Rutland's precise, societally conditioned obsessions–are metaphorically revealed or underscored by the backgrounds. Extending that to thematic traits, the entire trip in *Marnie* might be viewed again as a movement from one sphere of influence to another, from freeways and artificial considerations (plot mechanics) in the dialogue, until they stop at the coffee shop, then continuing onto back roads and an increasingly wooded landscape where Rutland can confess his more primitive, "animal lust."

Extrapolation. Inversion.

On the most essential level, landscape can establish certain lines of force within the frame which in turn elicit a perceptual response from an audience. The Brenner house seen across the bay in *The Birds* is obstructing the vanishing points and it becomes the natural focus of the shot's lines of sight. Competing with it for attention are the vertical forms of pilings and masts in the frame's foreground; surrounding it are the dark blue of the bay (center) and gray overcast (top). The house remains the center of attraction but simultaneously is part of a compositional tension, a conflicting turmoil of shape, size, and color. Beyond this interior line of force, the composition may erect vectors or directional influences which are aimed at points outside the limits of the frame (towards an implied landscape which has an exterior duration). The one-way signs in *I Confess* functioned in that way; and that motif is picked up and taken much further in *Vertigo*.

A one-way sign appears at frame right when Scottie first watches Madeleine emerge from her apartment (indicating the direction of the subsequent action). Another figures in the rear ground of a following close shot of Ferguson in front of the McKittrick Hotel. In an isolated long shot of a street corner at night, while he walks across in silhouette in the direction of yet another one-way sign, the stop light to which it is affixed changes from yellow to red. All these can be read as visual renderings of, obsession at work on Ferguson, of the fixation or one-directionality of his mind. Perhaps the most telling usage of this iconic shorthand follows his stay in a sanitarium. First, a panning shot sweeps over the entire city–across the roofs where his illness began–then it dissolves to Madeleine's apartment, as the camera assuming Ferguson's point of-view seeks out the last vestiges of her. The one-way sign symbolic of his compulsion is even more prominent than before in the foreground; and after a low angle close shot of Ferguson, Hitchcock tightens on her car but still holds the arrow-shaped sign within the frame. The final instances of this particular icon are associated with Judy–at the rear of the hallway leading to her room hangs a similarly shaped sign marked "fire escape" and it is last seen when she returns home "transformed" to Scottie. It's interesting to note (although it's never specified in the film) that Ferguson lives at the foot of a nar-

Hitchcock's figurative use of landscape in *Vertigo* might even be roughly charted as:

NATURAL WORLD		ARTIFICIAL WORLD	
Chaotic		Ordered	
LANDSCAPE		CITYSCAPE	
FOREST	OCEAN	SKYLINE	GOLDEN GATE
The redwoods: escape into the past	The sea: sexuality	The skyline at night: Ferguson's fall and illness	The bridge: Madeleine's attempted suicides

BEHAVIORS

UNGUARDED	OPEN GUILTLESS	COMPULSIVE REPRESSED	OBSESSIVE SELF-CONSCIOUS

The mechanisms for precipitating Madeleine's "possession and death" and Scottie's mental breakdown and withdrawal

RECONCILIATION

EXPLORATION	PURSUIT	RITUAL

The Two Missions

row, corkscrew section of a one-way street. The only orientation given the audience is that it is at the foot of a hill (perhaps "on the brink" of something) and that its significant landmark is the Coit Tower ("That landmark—I remembered Coit Tower," perhaps an archetype for the ordered world overlooking it, perhaps selected for its corkscrew shape). The only time that Ferguson is actually seen driving to his apartment is in his final, frustrating surveillance of Madeleine, turning alternatively left then right several times as he follows her through the city and ending unexpectedly in front of his own door. All this might easily imply that he is "going in circles" or metaphorically caught in a cycle of regressive (non-therapeutic) behavior.

To some extent Hitchcock is continually externalizing his characters' emotions in terms of landscape. He may alter the terrain itself (tilting the camera to accen-

tuate the steepness of the hill Ferguson lives on) while still allowing for "extrapolated" values (the tower; the one-way street, the circuitous route Madeleine takes
to reach it). Or he may bring character and background into sharper interplay. In
the visit to the graveyard in Vertigo where he intercuts traveling POVs of the
genuine location with process shots of James Stewart on a treadmill; in Marnie
when the runaway sequence matches helicopter exteriors to studio shots on a
mechanical horse; in The Birds when Melanie and Mitch leave the party (genuine
exterior) to converse in front of a painted backdrops; in those earlier instances in
Notorious or I Confess–whenever Hitchcock distorts or removes his characters
from the "real world" in this obvious manner, he also communicates an emotional
detachment on a sensory level.

A more difficult example is Mission San Juan Batista in Vertigo. The actual mission has no towers which provides an opportunity to make the tower required by
the plot both a narrative "fact" and a fictional projection, possibly of Ferguson's
disturbed mind. First, the tower is matted in with a technical skill that makes it
very difficult to spot as a miniature; then the conclusion of the scene is photographed from an impossible angle–even more so than the one in North by Northwest–in which the camera seems to be suspended in mid-air, a number of yards
out from the edge of the tower. No knowledge of optical processes is required
for a viewer to appreciate that something is "wrong" with this shot, that it cannot
be and yet it is, which sensation in the audience is a fair equivalent of that which is
being experienced by the main character involved, so that manipulation of landscape by contravening "reality" or realism again brings the audience close to sharing in the dramatic emotion.

There is no actual, definable limit to the variables of landscape in Vertigo or in
Hitchcock or in film noir in general, from a panoramic cityscape at dusk with an
ominous neon sign at horizontal center like a red, open wound to the barely no-
ticeable, inverted process screen which makes Ferguson's final drive to the mission seem to be on the wrong side of the road, each usage in each film can inform
and color other usages, adjacent and distant. While landscape in Hitchcock and in
film noir, must conform to certain broader film conventions, the style of noir and
the style of Hitchcock overlap definitively in the way which both create externali-
zations of character emotion through visual imagery. The recurrent tropes in
Hitchcock, the rituals and polarities of order vs. chaos and artificial vs. natural, are
also preeminent tropes in film noir. In a very direct and tangible way, landscape
and cityscape defy the spectator to anticipate them, draw emotional impact but
resist systematic interpretation. Perhaps, in the final analysis, they cannot be intel-
lectualized with any degree of the meaning or potency which they possess experi-
entially; rather Hitchcock's landscapes remains as in Scottie Ferguson's
description of Madeleine's dreams "the fragments of the mirror."

Barbara Stanwyck plays a very different type of femme fatale than Phyllis Dietrichson as the title character in *The File on Thelma Jordon* with Wendell Corey as D.A. Cleve Marshall.

The Unintended *Femme Fatale*:
The File on Thelma Jordon and *Pushover*

Elizabeth Ward

One of the enduring ironies of *Double Indemnity*, which is arguably one of the most important *noir* films of the classic period, is the casting of its principals. In a credit block of stars that included Fred MacMurray, Barbara Stanwyck, and Edward G. Robinson, how many viewers not already familiar with the plot from James M. Cain's novel would have expected the star of *Little Caesar* to be the only good guy? The tough-talking, sometimes shady characters portrayed by Barbara Stanwyck in *The Lady Eve, Meet John Doe,* and *Ball of Fire* were not exactly shrinking violets–what heroine of Howard Hawks or Preston Sturges could be–but compared to Phyllis Dietrichson in *Double Indemnity* they were choir girls. And long before *Flubber* or "My Three Sons" and also before portraying the craven second mate in *The Caine Mutiny*, Fred MacMurray was more likely to be trading jibes with Claudette Colbert than tossing bodies on train tracks. While it's clear from the recollections of various of the filmmakers that MacMurray was not the first choice for Neff, his casting was ultimately the most inspired in a film whose performances are among the most gripping in *film noir*.

Film noir is after all about style; and style is, according to Raymond Chandler, co-scenarist of *Double Indemnity*, not only "the most durable thing" but also "a projection of personality." For the directors of *film noir*, the stylistic layering was never just a visual patina laid over a crime story. While a fog-shrouded street or ominous footsteps from an unseen figure might quickly create suspense, the real shock of *film noir* came in the behavior of its protagonists. And the easiest way to play with the viewer's head was to cast against type, to work counter to the expectations by creating a core confusion between type of film and type of actor. This piece then is a consideration not just of unintentional *femme fatales* in two later *noir* films, but also of the flip side of *Double Indemnity* in that they center on subsequent portrayals of *noir* figures by Barbara Stanwyck and Fred MacMurray.

As the title chracter in *The File on Thelma Jordon* (1950, directed by Robert Siodmak), Barbara Stanwyck plays a very different type of *femme fatale* than Phyllis Dietrichson in *Double Indemnity*, who Thelma nonetheless resembles in method and motivation, as well as inevitably physical appearance. Although she ensnares the innocent Cleve Marshall to ensure the the success of a crime to benefit her and another man, Thelma does something usually associated with male criminals in *film noir*: she falls for her victim. Where Phyllis was emotionally empty, a woman whose profession of love to her co-conspirator Walter Neff came only to avoid being shot by him, Thelma is a confused and reluctant criminal. While there may be contemporary critics such as Jean-Pierre Chartier who thought that, absent Phyllis' predatory sexuality, Walter would not be "responsible" for his actions but merely "a law-abiding young man seduced by a calculating bitch,"[1] this does not jibe with the filmmakers portrayal of Neff. While he may not have ever used his inside knowledge of the insurance business for personal gain, it had clearly crossed his mind before he met Mrs. Dietrichson.

Thelma's patsy is Cleve Marshall (Wendell Corey), who is not only an assistant district attorney, an occupation that, in theory at least, is more dedicated to upright behavior than selling insurance, but is actually guiltless when Thelma enters his life. While he never dumps any bodies on train tracks, shortly after meeting Thelma, Cleve is cheating on his wife and soon thereafter covering up the questionable circumstances of the death of Thelma's wealthy aunt. In a typical *noir* twist, Cleve does a poor job concealing a murder, Thelma is accused of committing it, but Cleve is assigned to prosecute her and, of course, his feeble attempts result in her acquital.

Below, Thelma (Barbara Stanwyck) leans over the body of her aunt in whose home she lives. Her lover, Cleve Marshall (Wendell Corey), came to visit and found a crime scene.

As conspirators and sexual partners Cleve and Thelma are as guilt-ridden and romantic as Walter and Phyllis were calculating and carnal. Whereas Phyllis keeps her little indiscretion with her step-daughter's boyfriend from Walter, Thelma tells Cleve that her shady boyfriend Tony Laredo (Richard Rober) is her estranged husband, something which the smitten Cleve actually believes. The crucial moment that will determine Thelma's unhappy fate in the *noir* universe is not when she tells that lie and not even when she murders her aunt, but when Cleve confronts her after the acquittal at her aunt's (now her) mansion. Cleve faces her squarely, like the straight shooter he is or used to be, but his presence in the room is shadowed by Tony Laredo. Literally a man of darkness, with an animalistic sexuality, Tony is irresistable to Thelma, something of an "homme fatal." She cannot break with Tony despite her feelings for Cleve, despite, or perhaps because of, his clean-cut normality and self-sacrificing love for her. As she looks from one man to the other, Thelma knows they are equally bound to her because they both know the truth; but she realizes that her deceptions have left her no choice, that she belongs in the dark shadows with Tony. Romantically, she attempts redemption when she causes Tony to swerve off the road in a flaming crash and confesses in a desperate belief that her dying avowal may permit Cleve to salvage his shattered life. But Cleve is also a *noir* figure, and Thelma's touch is just as fatal as that of a full-blown *femme fatale*. In the end, it is Cleve who walks off into the shadows. "Because of his children and because of the years," he resolves to carry on the sham of his career and his marriage, but without Thelma and without his honor, he is an emotional Sisyphus, bearing the weight of a tragic mistake, toiling uselessly in darkness for salvation.

Pushover (1954, directed by Richard Quine) also resonates back to *Double Indemnity*: it involves murder for money and a cool, beautiful blonde who seduces a man into betraying his profession and his colleagues. In portraying Det. Paul Sheridan, Fred MacMurray reprises key aspects of Neff. Both characters are similarly vulnerable, superficially clever but unwise, concealing romantic disillusionment behind a mask of cynicism. As in *Thelma Jordon*, the use of MacMurray inevitably recalls Neff; but ten years have passed and the evidence of that decade on MacMurray's face have a telling effect. Neff was an ambitious young man in a well-cut suit, glib, attractive, and on the make. Paul Sheridan is slower in movement and less prone to snappy patter, with a puffy face that betrays an inactive and unrewarding life as palpably as a rumpled rain coat. For Neff, it was not just Phyllis but the challenge of the cheat, outwitting his mentor Barton Keyes, a guy who knew all the angles. For Sheridan, the temptation is all Leona McClane (Kim Novak). Again the intricacies of *noir* narrative create the essential irony: Paul is assigned to approach and sweet talk Leona as part of his stake-out for she is the girlfriend of fugitive bank robber Harry Wheeler (Paul Richards). Although Sheridan's con is part of his police work, the effect is the same as with Thelma and Cleve. The final factor is the age difference between the vibrant young Leona and

Above, Det. Paul Sheridan (Fred MacMurray) and the younger woman whom he loves, Leona McClane (Kim Novak), in *Pushover*.

the veteran detective, so for Sheridan the chance at having the missing money is a chance to buffer the years between them.

In the police interrogation room early in *Pushover*, Sheridan's younger partner Rick (Phil Carey) sits pensively by the window and remarks, "money's nice but it doesn't make the world go 'round." Paul's retort: "Don't it?... I promised myself as a kid that I'd have plenty of dough." Sheridan's snort confirms that he knows that the dream is just about over. In this context Leona and the missing $200,000 are a last chance that he cannot pass up.

Like Walter and Phyllis in *Double Indemnity* the sexual attraction between Paul and Leona helps to sustain viewer identification with the criminal protagonists. On stake-out with Rick, Paul watches him pine platonically over Leona's neighbor, Ann (Dorothy Malone), a wholesome brunette. Once he has succumbed to Leona's overtures that he betray his badge and take both her and the money, Paul is both disdainful and jealous of Rick's innocent infatuation. As a middle-aged man MacMurray uses the same facial expressions he did as Neff to convey markedly different meanings.

The physical surroundings during Paul and Leona's moments together in his apartment are remarkably similar to those of the Neff/Dietrichson rendez-vous in *Double Indemnity*. The staging in *Pushover* is almost a mirror reverse of the former but significantly less glamourous, despite or perhaps because Leona's naive, breathless sexuality has replaced Phyllis' sophisticated, throaty lust. Unlike their knowing and unknowing counterparts in *Double Indemnity* and *File on Thelma Jordon*, this couple do not redirect the tension of their secret and only partially consummated liaison into a betrayal of the other. It is only Paul who believes the money is critical to sustaining their emotional attachment. When confronted by the police, Leona actually urges Paul to forget about the money. It is not until he is lying the street grievously wounded that Paul realizes and says "We really didn't need the money, did we?"

While *Pushover* is a *film noir* and Leona is a *femme fatale*, actually bringing doom both to Harry Wheeler, whom Paul kills, and then Paul who is shot by his own partner, she is far removed from the predatory Phyllis and even Thelma Jordon. As a young actress, Kim Novak easily imbues Leona with inexperience and captures the confusion of the character's mixed ambitions. Although he initially accuses her of manipulating him and although Leona's physical youth and beauty give her the power to do that, she is too guileless. Having been manipulated herself by Harry Wheeler, she now becomes as much Sheridan's victim as he is hers. While it may be her suggestion, he, in fact, controls all the elements of their criminal scheme and only gives her simple directions which she follows unhesitatingly. One of Leona's few moments of defiance occurs early on when Paul reproaches her for accepting Wheeler's favors. Vehemently refusing to settle for squalor, she turns abruptly from Paul and in a rim-lit medium close shot pointedly affirms that "Money isn't dirty. Just people." Paul's face is visible behind, as it registers weary understanding of what made her compromise between disgust with her prospects and disgust with Wheeler. His expression also foreshadows the self-immolation to which his own lack of prospects will lead as he contemplates destroying his connection with the law and society.

While Chartier also alluded to the "pure young girls" in *film noir* who constitute "some hope about future generations,"[2] that effect is negligible in *Double Indemnity* and non-existent in *File on Thelma Jordon*. While it is well exemplified in the relationship between Rich and Ann in *Pushover*, it it not without some irony of its own. The gradual and reasonable (they are of like age and appearance) development of the attraction between Rick and Ann strongly contrasts with the impulsive connection between Paul and Leona; and the conventional behavior of the career woman and the dedicated police detective reinforces the safety of social values as Paul and Leona are driven to desperation and destruction. But the high moral tone is severely undercut by the aspect of voyeurism in Rick, as he literally window shops for the right woman. Paul and Leona are brought together on orders from his police superior. Rick's intentions may be honorable, but watching

Below, Sheridan and his partner Rick (Phil Carey) staking out Leona's apartment in *Pushover*.

Ann without her knowledge is stalking. Ann, though, unquestionably fulfills the purpose to which Chartier alludes. Although Paul has taken her hostage in his attempt to escape and although her lover Rick saves her, she immediately runs not into Rick's arms but to aid her now-wounded captor. If there is a fundamental aspect of women in *film noir* and their relationship to social values, a conclusion like this embodies it. Ann understands the emotions which Paul has experienced even as he holds a gun on her, even as Rick shoots him down. Rick's view of the patriarchal structures that empower him is inflexible and, even if he were not a police officer, he would be likelier to resort to violence and confrontation to resolve crises. He places his loyalty to those values over his partner's life. Although she is unable to dissuade him and suffers herself as a result, Ann's first allegiance is to the value of human life. Leona and even Thelma share that inclination. Even Phyllis, whom male observers call a "calculating bitch," understands human impulse and empowers herself by exploiting it. Ultimately, what the unintended *femme fatale* reveals about *noir* and its deadly underworld, is that the doomed male is brought down as much by his own ego and his inability to understand the emotional truth—"We really didn't need the money, did we?"—as by any fatal woman's schemes.

Notes

1. Editor's Note: cf. Chartier's "Americans Also Make *Noir* Films," p. 23 above.

2. Editor's Note: cf. Chartier, p. 21 above.

Above, Paul Stewart as Joe Kellerton in *The Window*.

Translate and Transform:
from Cornell Woolrich to *Film Noir*

Francis M. Nevins

Cornell Woolrich (1903-1968), the Poe of the twentieth century and the poet of its shadows, is universally acknowledged–along with Dashiell Hammett, Raymond Chandler and James M. Cain–as one of the founding literary fathers of *film noir*. But if Woolrich's novels and stories were no longer available (a supposition which today, in the summer of 1998, is all too true), how accurate a picture of his world could be gleaned from the major Woolrich-based movies made in the author's lifetime–films which are now easily available thanks to the miracles of videocassette, cable and satellite? My aim here is to offer an answer to that question. [1]

The first movies with Woolrich's name in the credits were adapted (one of them in name only) from two of the mainstream novels he wrote in the late Twenties and very early Thirties, when he still had hopes of becoming the next F. Scott Fitzgerald. It wasn't until about four years after he began writing suspense tales for the pulp mystery magazines that one of those tales sold to Hollywood for $448.75 and became the basis for *Convicted* (Columbia, 1938), a 54-minute quickie without *noir* ambience nor any particular distinction except that the female lead was played by a not yet famous Rita Hayworth.

In 1940 Woolrich followed in the wake of Chandler a year earlier and made the move from pulps to hardcover with his first overt suspense novel, *The Bride Wore Black*. His next movie sale and the first one to interest us here came a year later, after the publication of his novel **The Black Curtain** (1941), which attracted studio interest with its powerful *noir* story of Frank Townsend's recovery from amnesia and obsession with finding out who and what he was during three and a half lost years. Although Hollywood films on the subject of memory loss would glut the market later in the decade, no movie on the subject had yet been made at the time Paramount paid $2,225 for the right to adapt **The Black Curtain**. During production the picture's working title was the same as that of the source novel but it was released as *Street of Chance* (Paramount, 1942), starring Burgess Meredith as Frank Thompson (the change in the character's name being as unaccountable as the title change) and Claire Trevor as Ruth, the woman who loved him in his interim identity. The cast included Louise Platt as Meredith's wife, Shel-

137

don Leonard as the sadistic homicide detective who's out to nail him, Frieda Ines-
cort and Jerome Cowan as the widow and brother of the man Meredith is accused of murdering, and Adeline de Walt Reynolds as the mute and paralyzed old
woman who holds the key to the nightmare.

Directing this 74-minute film was Jack Hively, who had recently come to Para-
mount from the B-picture unit at RKO where he'd helmed several of George
Sanders' cinematic exploits as The Saint. Its cinematographer, Theodor Sparkuhl,
had worked on most of Ernst Lubitsch's silent films in Germany before coming to
Hollywood. Hively and screenplay writer Garrett Fort more or less followed the
Woolrich storyline for the suspenseful first half of the picture. But as soon as
Meredith and Trevor return to the mansion where the murder was committed,
the movie diverges radically from the novel, scrapping the many weak elements in
Woolrich's final chapters and all too often substituting clichés from the low-
budget detective flicks in which Hively had his roots. The film's most crucial
changes, however, improved on the Woolrich novel vastly. Townsend's devising a
way of communicating with the paralyzed mute witness and thereby laboriously
learning the truth had been a throwaway element in the book but was transformed by Hively and Fort into some intensely dramatic on-camera scenes between Meredith and Adeline de Walt Reynolds. Even more important, the
director and screenwriter junked Woolrich's ending, in which the murderer turns
out to be a peripheral character, and worked out a much more effective climax
with Claire Trevor herself being exposed as the culprit and then being shot accidentally while struggling with Meredith over a gun. Thanks to these innovations, a
number of knowledgeable Woolrichphiles insist that the movie is better than the
novel. In any event, *film noir* specialist Robert Porfirio was right when he re-
marked that with its hapless and desperate amnesia victim and its sense of doom
and foreboding, *Street of Chance* "authentically captures the essence of Woolrich's
universe."[2]

The makers of the next Woolrich-based film went way beyond their predecessors and captured Woolrich not just thematically but also in terms of visual style.
In his novel **Black Alibi** (1942) Woolrich had set aside loneliness and despair, concentrated on what he called "the line of suspense," and turned out a masterpiece
with menace breathing on every page. The five long sequences in which a different young woman is stalked through the night by a killer jaguar, or her own fears,
or a madman hiding behind the animal's claws, are among the most terrifying he
ever wrote. RKO bought screen rights to the novel for $5,175 and assigned the
project to the production unit of Val Lewton, who in the early Forties was responsible for some of the most haunting low-key horror films every made. Lewton, born Vladimir Leventon, was almost exactly Woolrich's age and had spent
two years as a journalism student at Columbia University around the time Woolrich had been an undergrad on the same campus, and it's possible, especially in
view of both young men's creative interests and Russian ancestry, that in the early

1920s they had known each other. *The Leopard Man* (RKO, 1943) was produced by Lewton and superbly directed by Jacques Tourneur, another visual poet well suited to translate Woolrich to film. The 66-minute picture starred Dennis O'Keefe as press agent Jerry Manning, with Spanish-born Margo as the castanet dancer Clo-Clo (a sanitized version of the near-prostitute in Woolrich's novel) and Jean Brooks as the actress Kiki who becomes the bait for the climactic trap. Although meticulously reshaped by Lewton and Tourneur, the screenplay was credited to Ardel Wray, a young woman who had recently joined Lewton's unit as a writer. The picture follows Woolrich's storyline–except for a few matters like moving the setting from Latin America to New Mexico, substituting a black leopard for the novel's jaguar and involving the Clo-Clo character at least peripherally in each episode so as to create a semblance of unity–but adds to the cast a number of people not in the novel, turns one of them into the murderer, and scraps Woolrich's horrific subterranean climax in favor of a chase through a procession of black-robed hooded monks.

In his critical study **Val Lewton: The Reality of Terror** (1973), Joel E. Siegel points out that the film

> was a departure from the Lewton formula in several important respects....It was Lewton's first try at a straightforward murder story, and for the first time he included several sequences of explicit bloodshed. In an episode which haunts the memory, a little Mexican girl returning from the store where her mother has sent her to buy food is clawed to death while trying to get someone to open the door. Although the violence is mainly suggested after the child's shuddery walk home, the attack itself is shot from *inside* the house so that we can only hear what is happening–the fact of the child's death is revealed by a rivulet of blood trickling under the door.

"I saw *The Leopard Man* when I was eleven," Siegel says at the close of his discussion, "and seeing it again for this book, almost twenty years later, I discovered that almost every shot was fixed in my memory. The death of the frightened child, the young girl alone in the cemetery, those shots of the dancer clicking her castanets through the dark streets–these are artful images of fear that will long haunt those who experience them." Many of those images come either literally or in spirit from Woolrich's novel. With the next film based on Woolrich, studios stopped thinking of him just in terms of medium-budget thrillers and began recognizing the potential of his fiction for top-of-the-line A pictures. What made the breakthrough was his classic *noir* novel **Phantom Lady** (1942, as by William Irish). A man quarrels with his wife, goes out and picks up a woman in a bar, spends the evening with her, and comes home to find his wife dead and himself accused of her murder. His only hope of clearing himself is to find the woman who was with him when his wife was killed, but she has vanished into thin air and everyone in a position to know–the nameless bartender at Anselmo's, the jazz drummer, the peppery Latin entertainer–swears that no such woman ever existed. The man is convicted and sentenced to die, and his secretary who has long loved him joins with his best friend in a race against the clock to find the phantom lady and the reason why so many witnesses couldn't see her.

Universal bought screen rights to the novel and gave the project to associate producer Joan Harrison, who was just starting out on her own after several years with Alfred Hitchcock. *Phantom Lady* (Universal, 1944) was directed by German emigré Robert Siodmak from a screenplay by Bernard C. Schoenfeld. Franchot Tone starred as Jack Marlow, the counterpart of the novel's Jack Lombard, Ella Raines as Carol Richman, and Thomas Gomez as police detective Burgess. The cast included Alan Curtis as the convicted Scott Henderson, Elisha Cook Jr. as jazz drummer Cliff March, Andrew Tombes as the night bartender, and Regis Toomey and Joseph Crehan as menacing cops. The movie's plot tracks Woolrich for about half its length, then veers off on its own paths and becomes silly, giving away the denouement far too early and turning the novel's murderer into a stereotyped mad artist, complete with delusions of grandeur and symbolic migraine headaches and overdone hand gestures. But in terms of visual style much of Siodmak's film (to quote Robert Porfirio) captures "the essential ingredients of Woolrich's world, from the desperate innocent loose at night in New York City, a city of hot sweltering streets, to the details of threatening shadows, jazz emanating from low-class bars, and the click of high heels on the pavement. The whole *noir* world is developed here almost entirely through *mise-en-scène*."[3] The picture's best-known sequences–the cat-and-mouse between Raines and Tombes on the Third Avenue Elevated platform and the jam session where orgiastic shots of Cook's drum solo are intercut with Raines' "wordless sexual innuendoes"–come straight out of scenes in the novel. Tom Flinn in his essay "Three Faces of *Film Noir*" got it right when he praised Siodmak for "creating a sombre world of wet streets, dingy offices, low-ceilinged bars, crowded lunch counters, and deserted railway platforms, all unified by an atmosphere of heightened realism in which the expressive quality of the image is due entirely to lighting and composition." [Ed. Note: see p. 38 above]

By the end of 1945 Woolrich might easily have felt that in Hollywood he could do no wrong. During the last months of war and the first of uneasy peace, each of three major studios paid him sizable sums for rights to a different novel, and he made just under $20,000 that year in film money alone. Of the three pictures that resulted from these deals, the first to reach theaters was *Deadline at Dawn* (RKO, 1946). Woolrich's novel of the same name (1944, as by William Irish) was a loosely constructed episodic work whose action takes place on a single night in the bleak streets and concrete catacombs of New York. By using clock faces for chapter heads he made us all but see the passage of time as his protagonists–a young man on the run from a murder he knows he'll be accused of come morning, and a feisty terrified little taxi dancer who sees the city as a personal enemy out to destroy her–encounter all sorts of disconnected *noir* characters and incidents in their frantic race to escape Manhattan before sunrise. The movie nominally based on this novel was earnest, ambitious and largely unsatisfying, the work of four men whose roots were in the left-wing theater movement of the 1930s.

Producer Adrian Scott was blacklisted in the McCarthy era after refusing to kowtow to HUAC; director Harold Clurman (1901-1980) and screenwriter Clifford Odets (1906-1963) had been key figures in New York's Group Theatre during the Depression; and Marxist composer Hanns Eisler was commissioned by RKO on Odets' recommendation to write the film's music score. These men might have given us a fascinating politicized version of Woolrich's novel but opted for a conventional whodunit with pretensions to Higher Meaning, more tightly constructed than the book but with none of its characters, almost none of its suspense, nothing even of its plot except the springboard situation, and no political content either. Susan Hayward and Bill Williams starred as the couple remotely modeled on Woolrich's Bricky and Quinn (she's still a taxi dancer but since this is a wartime picture he is turned into a naively patriotic sailor), with Paul Lukas as a philosophical cab driver who furnishes free wheels as they try to find a murderer before dawn. Lola Lane played the victim of the crime, a predatory bitch of the kind endemic to *film noir*. Among the people Hayward and Williams encounter on their quest are Osa Massen as a beautiful crippled woman, Joseph Calleia as Lane's gangster brother, Jerome Cowan (who had also been in *Street of Chance*) as a Broadway hanger-on plagued by Lane's blackmail demands, Marvin Miller as a blind pianist once married to Lane and still in love with her, Steven Geray as a pathetic little immigrant with a platonic crush on Hayward, and Joe Sawyer as an alcoholic ballplayer with a parallel passion for Lane. Precious few of these characters come from Woolrich's novel (although Miller's sightless piano player is true to the Woolrich spirit) and most of them are wistful wimps, each with a tag line of dialogue repeated *ad nauseam*: Hayward's mournful "I hear the whistle blowing"; Williams' self-deprecating "Non compos mentis" and his naive "....and that's the truth!"; Lukas' gently knowing "Statistics tell us"; Geray's meek "Meaning no offense."

In his autobiography ***All People are Famous*** (1974) Harold Clurman dismissed the film as "run-of-the-mill" and "of no importance." What he remembered best about the project, he said, was the time a censorship functionary visited the set to complain that Susan Hayward "was showing too much cleavage; but Miss Hayward and I insisted that this was one of the more pleasing features of the picture." Clurman's casual attitude was resented by the RKO front office, "perhaps because I finished the film on time and it proved moderately profitable." He never directed a movie again. In his critical study ***Odets the Playwright*** (1985) Gerald Weales shrugs off the *Deadline at Dawn* script as "of minimal interest." One can appreciate his lack of enthusiasm for a screenplay whose protagonists step out of the apartment building where a woman was murdered and, trying to put themselves in the killer's place, decide that the first thing he must have done after the crime was to cross the street to the Nedick's stand and purchase a soothing glass of orangeade.

But the picture is far from a total loss. Every so often, as Robert Porfirio puts it, "by virtue of *mise-en-scène* alone, *Deadline at Dawn* captures...the quiet desperation of the nighttime people in New York City."[4] The anguished confrontation between the soon-to-be-murdered Lola Lane and her blind pianist ex-husband Marvin Miller is a *noir* classic, and eerily similar to the scene between the soon-to-be-murdered Constance Dowling and her alcoholic pianist ex-husband Dan Duryea in the next Woolrich-based movie, *Black Angel*. (Nothing remotely like these scenes occurs in either Woolrich source novel.) In the outdoor sequences, which of course were shot in the studio, Clurman and cinematographer Nicholas Musuraca superbly caught the Woolrich image of the city in deep night. And amid Odets' bizarre notions of dialogue come a few lines which breathe the Woolrich spirit, for example when Lukas tells how his wife had deserted him long ago and then says: "For the first six years I shaved every night before I went to bed. I thought she might come back." It's by moments like these that *Deadline at Dawn* is redeemed.

If that film was the weaker for having junked most of its source novel, the next movie based on Woolrich proved that the same procedure could result in a powerful picture true to his bleak view of life. In his wrenching episodic novel *The Black Angel* (1943) Woolrich had described in first-person narration a terrified young wife's race against time to convince the police that her husband, convicted and sentenced to die for the murder of his mistress, is innocent and that one of the other men in the dead woman's life is guilty. Adopting a new persona each time, she invades the lives of four emotionally vulnerable men–a Bowery derelict, a drug-pushing doctor, a Park Avenue socialite and a lovelorn gangster–and destroys each of them, innocent and culpable alike, her obsessions growing to madness as she ruins others and herself to save her man from Mr. Death.

On a literal level the movie based on this book has little in common with its source, yet paradoxically it's more Woolrich-like than many a more faithful adaptation of his fiction. *Black Angel* (Universal, 1946) was directed and co-produced by Roy William Neill, who is fondly remembered for his Sherlock Holmes series with Basil Rathbone and Nigel Bruce. Neill and screenwriter Roy Chanslor set out to tighten the novel's structure, reduce the number of male characters, make the female lead more sympathetic, and at the same time preserve the Woolrich qualities of suspense and emotional anguish. June Vincent starred as the title character Catherine Bennett and Dan Duryea as the alcoholic pianist Martin Blair, who is a composite of two men in the novel (the heartbroken drunk Martin Blair and the haunted socialite Ladd Mason) supplemented with touches of Marvin Miller's blind pianist character in *Deadline at Dawn* and with a few of the traits of Woolrich himself. In the movie an M-monogrammed matchbook leads the black angel not to several men as in the book but only to one, nightclub owner Marko (Peter Lorre), who is more or less the counterpart of Woolrich's love-struck gambler McKee. Broderick Crawford played Captain Flood, promoted from Woolrich's plainclothesman of the same name, and the key role of the predatory murdered woman, Mavis Marlowe, was enacted by Constance Dowling.

One of the major alterations Neill and Chanslor made is that the cinematic black angel doesn't carry out her quest alone as in the book but is joined by Dan Duryea's Marty Blair character. Woolrich's Marty had killed himself after his brief encounter with the angel; Duryea not only lives through the picture but is recovering from his alcoholism by the fadeout. Duryea falls in love with June Vincent somewhat as Woolrich's Ladd Mason had with the black angel, but in the movie Vincent doesn't return his love but stays loyal to her convicted and philandering husband. Despite these changes and many more, every frame of this magnificent *film noir* is permeated with the Woolrich spirit. From the opening sequence with its complex boom shot from the street to the interior of Mavis Marlowe's penthouse, through the climax with its expressionist re-creation of Marlowe's murder through Marty's drunken consciousness, Neill and cinematographer Paul Ivano invest every shot with a visual style that translates Woolrich into film precisely as any novel needs to be translated: with total fidelity to its essence and little if any to its literal text. If all but one of the movies based on a Woolrich book had to be destroyed, I would opt to save *Black Angel* for future generations. It was Roy William Neill's best film, and his last. He died suddenly a few months after its release.

Woolrich himself thought the picture a disaster. Early in 1947, after receiving a letter in which the poet and Columbia University professor Mark Van Doren mentioned having recently seen the movie, Woolrich went to see it himself at a neighborhood theater. "I was so ashamed when I came out of there," he wrote to Van Doren on February 2. "All I could keep thinking of in the dark was: Is *that* what I wasted my whole life at?" Woolrich's talent for film criticism was as meager as his contempt for himself was boundless but at least (whether out of good sense or lack of clout) he never tried to tell moviemakers how to adapt his work.

The most controversial of that year's Woolrich-based movies was *The Chase* (United Artists, 1946), an 86-minute picture directed by the erratic Arthur Ripley from a screenplay by playwright Philip Yordan that was very loosely derived from Woolrich's **The Black Path of Fear** (1944). In the book Bill Scott escapes from Miami to Havana with Eve, the wife of American gangster Eddie Roman, whose Cuban agents kill the woman and frame her lover, leaving Scott a stranger in a strange land, menaced on all sides and fighting for his life. It's an uneven novel, combining prototypical *noir* elements–love discovered and then snuffed out, a man alone hunted through a nightmare city–with an ambience of dope dens and sinister Orientals and secret passages and hair's-breadth escapes straight out of the cheapest pulps. Ripley and Yordan scrapped not just the pulp stuff but most of Woolrich's plot too, and tried to capture the book's essence visually. Robert

Cummings, whose lighthearted manner made him a most unlikely *noir* protagonist, starred as Chuck Scott, with the lovely French import Michele Morgan as Lorna Roman, Steve Cochran as the vengeful husband Eddie and *Black Angel's* Peter Lorre as Eddie's hitman Gino.

As retold on screen, the story avoids Woolrich's flashbacks and proceeds in chronological order. Scott is a down-at-heels war veteran who becomes Eddie Roman's chauffeur after returning the gangster's lost wallet intact and eventually falls in love with Lorna and agrees to flee with her to Cuba. So far so faithful to the novel, but then Ripley and Yordan start playing games with the storyline and make it go haywire. The day he's to elope with Lorna, Chuck suffers a relapse of the malaria he contracted in the Navy and *dreams* the events that make up the bulk of the book: the stabbing death of Lorna in the Havana nightclub, his own arrest by and escape from the Cuban cop Acosta (Alexis Minotis) and his encounter with the prostitute Midnight (Yolanda Lacca). In due course he discovers that Lorna was killed by Eddie's pet assassin Gino but at this point he is himself shot to death and awakens from his fever dream. Unfortunately Chuck's malaria is compounded by a case of *film noir's* favorite disease, amnesia: he has no recollection of his plans to escape from Miami with Lorna until a military doctor (Jack Holt) pulls him out of his forgetfulness. At the film's climax Eddie and Gino die gruesomely in an auto wreck that causes most viewers to giggle, while Chuck and Lorna disembark at Havana and find the same coachman and nightclub that figured in Chuck's dream.

Of all the Woolrich-based features *The Chase* is the one most likely to provoke an argument among aficionados. Robert Porfirio ranks it second only to Siodmak's *Phantom Lady* as a "cinematic equivalent of the dark, oppressive atmosphere" of Woolrich, thanks to its dreamlike ambience, "especially at the conclusion, which collapses the distinction between dream and reality; its eroticism, particularly in the scene where Roman sexually badgers and then abuses his female barber and manicurist; its unprecedented elements, such as the dreamed death of the hero; and its aspects of cruelty and ambivalence...."[5] Others (myself included) ridicule the picture as a chaotic botch, full of unintentionally funny blunders. In any event it was the last A feature adapted from his work for almost two years.

Three more Woolrich-based movies were released in 1947 but all of them were low-budget efforts, based not on his novels but on short stories or novellas the rights to which cost less, and staffed on both sides of the camera by relative unknowns. One of the trio, however, turned out to be the finest by far of the low-budget thrillers adapted from Woolrich's shorter fiction. *Fear in the Night* (Paramount, 1947), directed and written by Maxwell Shane, is a 71-minute gem of *noir* on a shoestring that keeps remarkably faithful in both script and visual style to the plot, characters and spirit of Woolrich's 1941 novella "And So to Death," which is better known under its reprint title "Nightmare." Shane signed a young Hollywood newcomer named DeForest Kelley (who two decades later became

Star Trek's Bones McCoy) to play Vince Grayson (Vincent Hardy in Woolrich's story), the hapless bank teller who wakes up from a nightmare about committing a murder in a mirror-walled octagonal room only to find objective fragments from the dream in his pockets and on his body. Paul Kelly portrayed Vince's plain-clothesman brother-in-law Cliff Herlihy (Cliff Dodge in Woolrich's story), who becomes determined to find out whether his wife's brother is a mental case, a murderer or the victim of a Svengali. Ann Doran was cast as Cliff's wife Lil and Kay Scott as Vince's girlfriend Betty Winters (the only major character invented by Shane), with Robert Emmett Keane playing the evil hypnotist. Where Shane changed Woolrich's story–for example at the climax, which is filmed from a de-tached viewpoint rather than confined to the narrator's consciousness as "And So to Death" was–the alterations are improvements. He also created some memora-ble visual correlatives for Vince's hallucinations: not just the eerie opening se-quence recounting the bloody dream of murder but the superimposition of an extreme close shot of DeForest Kelley's eyes over repeat footage of the stabbing whenever his thoughts flash back to the nightmare. Shane's direction of the prin-cipal players superbly caught the contours of Woolrich's characters, with DeFor-est Kelley turning in a near-somnambulistic performance as the haunted dreamer and Paul Kelly evoking both the humanity and the sadistic streak in the prototypi-cal Woolrich cop. Nine years later Shane wrote and directed a bigger-budgeted but inferior 89-minute remake, *Nightmare* (United Artists, 1956), filmed on loca-tion in New Orleans with Edward G. Robinson as the cop and Kevin McCarthy as the young man who dreamed of a murder in a mirrored room.

Of the three Woolrich-based movies that reached the nation's screens in 1948, two were mediocre quickies based on his shorter fiction and the third and most ambitious was *Night Has a Thousand Eyes* (Paramount, 1948), adapted from his novel of the same name (1945, as by George Hopley). Of all Woolrich's books this is the one most completely dominated by death and fate. A simple-minded recluse with apparently uncanny powers predicts that millionaire Harlan Reid will die in three weeks, precisely at midnight, by the jaws of a lion, and the tension rises to unbearable pitch as the doomed man and his daughter Jean and the sym-pathetic young homicide detective Tom Shawn struggle to avert a destiny which they at first suspect and soon come to pray was conceived by a merely human power. It's the kind of waking nightmare that is the essence of *noir*, and Woolrich makes us live the emotional torment and suspense of the situation until we are lit-erally shivering in our seats. The movie doesn't, and what it substitutes is bland fare indeed. John Farrow directed the film from a screenplay by Barré Lyndon and hardboiled mystery writer Jonathan Latimer (1906-1983), but their version had little connection with the novel and almost none of its power and terror. Edward G. Robinson starred as John Triton, the cinematic stand-in for Woolrich's haunted prophet Jeremiah Tompkins, with Gail Russell as Jean Courtland (Jean Reid in the novel), John Lund as her boyfriend Elliott Carson (who doesn't exist in the novel), and William Demarest as a skeptical and middle-aged Lieutenant Shawn. The picture opens with a striking scene vaguely like the novel's beginning as Russell, pursued by Lund, wanders trancelike through a railroad yard to a high bridge from which she feels a compulsion to jump to her death. Lund saves her and brings her back to the coffee shop where Robinson is waiting. In a flashback sequence that's exceptionally long even for *film noir*, Robinson tells the young couple how years ago, while working as a phony vaudeville mindreader, he suddenly found himself endowed with what he claims is true clairvoyant power—primarily the power to foresee deaths and disasters. He correctly predicted the death of Russell's father in a plane crash and in due course he reveals his prevision that she will die at the feet of a lion at precisely 11:00 P.M. The film then mutates into a standard whodunit padded with discussions of whether there's a scientific basis for ESP. Finally Robinson convinces the police that his powers are real, rushes to save Russell from the idiot plot by one of her father's business associates to kill her, and is mistakenly shot to death by the detectives who were her bodyguards. In his pocket the police find a note in which he'd predicted his own death that night.

"What I hoped to establish," Jonathan Latimer claimed in an interview near the end of his life, "was a real sense of terror that these things were coming true." This is precisely what Woolrich wanted too, but the radical alterations of Farrow and the writers frustrated that hope and resulted in a silly and unsuspenseful film version depending on the intermeshing of several ridiculous contrivances. The film's strong points are Farrow's stylish direction and Robinson's fine performance as a sort of Woolrich surrogate, a man whose gift has turned him into a half-crazed recluse obsessed by the inevitability of fate. But one senses the hand of the devoutly Catholic Farrow in the climax where Robinson becomes a Jesus figure, choosing to go to his own death so that his quasi-daughter might live.

Until this point Hollywood's tendency had been to make A pictures with decent production values out of Woolrich's novels and B quickies out of his shorter work. The next Woolrich-based film, however, was so well made and successful that it broke the tradition, proving that a big hit could be adapted from a shorter work of Woolrich and thus in a sense paving the way for Alfred Hitchcock's *Rear Window* a few years later. Woolrich's 1947 novella "The Boy Cried Murder," also known as "Fire Escape," opens one night during a heat wave when 12-year-old Buddy climbs out on the fire escape of the New York tenement he and his working-class parents live in, and witnesses a brutal murder committed by their upstairs neighbors. But because he has a reputation for spinning tall stories, no one will believe him, not his parents, not the police—only the killers, who set out to make the boy their next victim. Woolrich squeezed every ounce of tension from this powerful *noir* premise, and was rewarded when "The Boy Cried Murder" sold to a studio almost at once.

Former cinematographer Ted Tetzlaff directed *The Window* (RKO, 1949) from a screenplay by Mel Dinelli, who had earlier scripted another they-won't-believe-

Above, John Triton's (Edward G. Robinson) psychic act in *Night has a Thousand Eyes*.

I-witnessed-a-murder thriller, Robert Siodmak's *The Spiral Staircase* (RKO, 1946). Bobby Driscoll starred as Tommy Woodry, with Arthur Kennedy and Barbara Hale as his hardworking and long-suffering parents, and Paul Stewart and Ruth Roman as the deadly couple upstairs. Tetzlaff and Dinelli kept the film close to both the storyline and specific incidents in Woolrich's tale, and most of their alterations—like constructing scenes where the boy who was Woolrich's viewpoint character is not present, or expanding the climax in the condemned building where Tommy is stalked by the killers—stay faithful to Woolrich's intent and add to the picture's suspense. Tetzlaff took pains to find visual correlatives for Woolrich's *noir* mood, playing off the neorealist look of the characters' sweltering tenement existence against the expressionist duels of light and shadow in the night-time terror sequences. In a few respects *The Window* softens "The Boy Cried Murder": Tommy's parents are portrayed as decent and caring people, without the brutal edge Woolrich gives them, and the victim whose murder the boy witnesses is not carved up with a razor as in Woolrich but transported whole out of the tenement and across the rooftops. The movie ends happily, but then so does the Woolrich version. Lacking any major stars and running a scant 73 minutes, *The Window* transcended its modest circumstances to become a runaway box-office success, and even today it stands up nicely as one of the many American suspense films which, while neither as visually innovative nor as existentially multileveled as the masterpieces of Hitchcock, are squarely in the Hitchcock (and Woolrich) tradition of nonstop nail-biting terror.

At the end of the decade only four of Woolrich's major crime novels were still unfilmed: two which would be brought to the screen in the late Sixties by Francois Truffaut, plus **Rendezvous in Black** (1948) and **I Married a Dead Man** (1948, as by William Irish). The latter was the source of the final Hollywood feature based in Woolrich's lifetime on one of his novels. Helen Georgesson, a pregnant woman with nothing to live for and in flight from her sadistic lover, is injured in a train wreck while in the ladies' room with Patrice Hazzard, another pregnant woman. Wrongly identified in the hospital as Patrice, who had died in the train disaster, Helen goes along with the deception, pretends to be the daughter-in-law whom Hugh Hazzard's wealthy parents had never met and enters what seems to be a heaven-sent new life, even falling in love with Hugh's brother Bill. Then the real father of her child invades her world, and the miraculous second chance becomes a curse from the evil god at the heart of being. The novel's radically offbeat climax offers two options, each of them unthinkable: either Helen the viewpoint character has been lying to us throughout, or Bill who desperately loves her has been lying to Helen. In the world of Woolrich logic doesn't work and we are abandoned to the powers of darkness.

This hardly seems the kind of novel that would command Hollywood's attention but it made a strong impression on director Mitchell Leisen, Paramount Pictures' specialist in sophisticated comedies and so-called women's films. Leisen shared his enthusiasm with one of the studio's top stars, Barbara Stanwyck, and suggested that she pressure Paramount into buying screen rights so he could adapt the novel into a Stanwyck vehicle. Such was the genesis of *No Man of Her Own* (Paramount, 1950). Stanwyck as the tormented Helen Ferguson was supported by John Lund (who had also had a major role in Paramount's *Night Has a Thousand Eyes*) as Bill Harkness, Lyle Bettger as menacing Steve Morley, and Milburn Stone as a homicide detective.

According to David Chierichetti's **Hollywood Director** (1973), Leisen contributed a great deal to the script, which was credited to Sally Benson and Catherine Turney. Stanwyck, Leisen recalled, "did all of her own stunts in the picture. To stage the train wreck, we built the set of the ladies' room inside an enormous wheel, about twenty feet in diameter. We rotated the wheel to make the train crash and roll over, and Barbara and Phyllis Thaxter were right in there, falling from side to side."

No Man of Her Own is a well-acted and stylishly directed movie, with the peace and serenity of the Hazzard household counterpointing the anguish and suspense of the sequences with Stanwyck in jeopardy. But even though the 98-minute film stays strikingly faithful to the novel's plot almost to the fadeout, Woolrich's *noir* spirit is lost. Part of the problem lies in the casting. Beautifully coiffed and suffering nobly in the best weepie tradition, Stanwyck looks at least twenty years too old to play Woolrich's terrified and inexperienced Helen. Even more fatal was Leisen's decision to scrap Woolrich's impossible but inevitable ending and instead have a character who had made a split-second appearance in an early scene suddenly come back into the picture and blurt out a confession which cuts the Gordian knot and assures Stanwyck and Lund of happiness-ever-after. It's the closest Mitchell Leisen ever came to *film noir* and ranks among the best of his later pictures, but in the light of Woolrich's novel one can only say: So near and yet so far!

By 1950 competition from the new medium of television was forcing studios to make fewer and fewer features each year, and the hitherto steady stream of Woolrich-based movies suddenly dried up. But TV discovered Woolrich's potential very early in its history, and both live and filmed versions of his fiction proliferated throughout the Fifties. It wasn't until 1954 that another U.S. feature based on that haunted man's work came to the big screen.

Below, Harkness (John Lund) and Helen Ferguson (Barbara Stanwyck) in *No Man of Her Own*.

Its source was the story "It Had To Be Murder" (1942), which is usually re-printed under the more evocative title "Rear Window." The narrator Jeffries, con-fined to his New York apartment with a broken leg, whiles away the lonely nights by staring out his rear window and through those of his neighbors, observing their lives like a curious god. He soon comes to suspect on circumstantial evidence that one of them, jewelry salesman Lars Thorwald, has murdered his wife and dis-posed of various parts of her body around the city. Conceptually the story has much in common with 1947's "The Boy Cried Murder," with the major difference that in "Rear Window" we don't know all along that the viewpoint character's murder accusation is correct but are made to oscillate between agreeing with him and thinking he's the victim of a diseased imagination. Finally Jeffries sees that Thorwald has discovered his invisible observer's identity, and waits alone and helpless in his invalid's chair for a visit from the murderer. This carefully con-structed story, rich in tension and detailed setting and *noir* ambience, brought Woolrich for the first time to the attention of his cinematic counterpart, the di-rector whose name is synonymous with suspense.

Thanks to Donald Spoto's biography **The Dark Side of Genius** (1983), which mentions Woolrich only in passing, we can see that he and Alfred Hitchcock were soul brothers, sharing not only a sense of the world as a hideous and terrifying place but also a longing for physical relationships which the homosexuality of the one man and the obesity of the other seemed to put forever out of reach. *Rear Window* (Paramount, 1954), directed by Hitchcock from a John Michael Hayes screenplay, starred James Stewart as Jeffries and Grace Kelly as his fashion-de-signer girlfriend Lisa Fremont. Thelma Ritter was featured as the friendly-snoopy visiting nurse Stella, Wendell Corey as skeptical but open-minded Lieutenant Doyle, and Raymond Burr as Thorwald. In preparing the film Hitchcock and Hayes had to find a way of turning a short story into a picture that would hold the attention for two hours' running time. This they accomplished by integrating into the movie a host of major and minor characters and an abundance of themes that were either absent from the Woolrich story or barely hinted at, while at the same time keeping the story's plot structure almost exactly as Woolrich had put it to-gether. The measure of Hitchcock's genius is that the fusion of new and genuinely Woolrichian elements produced not a patchwork but a beautifully unified film.

One aspect of the movie that has been praised as uniquely cinematic is the way Hitchcock limits our viewpoint throughout all but a few seconds of the movie to what the immobilized Jimmy Stewart can see from the windows of his apartment. Reading the story, which Woolrich had submitted under the title "Murder from a Fixed Viewpoint," we learn that this is simply a translation of its material into vis-ual terms. The characters on the other hand owe very little to Woolrich. Jeffries in print is not only a man immobilized but, like so many Woolrich protagonists, a man alone, indeed virtually a blank slate, with no one even to talk to except the compassionate black houseman Sam whom Hitchcock dropped from the film. But by adding the Grace Kelly and Thelma Ritter characters, who have no counter-parts in Woolrich, and by expanding Wendell Corey's role as the police detective, Hitchcock opened the door to the network of relationships which distinguish the stunningly complex character Jimmy Stewart plays in the film.

One of the blank-slate aspects of Woolrich's Jeffries is that we're never told what he does for a living. In the film he's a professional photographer, whose job involves a sort of spying on people, so that it's completely in character for Stewart to pass the long hot days and nights peering into his neighbors' lives through his telephoto lens. By limiting us to Stewart's viewpoint, Hitchcock in effect tells us that we in the audience are sick voyeurs just like his charming protagonist.

> Jeffries: I wonder if it's ethical to watch a man with binoculars and a long-focus lens. Do you suppose it's ethical even if you prove he *didn't* commit a crime?
>
> Lisa: I'm not much on rear-window ethics....Look at you and me, plunged into despair because we find out a man *didn't* kill his wife. We're two of the most frightening ghouls I've ever known.

This too is not a pure Hitchcock innovation but an elaboration of an element in Woolrich's story. "Why is [Thorwald] so interested in other people's windows, I wondered detachedly. And of course an effective brake to dwelling on that

Below *Rear Window*: Grace Kelly as Lisa and James Stewart as Jeffries.

thought too lingeringly clamped down almost at once: Look who's talking. What about you yourself?"

Another central motif of the movie stems from the barest hint in the story. As presented by Woolrich, most of Jeffries' spying is concentrated on Thorwald, and the other neighbors into whose lives he peers are given only a few poignant paragraphs. Hitchcock creates more neighbors–Miss Lonelyhearts, Miss Torso, the composer, the honeymooners, the middle-aged couple with the dog–and makes each a vivid character in his or her own right. Even more important is the thematic use Hitchcock makes of the neighbors, each representing Stewart's vision of one of his own possible futures if he makes a real commitment to Grace Kelly. This motif, like the Kelly character herself, has no basis in Woolrich whatsoever.

On the level of plot Hitchcock followed the story quite closely, keeping intact the springboard situation, the did-he-or-didn't-he oscillations and the hair-raising suspense climax. But thanks to all the nuances of theme and character and mood that he grafted onto the story's structure–not just the ones already mentioned but the heat wave and the steady stream of light bantering dialogue with dark implications–*Rear Window* the movie evolved into something worlds removed from "Rear Window" as Woolrich wrote it: richer, lighter, deeper, less obsessive and claustrophobic but no less suspenseful.

Whether Woolrich was happy with the picture is unclear, and in fact he may never have gone to see it. "Hitchcock wouldn't even send me a ticket to the premiere in New York," he told his literary agent many years later. "He knew where I lived. He wouldn't even send me a ticket."

By the mid-1950s TV had left the movie business in a shambles and most of Woolrich's media money was coming from the sale of small-screen rights to shorter fiction: $9,350 in 1955 alone and a staggering $13,650 in 1956. By far the finest of the Woolrich-based telefilms was "Four O'Clock," a 60-minute film broadcast September 30, 1957 on NBC's brief-lived anthology series *Suspicion*. Alfred Hitchcock himself directed the picture, from a script by Francis Cockrell based on the 1938 story "Three O'Clock" which for my money is the most powerful tale Woolrich ever wrote. Paul Stapp lies in his own basement, gagged and bound with clothesline to a thick pipe within a few feet of a bomb set to explode in ninety minutes. Woolrich makes us share those minutes with Stapp, his frozen eyes fixed on the clock as its hands plunge inevitably towards the hour of three; makes us live in his crawling flesh, descend with him into madness, recognize this warped man as the carrier of our common fate. In making *Rear Window* Hitchcock had radically expanded the source story and altered its tone from *noir* to monochromatic so as to suit his own needs; in making "Four O'Clock" he had a source story that perfectly captured his own existential nightmares and therefore made only minimal changes. The result is an absolute masterpiece, pure Hitchcock and pure Woolrich simultaneously, and perhaps the most unremittingly suspenseful film in the director's long career. No one knows why he changed the

Woolrich title but my guess is that with his Catholic roots he caught in the original the subliminal allusion to the death of Jesus and was afraid of it. E.G. Marshall was magnificent as Stapp, with Nancy Kelly and Richard Long in the principal supporting roles. If ever a little-known film deserved a high-profile revival, this is it.

The only other first-rate telefilms based on Woolrich came a few years later. The NBC anthology series *Thriller* (1960-62), hosted by Boris Karloff, frequently featured episodes based on works by top mystery writers, and in 1961 the production company paid Woolrich $4,600 for the rights to three of his best known stories. The first of these to be broadcast was "Papa Benjamin" (March 21, 1961), an efficient and workmanlike but unmemorable version of Woolrich's 1935 novella "Dark Melody of Madness" in which a jazz composer is put under a curse when he learns too much about a voodoo cult.

Two weeks later came the far superior "Late Date" (April 4, 1961), which was based on another 1935 Woolrich classic, "Boy with Body." The inspired direction of Herschel Daugherty combined with Donald S. Sanford's adaptation and a spine-tingling Jerry Goldsmith music score to create an exceptional exercise in suspense. As in Woolrich's story, a young man (Larry Pennell) finds that his beloved father (Edward Platt) has murdered his promiscuous stepmother and desperately tries to conceal the crime by carrying the woman's body out of the seaside town where the family lived and over to the roadhouse rendezvous where her current lover is waiting for her. The picture does full justice to Woolrich's nail-biting account of the boy's journey with the rug-wrapped body and, even with his original ending reversed for TV at the demand of censors, remains one of the finest examples of *telefilm noir*.

The last and finest of the *Thriller* segments based on Woolrich was "Guillotine" (September 25, 1961), directed by Ida Lupino from a script by Charles Beaumont based on the unforgettable Woolrich story first published in 1939 as "Men Must Die." Like "Three O'Clock," this tale is a gem of existential suspense rooted in the protagonist's knowing the exact moment of his gruesome death and flailing wildly to avert his fate. In late 19th-century France, Robert Lamont (Alejandro Rey) approaches the hour when he is to be guillotined while his girlfriend (Danielle de Metz) desperately tries to poison the obese headsman (Robert Middleton) on his way to the scaffold. Even if you know the story well before you watch this film, you are left gasping with fright.   By the last year of Woolrich's life only three of his major suspense novels–*The Bride Wore Black* (1940), *Waltz into Darkness* (1947, as by William Irish), and *Rendezvous in Black*–had not been filmed. But producer-director Hall Bartlett had been paying Woolrich $1,000 a year since the mid-1950s for an option on *The Bride*, and a $4,500 lump-sum payment in 1965 left Bartlett the owner of all screen rights in the novel. Unable to secure his own financing for the picture, he sold his interest to Les Films du Carrosse, the production company of director Francois Truffaut, to whom it fell to make the last Woolrich-based picture released in the author's lifetime–and one of the most fascinating. In *La Mariée était en Noir* (Les Films du Carrosse/Les Productions Artistes Associés/Dino de Laurentiis S.P.A., 1968; U.S. title *The Bride Wore Black*), directed by Truffaut from an adaptation by himself and Jean-Louis Richard, Jeanne Moreau starred as Julie. It was an all but inevitable choice, for in his classic *Jules et Jim* (1961) Truffaut had also cast Moreau as an unknowable man-destroying woman of the most sympathetic sort. The five men who are Moreau's prey were portrayed by Michel Bouquet, Charles Denner, Claude Rich, Daniel Boulanger and Michel Lonsdale, with Jean-Claude Brialy as the friend of the first victim. The 107-minute film was photographed by Raoul Coutard, and the music score was by Hitchcock's favorite composer, Bernard Herrmann.

Reviews were ecstatic. Every one of Moreau's victims, said Renata Adler in the *New York Times*, "is a gem of characterization, lines witty and right, acting subtle and thought out, the decor of their lives and even the manner of their deaths inventive and expressive of personality." What almost no one bothered to point out was that Truffaut had pulled off one of the neatest feats in the history of cinematic adaptations of novels. He moved the action to France and Switzerland, junked the character of homicide cop Lew Wanger and indeed the entire detective element, scrapped almost everything in Part Five of Woolrich's novel including the wild coincidences revealed at its climax, and yet kept true to the spirit and structure of much of the book. He even found room for a number of tiny details from the novel, filming the bit where the maid adds water to Michel Bouquet's gin bottle, for example, and changing most of the victims' names either not at all or just enough to make then pronounceable in French, so that Ferguson (Charles Denner) becomes Fergus, with the accent on the second syllable as in Camus. But since his own view of the world was not bleak but life-loving and optimistic in the tradition of his mentor Jean Renoir, Truffaut dropped the corkscrew twists and dark metaphysics of Woolrich's novel and used characterization, camerawork, color, music and nuance rather than plot manipulations to show us that by her fanatical crusade Julie has destroyed herself.

In *The Cinema of Francois Truffaut* (1970) Graham Petrie writes eloquently of this movie's power. He describes how Truffaut obtained the effect "almost literally...of a dance in which music and camera combine, the one adapting and suiting itself to the needs of the other." He discusses the made-for-each-other relationships between the bride and her victims, with Julie "using [the men] coldly and deliberately for her own purposes" while they in turn ironically "attempt to manipulate her for their own satisfaction." He praises Truffaut for pulling our sympathies in several directions at once, so that "we find ourselves drawn into complicity with [Julie], into sharing her sense of her victims as pure objects to be manipulated and disposed of *at the same time as* we are made uncomfortably aware of their reality and humanity. One side of us wishes her to succeed...while another keeps reminding us that not only are these people like ourselves who are being killed but their elimination is fanatically wrong-headed." Truffaut's "romanticism and the mysterious and dreamlike atmosphere which he creates combine with his typical attention to the details of human experience to produce a work of complex and evocative beauty, for whose subtleties the original can take little credit." You'd never know from Petrie or almost any other Truffaut scholar that not just the plot of the film but its essence stems from Woolrich's novel, or that many of Truffaut's alleged innovations, such as the strategies for dividing our reaction, come straight out of the Woolrich repertory. In *La Mariée était en Noir* Truffaut did to Woolrich source material precisely what his idol Hitchcock had done fourteen years before in *Rear Window*: kept much of the plot even to precise details but transformed it into a totally cinematic and personal work that will be seen and loved for generations to come.

What Woolrich would have thought of the movie will never be known. He was still alive when it opened in New York but confined to a wheelchair and unable or unwilling to make the effort to go see it even with Truffaut himself at the screening and anxious to meet him. A few months later Woolrich was dead.

By that time Truffaut was preparing if not actually shooting another film rooted in a Woolrich *roman noir* but transformed by his cinematic power and open-to-the-world humanism into an extremely personal and moving work, based this time on Woolrich's novel **Waltz Into Darkness**. The theme had appealed to Truffaut at least as far back as *Jules et Jim*, and what attracted him to this particular Woolrich book, he said, was that it gave him a chance to do a story about a man obsessed with and ruined by a woman in the vein of several movies he admired such as Josef von Sternberg's *The Blue Angel* (1930), Jean Renoir's *La Chienne* (1931) and Fritz Lang's *Scarlet Street* (1945). But Truffaut saw relations between the sexes rather differently from Woolrich, and in *La Sirène du Mississippi* (Les Films du Carrosse/Les Productions Artistes Associés/Produzioni Associate Delphos, 1969; U.S. title *Mississippi Mermaid*) he once again kept most of a Woolrich plot while radically altering its meaning, replacing the grim and feverish tone with his own life-affirming optimism. The 123-minute film was both directed and scripted by Truffaut, with photography by Deny Clerval and music by Antoine Duhamel. Jean-Paul Belmondo starred as Louis Mahé and Catherine Deneuve as Marion/Julie, with Michel Bouquet as the private detective Comolli (Walter Downs in the novel), Nelly Borgeaud as Berthe Roussel, and Marcel Berbert as Louis's business partner Jardin. Truffaut changed the time from the 1880s to the present and the principal setting from New Orleans to the French-owned tropical island of Reunion in the Indian Ocean. Louis Mahé (Jean-Paul Belmondo), the island's richest tobacco planter, has sent away for a mail-order bride. Almost as soon as Julie Roussel (Catherine Deneuve) steps off the boat, Louis realizes she's not the woman he sent for, but she's so adorably beautiful and sweetly mysterious that he falls in love with her anyway and marries her. Then one bright day she vanishes from the island, along with most of Louis' money. Heartbroken and vengeance-driven, he pursues her, catches up with her in the south of France, listens to her story, falls in love with her again, and commits murder to save her from the investigator he himself has put on her trail.

As Vincent Canby suggested in his *New York Times* review, the picture is less a suspense thriller than an exploration of loneliness and love. Even the opening credits, he points out, "are presented against the background of a newspaper's 'personal' ads. On the soundtrack voices are heard, first one, then another, and then a kind of chorus of controlled desperation ('Young girl, serious, pretty...' 'Bachelor, 35, interested in music...'). Everyone is searching for love." But so was Woolrich's *Waltz Into Darkness* an exploration of loneliness and love, although in a wildly different key. What distinguishes the film is not the theme but how Truffaut reworked that overheated and bizarre novel into his own Renoiresque design. Some of the alterations are obvious and major, for example the conversion of Woolrich's nameless metaphysical female demon into a sensuous, fully individualized woman with a vibrant sexuality and no trace of the religious aura that surrounds her in the novel. Other Truffaut contributions are subtle and close to unnoticeable, like replacing the Woolrich woman's murder of the canary with Deneuve's mere indifference to the bird's natural death. The most radical departure from the novel comes at the film's climax: overcome by Belmondo's love,

Below, Truffaut's doomed version of Woolrich's fugitive couple, Catherine Deneuve as Julie/Marion and Jean-Paul Belmondo as Louis in *La Sirene du Mississippi*.

Deneuve stops slowly poisoning him, saves his life and marches off absurdly into the snow with him to start their relationship over. No one who sees this movie could mistake Truffaut for a pessimist.

As Graham Petrie put it, Truffaut's "characteristic generosity towards his people...leads him to soften the character of Marion and make her much less calculatingly vicious and amoral than the [woman] of the book; Marion is frivolous with a core of hardness, but much more genuinely attached to Louis throughout than her counterpart in the novel. The result is that the weakness of the novel is exactly reversed: Truffaut creates a sense of genuine love and tenderness between his characters which makes Marion's attempt to poison Louis difficult to take, while [Woolrich] presents a near-degenerate...who is perfectly capable of poisoning her husband but less so of repenting." In other words, Truffaut took almost all the *noir* out of the novel, substituted the full spectrum of colors–physical, psychological, emotional–and created a movie so lovely and fascinating that even Woolrich's staunchest admirers must forgive him.

Except for a haunting segment of the 1993 cable series *Fallen Angels* based on Woolrich's story "Murder, Obliquely," (starring Laura Dern and Alan Rickman), the films adapted from his work since his death have been at best mediocre. Thirty years after his death most of Woolrich is out of print and most of his influence on motion pictures is history. But his doom-haunted world remains alive for countless readers with good memories and–sometimes in radically altered form– for countless devotees of *film noir*.

Notes

1. A full account of the movies, radio plays and live and filmed television dramas based on his suspense novels and stories will be found, in perhaps excruciating detail, in chapters 24 through 26 of my book **Cornell Woolrich: First You Dream, Then You Die** (1988).

2. Editors' Note: cf. the entry in **Film Noir: An Encyclopedic Reference to the American Style**, p. 271.

3. Ibid., p. 226.

4. Ibid., p. 86.

5. Ibid., p. 55.

Film noir and Samuel Fuller's Tabloid Cinema: Red (Action), White (Exposition) and Blue (Romance)

Grant Tracey

> "A film is like a battleground. There's love. Hate. Action. Violence. Death. In one word, emotions."
>
> > Samuel Fuller discussing cinema with Jean-Paul Belmondo in Jean-Luc Godard's *Pierrot le Fou* (1965)

In *More than Night*, James Naremore situates the initial critical reception to *film noir* within a Parisian context of surrealism and existentialism. The surrealists found in American *noir* the dynamism, cruelty and irrationality that they valued.[1] Because surrealists sought to destroy bourgeois art, they valued *noir*'s graphic style and narratives that seemingly disoriented the spectator and attacked conventions of logical action and linear coherence. Thematically, American *noir* suggested moral disorientation, an inversion of capitalist ideology, and possible revolutionary destruction.[2] The existentialists, Naremore contends, admired American *noir* because of its absurdity and its promise to give spectators Andre Gide's notion of "a foretaste of hell."[3] Through these two cultural paradigms a group of French Critics in *Cahiers du Cinema* of the 1950s, and then their American and British counterparts in the 1960s and 70s, praised American *noir* and American auteurs, such as Samuel Fuller.

But the interests and themes in Samuel Fuller's *noir* films exist within a different context than that in which the French critics first situated *noir*. Fuller is neither surreal, nor overtly existential. No doubt, Fuller's American *noirs* are influenced by the style and look of his predecessors, and his films play with *noir*ish preoccupations such as alienation and obsession, but Fuller is ultimately a modernist. His films don't give us a "foretaste of hell," nor do they deconstruct capitalism.

Opposite, images reveal the "tabloid" theme directly inserted into the narrative. Top, in the Fuller-scripted *Scandal Sheet*, crime reporter Steve McClery (John Derek, right) shows pictures of a murder victim to his editor Mark Chapman (Broderick Crawford), who is actually the killer. Bottom, in *The Crimson Kimono*, witness Christine Downs (Victoria Shaw) discusses a headline murder case with her roommate (Pearl Lary).

Fuller's films are hopefully democratic and contain a certain residual humanism, a desire to expose the world for what it is and to force us to want to change it, to make it better. His poetics, as Lee Server has explained, are grounded within the traditions of the American tabloid press.[4]

Fuller says that he plotted his potboilers on a blackboard with different color chalk to make sure the compositions of red (action), white (exposition) and blue (romance) were balanced.[5] Fuller's collision of these three modes distinguishes his craft and has been, in part, informed by his work as a crime reporter, 1929-31, on Bernard Macfadden's *Evening Graphic*, a poor imitation of the *New York Daily News*. The *Graphic* specialized in sensational stories of sordid love, gangland crimes, and murder. Fuller found parallels between film-making and reporting; the cinematic close-up, for example, was like a headline. And although Nicholas Garnham,[6] J. Hoberman,[7] and Lee Server acknowledge Fuller's connection to the tabloids, no one has systematically analyzed how his films extend the tabloid aesthetic and what that narrative style means for how spectators interact with Fuller's cinema fist. Fuller's fist affirms and denies our expectations and assumptions about *film noir*. He exploits the notion of *film noir* as catharsis and takes it to different ends.

Often Fuller seeks to jar viewers, to roust them from story world reveries to contemplation of larger social ills. In this way, Fuller's cinematic syntax goes against the cathartic effect of most *noirs*. *Film noir*, according to Alain Silver and Elizabeth Ward, portrays varying dark moods in American society (obsessions with McCarthyism, fear of nuclear devastation, an inability to conquer ennui and post-war disillusionment, paranoia of big business and governments), and by presenting these themes and images, *noir* relieves our collective nightmares.[8] Fuller's *noir* cinema is anti-cathartic. He wants the nightmarish effect without the immediate relief. Fuller, like a dark WeeGee photograph of a dead gangster sprawled across a New York City street, wants the impact of his films to linger long after we watch and experience them. And his cinema demands even more than that. Fuller has a tabloid eye, exposing truth and asking that we do something about injustices. This article, borrowing the paradigmatic narrative structures laid out in Seymour Chatman's *Coming to Terms* and David Bordwell's *Narration in the Fiction Film*, will demonstrate how Fuller's *Pickup on South Street* (1953), *Crimson Kimono* (1959), *Underworld U.S.A.* (1961) and *The Naked Kiss* (1964) create a hybrid: the look and feel of *film noir* combined with the drive and impact of tabloid poetics: scenes charged with collisions, expository pauses or mini-editorials on larger discursive issues, and "objective" yet caring reporting.

Fuller's Tabloid Paradigm: - Collisions

Fuller clashes narrative modes (romance, action, exposition) within and across scenes to create a variety of collisions in his *noir* films. Like the layout of different stories on a newspaper page ("Co-Ed Murder Suspect to Tell All," "Saw Parade of

Beauties Unclad in Worker's Room," "Furriers Fail to Quit in Needle Strike"[9]) the punches of a Fuller film constantly shift narrative modes. These shifts suggest a lack of rational normality and reveal a *noir* universe spinning off kilter. Romance (blue) is at the center of this irrational chaos, for it is obsessive and dangerous. In Fuller's tabloid *noir*, romance must be buried, repressed through the contrapuntal shock edits of violence, or the sudden emotional explosions within a scene (red: action).

Two scenes from *Pickup on South Street*, with Jean Peters (Candy) and Richard Widmark (Skip McCoy), clash tenderness with violence. The film concerns a reluctant hero figure, a pickpocket who accidentally grifts some government secrets from a red agent. Unpatriotic and somewhat of a dislocated loner, he seeks to cash in the microfilm and make a "big score." The institutions of America don't speak to him. "You waving the flag at me," he, with traces of Frank Sinatra cool, tells two cops who ask for his help. Candy, who Fuller in an interview had described as a "half-assed hooker," desires to fit into the collective, and after falling in love with Skip tries to bring him in line with the desires of the police. But during their first encounter, they know little about each other, so that it begins in the expository mode (white). Candy bluntly asks Skip how he became a pickpocket. To show Skip's distrust and dismay over the directness of the question, Fuller rapidly cuts to a medium-close up reverse shot of Widmark. Enraged, Skip violently shoves

Above, Kelly's violent assault on her pimp at the beginning of *The Naked Kiss* dislodges her wig which she calmly replaces. Below, another prostitute Candy (Jean Peters) with Mo (Thelma Ritter) in *Pick-up on South Street*.

her away. "How did I become a pickpocket? How did you become what you are?" (red: action). The second scene also starts with exposition (a discussion of how Mo, Thelma Ritter, was murdered), and then Candy cries. Widmark, angry, butts his cigarette on the floor, strides aside and snaps, "Aw, shut-up." Then he pauses, feels remorse and tenderly apologizes to Candy (blue: romance). But, seconds later, the scene's mood swings again when Skip decides to sell the microfilm to the communists: "He better have that 25 grand ready." Fuller eclipses blue and white with red. Candy, now desiring to have herself and Skip accepted by the collective, violently smashes a beer bottle over his head and becomes the film's moral center. These radical shifts in narrative modes reflect a lack of coherence in love and the chaotic irrationality within Fuller's *noir*ish universe.

The Naked Kiss cranks up the collisions another notch as the violent switches in mood culminate in death. Kelly (Constance Towers), another former prostitute and now an obstetrics aid for handicapped children, arrives with her wedding dress at the house of her fiancé, rich philanthropist J. L. Grant (Michael Dante). She stands aglow in the hallway, twirling, and Fuller rapidly cuts-in to a close-up of her face as it spreads from joyous abandonment into disgust. Her lips press together, and a six-year old girl emerges from shadows to skip out of the room. Grant, only slightly surprised at being caught molesting a child, lurches slowly forward and in a tight claustrophobic close-up confesses, "Now, you know why I never could marry a normal woman. That's why I love you. You understand my sickness." Fuller crowds the frame with Dante's leering face and creates an intense unease. As Dante drops to his knees, he informs Kelly that "our marriage will be a paradise because we're both abnormal." Kelly, seething, seizes a phone and clubs him to death with the receiver. The moment shocks us because not only does Fuller negate the possibility of a healthy, loving relationship, but he also questions our own obsessive desires for normalcy. As we discover later in the film, Kelly killed Grant not because she caught him molesting a child, but because he had called her abnormal, *twice*. Kelly, like Candy, wants to assimilate into society, but Grant's marking her as strange other causes her to lash back with film-*noir*ish disillusionment.

Fuller's tabloid poetics, shock edits within scenes, replicate what Thomas Elsaesser defines as an element of film melodrama: radical swings of emotion that create a mood of "dramatic discontinuity."[10] This "dramatic discontinuity" is a strong component to *film noir* and something the French surrealists praised about *noir*'s style. But Fuller's editing across scenes also moves outward from the story world's psychological concerns of character and discontinuity to larger social issues and a cry for continuity and order. In this manner, his jumping from syzuhet (story) to fabula (discourse), Fuller's films are indebted to Soviet, Historical-Materialist narration (1925-33), especially the work of Sergei Eisenstein.

Eisenstein and other Soviet filmmakers, David Bordwell has shown, transcended the Hollywood paradigm of invisible storytelling.[11] In Hollywood editing,

Above, Detectives Joe Kojaku (James Shigeta, left) and Charlie Bancroft (Glenn Corbett) watch as Christine (Victoria Shaw) looks at mug shots in *The Crimson Kimono*.

visual style is almost always subordinated to the dictates of the syzuhet. By contrast, Soviet montage editing deliberately lacked Hollywood's reliance on shot/reverse shots and eyeline matches of the ABA pattern (character looking off camera/shot of what character sees/return to character looking). Because Soviet film narration was locked into larger societal discourses–an historically contextualized cultural fabula that detailed the successful struggles of revolution or recorded noble, heroic failures–the syzuhet (linearity of the filmed story) was always a given because of its redundant narrative objectives; therefore, style in Soviet films was something that could be played with more freely, and the goal of montage wasn't merely aesthetics. It was grounded in emotional/sociological impact: to move the spectator from enjoyment, or losing oneself in the syzuhet (story) to the fabula (discourse), forcing viewers to contemplate the larger master narrative of historical oppression and the accompanying movement to socialist activity.[12]

Fuller's vulgar modernism, borrowing from the Soviets, uses crosscut collisions to further discomfort us and make us link story troubles to fabula troubles (greater issues of violence, crime, prejudice within society).

In *Crimson Kimono*, Fuller tells an interracial love story about a Nisei cop (James Shigeta as Detective Joe Kojaku) and a white artist (Victoria Shaw as Chris Downes). Their love challenges Joe's friendship with his Korean-War buddy, a white cop (Glenn Corbett as Sgt. Charlie Bancroft). While detailing the interracial love story, Fuller, the tabloid journalist, shows us vantage points, stories, outside the hegemonic norm. He explores notions of Asian identity that had rarely been looked at honestly in Hollywood films of that or any prior period. Joe's love for a white woman is not the real conflict to Fuller's story, a lack of love for his own Asian ancestry is. Fuller's portrayal of Joe's obsessions moves the narrative to a larger context of racial identity and acceptance.

Moreover, because Fuller, like most *film noirs*, regards love as obsessive, he refuses to tell a standard romance story that spectators can lose themselves in. Instead, Fuller constantly reminds viewers of the dangers of love. His use of jarring crosscuts suggest that love interferes with professionals doing their jobs and threatens lives. In *Crimson Kimono*, Fuller interrupts an early love scene between Charlie and Chris with a phone-call from Joe. Corbett says, "Don't do anything foolish, Joe. I'll be right there." A shock edit follows as a hand chops down on a pool table, and then Fuller cuts to an extreme-close up of Shigeta's face perspiring. Corbett jumps in and together they sprawl and brawl with a big man in a pool hall. Because Charlie was away romancing Chris, Joe was placed in greater danger, having to initially face a suspect alone. Later, Fuller also breaks down a parallel love scene between Shigeta and Shaw. As they romance, Fuller crosscuts to

Below, Detective Driscoll (Larry Gates) questions young Tolly Devlin (David Kent) about his father's murder while Sandy (Beatrice Kay) looks on in *Underworld U.S.A.*

Corbett looking for a suspect in seedy back alleys, and then busting into a woman's apartment. He too, because of romance, now faces a possible suspect alone. For Fuller, love often kills.

In *Underworld U.S.A.*, Fuller uses an explosive crosscut sequence to suggest a glaring absence of father-as-role model and to darkly portray the negative influences of the city streets. Fourteen-year-old Tolly Devlin meets Sandy (Beatrice Kay) in back of her club. He claims that his "old man" is teaching him how to hustle, and she quotes some headline philosophy: "Oh, sure. Dodging truant officers, rolling drunks, lying to welfare workers. He's teaching you to hustle all right. Right into the electric chair." As one of Fuller's mother figures, she dresses a wound on Tolly's face and gives him a polka-dot tie for New Year's. "Auld Lang Syne" plays on a music box and a moment of communion occurs between a woman who can't have children and her surrogate son. Fuller suddenly mars the sentimental moment as he crosscuts from the gift-giving to long angular shadows on a brick wall and Tolly's father being beaten to death in a back alley. The killing (off-centered compositions, low-key lighting and dramatic use of bricks cut in diagonal lines) captures a *noir*ish flavor, but more importantly, from a tabloid perspective, the cutaway raises larger social issues. Fuller's reporter's eye tells us that, even while alive, Tolly's father, with his lessons on hustling, was a terrible role model. Now, with him gone, Tolly seems even more cast adrift in a chaotic world. How can kids with Tolly's background ever make it?

Exposition

Fuller's characters often provide viewers with tabloid editorials, informing us of larger problems in our society. When Richard Widmark quips, "you waving the flag at me?" he incinerates an entire spirit of McCarthyism. The right-wing police in *Pickup* will use whatever emotional and patriotic means necessary to achieve what they want, including manipulating Candy and placing her in danger with Joey in order to get back the microfilm. Their patriotism seems deluded, as Joey savagely beats Candy, nearly killing her. Similarly deluded was the McCarthy-like patriotism and paranoia of the early 1950s. This Cold War fervor was used by many, including Richard M. Nixon, for private gains (Nixon won political power through red-baiting). Ultimately, McCarthyism was a convenient tool to keep gatekeepers in power and the marginalized outside the norm. "Communists" are what the Beat writers and poets, such as Jack Kerouac and Allen Ginsberg, were branded, because they sought an authentic way of living. The right feared how the Beats might challenge American mores and proprieties. Others too–actors, civil rights leaders and women's activists–were victimized. Within this historical context of convenient red-bashing disguised as Cold War patriotism, Skip's refusal to play ball, in 1953, is alarmingly refreshing.

Exposition is the newspaper reporter's and director Fuller's mode of social relevance, the opportunity to interrupt the story with a lesson. Half-way through

Underworld U.S.A., Tolly's narrative seems to stop. He (Cliff Roberston) has discovered the names of those who killed his father, rescued Cuddles (Dolores Dorn) from Gus, and infiltrated his way into Connors' organization. Fuller suddenly pauses the narrative for an expository, tabloid editorial. District Attorney Driscoll (Larry Gates), in long-shot and medium-long shot, lectures his men and the audience with two minutes of social commentary: "The syndicate bosses command the rackets like generals in the field command divisions. . . . They all have substantial business fronts, pay taxes, wear respectable suits. . . . Lording it over all of them is Earl Connors. Their chief of staff. Shrewd, warm, charitable. An animal." Driscoll's editorial commentary describes why it is hard to crackdown on a "legitimate" army. He continues his essay: "The most vicious increase in vice is the teenage dope addict. And the recruitment of school girls into the ranks of prostitution. . . . Our job is get people to prosecute. Getting anybody to talk is tough. Families of informers have been butchered, burned, bludgeoned to death." Driscoll's words are sensational, alliterative, like copy from a tabloid, but they directly speak against the structure and power of organized crime. He argues that more people need to come forward and that the police need to do a better job of protecting their informants. Driscoll's expository essay succeeds in pausing Tolly's story in favor of opening up the narrative to its larger context. The expository mode shifts the discourse from one man's melodramatic drive for revenge to larger questions that implicate the viewer in the war on crime.

It is at this level of discourse or fabula that Fuller's tabloid poetics further move his films beyond catharsis and outside of Paul Schrader's definition of *film noir*. For Schrader, *noir* grows out of an historical mood of "cynicism, pessimism and darkness,"[13] and the themes often involve an anti-hero stuck in the past and present and dreading the future.[14] Some of Fuller's heroes, such as Skip McCoy and Tolly Devlin fit this paradigm as they often live for the moment or seek vengeance for something that happened to them in the past, but the female characters: Candy, Kelly and Cuddles, all seek a future of acceptance and assimilation. The two above scenes look at characters making editorial commentary, but Fuller often transcends story exposition for discursive exposition. When he does that, his films are inflected with hope, a desire to emerge from the darkness and make the future a better place. Fuller's characters may be shrouded in *noir* darkness, but his overall narrative purpose is rarely cynical.

In order to make the world a better place, Fuller's expository essays describe a social problem and argue for change. His texts occasionally shift from the dominant narrative mode (the focal point of characters within the story plane) to a different discursive formation, one unmotivated by character, just exposition. Exposition, Chatman suggests, combines both the descriptive and argumentative modes.[15] It is descriptive because it abstractly defines a social problem; it is argumentative because it indirectly requests that the audience do something about the problem.

Red and Blue in *The Crimson Kimono*: above, Joe seems more comfortable fighting Shoji (Fuji) with his partner than, below, romancing Christine at the piano..

Midway through *Crimson Kimono*, Fuller offers a mini-essay on segregation/integration. The sequence begins with a long-shot of Evergreen Cemetery in Los Angeles. Fuller cuts to a white column with a soldier on it. This is followed with a shot of a huge stone and an Eisenhower quote that salutes "the men who gave for their country." Cut to another huge stone and a quote by Mark W. Clark, General, U.S.A.: "The soldiers who lie here symbolize the fealty and courage of Nisei troops . . . may they rest in honored peace." Cut back to long shot of the white column. This sequence both separates Nisei soldiers (they have their own monument) and links them (through the words of white generals) to the mainstream. This is the larger theme in the film (Kojaku's liminality and his troubled relationship with Charlie) and perhaps suggests, by Fuller, the need for greater, *real* integration in our society (separate is not equal). The ending of *Crimson Kimono* is also descriptive. James Shigeta (Detective Joe Kojaku) guns down the female killer and her story of obsessive love strangely mirrors his own: "It was all in my mind." As she collapses in Kojaku's arms, Fuller cuts to a series of Asian faces, looking. These cut-ins aren't achieved through eye-line matches and are thus unmotivated by character. Instead, these close-ups function as descriptive commentary that punctuate a theme: Joe Kojaku's fear of his own skin, his own people, and their collective gaze at his guilt.

Below, a frame within a frame: Kelly (Constance Towers) can never convince Griff (Anthony Eisley) that she has changed from what she used to be in *The Naked Kiss*.

The Naked Kiss boldly offers a different kind of descriptive pause. Fuller takes on patriarchy and directly assaults the spectator with a bizarre opening. Constance Towers (Kelly) forcefully socks her pimp, Farlunde (Monte Mansfield), as he staggers backwards into his swank apartment. The camera shakes and shimmies like cinema-verite-style documentary as she continues to pummel him. Fuller actually attached the camera to Mansfield in order to create a disorienting and off-kilter mood. But the triumph of Fuller's flashy technique is that Kelly's punches directly assault the audience, pulling us simultaneously into the story (the opening has to be admired on a level of unbridled audacity) and into the text's larger discursive concerns (the role of women in society). Kelly is victimized by men. Her pimp shortchanges her. Later when she arrives in Grantville, the town sheriff, Griff (Anthony Eisley), sleeps with her and falsely finalizes Kelly as a whore. When Kelly involves herself with handicapped children, he refuses to believe in her transformation. Maybe by the end of the film, he acknowledges her agency and ability to be different from the woman he had defined. However, she cannot stay in their world, and leaves on the next bus. Within the larger narrative context, Fuller's slam-bang opening becomes double-voiced: a story-based attack on a pimp, but also a discursive-based attack on men and how they define women and the limits they place on them. Kelly's punches directly assault the male spectator and display a displaced female rage that would get more fully articulated amongst the feminists of the 1960s and 70s.

Underworld U.S.A. uses three descriptive pauses to move from story to discourse and thereby open the text up to larger social issues. After hit-man Gus (Richard Rust) murders Mencken's daughter with his automobile, Fuller fades the scene with a haunting tableau: a mangled bicycle, the girl's body lying on its side in the street, two discarded shoes. The narrative pauses for an image that resembles a WeeGee crime scene photograph. Later, following police Chief Fowler's arrest for being on the mob's payroll, he asks his daughter to leave the room and nimbly grabs a gun. A shock cut-in follows: an extreme close-up of Fowler's face. "God forgive me," he prays, and then pulls the trigger. And like the murder of the Mencken girl, this scene ends with a narrative pause. Fowler's bullet lodges behind him in a large-framed photograph of uniformed police officers. The lingering fade to close the scene is a form of narrative description; it echoes the words his daughter, Connie, spoke earlier about the lowest crooks being cops. And finally, Tolly, too, pauses the narrative. After Tolly crashes into Connor's headquarters to save Cuddles, he drowns the kingpin in a swimming pool and is shot by one of his henchmen. Mortally wounded, he stumbles out of the complex, and dies in the same back alley where his father was beaten to death. Cuddles and Sandy find him, his hand a tight fist. The camera tracks in on the fist and then freeze frames into a grainy image.

All three frozen images—the tableau of the dead girl and the mangled bicycle, the bullet lodged in a framed photograph, and the grainy newspaper still of Tolly's fist—

circumscribe the action and invite a viewer to ascribe meaning, to "write a caption." To use Chatman's terms, all three images momentarily halt story time and ask that we ponder these images and consider them separate from story as part of the text's larger discursive statements on crime:[16] the dead girl isn't just a girl, but a victim—nobody is innocent or safe; gangsters are immoral (Head mobster Connors wants to spread drugs in the schools—"don't tell me that a needle has a conscience"); the lodged bullet suggests Fowler's corruption and corruption within police departments across the country; Tolly's fist doesn't represent only his pain, but the drive and failure many experience trying to fight their way out of the gutter.

Fuller's cinema fist is not the usual *noir*ish one of catharsis, but a *noir*-tabloid hybrid of subtle social activism.

Caring but Objective Reporting

In 1976, Robert Porfirio outlined several existential motifs in *film noir* such as the non-heroic hero, alienation and loneliness, and existential choice. For Porfirio, existential *noir*s place characters in a world with no moral absolutes,[17] and yet these characters persevere. A non-*noir* and yet existential classic, Nicholas Ray's *Rebel Without A Cause* (1955), fits Porfirio's paradigm perfectly. The story concerns youths trying to authenticate their existence through ritualized games such as the "chickie run." These youths, as the Planetarium sequences attest to, live in a world in which if God does exist he is an indifferent God.

Porfirio's paradigm can be applied to several *noir*s, such as *The Killers* (1946), *Brute Force* (1947), *He Walked By Night* (1948), and non-*noir*s of the post-World War II period but it doesn't work within the tabloid poetics of Samuel Fuller. Por-

Fuller's "moral spin" on characters can make a prostitute the "moral center" as enacted by Jean Peters in *Pickup on South Street*, Constance Towers, below left, in *The Naked Kiss*, and Dolores Dorn as Cuddles, below right, in *Underworld U.S.A.*

firio contends that the term "hero" never fits with the profile of the *noir* protagonist because he exists in a world "devoid of the moral framework necessary to produce the traditional hero."[18] Fuller's filmic worlds may be unseemly at times, but he's never indifferent. Fuller always inflects his tabloid texts with a moral frame.

As has long been noted, Fuller's stories feature political sloganeering,[19] bombast, and characters speaking in headlines, but they also contain a strong element of the newspaper tradition: objective yet caring reporting. According to historian Bill Stott, restraint had become one dominant mode of reporting in the 1930s. Adjectives were eschewed for concrete nouns and verbs to create an objective, documentary voice; but Stott maintains that behind a Walker Evans photograph was a presence, a moral voice, that demanded that we care about the plight of the sharecropper.[20] Fuller's narratives replicate this paradox: apparent neutrality couched in judgment.

Fuller presents characters that are ambiguous and even dubious, but within his mise-en-scene is a system of intelligence, a series of textual cues that place a moral spin on the characters within the story world. Seymour Chatman analyzes the difference between story and discourse on how the spectator is positioned while viewing. Chatman suggests that within a varying degree of textual cues rests both a narrator and filtered characters. The narrator exists only on the discursive plane and works in conjunction with the film's presentation to give us a slant, a point-of-view on the cinematic story. Characters work within the story plane to give the viewer first-hand, as opposed to the narrator's reported perception, emotions to the events.[21] Fuller's characters are both fallible and infallible narrative filters. At times the focal point of a character can be aligned with the narrative slant of the scene (the textual intent)[22] or, in the case of fallible filtration, outside of it and the overall ideology of the film.[23]

In Fuller's hard-hitting *Pickup On South Street*, Jean Peters, the film's eventual moral center and catalyst for Richard Widmark's redemption, moves from being a fallible to an infallible character filter. The film opens with her on a subway. The eyeline matches of Government agents and pickpocket Widmark penetrate her. She is the object of their look, but her gaze is absently distracted. She doesn't return their looks. This lack of knowledge, both about being watched and the dangerous spy mission that Joey (Richard Kiley) has sent her on, illustrates her lack of authority within the text. Later, Candy comes to knowledge during a meeting with her ex-boyfriend and his "friends." Peters in long-shot and medium close-ups moves about a room, talking about how Widmark has accused her connections of being "commies." They say nothing, but a series of static, close up cut-ins–a man smoking a cigar, another holding a cigarette in a holder, Joey's squinty, sweaty eyes–visually separates her from them. Fuller's use of Candy's eyeline matches illustrates their guilt and links her to the narrative slant (communists in Fuller's world view are totalitarian and therefore evil). Moreover, Candy's looks are interrogative; in contrast to

Above, *Underworld U.S.A.*: Cuddles relunctantly leads Tolly (Cliff Robertson) to a cache of drugs hidden in a cartridge box.

her earlier distracted gaze on the subway, she is now an infallible, knowing character who can distill right (freedom) from wrong (totalitarianism).

In *Underworld U.S.A.*, Fuller further plays with the paradox of "caring but objective reporting." He creates conflict between story and discourse, a rift between the perceptions of a reliable narrator and an unreliable character (rendered by his sharp contrast of mise-en-scene and editing versus Tolly Devlin's sensibilities). The distance between the two haunts the spectator.

During a confession scene, Fuller's narrative slant prevents viewers from accepting Tolly's judgement. Cuddles, Tolly's girl, has decided to tell District-Attorney Driscoll that she saw Smith, one of the three men against whom Tolly seeks revenge, kill a woman years ago. Robertson, background frame left, watches. Suddenly shot two of the sequence cuts away from Driscoll and Cuddles to rapidly track-in on Tolly. Offscreen, Driscoll asks Cuddles, "What prompted you to contact me?" The link between the cutaway tracking shot and Driscoll's question creates an interest-focus around Cuddles. Her actions are motivated by her love for Tolly. She'll state this directly, in shot three; however, Driscoll's empty phrasing, "Thank-you for your courage. There aren't many citizens who'll run this risk for society," makes her gesture of love appear unappreciated and misguided. The final shot ends with a close-up of Tolly. He smirks and looks away. "Sucker," he whispers with disdain. Tolly and Driscoll's cynicism is accurate–she is a sucker for wanting to help them. Driscoll's cynicism is driven by the reality that he can't protect witnesses; Tolly's cynicism indicates an abuse of love. Cuddles, through the cutaway tracking shot, embodies an opposing force, a character who honestly states her feelings: "I did it for Tolly." Thus Tolly's finalizing remark is one of fallible filtration. It condemns Cuddles' sentimentality but it also, on the level of narrative slant, indirectly criticizes his own lack of feeling.

This latter point is embellished near the narrative's conclusion, in a scene that has both a moral spin and collides narrative modes (blue with red). Cuddles openly confesses her love for Tolly, how she desires to have his children (blue). Robertson, in a chilling moment, suddenly begins to laugh, his forehead apparently splitting with paroxysms: "You must be on the needle. Me, marry, you?" (red). Cuddles has openly exposed her emotion and Tolly's cold reaction is, perhaps, the film's cruelest moment. Seconds later, surrogate mom Sandy, in a classic Fullerian editorial, passes her own expository essay on Tolly's cruelty: "[You're] a scar-faced ex-con, a two bit safe cracker. A penny thief who don't know when he really made the big time. Where do you come off to blast her. She's a giant . . . You're a midget."

Fuller's tabloid cinema, like the goals of existential thinkers Jean-Paul Sartre and Albert Camus, is concerned with social justice, but Fuller's context of creative inception differs from the context of critical reception initially defining *noir*. Unlike Porfirio's definition of *film noir* existentialism, Fuller insists on providing a moral framework to his scenes. Moreover, as a filmmaker with an agenda, Fuller often collides narrative modes and combines gritty story telling with a desire to move us beyond story (through editing and expository essays) to larger discursive issues. And whereas several arresting filmmakers, including legends such as Robert Aldrich (*World For Ransom* [1954], *Kiss Me Deadly* [1955], *Hustle* [1975]), Joseph H. Lewis (*My Name is Julia Ross* [1946], *Undercover Man* [1949], *Gun Crazy* [1949], *The Big Combo* [1955]), Robert Siodmak (*Phantom Lady* [1944], *The Killers* [1946], *Criss Cross* [1949], *File on Thelma Jordon* [1950]), and the American efforts of Fritz Lang (*Scarlet Street* [1945], *The Woman in the Window* [1944], *The Big Heat* [1953], *While the City Sleeps* [1956], *Beyond a Reasonable Doubt* [1956]), clearly did their best work in *film noir*, Samuel Fuller's non-*noir* films, including *The Steel Helmet* (1950) and *Verboten!* (1959), are equally entertaining and enmeshed within the tabloid aesthetic detailed in this article. In *Steel Helmet*, Fuller offers editorial essays on racism experienced by blacks in 1950 and Niseis during World War Two. He also has Sgt. Zack offer us essays on fighting a guerilla war. In *Verboten!*, a story about a post-war Hitlerite wolfpack in West Germany, Fuller constantly moves outward from story to discourse to remind us, through grainy 16mm documentary images, of the horrors of the holocaust and to ensure that it never happens again. Because Fuller is a talented auteur with a shockingly graphic visual style and pile-driving story-telling skills, he is not subsumed by the themes

Tabloid cinema irony in *Underworld U.S.A.*: Conners (Robert Emhardt) points to a meaning-ful headline held by his associate Gela (Paul Dubov), above. Before the film is over, Con-ners will float dead in his pool by another headline that reads "Connors defies Uncle Sam."

or issues of *film noir*. Instead, he uses, in these four films, shades of *noir* to darkly paint variations on his own tabloid preoccupations.

Notes

1. James Naremore, ***More Than Night. Film noir in its Contexts*** (University of California Press, 1998), p.17.

2. Naremore, p. 22.

3. Naremore, p. 23.

4. Lee Server, ***Sam Fuller: Film is a Battleground*** (North Carolina: McFarland and Company, 1994), pp. 4-5, 12-17.

5. Server, p. 55.

6. Nicholas Garnham, ***Samuel Fuller*** (New York: Viking Press), pp. 25-26.

7. J. Hoberman, "Three Abstract Sensationalists" in ***Vulgar Modernism*** (University of Temple Press, 1991), pp. 22-32.

8. Alain Silver and Elizabeth Ward, eds., ***Film noir: An Encyclopedic Reference to the American Style*** (Woodstock, New York: Overlook Press, 2nd Edition, 1988), pp. 1-2.

9. *The Evening Graphic* (20 June, 1929), p. 5.

10. Thomas Elsaesser, "Tales of Sound and Fury: Observations on the Family Melodrama" in ***Film Theory and Criticism***, eds. Gerald Mast, Marshall Cohen and Leo Braudy (Oxford University Press, 4th Edition, 1992), p. 528.

11. David Bordwell, ***Narration in the Fiction Film*** (University of Wisconsin Press, 1985), pp. 239-239

12. Bordwell, p. 239.

13. Paul Schrader, "Notes on *Film Noir*," in ***Film Noir Reader***, eds. Alain Silver and James Ursini (New York: Limelight Editions, 1996), p. 53.

14. Schrader, p. 58.

15. Seymour Chatman, ***Coming to Terms: The Rhetoric of Narrative in Fiction and Film*** (Cornell University Press, 1991), p. 6.

16. Chatman, p. 49.

17. Robert Porfirio, "No Way Out: Existential Motifs in *Film Noir*," in ***Film Noir Reader***, eds. Alain Silver and James Ursini (New York: Limelight Editions, 1996), p. 81.

18. Porfirio, p. 83.

19. Garnham, pp. 25-26.

20. William Stott, ***Documentary Expression and Thirties America*** (Oxford University Press, 1973), p. 37.

21. Chatman, pp. 143-49.

22. Chatman, pp. 154-60.

23. Chatman, pp. 149-54.

Above, disturbed musician Stan Grayson (Kevin McCarthy) plays the clarinet in a New Orleans night club in *Nightmare*.

Dark Jazz: Music in the *Film Noir*

Robert G. Porfirio

1. Pre-*Noir*: Expressionism, Violence, Death and Sexuality

The juxtaposition of jazz in the broadest sense of the term with an expressionistic decor can be detected in the Hollywood musical almost from its inception (*Broadway*, 1929; *King of Jazz*, 1930), especially at Universal where the "Germanic" influence was most pronounced and effected even in a traditional "folk opera" like *Showboat* [Figure 1, from the "Old Man River" montage with Paul Robeson]. Yet the confluence of expressionism and jazz was already inherent in Weimar culture and cannot be easily rationalized in terms of that culture's interest in African "primitivism" or popular Americana. Aside from the romantic mystique attached to its origins, the improvisational nature and affective qualities of jazz were quite compatible with the expressionistic quest for "deeper meanings" that focused upon heightened states and the unconscious in order to probe "the secrets of the soul." Still, jazz, with its sources in the black American demimonde and its unfortunate association with brothels, speak-easies and "dope," did lend itself to sensational popular image that in turn reinforced its association with sex, violence and death, three themes dear to "Germanic" hearts. To no one's surprise, Hollywood capitalized upon these associations, emphasizing the strident and violent aspects of the music over its warm and sentimental side and this emphasis culminated into those popular jazz scores of the mid 1950's that gave aural significance to contemporary urban "problems" (e.g. Elmer Bernstein's score *for The Man with the Golden Arm*). And while an early all-black short like *Black and Tan* (1929 RKO, directed by Dudley Murphy) used Duke Ellington's music as a springboard for a film whose visual expressionism synthesized hallucination, orgasm, and death in a haunting manner, the typical Hollywood musical of the 1930's was much less ingenious in its exploitation, except for a few brief "interludes" such as Berkeley's "Lullaby of Broadway" sequence of Gold Diggers of 1935. Surprisingly, the gangster film relied very little on the use of jazz , and it remained for the next generation, and particularly for the *noir* cycle to promote that special relationship between jazz and urban violence.

Even before the cycle began in earnest, Warner's *Blues in the Night* (1941, directed by Anatole Litvak) combined some of the visual marks of the *noir* style with an older gangster idiom to depict the story of the trials and tribulations of a

(white) jazz band. But it was an early entry, *Among the Living* (1941), that used the music's dissonant milieu to prompt one of Paul Raden's (Albert Dekker) homicidal attacks. This association of jazz with disturbed mental states that was made even clearer later in *The Blue Dahlia* (1946), where the amnesiac Buzz (William Bendix) refers to it as "jungle music." Appropriately, it was those entries directed by Robert Siodmak that propelled the triad of jazz, violence and sexuality within the cycle, most memorably through certain expressionistic interludes in *Criss Cross* (1949), *The Killers* (1946) and *The Phantom Lady* (1944). Yet jazz could almost be used to express quieter moments and nostalgic reveries (especially when nudged in the direction of blues); and though Al Robert's remembrance of his songstress fiancée (Claudia Drake) in *Detour* (1945, directed by Edgar Ulmer) was bathed in his warm glow, it was shot in a typically expressionistic fashion [Figure 2].

Coming at the end of the cycle, *Nightmare* (1956, a more stylized version of the earlier *Fear in the Night*, 1947) rather self-consciously deployed its *noir* conventions, exploiting the bizarre surroundings of its New Orleans locale and casting its victimized hero, Stan Grayson (Kevin McCarthy) in a role of jazz arranger and clarinetist. Grayson's dark odyssey through a succession of Bourbon Street "jazz joints" as he attempts to identify the unusual jazz piece associated with his "nightmare" is particularly blatant in this respect: the collage of discordant sounds, the chiaroscuro lighting, the oblique angles, all heighten the effect of the setting. At one of the "joints" he appears to discover the girl in his "nightmare," his first view of her distorted by that split-mirror effect which by then had become something of a visual cliché [Figure 3]. Though this unnamed blonde (Marian Carr) turns out to be someone else, she is a fitting denizen of this world, capturing its essence with her seductive voice when she tells Stan, "Look around, maybe everyone here has lost their marbles." Finally even the dissonance of jazz is enhanced as an aural effect and not simply by Stan's "blurry" memory, for he discovers that the crucial piece of jazz is actually a familiar tune rendered "strange" by being played back too slowly on a phonograph.

DOA (1950) begins its Germanic bias in its source material (the German Film, *Der Mann, Der Seinen Morder Sucht* [1931], directed by Robert Siodmak and partially scripted by Billy Wilder) as well as in Rudolph Maté's and Ernest Laszlo's expressive use of its authentic locales. Its expressionistic influence, however, is most pronounced in the jazz sequence at "The Fisherman Club" whose Dantesque proportions mark it immediately as the nodal point between the mundane tone of the earlier part of the flashback and the macabre tenor of what is to follow. It also serves as a barometer for the complex ambivalence provoked by jazz; a jaded white bartender describes the frenzied white patrons as "jive crazy," declaring his preference for Guy Lombardo while the black group plays on, sweating in agony as the Fisherman himself thrusts his saxophone in an apparent gesture of defiance [Figure 4, second from left: actually Illinois' Jacquet, known for using the upper register of his tenor sax to produce irresolvable high "hot" notes). Finally, "The Fisherman" is the major locus for a network of metaphoric associations, integral to *DOA*'s structure, not the least of which the association of jazz, sex and death: it

represents Frank Bigelow's further descent from the security of the small town of Banning and his fiancée, Paula, into San Francisco's demimonde; the thrill of illicit sex is implicit not only in the milieu but in the person of Jeanie, (Virginia Lee) a "jive

crazy" blonde whom Bigelow tries to pick up and whose hip response to every-thing is "easy"; Jeanie's presence coincides with that of the furtive figure of Halli-day (William Ching) who is able to "slip" Bigelow the poisoned drink precisely because Bigelow is distracted by Jeanie; a sporadically audible "blues" tune sung by a female vocalist ("I wanted to kiss you...I tried to resist you...") indexes the sexual potential of Jeanie as well as the lethal potential of the milieu; and as Bige-low recalls a "blurred" variation of this tune on subsequent occasions, it becomes an index to the perverse nature of the whole world.

2. Expressionism and the Libido

The earlier expressionistic obsession with the debilitating effects of the Weimar night life (particularly as it involved the Berlin milieu and the *femme fatale*) made the emigrés willing exploiters of the popular association of jazz with death, drugs, and sex, while jazz's own improvisational qualities could be conceived in terms of the Freudian "unconscious." Robert Siodmak was probably most prone to this exploitation and it can be observed in many of his *noir* films, most notably in the "jam session" scene from *Phantom Lady*. Yet here the *femme fatale* is ironically the innocent heroine, "Kansas" (Ella Raines), posing as a tart to wheedle some information out of the trap-drummer Cliff Milburn (Elisha Cook, Jr.) as part of a last ditch effort to save the life of her employer, Scott Henderson, (Alan Curtis); and it is Milburn who takes her to the late-night jam session. But this situation in turn was borrowed from the original novel of the same name by Cornell Woolrich, easily the most expressionistic writer of the "Black Mask School" and one who had already demonstrated an interest in the power of drugs to unleash the passions with such short stories as "C-Jag" (1940) and "Marihuana" (1941). In the novel, Woolrich uses the jam session episode to capture the dangerous eroticism of both drugs and jazz with his own distinctively overwrought prose style:

Left, **Figure 4**, Iliinois' Jacket in D.O.A.

Opposite below, **Fig-ures 5 and 6**, Elisha Cook, Jr. and Ella Raines in *Phantom Lady*.

> The next two hours were sort of a Dantesque Inferno. She knew as soon as it was over she wouldn't believe it has actually been real at all.... It was the phantasmagoria of their shadows, looming black, wavering ceiling-high on the walls. It was the actuality of their faces, possessed, demonic, peering out here and there on sudden notes, then seeming to recede again. It was the gin and marihuana cigarettes, filling the air with haze and flux. It was the wildness that got into them, that at times made her cower into a far corner....

In Siodmak's version "Kansas" does a good deal less "cowering," and he draws adeptly from his expressionistic arsenal to heighten the erotic and oneiric elements. Since the jazz sequences invariably represent a break in the temporal order, Siodmak exploits this in a manner that would become a characteristic trope: eliminating diegetic dialogue throughout the whole sequence (approximately 3 minutes) in favor of the jazz so that visual, editorial, and acting styles might all benefit from a greater formative range. The sequence itself begins as Cliff, snapping his fingers in time with the music, leads "Kansas" down a dark alley and then opens the door to the "jazz den," the camera trucking backward ahead of them and then forward slightly to enter the "den" before them. From this point on, the jagged editing and oblique angles serve to defamiliarize the surroundings in accord with the polyphonous music, as Cliff weaves "Kansas" through the band to a chair, before taking his place behind the drums. The phallic power of the instruments, revealed in turn by camera movement or cutting, seems to alternately repel and attract the girl, finally motivating her to rise and pour a drink for Cliff. He pauses just long enough to consume the drink and kiss her clumsily, her displeasure suggested by the subtle gesture of her clenched fist and slight grimace. But it is when "Kansas" attempts to fix her makeup at a mirror which "rocks" with each pulsating beat of the piano that the unreality of the place is marked by the typical Germanic trope, just as Cliff prepares to go into his solo [Figure 5] and the remainder of the sequence (approximately 1 minute) is cut to a tempo that matches Cliff's solo riff with a progression that is unmistakably sexual. "Kansas" nods her approval as he begins [Figure 6] then approaches Cliff to coax him on with periodic thrusts of her body [Figure 7]. The libidinous nature of the jazz is barely veiled in

metaphor here, either by the amount of intercutting between the girl and the drummer [Figures 7-12] or by the high-angle shot of him playing a drum between his legs. At one point "Kansas" throws back her head in laughter which is completely masked by the din of the music. As Cliff reaches the climax of his riff [Figure 10] she beckons with her head [Figure 11] and he responds by throwing away his "drum stick" [Figure 12] and following her to the door, bowing to his fellow

musicians with a slight flourish before departing. Such a stylized "musical interlude" would seldom be equaled by the Hollywood cinema!

3. Style and Musical Parody

By late 1952, when the "Girl Hunt" ballet sequence in *The Band Wagon* was designed, the cycle's narrative and visual conventions were familiar enough to be gently parodied. Since this was done as a modern ballet it achieved a surreal quality the original lacked: the visual density of the *film noir's* photographic iconography was reduced to its essentials as painted backdrops and its discursive irregularities were heightened into a series of actions (all danced) which refused to cohere into a story . This quality is evidenced in the sequence's opening shot [Figure 13], a backdrop of a deserted city street which in its austerity is reminiscent of painting by Edward Hopper.

Look carefully at the stairwell which Rod Riley (Fred Astaire) is climbing in Figure 14. Only the first level is tangible, the rest is a painting which aptly leads nowhere. Close to the end of the sequence when his battles are momentarily over, detective Riley takes out a cigarette and a woman suddenly shows up to light it [Figure 15]; she looks strikingly similar to the other *femme fatale* (both are played by Cyd Charisse) whom Rod was forced to shoot earlier in the scene reminiscent of *Double Indemnity*. As Rod's voice-over narration again warns of a woman's lethal untrustworthiness, the two walk off into the stillness of the night, disturbed by the shriek of a jazz trumpet which serves as a solemn reminder of the well-known affinity of sexuality and death.

Opposite, **Figures 7, 9, and 11** (left, top to bottom) and **8, 10, and 12** (right) from *Phantom Lady*.
This page from *The Band Wagon*: right, **Figure 13**; below, **Figures 14** (left) and **15**.

4. Aural Structure and Effects in a Sequence from *The Dark Corner*

The accompanying eight frames were drawn from a rather long (over 9 minutes) and complicated sequence (over 50 separate shots, many of them compounded by moving camera) from *The Dark Corner* whose quintessential *"noirness "* derives from the manner in which the narrative's central conflict is expressed through its visual and aural forms. The conflict permits the detective-hero, Bradford Galt (Mark Stevens), to be framed for the murder of his treacherous ex-partner, Tony Jardine (Kurt Kreuger), by a hoodlum named Stauffer (Willliam Bendix) according to the plan of Hardy Cathcart (Clifton Webb), a wealthy art dealer jealous of his wife's affection for Tony. It is not my intention to submit this sequence to any sort of reading, but rather to suggest how aural structure complimented visual form in generating that tension charged atmosphere for which the *film noir* is duly recognized. My choice here demonstrates specifically how the *noir* cycle achieved an aural expressionism despite its progressive adherence to conventions of "realism" the latter evidenced by the fact that sequence's sounds are all diegetically motivated. Therefore, while the accompanying frames obviously display the *noir* penchant for mannered lighting as a means of synthesizing exteriors with studio interiors, they were selected principally to locate its major aural transitions and should not necessarily be regarded as among the most essential or "representative" shots in the sequence under consideration.

The segment itself begins with an exterior scene during which Brad attempts to persuade his secretary Kathleen (Lucille Ball) to wait for him inside a Newsreel theater [Figure 16] for an hour while he returns to his apartment to meet with Stauffer, whom he knows as "White Suit" and from whom he is to buy some in-formation. The only sounds here are some background noises of traffic, trolley bells, and ticket dispenser, aside from the dialogue itself; it is structurally signifi-cant that there is no further dialogue until some five minutes into the sequence when these two characters are reunited. As Kathleen reluctantly enters the thea-ter the scene shifts to Stauffer secretly gaining access to Brad's apartment through an open bedroom window off the fire escape [Figure 17]. Behind his furtive ac-tion can be heard the naturalistic noises of traffic, trolley bells and a "honky-tonk" piano playing "Red, Hot and Beautiful" (by Jimmy McHugh), ostensibly emanating from a nearby arcade whose proximity to Brad's apartment has been indicated in an earlier scene.

While Stauffer cautiously makes his way into Brad's living room a slow orches-tral version of "Mood Indigo" begins to fade up, first in counterpoint with the noise of the piano and traffic, then displacing the piano entirely as Stauffer moves toward the entry door at the front of the living room (and, presumably, closer to an adjacent apartment which is its source). Stauffer next removes a handkerchief and a bottle of fluid from his coat pocket and sits in a chair facing the entry door.

The scene then shifts to Brad as he walks down a dark street toward his apartment building [Figure 18] , behind which are the off-screen noises of traffic interwoven with the sounds of a "streetplayer's" rendition of Brahms' "Wiegenlied" (actually performed by *both* accordion and violin.). The comforting qualities of this familiar lullabye, which escorts Brad into the apartment building (the camera remains stationed outside to continue to motivate the music and as Brad enters the elevator he is viewed through the glass of the building's front door), function at once to connote his guileless vulnerability and to generate an ironic tension in the viewer who is aware of his danger.

A series of intercut shots–Stauffer waits inside the apartment; Brad exits the elevator into the corridor; Stauffer, alerted by the elevator noise, prepares for Brad's arrival by dousing his handkerchief with ether [Figure 19] and positioning himself to one side of the entry door; Brad innocently lets himself in, is waylaid by Stauffer and eventually subdued by the ether–maintains a respectable level of aural "realism," enhancing the volume of "Mood Indigo" on corridor shots, muting it on apartment interiors while fading up the traffic noise and mixing both with the loud sounds of the scuffle. The same aural "realism" prevails in a similar series of intercut shots which follow: Stauffer, alerted next to the arrival of Jardine by the

Below, **Figures 16** and **18** (left, top and bottom) and **17** and **19** (right) from *The Dark Corner*.

noise of the elevator, positions himself to the side of the door with a poker in his hand while Jardine locates the apartment and rings the buzzer; Stauffer opens the door from the side and the unsuspecting Jardine enters the darkened apartment as the camera pans down to the floor, to indicate Jardine's murder only by his shadow and the sound of the clubbing blows, each followed by a groan: Stauffer then pulls Jardine's body completely into the apartment and shuts the door, once again muting the sounds of "Mood Indigo."

As the scene shifts to the exterior shot of Kathleen waiting anxiously for Brad outside the theatre [Figure 20], there is an abrupt transition to a much louder level of traffic noise that in turn is quickly displaced by the "Mood Indigo" in the following scene during which Stauffer messes up the apartment and places the poker in the unconscious Brad's hand before departing through the window. While Brad awakens from his stupor and begins to realize what has happened, Kathleen's opportune arrival is indicated aurally by the simultaneous sounding of the buzzer and the abrupt displacement of the jazz with Beethoven's *Minuet in G*, as if somebody nearby was practicing the piano. Since it is Kathleen who will be the stabilizing influence in the life of the oppressed hero, reviving his spirits when they are down and suggesting possible remedies to his predicament, the minuet

Below, **Figures 20** and **22** (left, top and bottom) and **21** and **23** (right) from *The Dark Corner*.

serves a major paradigmatic function, announcing her presence even prior to her muffled cries for "Brad" and a shot of her outside the door [Figure 21] as she tells him that she intends to stay there all night unless he lets her in.

Brad does open the door, of course, explaining to her how thoroughly he has been framed, rejecting the idea of going to the police, and dismissing her offer of aid while the "Minuet" begins to fade out. For a few moments their dialogue exchanges are without any background noise, but when Brad orders her to go and starts to exit towards his bedroom, dragging Jardine's body after him, a muted orchestral version of a swing piece, "I Don't Care who Knows It" (by Jimmy McHugh) suddenly fades up. It continues to play behind a series of alternating shots during which Kathleen straightens up the living room [Figure 22] and washes the poker in the kitchen sink before returning it to the fireplace while Brad hides Jardine's body under his bed and washes up in the adjacent bathroom [Figure 23]. The choice of that particular tune for its sentimental meaning seems clear enough here for Kathleen, once having coyly resisted Brad's advances, is now ready to commit herself to the full extent of helping him cover up a murder, and this meaning is reaffirmed when Brad re-enters the living room, sees what she has done and kisses her, an act punctuated by a harp glissando that segues into the next swing piece (appropriately titled "Do You Love Me ?"). However, since neither of the last two tunes were widely known at the time of the film's production, one can move beyond the merely affective sentimentalism of the former to consider it as a source of dissonance in conjunction with the visuals behind which it initially appears (and also beyond the purely literary "irony" of its title, "I Don't Care Who Knows It"), a syntagma whose alternations bear the symbolic weight of ritual: Kathleen "gets rid" of the broken glass/Brad "gets rid of the body" and "straightens up" his appearance; Kathleen washes the blood off the poker/Brad washes his hands, etc.

Yet dissonance is operative at the plane of diegesis itself where variations of volume level "placed" the source of the other music (except for the original "honky tonk" piano) near the corridor close by the front of the living room, whereas this piece is recognizably louder in Brad's bedroom and, conjoined with traffic noises, seems to emanate from somewhere outside the same open window through which Stauffer entered [see Figures 17 and 23]. Indeed, much of the whole sequence's tension is the product of the dissonant interaction of music, effects and visuals, a tension falsely resolved with the couples' embrace (and the glissando), though they will soon leave on an unsuccessful quest for "White Suit." As one might expect, tension is only finally resolved at the conclusion of the film with the death of Cathcart and the "cleansing" of Brad's reputation, after which Kathleen makes plans for their hasty marriage, "I told you I play for keeps!" while the Cyril Mockridge score moves to the resolution of its finale.

Above, Kit (Martin Sheen) walks towards the horizon while contemplating one of his killings in *Badlands*.

Mad Love is Strange: More Neo-*Noir* Fugitives

Linda Brookover and Alain Silver

In the transition from classic period to neo-*noir* many filmmakers of the 1970s brought a consciousness of the existing canon of fugitive couple *noir* films to their newer work. The two examples to be addressed here, *Mississippi Mermaid* (*La Sirène du Mississippi*, François Truffaut, 1970) and *Badlands* (Terrence Malick, 1973), evince this on several levels.

François Truffaut, as a critic for *Cahiers du Cinéma* in the 1950s, was enthusiastic, impressionable, and occasionally over the top. While less manifestly analytical than Rohmer, Chabrol, or Godard, Truffaut was both auteurist and generic experimenter. While they made forays into neo-*noir*, Charbrol, Godard et al never embraced Truffaut's allusory approach. *Mississippi Mermaid* is, at once, a most derivative and a most individualistic work. The sources are wide-ranging, from the all of *noir* movement's femme fatales and its sub-group of fugitive couples, through the perverse Romanticism of William Irish/Cornell Woolrich (from whose novel, *Waltz Into Darkness*, the film is adapted), to specific movies such as Hitchcock's *Vertigo* and Joseph Lewis' *Gun Crazy*. Coming after such mannered neo-noirs as *Shoot the Piano Player* and *The Bride Wore Black* (also from Woolrich), *Mississippi Mermaid* relies on a pot-pourri of sources.

Under the titles, the camera scans the personal columns of a newspaper. Flat voices read the contents: "Man, 35, seeks woman of similar interests..." etc. A man about 35, Louis (Jean-Paul Belmondo), picks up a wedding ring and hurries to a dock to meet Marion, a fiancée acquired through correspondence via the personal columns. He meets the passengers of the freighter "Mississippi," but she isn't there. He starts to leave. A voice calls his name. The camera pans to a dazzling young blonde in a white hat and dress, windswept, holding a golden cage. She has lied and sent a friend's snapshot. Is he displeased? No, rapturously surprised. Besides, he lied also. He doesn't just oversee the plantation, he owns it. As the siren of the title (or mermaid of the translation), Marion Vergano (Catherine Deneuve) carries a mythic identity as well as a golden cage. Enchantress, femme fatale, liar, she will grant Louis a few weeks of that rapture then empty his bank accounts and disappear.

In the *noir* context, Truffaut's concerns will never be focused on the details of the thefts, deceits, and murders that occur. It is rather Louis' obsession. Marion arrives with her golden cage to inspire Louis' worship: "Do you know what it means to be adorable?" he asks his deified wife, "It means worthy of adoration." Being worthy of adoration, Marion is also worthy of pursuit when she escapes from her husband. The twist for the vengeance-seeking Louis is his discovery of Julie, the real woman who was pretending to be Marion, the real woman whom he will love. What a tearful Julie asks Louis near the end of the picture, "Is that love? Does love hurt?" is the central question of the film, the question which resonates back to Woolrich, to *Vertigo* and *Gun Crazy*, to the entirety of *film noir*.

Like the obsessed figures of the classic period of *film noir* Louis will alternate between trust and suspicion, between love and fear, as Marion/Julie's enchantment waxes and wanes. The scene where Louis first catches up to Marion-now-Julie across from the cocktail bar where she is a "hostess" exemplifies this alternation. Unable to kill her as he planned, Louis slumps in a chair, and Truffaut intercuts medium close shots of him with those of her as she walks back and forth confessing the details of her past. Only when she finishes does Truffaut frame them both in medium shot, physically uniting them as he accepts her for a second time ("I believe you...I love you"). Julie remains an enchantress for the entire picture, a point Truffaut reinforces with her constant re-seductions of Louis but also with third party reactions. Comolli, a detective Louis early on hires to find her, reports how she is easy to trace because people are singularly struck by her beauty. This striking beauty even inspires comic relief, as when Julie casually changes her blouse by the side of a country road and sends a passing car's distracted driver out of control into a ditch.

The authenticity of Julie's feelings for Louis, like those of most femme fatales of the classic period, remains ambiguous. In a sense this constitutes the principal suspense of *Mississsippi Mermaid*. Where *The Bride Wore Black* was a more superficial homage to Hitchcock out of Woolrich, even including a Bernard Herrmann score, *Mississippi Mermaid* revisits Hitchcock's darker themes. The need for trust is as important as love in the manner of *Notorious* and *Marnie*. The many direct allusions—Marion and Julie are rough anagrams of Madeleine and Judy, the two characters portrayed by Kim Novak in *Vertigo*; Louis' drive into town after Marion's departure parallels the flight of another Marion in *Pyscho*, with the voiceovers acting as sort of flash-forward in the protagonist's mind—are handled with controlled integration into the narrative of *Mississippi Mermaid*. The parallel visualizations with Hitchcock are also seemlessly inserted. As is the restaging of the celebrated sustained shot from *Gun Crazy*, with the camera fixed in the back seat of a car for an entire sequence as Louis and Julie anxiously evade pursuers, effectively mirroring the robbery in Western garb in Lewis' picture.

Because *Mississippi Mermaid* is primarily a fugitive couple story, like *noir* filmmakers of the classic period, Truffaut's emphasis is on the psychology and determinism of fugitive love which he defines with a subtle visual precision. The first indicator is Julie's nightmare, where the widescreen frame is masked clautrophobically. Equally telling is the first shot of Louis' return to the island, as he walks down a constricted pathway and veers off into darkness before reaching the house of an associate to whom he will confess, "I am outside society." In the end, Julie "becomes" Marion again for Louis' sake. But as Louis predicted in his despairing comment, they cannot return to society. Their "mad love," their relentless self-involvement enmeshes them in a fatal struggle with the social order. Comolli, its representative, is murdered. Other of its fundamental tenets are broken. So they are forced to remain fugitives.

Like Woolrich and Hitchcock, Truffaut is a dark neo-Romantic whose narratives can be conspicuously emotional to the point of extravagance. In all contexts, from neo-*noir* to Luis Bunuel's description of *amour fou* which "walls the lovers off...and brings them to destruction," Louis and Julie seem doomed. Truffaut's last shot frames them walking off into the drifting snow until they are no longer visible and the frame goes white.

Very different from the obsessed love of Louis and Julie and those of classic *film noir* fugitive couples, are Holly and Kit, *Badlands'* lovers whose lukewarm relationship is the catalyst for crime. Based on the true story of "Mad Dog Killer" Charles Starkweather and Caril Ann Fugate whose 1958 killing spree left 11 people sense-

Below, Louis (Jeal Paul Belmondo) contemplates killing his fugitive wife, Julie/Marion (Catherine Deneuve) in *La Sirène du Mississippi*.

lessly murdered, *Badlands'* off-handedness in portraying a killing spree in the American heartland engendered negative responses from some contemporary re- viewers for its detached and amoral viewpoint. Filmed in 1972, a few years after *Bonnie and Clyde* was a box-office hit, *Badlands* has long been accorded the eso- teric status of cult classics. Twenty years before the excesses of *Natural Born Kill- ers*, *Badlands'* mix of ingenuous angst and sudden death make Kit and Holly ring truer than Oliver Stone's twisted fugitives in a post-modernist context.

Part homage to the fifties, part naive *noir*, the first person narrative is straight out of Holly's movie mags, which she reads to her personal James Dean as they travel the back roads of the Dakotas. The landscape of this film, framed by her dark narrative, is spectacular; but at the same time she is detached, as if recalling another lifetime. Several different cinematographers gave *Badlands* a stylish period look without the dark corners of *noir*. Its horizontal aspect created by the meeting of land and sky runs counter to many of the vertically oriented visuals of *film noir* and German expressionism and is closer to the rare examples of open landscapes of the classic period such as *Nightfall* or *Ace in the Hole*. The film's first-time direc- tor Malick (who appears in a *Badlands* cameo at the door of a rich man's house where Kit and Holly are spending a few hours before borrowing his Cadillac) uses landscape as a mute witness to the unspoken emotional intensity of his characters in *Badlands* and his only other films to date, *Days of Heaven* (1978) and *The Thin Red Line* (1998).

The protagonist of *Badlands,* erstwhile garbage collector Kit Carruthers (Martin Sheen), meets 15-year-old Holly Spargis (Sissy Spacek) after being fired from his job. The fateful quality of the meeting is both reinforced and mocked by Holly's voiceover narration, a modality which will carry over to most of the film's events. Holly is delighted that good-looking Kit likes her despite her self-deprecating be- lief that she is not very pretty or interesting. For that, she is willing to follow him anywhere, at least, up to a point. In her own self-centered way, she explains that it was "better to spend a week with one who loved me for what I was than years

Below, Kit prepares to do battle in their sanctuary in the woods as Holly (Sissy Spacek) runs for cover.

of loneliness." Similarly when Kit asks for Holly's hand, he rationalizes that if she ever wanted to go away, he would just let her and that would be okay.

Holly's father (Warren Oates) prescribes more music lessons to keep Holly occupied; but she and Kit meet in secret and get busy on their own. There first sexual outing evokes the same blasé reaction from her as do the later deeds of her man, Kit: "Is that all there is to it? Gosh what was everybody talking about?" He, on the other hand commemorates the day by finding a special rock. So it goes with their relationship in which she rides along towards her next stop in life, and he races towards his fifteen minutes of fame in the days when tabloid news was in print and not in syndication.

Rejected by Holly's father, Kit walks into their house with a gun in his pants and casually shoots Mr. Spargis to death. While Holly looks on blankly, he drags the body to the basement, casually picks up an old toaster while he's down there, and then sets fire to the house. As it burns, we see both Holly's dollhouse and the family's household possessions outlined in flames. Visually the suggestion is that in Holly's adolescent perception, both are the same, the dollhouse and the Spargis house, the young rebels of her movie magazines and Kit, fact and fiction, model and real life intermixed inextricably. For his part, Kit searches for his mythic dimension, his way to somewhere, and begins to record messages for posterity. At first they are an attempt to cover the crime, but quickly evolve into odd bits of advice for future, would-be fugitive couples, homespun comments such as "listen to your parents and teachers, they usually have a handle on things" or just "be open minded."

"We built our house in the trees with tamarisk walls and willow floors," recounts Holly in one of her more poetic moments. Her pointedly rural accent and meticulous inflection create an unrelenting and dark tension in her narration. Mallick's script infuses it and the dialogue with a banality that contrasts chillingly with the violence. While the voiceover tradition is deeply imbedded in *noir* history, no other femme fatales address the viewer directly. The idyll in the forest again reinforces the perpective of playing out a pulp drama. The dichotomy between the seeming indifference of Kit and Holly to their situation and the casual violence of a scene in which Kit guns down three local searchers in the woods plays a lack of emotion against a lack of constraint that colors all aspects of the couple's love.

Their romance in its early stages is both mundane and bizarre: Holly with her hair in curlers playing house in their own Tarzan-and-Jane treehouse which Kit has handily outfitted with booby traps. Kit is enjoying his heroics as protector and provider. Their dance to Mickey and Silvia's "Love is Strange" is one the most darkly comic moments of the film. Swaying languidly, eyes closed, Holly barefoot, Kit is his cowboy boots, the music and their aspect in wooded hideaway are stranger than the most outlandish images of *Natural Born Killers*. Holly has already realized that her destiny lies elsewhere, and that she has Kit wrapped around her little finger but doesn't really care. His fingers are itching for the trigger, even shooting fish in the stream, which, of course, attracts attention and forces him to fight and flee again.

Kit neatly slays the bounty hunters and they tear off to their next hideout where three more people are shot. Holly sits with mortally wounded Cato, an old trash collecting buddy of Kit's and talks to him in her bored Texas teenage voice about the spider he has in a jar near the bed. Upon his death, Kit coldly surveys Cato's possessions pronouncing them "junk" and they are away after he places the latest victim in the root cellar to keep him out of the sun. While he may show a few odd moments of conscience as he paces angrily back and forth talking to himself, Kit is lost in his own fugitive-couple, desperate-character fantasy. By now, it is out of sympathy for Kit that Holly stays with him. As she off-handedly remarks with no sense of belaboring the obvious, "I got to stick by Kit right now. He feels trapped."

Headed for Canada, they stop one night on the plain between the gas fires of Missoula and the bright lights of Cheyenne and dance again, this time to Nat King Cole's "A Blossom Fell,"; but by now Kit has lost Holly. As the lyric asserts with unabashed irony: "I saw you kissing someone new against the moon...the dream has ended for true love dies, the night a blossom falls." Although Holly quit listening to him days ago and told him she would "never tag a long after hell-bent types again," Kit is lost in his own mythos; and Holly understands that: "Kit knew the end was coming. He dreaded being shot down alone without a girl to scream his name." He maintains throughout the film, though, that they "had fun which is more that he could say for most"; so resigned to his fate, Kit knows he shouldn't expect miracles now. Holly waits calmly for her inner cue to disengage, and ultimately she simply refuses to go on with him. Though he is distressed, he is compelled to offer a last chance, a meeting at the Coolie Dam on New Year's Day sometime in the future. Kit's self-image requires him to play the gallant and takes full responsibility for the killing spree. To do that he even stage manages his own capture.

About Kit's apprehension, Holly wonders, "Was it despair?" Instead of running, he deliberately stops and, since rocks had special meaning to him, makes a stone marker on the spot where he is to be caught. He later handcuffs himself and marches amiably off to his end. The key question the police asked was, "Kit, do you like people?" Having thoroughly enjoyed his arrest, throwing souvenirs to the crowd, Holly reports that Kit went to sleep in the chair while they were reading his confession. Holly dismisses the entire affair as just another of life's episodes for which her punishment was a year's probation and a few nasty looks from the people in town. She ends up marrying her lawyer's son and leads the life one thinks her father had meant for her.

For Kit being part of a fugitive couple is the existential self-expression of the unhappy garbage collector. Holly is less love object than decoration: he would "love" her or anyone else that had been in her place. Holly just happened to be

there, a detached observer who never once got her hands dirty. His farewell to Holly is a promise that there are plenty of boys out there waiting for her and that she would have a lot of fun: "The dream has ended for true love dies."

While the dream seems to end differently for Kit and Holly than Louis and Marion, several aspects overlap. The dream, the myth, the act of fugitive love stand apart from the protagonists, who may perceive it and live it but cannot guide it to a happy ending. Some classic period fugitive couples do survive. Most perish. But only the neo-*noir* can be crushed by the myth itself.

Passion and indifference in the neo-*noir* fugitives: above, Kit and Holly's idyll at the rich man's house, a mixture of fascination and boredom. Below left, "Julie" fends off her husband as they lie in bed. Below right, true to their fugitive couple status, Holly and Kit are most amorous in the back seat of a car.

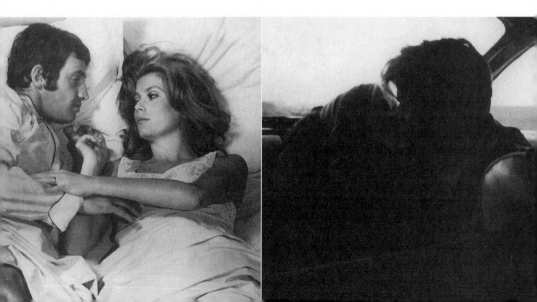

Above, a desperate Evelyn Mulwray (Faye Dunaway) brandishes a gun in *Chinatown*.

Son of *Noir*

Richard T. Jameson

It's a good idea to recall periodically that no director at, say, RKO in the Forties ever passed a colleague on the lot and called, "Hey, baby, I hear they're giving you a *film noir* to do next." The term was a critical response, on the part of some French film freaks, to a body of American movies that had been piling up during the war years, a body that continued to grow in size as the postwar films themselves became increasingly darker and more intense in mood.

Film noir–the phrase–crossed the Channel and passed into English film criticism, where it began to suggest (as almost any colorful phrase has a way of suggesting in English film criticism) some kind of hothouse specimen. Characteristically, American francocinéphiles grafted it onto their own critical vocabulary in order to celebrate not the wondrously rich heritage of their homegrown cinema, but rather the grubbily exotic blooms of Godard (*Breathless*) and Truffaut (*Shoot the Piano Player*), themselves in large measure derived from the genuine, originally American article.

More than a decade has gone by and *film noir* has finally been discovered at home. Not every workaday reviewer employs the term, but many of them have a vague idea what it's about, and whenever a new movie comes along in which the atmosphere is wishfully sinister and oddball characters proliferate to the confounding of any hope of lucid plot explication, they've learned to dive for prototypes in *The Big Sleep* the way a seal dives for a fish.

Some filmmakers operate along similar lines. Super-commercialized nostalgia trips of every description inundate theater screens; nostalgia should take longer than "youth films" to wear out its welcome at the box office, but the end will come. Meanwhile, it's been at least partially instrumental in polluting one of the loveliest waterholes directors and critics liked to share.

Once upon a time, a director might segue into a discreet quotation from a predecessor's work, nod respectfully, and proceed about the business of getting his own film made. Not many people were expected to "get it," so the gesture remained a sort of semi-public acknowledgement that one man's film grew out of, and drew strength from, an honorable cinematic tradition. Too frequently nowadays, the *hommage* serves as a means of borrowing validity for essentially invalid, half-thought-out, insincere, and sometimes campily patronizing work. Eminently *homage*-worthy items like *Out of the Past* and *Gun Crazy* will not serve to provide material because general audiences cannot be relied upon to pick up on the references. But with Warner's Bogey you're home free.

Hence, we find a recent, schlocky addition to the private-eye sub-genre, *Shamus*, featuring Burt Reynolds being ushered into a refrigerated room with his client-to-be where he must don an overcoat to ward off the freezing cold. The protractedness of the setting-up and the quotation-marked wryness of Buzz Kulik's direction leave no room for doubt: the scene exists primarily as a one-to-one inversion of Bogart's interview with General Sternwood in the steaming conservatory. The rest of the film is consistent with this dubious opening, flaunting its duplication of scenes and details from previous pictures, and pretending to have updated the material simply by exploiting the star's pop-certified machismo value.

Not that generic self-consciousness is necessarily all bad. Nowhere has it proved so explicit a virtue as in the marvelous, and scarcely shown, *Gumshoe* of Stephen Frears (very much to the star-as-auteur point) Albert Finney. Frears served as Finney's personal assistant on *Charlie Bubbles*; and that film's image of Charlie (Finney) using a toy gun to pop off the objectionable members of his household deployed across a panel of closed-circuit TV screens anticipates the multi-layered, magically resonant structure of *Gumshoe*. In it, Finney plays Eddie Ginley, a Hammett-obsessed (also Bogart-obsessed, movie-obsessed, performance-obsessed) bingo caller and patter artist who advertises himself as a private dick in the Sam Spade mold, just for a lark, and then finds himself involved in a real case.

A minor masterpiece of faultless footwork, this crammed (less than an hour and a half in running time), nimble pre-nostalgia piece describes a stand-up comic in a trenchcoat trying to come of age. In an incestuous way completely consistent with private-eye thriller plotting, Neville Smith's screenplay enables Eddie to pay off by means of melodramatic ingenuity, those very psychic wounds that have necessitated his fantasy-embracing lifestyle. It's his in-laws who are guilty, including the girl who dropped him to marry his upwardly mobile brother. And Eddie gets to lock them all up in that most characteristic chunk of *noir* iconography, an automobile–to which he holds the key.

The film ends with Ginley sitting down in his apartment with teacup and cigarette–and trenchcoat and hat. As Fifties style rock music blares from his phonograph, he repeats in voiceover the opening hard-guy soliloquy about this being "just like any other morning" to the rest of the folks in Liverpool, but with this difference for him: "I had to start learning to get along without the family." The ambiguity of this last lengthy take is profound. Is Eddie locked forever into the clinical pathology of playing his absurdly stylized role, or has the fantasy succeeded in delivering him from his demons and freeing him to become an adult?

Gumshoe is highly self-aware about its exploration and exploitation of a genre, but it never descends to trivializing cuteness (despite the fact that a lot of it is very funny) because it is committed to a fundamentally serious treatment of the problem of finding, or making for oneself, a personal way-of-being. Such seriousness was not apparent during one's—my—first look at Robert Altman's *The Long Goodbye*. Ringing in my mind's ear were some quotable quotes from Altman and/or screenwriter Leigh Brackett, to the effect that Philip Marlowe would be pathetically out of place in the Seventies, that this film would put him out of his misery, that the myth of friendship was just that, etc., etc., etc.

And indeed the revisionism of this particular Altman film sits less well—on an initial encounter, at least—than that of his previous work. One may cherish many Western archetypes that get demythicized in *McCabe and Mrs. Miller*, but one is unlikely to come to the theater cherishing the character of John McCabe as created in some obscure novel. Not so, pretty obviously, with Marlowe, whether out of Chandler or Hawks-Bogart. Marlowe exists, Marlowe is something, and the characters and relationships in the novel **The Long Goodbye** are remarkable enough that the mauling they took in the adaptive process could not be assimilated without considerable pain and resentment.

There is no suggestion here that Altman had to be faithful to the letter of Chandler's original; but I do suggest that if you're going to demonstrate the outdatedness and the fallaciousness of an artist's vision, you can't expect to be applauded—or to prove anything, for that matter—if you bash what you're criticizing out of shape and then point at it and say, Wow, that's some silly shape! One example: showing the audience, but not Marlowe, that Terry Lennox's knuckles are raw from the pounding he's given his wife, so that Marlowe seems, at a glance, more of a fool than he really is for believing in his friend. Another: reducing the disturbed but articulate novelist Roger Wade to a lumbering barbarian who can't get two sentences in sequence—and who, in addition, is tricked up to evoke, visually, associations with Hemingway, a particularly trendy target-of-opportunity for simple-minded denigration these days.

There was a self-righteous tone to many of the directorial remarks preceding the release of *The Long Goodbye*, as though it were the hip contemporary filmmaker's responsibility to purge us of all those debilitating illusions Hollywood had put in our way. Certainly the "Hooray for Hollywood" voiceover that initiates the movie and at the end underscores the onscreen high jinks of Elliott Gould's Marlowe seems to make the point explicitly enough. One felt—I still feel—that it was indeed Elliott Gould, not Philip Marlowe or any variation thereof, whom we saw exuberantly hoofing toward the bleary luminescence at the end of that Mexican road, relieved henceforward of any obligation to lend credence to outmoded creatures of the morbidly romantic imagination, turned loose in Real Life without a Scenario, movies without a Hollywood. (And I must admit that Altman's and Gould's *California Split* stunningly makes good on the promise I'm inferring here.)

In one respect I have to concur with Altman: *film noir* is terrifically romantic. The uncompromising deadendedness of *Gun Crazy* nevertheless includes room for some sense of voluptuous consummation in the camera's soaring up and away from the shattered bodies of Bart Tare and Annie Laurie Starr lying together in the swamp mist. It's heady stuff, and I've been present when it worked its black magic on an audience that had conspicuously come to jeer a presumed potboiler exhumed to satisfy some genre freak's notion of aesthetic merit. Must audiences, and filmmakers, be saved from such transcendent morbidity?

The *films noirs* of the classic period (and Paul Schrader in part defines *noir* as a period in American film history, in his invaluable Spring 1972 *Film Comment* piece "Notes on Film Noir" [reprinted in the first *Film Noir Reader*]) individually and cumulatively stood as a bitter response to a decade and a half of self-imposed screen optimism–and probably not an entirely conscious response. If the *films noirs* (or *noir* descendants) of today are any sort of response it must be of a markedly different kind. Of nostalgia-tripping, recreating the artifacts of the past for the sake of doing so, we have already spoken briefly; it is a decadent process, and if anything is illuminated thereby, it's the calculated self-interest of people who want to sell what the public is buying. That in itself is a cynical response to a cynical era hungry for optimism–an almost precise reversal of the climate in which *noir* was born.

If we admire the post-World War Two *films noirs* as healthily subversive gestures ("American movies...in the throes of their deepest and most creative funk," in Schrader's phrase), what are we to say about professional-despair pix like *Badge 373*, *Busting*, and most of their fellow copy movies? or the programmatic mutual-annihilation games monitored by Michael Winner: or the abstract loathsomeness of Equal Opportunity employer Marty Augustine in *The Long Goodbye*? Rather than reactions against blinkered optimism, such gestures fall in line with a general negativity that is enforced by a fear of being caught out as some kind of idealist. "Everybody knows" that "everybody's corrupt," so by all means let's do business.

In such spiritually dead air, resonance becomes increasingly difficult to achieve. One sees it in the debasement of standard *noir* icons. The car, for instance, has virtually lost its capacity to convey nuances of character and event, to participate in anything like the sleek ripple and jagged surge of the old *noir* textures. In *The Big Sleep*, *Out of the Past*, *They Live by Night*, *Gun Crazy*, *The Asphalt Jungle*, we never thought about the machine as much as the fact that it bore, and was sometimes violently guided by, Bogart, Mitchum, Farley Granger, John Dall, Sterling Hayden. McQueen's and Hackman's epoch-making drives aside, in contemporary *noir* (or potentially *noir* movies) one car, like one hilltop or one road barrier or one pedestrian with a shopping cart, is indistinguishable from another; and directors are so involved with racking up the requisite number of crinkled fenders, powdered headlights, violated intersections, and driven-through showroom windows that the minimal niceties of relative location and trajectory are mostly abandoned.

In this sense Robert Altman, for all his abuse of hallowed archetypes, deserves to be exonerated of any real or implied charges in the preceding few paragraphs. It took me a second, long-delayed look at *The Long Goodbye* to confirm that; others may have been more perceptive the first time around. At any rate, if *The Long Goodbye* isn't fair to **The Long Goodbye**, nevertheless it is one of the few Sixties-Seventies films to establish and make expressive use of a contemporary *noir* environment—an environment, that is, in cinematic terms more concrete, more ordered, more strongly and responsibly *felt* than the vaguely journalistic soothsaying which provides the moral and aesthetic fibre of the facile-negativity school.

For any contemporary *noir* cinema would need a good deal of reinventing. Barring the possibility of (very sympathetic) antiquarian experiments like Bogdanvich's black-and-white films, the new *film noir* must be in color and, if not wide-screen, at least wider-screen than anything out of the classic *noir* period. Obviously there will be nothing directly comparable to the tall, inky-shadowed, vertically-speared frame environment of Anthony Mann and John Alton: *T-Men, Raw Deal, Border Incident*, and the outrageously dynamic *The Black Book* (called *Reign of Terror* on TV), which happens to be a splendid *film noir* set during the French Revolution.

John Frankenheimer's *99 and 44/100% Dead* has comic-strip-style title art exploding into a scarcely less subdued real-life shot of an American flag crackling above the scene of a gangland rub-out, and features athletic action sequences angled and assembled like something out of National Comics. Blake Edwards' 1976 *Gunn*, a Technicolor revisit to his *Peter Gunn* television series, takes a fetishistic delight in liquid or liquid-looking surfaces, streamlined hot and cold color matches, lubricious camera movements, and even slipperier patterns of conversational flow (reflecting, according to Andrew Sarris, "the very, very contemporary view of individual lives as being composed less of experiences than of auditions"), from the opening image of a motor yacht slipping out of the darkness to the cool burbling of a Henry Mancini motif.

The Long Goodbye was photographed by Vilmos Zsigmond, the master cinematographer who previously shot *McCabe* and *Images* for Altman, and who has made a specialty of finding ways to capture true and evocative film images by means of the light naturally available on the scene. (Several times during the picture, and still more rigorously in his subsequent *Cinderella Liberty*, Zsigmond gets a viewable something on film relying on nothing but the flare of a match.) His dusky color eye only *seems* to slur the chromatic textures of Marlowe's world. The colors are there, fully saturated. But the three o'clock in the morning of the soul when Elliott Gould goes searching for his cat's favorite brand of pet chow seems to overlay the whole film, so that everything looks soaked in muggy heat, fuzzed over less by optical unsharpness than by the weariness of a sensibility that expects no surprises,

The Long Goodbye: above, outside his Hollywood apartment, a laconic Philip Marlowe (Elliott Gould) encounters gangster Marty Augustine (Mark Rydell). Below, Marlowe in Malibu with Eileen Wade (Nina van Pallandt) at the opposite end of the frame.

no matter how comically shitty life's ineptitude becomes. Yet the sensibility, and Gould/Marlowe, remains ambulatory ("It's okay with me" is his formula for all–or almost all–occasions), and so does Altman/Zsigmond's camera.

Cruising about the periphery of a conversation or cutting across the path of one character in a volatile two-shot, the camera keeps seeking a meaning that is almost never precisely connected–and so the camera movements aren't either–to anybody's line of march. When it is, we often don't realize it until a take is well underway: Marlowe and Mrs. Roger Wade (Nina van Pallandt) take up opposite ends of the Panavision frame playing verbal games with one another. The camera moves in; sure, fine, standard intensification tactics–it's OK with me, Bob. But it *keeps* moving in, and we become aware that out there in the night through the window beyond and between our ostensibly principal parties, the white blur of Roger Wade (Sterling Hayden) is walking into the Pacific Ocean.

Film noir stylists of the classic period used to delight in toying with mirrors, puddles, windows, anything that might suggest another–distorted or truer–face of reality. The lens-flare, telephoto-blob contingent of contemporary filmmakers have made us yearn for the clarity of straight-on, in-focus imagery. *The Long Good-bye* suggests a valid approach to what are elsewhere usually pointless or simplistic exercises in "visual" (the quotation marks are permanent) narration: Marlowe waits outside on the beach in an earlier scene while the Wades alternately yearn toward and snipe at one another in a mutual marital agony of which any *noiriste* might be proud. Sometimes we are inside with the Wades, looking out; at others, outside with Marlowe. Rarely is the camera still; and if it is, the lens is not, zooming in or out, closing on the distant nonparticipant (Marlowe) and losing the combatants; and just about the time the zoom loses the Wades, a polarizing filter is shifted and the Wades are back again in a windowglass reflection more vivid than the actual man on the beach.

It's a cinematographic tour-de-force, and not merely on a look-at-my-new-toy level. Marlowe is implicated in that conversation–*we* are implicated in that conversation–and the never-easeful drift of that privileged private eye elucidates quicksilver transformations in the reality before us that the long-suffering Wades lost control of eons ago. The very fluidity of that reality becomes charged with not so much explosive as implosive force. The zooms that seem to be sucking the life out of the characters–and the roiling white waves that tumble relentlessly toward the glass-walled environment–hold everything in a suspension that mere human beings cannot indefinitely endure. There is no purgative explosion when Roger Wade walks into that sea with his burden of guilt, partly because the guilt is half-imaginary, but also because his demise is an everyday, one-step-at-a-time process that simply reaches an endpoint.

I've refrained from saying anything so far about the latest clear triumph in the revivification of the *film noir*, Roman Polanski's *Chinatown*, mainly because I've already enjoyed the opportunity of discussing it at some length in *Movietone News*

#33. *Chinatown* does function on a principle of explosion; but, although its finale is as aesthetically fulfilled and dramatically forceful as any I know of, the explosion does not purge, as Marlowe's implicitly does. It seems, instead, one in a series of inevitable disasters–inevitable and virtually innate, gathering themselves toward horrible maturity. As Professor Abronsius says in Polanski's *Dance of the Vampires*, "It's in the order of things."

It makes perfect sense that some of the best of the new *films noirs* should have been made by men whose personal stylistic drift and thematic preoccupations are congenial to *noir* itself. Blake Edwards has always found his meaning in delirious style rather than literarily respectable substance. Altman's distrust of institutional-ized formality has (as with early Godard) become the very basis of brilliant new forms. Polanski's visions of the horrific are at the same time eerily matter-of-fact, as though he were merely confirming what he long ago learned to be true, and pragmatically accepted. There is a tremendous sense of *objets trouvés* about his art: the forceful yet mysterious image of the lifebuoy in *Knife in the Water*, the spoiling potatoes in *Repulsion*, the improbable and perfectly appropriate Gothic castle of *Cul-de-Sac*, and so on.

Below, *Chinatown*: corrupt scion Noah Cross (John Huston) tries a less violent approach to discourage private detective Jake Gittes (Jack Nicholson) whose bandaged nose is evidence of an earlier assault.

In a season when *Stings* and *Gatsbys* ought to have hopelessly tainted the pe-riod-piece genre, the reconstituted L.A. of 1937 in *Chinatown* crawls with an authenticity far beyond production department research. When Jake Gittes (Jack Nicholson), matrimonial peeper *extraordinaire*, is about to be interrupted in his clandestine inspection of a municipal bigwig's office, Polanski signals the intrusion by way of a sudden flash of white light on a translucent office-door window in the background. It is a piercing evocation, not only of the ambience in numerous Ray-mond Chandler locations, but also of the half-forgotten memories of anyone who ever waited in, say, some evil-smelling dentist's office in a building mercifully (sadly?) demolished since.

"Chinatown" itself is the most central–and at the same time all-embracing–*ob-jet trouvé* in the film. It's just that the full implications of the phrase and the place must be *trouvé* by the viewer, even though some of them are part and parcel of the detective quester's own past. In large measure Chinatown *is* the past, that country of guilty legend which, one way or another, the best *films noirs* describe. Everyone of consequence in the film doubles back upon himself in some way, re-peating prior mistakes, even causing them to be repeated against the best of con-scious intentions.

This is figured in no more forcefully than in Faye Dunaway's incarnation of the eminently untrustworthy, irresistibly alluring *film noir* female. Hers is the stellar performance in a film which is graced by impeccable playing of the tiniest role. The character is incessantly surprising, compelling, troubling. She always seems to be listening for a signal beyond the range of normal hearing–in the tones of the person she's speaking with, in a space beyond the edge of the frame, maybe somewhere within herself. In her plight, the still-figurative incestuousness of *Gum-shoe* becomes overt. A quintessential *film noir* character, she carries the sign of her fatal imperfection on her own person, in the form of a black flaw in the green of her iris. Her lover takes note of it with sardonic tenderness; the police shoot it out of her head, as conveyed by an intolerable makeup effect that suggests that the explosion we spoke of a while ago comes from the core of her being.

Chinatown, it should be noted emphatically, requires no second, settled-down look to confirm its validity (although it surely rewards a second viewing, and still others). It plays straight with the genre, and the closest it comes to winking at the audience is to feature a hero who has to walk through half the movie with a ban-dage on his nose. It has a good story to tell, people worth introducing to us, moods to savor and explore. With consummate professionalism, it gets the job done. In 1974, *film noir* is still possible, and has no apologies to make to anybody.

"Plots [that] revolve around betrayal on a personal basis": above, the Pandora-like Gabrielle (Gaby Rodgers) shoots Hammer (Ralph Meeker) in *Kiss Me Deadly*. Below, Mike Swale (Peter Berg) and Bridget Gregory/Wendy Kroy (Linda Fiorentino) in *The Last Seduction*.

Writing the New *Noir* Film

Sharon Y. Cobb

Wet streets at night. Flashing neon in the window of a seedy bar. Smoke-filled rooms. All images of desperation, alienation. All images of Classic *Film Noir* which many film historians believe began with *The Maltese Falcon* (1941) and ended with *Touch of Evil* (1958). The term "Film Noir" is said to have been coined by Nino Frank in 1946 post-World War II Paris to refer to the release of a flood of American crime films. Other examples of Classic *Noir* are: *Double Indemnity* (1944); *Detour* (1945); *The Big Sleep* (1946); *White Heat* (1949); *DOA* (1950); *Gun Crazy* (1950); and *Kiss Me Deadly* (1955).

With the release in 1992 of Quentin Tarantino's *Reservoir Dogs* and then his *Pulp Fiction* in 1994 has come a revived interest in stories about antiheroes, desperate characters and the criminal element. The commercial and critical success of *Pulp Fiction* has opened Hollywood doors to more edgy, dark stories and generated a renewed ability to produce films some label New *Noir*.

But if the period of Classic *Noir* ended in 1958, the real revival of *Noir* was launched by *Chinatown* in 1974. Other films that could be called New (or Neo) *Noir* due to their cinematic style or content include: *Raging Bull* (1980); *Thief* (1981); *Body Heat* (1981); *Blood Simple* (1984); *Jagged Edge* (1985); *Manhunter* (1986); *Blue Velvet* (1987); *The Grifters* (1990); *Basic Instinct* (1991); *Reservoir Dogs* (1992); *Love Crimes* (1992); *Final Analysis* (1992); *Guncrazy* (1992); *Red Rock West* (1992); *Pulp Fiction* (1994); *The Last Seduction* (1994); *The Usual Suspects* (1995); *The Professional* (1994); *Fargo* (1996), and *L.A. Confidential* (1997).

Writing New *Noir* can be intriguing, especially since protagonists are primarily antiheroes and their motives are usually dishonorable. Capturing "the truth of the character" on paper is sometimes tricky due to the fact that many *Noir* characters are liars, at times even deceiving themselves.

Another challenge for writers is that *Noir* characters are "unsympathetic." In other words, the audience feels little sympathy for the characters and their situations because they are not likable personalities and they do forbidden things. If movie audiences can't feel sympathy for the characters, then they care little about what happens to them and cannot connect to the story on an emotional level. So, the keys to linking the audience to *Noir* characters are understanding and intrigue. A viewer may not especially like a *Noir* protagonist, but if there is enough under-

More "plots [that] revolve around betrayal on a personal basis" and manipulated men: above, Ned Racine (William Hurt) in *Body Heat*. Below, Roy Dillon (John Cusack) in *The Grifters*.

standing of why a character is the way he is, of how he got to this wretched place in his life, then the audience will be interested in what happens in the end. Another connection is fascination with intriguing characters. We may not choose to live our lives like the *Noir* protagonist, but we certainly are captivated by his big screen life of danger and sexual impulsivity.

In *L.A. Confidential* one of the protagonists, a never-by-the-rules cop named Bud, became a cop to "get even" after watching his father beat his mother to death. His anger takes the shape of revenge on any perpetrator of domestic violence that crosses his path. He's a violent man, but we understand the seed of his rage, therefore we see him in a somewhat more sympathetic light.

Understanding the New *Noir* genre and its idiosyncrasies is the first step to crafting a compelling *Noir* story. Using themes commonly found within the genre and developing desperate characters who drive the story forward with their reckless acts of deception all contribute to creating a fresh take on *Noir*.

The following are some of the elements essential to writing a good New *Noir* screenplay.

1. NEW *NOIR* GENRE

New *Noir* plots revolve around betrayal on a personal basis with one character betraying another, or more extensively when stakes are raised and betrayal has nationwide or even worldwide consequences. In *Body Heat* Matty convinces Racine to kill her husband, then double crosses him. The same plot was used in *Body Heat*'s inspiration, *Double Indemnity*, which was released thirty-seven years earlier. In *The Grifters*, released in 1990, Lilly robs her gangster boss and also betrays her own son. Jerry Lundegard, William Macy's character in *Fargo*, betrays his father-in-law and his wife by staging the wife's kidnapping, hoping to collect ransom from the father-in-law, until things go very wrong.

2. NIGHTMARES & CRIME

Noir stories symbolize our subconscious fears, our darkest ruminations, our worst nightmares. New *Noir*, as well as Classic *Noir* films, includes the presence or portent of crime. Dramatic tension is derived from the anticipation of violence from characters with little or no socially redeeming qualities. A good example of a film that uses this brand of suspense to the fullest is Quentin Tarantino's *Reservoir Dogs*. After a botched robbery, with one of the men bleeding to death and the police closing in, thieves clash as they try to figure out who was the "snitch."

3. GOOD VS. EVIL

In *Noir* good and evil are confused and sometimes indistinguishable. Moral ambivalence and complicated discrepancies in character motivation encourage the audience to feel the torment and insecurity of the protagonist. When Nicolas Cage's character in *Red Rock West* is mistaken for a hitman and hired by both a

Plots that revolve around *loyalty* on a personal basis: above, Anita (Drew Barrymore) and Howard (James Legros) in *Guncrazy*. Below, Detectives Bud White (Russell Crowe) and Ed Exley (Guy Pearce) in *L.A. Confidential*.

husband and wife to kill the other, he crosses the imaginary line between good and evil. He justifies his actions. In *L.A. Confidential*, Bud stands by while his fellow police officers beat prisoners (evil), yet at risk of being suspended he won't testify against his partner (good or heroic). Most *Noir* characters do not think of themselves as evil or bad, and if the story is told skillfully, the line representing good and evil will blur for the audience as well.

4. PROTAGONIST IS ANTIHERO

The main character/s are not heroes at all, but the antithesis of heroic. They are desperate characters, with little hope of positive change in their lives. They live on the outskirts of normalcy, surviving as best as they can in a chaotic world both inner and outer. Their behavior is not courageous and is usually obsessive. The title of the film, *The Usual Suspects*, implies that the story is about criminals, and it is. Not only is the film about crime and criminals, the entire cinematic story is a lie made up by Kevin Spacey's character (whose real story identity in the film shall not be revealed for those who haven't seen this edgy film yet). *The Professional* was about a hitman (an unsympathetic profession) who risks his life to take in an orphan (an heroic act), but ultimately he is a cold-blooded killer.

5. CRIMINAL POINT OF VIEW

When the protagonist is a criminal, the story is told from his/her point of view. The narrative is manipulated so audiences will identify with him. In the films just mentioned above *The Usual Suspects, The Professional, Reservoir Dogs , Pulp Fiction, The Grifters* the stories are told from the criminals' perspective. We may not agree with their lifestyles, but seeing the world through their eyes, seeing that they are human, somehow connects us with them, as if they represent a frightening, dark-side of ourselves. They are not heroes, but they are compelling to watch. Their stories deliver to us the thrill of danger, without the risk of the consequences.

6. NO REDEMPTION

Unlike other genres, the *Noir* protagonist rarely redeems himself in the end. He may regret being caught for his criminal, or even murderous, behavior, but he seldom learns from his mistakes and almost never performs some courageous, selfless act to redeem himself at the end of the story. Even when Jerry Lundegard in *Fargo* discovers that the orchestrated kidnapping of his wife has gone terribly wrong and his father-in-law has been killed, all he's worried about is covering up his own theft of the cars from the car lot that he manages, not the well-being of his innocent wife. An exception to this is found in *L.A. Confidential* when Bud saves Ed, a former nemesis, after their own fellow officers come to kill them.

7. ISOLATION

The *Noir* protagonist almost always experiences a sense of isolation, either physical and/or psychological, and this isolation and alienation is pronounced.

In *Fargo*, as Jerry Lundegard's scheme to con money from his father-in-law goes wrong, he becomes more and more withdrawn, isolated from the people around him. Another similar genre, the thriller, also counts on an isolated main character to heighten suspense and create a sense of danger and insecurity for the protagonist.

8. FEMME FATALE

In many *Film Noir* movies the main character's only source of hope may be a female character, the femme fatale, who is integral to the main plot of the story.

She represents a better life. She is usually wealthy, beautiful, intelligent and illusive. But the femme fatale always has her own agenda and after using the protagonist for her own gains, she will deceive him. An example is *Basic Instinct*. Nick (Michael Douglas' character) is attracted to Catherine Tramell (Sharon Stone's character) and risks his life, knowing she's a murder suspect, to satisfy his obsession with her. Kim Basinger's character in *L.A. Confidential* is a "victim" of her own beauty who serves as a Veronica Lake look-alike call girl. She lures Bud into a sexual relationship, but then betrays him by having a sexual encounter with Bud's fellow detective, Ed, which is photographed by another character to use for blackmail.

9. *NOIR* SEX

The protagonist falls in lust with the femme fatale and becomes obsessed with her. The femme fatale turns up the heat by flirting and luring the protagonist into a sexual relationship. Many New *Noir* films feature highly erotic "love scenes" which leave the main character wanting more. His professional objectivity becomes increasingly compromised by obsessive thoughts of when his next sexual encounter will be with the woman of his fantasies. Again *Basic Instinct* is a prime example of this, with Catherine teasing Nick in front of the other detectives during questioning. *Body Heat* also features a classic femme fatale in Matty's character, seducing Racine, using him, then betraying him. As the title suggests, *Body Heat*, gives us a passionate, lustful relationship between the two main characters.

10. BETRAYAL & VIOLENCE

Not only will the protagonist be beguiled and betrayed by the female character but violence, in one form or another, will be a result of the two characters' alliance. Again *Basic Instinct* and *Body Heat* demonstrate the juxtaposition of high sexuality and potential or acted out violence. Sex and violence collide in this symbiotic co-dependence between the anti-hero and femme fatale.

11. FOR ADULTS ONLY

There are few children in New *Noir*, or Classic Film *Noir* casts. Children represent optimism and a potentially promising future, and since *Noir* symbolizes our worst nightmares, hope is out of place. An exception is *The Professional*, where the child is a next door neighbor who is orphaned after her entire family is murdered while she's out at the grocery store. The hitman takes her in (reluctantly) and she talks him into training her in the art of killing.

12. PLOT TWISTS & REVERSALS

Tension in *Noir* stories is generated as much by plot twists is it is from anticipated violence. *The Usual Suspects* is rich with unexpected twists and reversals of expectation. When we think we know what's really going on, we are deceived again. Complications and story direction changes makes *Fargo* both suspenseful and entertaining. Jerry Lundegard's plans go wrong, time after time, and when he thinks things can't get any worse, they do. In *L.A. Confidential* there are so many primary characters, subplots, plot twists and surprises that audiences must pay close attention to follow the story. And like a giant jigsaw puzzle, the pieces, which at first seem unrelated, fall together to create one big picture of deception in the end.

13. CINEMATIC STYLE

Evoking Classic *Noir* images–the wet streets at night, the dramatic contrast between light and shadow, the stark symbols of isolation–requires a discreet written narrative. Screenwriters are forbidden from "directing on the page" by specifying shot angles and details, yet by integrating *noir*ish images into scene description, a writer can bring a *Noir* texture to a script. By choosing locations which emphasize noir-based themes a writer can vividly set the scene for a New *Noir* story. Some typical *Noir* locations are lonely bars, abandoned dark streets, and seedy motels, any place that arouses our feelings of isolation, fear, and warns of violence.

Not only have films used the *Noir* genre successfully, but television has also aired several series that could be considered *Noir*. Some people refer to this as Cable *Noir*, Pop *Noir* or TV *Noir*. Some classic examples are: *Dragnet, The Fugitive*, and *Peter Gunn*. More current TV *Noir* includes: *Miami Vice* and *Fallen Angels* (Showtime).

New *Noir* is an evolving genre and presents opportunities for screenwriters to redefine the genre as Hollywood's fascination with crime drama, antiheroes and violence grows. And movies about the sinister side of human behavior will always, like the femme fatale, lure audiences into dark theaters to safely experience their worst nightmares on screen.

Above, Joe Pesci, as Leon "Bernzy" Bernstein, poses in the manner of "Weegee the Famous" in *The Public Eye*.

Blanc et Noir: Crime as Art

Linda Brookover

Joe Pesci's portrayal of Leon "Bernzy" Bernstein, New York City's crime-chasing photographer in *The Public Eye* (1992) is a different take on *film noir*'s ubiquitous private eye, a character who shoots with a Speed Graphic camera instead of a snub nosed .38. The character is derived from the celebrated shutterbug, "Weegee the Famous," a "character" created in the 1940s by free-lance photographer Arthur Fellig, a master of self promotion who elevated his crime photos to works of art. His captions sometimes had the cynicism of hard-boiled prose (for a shot of a corpse under a letter box: "Special Delivery") or sometimes a clipped detachment ("Corpse with revolver," "Drunk in Bowery"). The quality of stopped motion makes his photos look more like stills from a movie; yet they are portraits of urban life at its most fragile moments. Working almost exclusively at night, Weegee was able to capture the essence of his underlit subjects against an infinite background of black. The use of infrared film allowed him to shoot at close range in almost complete darkness and capture the shocking and sometimes vulgar faces of death. Weegee had a sixth sense for capturing passion, for urban life at its edgiest moments. His POV is felt in the portraits of New Yorkers as they unwittingly play out the drama of daily life for the unflinching eye of his 4x5 Speed Graphic. A case of parallel art movements, Weegee's photography and *film noir* were the expressions of an era when the American dream began to crumble and crime stories in the news helped initiate a cycle of film violence that has yet to end.

Born Usher Fellig in the Austro-Hungarian Empire in 1899, he was renamed Arthur upon his arrival to the U.S. via Ellis Island in 1910. The name "Weegee" is probably a phonetic spelling of Ouija, a popular game known for its divining powers which described Fellig's uncanny ability to arrive at the scene of a crime before the police. He stamped his street photos not only with his pseudonym but with his own sense of alienation from New York's elite society. Growing up in the tenements of the Lower East Side, the son of a pushcart vendor and second of seven children, he was on intimate terms with urban squalor. His love for New York and its common-man denizens shows in his depiction of children playing in the spray of a hydrant or sleeping on the fire escape of a dingy apartment building in the summer heat. His intrusive style also reveals his disdain for the wealthy and powerful figures that dominated the social scene.

Best known, however, for his crime photos, Weegee was a voyeur whose invasive images belied the adage that "crime doesn't pay." His relentless pre-dawn prowls often earned him a hundred dollars a week, which in that era was quite a respectable sum. His 1941 one man exhibition at the Photo League in New York was aptly titled "Weegee: Murder is My Business." His captioned photos sold for

a mere $3.00 each, which made him as much hustler as photo-journalist; but unlike his fellow street photographers, he worked with the obsessiveness and the eye of an artist. Weegee transcended the professional objectivity of a news photographer by stepping into the picture at a critical moment and capturing the darkest emotions of the city in life and in death. Good and evil, rich and poor, Weegee's subjects were the black and white of life's circumstances. His talent for catching them off guard rendered many unselfconscious portraits of New Yorkers watching their apartment building burn or gathering at a murder scene. His compassionate photography is unsentimental in the same way that *noir* characters and films can be violent and passionate but devoid of attachment. Weegee's voyeuristic Speed Graphic celebrated the common man and mocked those who led lives of privilege and wealth. When a Speed Graphic was too obvious he took a pocket camera and infrared film into the unlit recesses to capture people watching movies, milling around fires and crime scenes, huddled in the smoky rear booths of cheap restaurants, aspects of everyday life that normally passed unnoticed.

His career as newspaper photographer, photojournalist and early paparazzi took several turns before including moving pictures. Weegee published his first book of photos, **Naked City**, in 1945, the year that Hollywood released such *noir* films as *Conflict*, *Mildred Pierce* and *Scarlet Street*. Weegee's breakthrough book propelled his work into another realm, eventually leading to his marginal involvement in filmmaking particularly *film noir*. It was his **Naked City** that inspired the classic period *film noir* of the same name. As *noir* fate would have it, Weegee's career in movies was undistinguished compared to his career in photography. It included a number of bit parts in which he played seamy New York roles like the ones in the 1948 Jules Dassin/Mark Hellinger *Naked City* and Robert Wise's 1949 *The Set-Up*. The 1951 production of *Journey Into Light* (aka *Skid Road*) featured characters that could have stepped right out of Weegee's photos. On television in the 50s the look of shows such as *M Squad* and *Harbor Master* reflected Weegee's imagery and *The Man with Camera* reflected his life, albeit a more Hollywood rendering with Charles Bronson as the series star. Weegee was a technical advisor on this 1958-59 show based on sanitized versions of his exploits as a crime photographer. He also was a technical consultant to Stanley Kubrick on *Dr. Strangelove*.

It was thirty years later that the nature and aesthetic of Weegee's work was dramatized in the neo-*noir* film, *The Public Eye* (directed by Howard Franklin). The opening scenes of the movie feature some of Weegee's most famous photos as they appear in the developing tray. Bernzy, the Weegee character, works out of his car and lives the rundown life of many a private dick. In *The Public Eye*, Bernstein roams the streets in his car/photo studio, traveling from one dark urban landscape to another, his portable photo lab in the trunk. When Bernzy rises at 2 PM and grimaces at his own reflection in the mirror, he is the daylit equivalent of the images he stalks at night: worn yet resilient, ugly yet beautiful. Like Weegee, this character is at home with cops and crooks as well as New York's hoi polloi. It

Opposite, the actual Weegee the Famous poses in front of a theater showing *The Naked City*.

Above, a Weegee photo: "Alone in their dream."   Below, alone in a different dream: Joe Pesci as "Bernzy" and Barbara Hershey as Kay Lovitz in *The Public Eye*.

is this fine line that Pesci as Bernstein walks in *The Public Eye* when he has fore-knowledge of a murder which he chooses to photograph rather than to stop.

The Public Eye, co-stars Barbara Hershey as Kay Levitz, a beautiful night club owner who calls on Bernzy for help with the mob who has an interest in her late husband's club. He accepts and the son of poor immigrant parents is admitted into the glamorous world of an uptown nightclub which he views completely as an outsider. In inevitable *noir* fashion, Bernzy is drawn into a mostly unrequited infatuation with Kay, which eventually leads into participating in a crime. As he slowly dares to fall in love with Kay, he collects photographs of the club and its patrons for the book he hopes to publish one day. It is this photo book that is central to *The Public Eye*'s neo-*noir* evocation of such classic-period mainstay emotions, alienation and obsession. Berny's infatuation with Kay may never quite reach the impulsive intensity of *amour fou*; but his monomaniacal compilation of images for his book certainly does. Rejected by mainstream publishers, Bernzy's work is more than obsession, it is his existential affirmation, a *noir* icon both in theme and in content. Like many of her *noir* antecedents, Kay can be genuinely moved, in this ironic instance by the emotion contained in Bernzy's photographs, especially by the his juxtaposition of one photo of her captioned "Beauty" with a battered prizefighter labeled "Beast."

In *The Public Eye*, the quest for recognition as an artist runs parallel to the quest for love. Bernzy points his camera at a sailor kissing a girlfriend good-bye and lurks in the shadows of unfulfilled longing. A moment later a hooker propositions him. Artie, a newspaper columnist who has broken through on Broadway, tells him bluntly, "No woman could love a shabby little guy who sleeps in his clothes, eats out of cans and cozies up to corpses so much that he begins to stink like one." Professionally, Bernzy can sustain his pose of self assurance even cockiness, even if grilled by cops or slapped by mobsters. But the rush of human feeling can only come to him filtered through the lens of his camera. Kay draws on her own feelings of unfulfilled artistic aspiration as a way to get to Bernzy. Her suggestion that she understands Bernzy as an artist with remarks such as "You are not like those other guys, you believe in something" or "you're the real thing or you'd have given up long ago" is as seductive for him as any physical allure.

Bernzy retreats from the club one night after he had begun to show Kay his book and she is called to hobnob with some important clientele. He finally trusts her enough to disclose his affection via his photos but is jealous of the attention she must pay to her business. Kay follows him into an alley where he has been drawn to a photo op. She catches him propping up a drunk in a white dinner jacket for his portrait and witnesses the tenderness with which Bernzy arranges the man's hair and his lapel which she finds both compelling and repulsive. Wearing a cape and looking more like Snow White than the Wicked Queen, she shows up later at his apartment where photographs hang out to dry above his bed, like black and white dreams that occupy his solitary slumber. Pesci and Hershey are unlikely lovers, yet for a short time, he allows himself to believe the dream. Pesci plays these few scenes with a shyness atypical of his usual character roles. His portrayal of a man in love is as charming as the delighted smile which spreads over Bernzy's face when Kay identifies herself as his girlfriend. As with most classic period characters, Bernzy's particular hubris is what threatens his very existence, as he lets Kay play him, drag him more deeply into peril and under her spell. Unable to express his love in a straightforward manner, Bernzy is driven to take greater chances. For as Artie reminds him, he would "never be in this mess if he were capable of expressing three human emotions."

Fame, recognition, and simple respect are what drive Bernzy to point his camera directly at a loaded gun during the restaurant massacre. Is this the romantic notion of sacrificing all for art? Or is it the simpler despair of a man exploited by a beautiful woman? When the gunman spots him under the table, Bernzy is ready to die. He half expected that his specially-rigged camera on wheels might capture the moment of his own death. But as fate would have it, Bernzy's number isn't up, as a stray bullet brings down his would-be assassin. Instead of dying, he becomes a hero; but he does not get the girl. When Bernzy discovers that Sal, his turncoat informant, ended up dead, he also realizes that Kay has been bought and knows that their complicated relationship cannot continue. Having been willing to sacrifice his life for art or love, Bernzy is liberated, free to return to his relentless stalking of the dark streets.

Below, Joe Pesci as "Bernzy" confers with Stanley Tucci as Sal Minnetto, a small-time gangster whose help Bernzy has extorted in *The Public Eye*.

The glamorous veneer of *The Public Eye's* New York night life is as much inspired by the Weegee photos, as it is by the classic underworld of *film noir*. Cinematographer Peter Suschitzky maintains the lighting scheme from black and white to sepia to color, recreating both the underworld ambience of 1940's New York and the feeling of intimacy that Weegee himself created in his photography.

Despite some criticism that *The Public Eye* is merely a *noir* pastiche in style and plot, it is the alienation of the characters that place it firmly within the neo-*noir* genre. The short, unattractive Bernzy is a classic *noir* outsider reminiscent of Mickey Rooney's *noir* portrayals in *Drive a Crooked Road* (1954) and *The Strip* (1951). Bernzy and Kay are both imposters: he as a detective, she as a blueblood in the glitz and dazzle of club society. They are both in the business of the night. She entertains celebrities and mobsters, he photographs them. In the end the comment that rings truest is simply that "they call them shutterbugs, because they are insects...vermin."

Until his involvement with Kay, Bernzy's greatest involvement in crime had been a little set dressing for some of his photos: he liked to place the dead guy's hat in the shot. He'd dress as a priest to hop into an ambulance and get a forbidden shot. Kay's solicitation causes him to break his own rule. He crosses the line and gets involved, both in crime and in love. Once he falls for the inaccessible femme fatale and becomes a patsy in a mob hit which he aims to photograph, the *noir* formula would suggest Bernzy's demise. Although he survives, as with many *noir* protagonists of the classic period, the price of physical survival is an emotional death. The intensity of his desire for recognition and to prove himself to Kay motivates him to go to the extremes only a true artist would. He declares his love for her, facing the wall, saying "you don't know what I would have done for you." She admits that she has betrayed him in order to hold on to the night club, with only a "don't hate me too much." In the end, Bernzy ends up with respect and admission to the Stork Club; but he is alone and obsessed, unable to shut off the police radio that blares non-stop inside his car and inside his fevered brain.

Above, Deckard (Harrison Ford) is pursued amid dark, blighted tenements by the Roy (Rutger Hauer) in *Blade Runner*.

Noir Science

James Ursini

In the seminal essay section of the first *Film Noir Reader*, we tracked the chief critical disputation surrounding *film noir*: namely, what exactly is "this thing called *noir*"? Is it, as Damico in *"Film Noir*: A Modest Proposal" and Higham-Greenberg in *Hollywood in the Forties* propose, a genre "rooted in the nineteenth century's vein of grim romanticism..."? Or could it possibly be, as Silver-Ward argue in *Film Noir: An Encyclopedic Reference to the American Style*, a mode or style of filmmaking which pervades all genres even though it found its most copacetic residence in the crime-detective genre?

The most compelling argument for *film noir* as a style or mode seems to be the fact, as Silver-Ward point out, that *noir* informs all genres, even ones as disparate as the western (e.g., *Duel in the Sun, Blood on the Moon*) and science fiction. However, over the decades since *film noir* was first named by those perceptive French critics Nino Frank and Borde-Chaumeton, there has been little serious exploration of this thesis. Even Silver-Ward in the original edition of their encyclopedia devoted only a few pages in one of their many appendices to the subject of *noir*'s influence on genres other than the crime-detective subset. With this essay I hope to begin a process which will rectify this omission. For in exploring *film noir*'s sway over various genres, one can discover more not only about *film noir* itself but also about the conventions of the identified genre.

Film noir and the movie genre science fiction were linked at birth. Several of what critics like Durgnat ("Paint It Black") considered proto-*noir* films are also science fiction films. In the forefront of those films is Fritz Lang's *Metropolis* (1926).

In *Metropolis* Lang creates a shadowy, stylized, expressionistic future world which reifies what Place-Peterson ("Some Visual Motifs of *Film Noir*") point to as the key to *film noir*'s visual look, "*mise-en-scene* designed to unsettle, jar, and disorient the viewer in correlation with the disorientation felt by *noir* heroes." The angst-filled protagonist in this case is Freder (Gustave Frölich), the son of the "master" who designed and rules Metropolis with an iron hand. Freder lives in luxury and decadence befitting his station. The spectator first sees him cavorting in a garden featuring wild peacocks, an elaborate fountain, and beautifully costumed women. As Freder reaches to caress one of his female "playthings," Maria (Brigitte Helm), a representative of the dark underworld city where the workers live and toil, enters dramatically surrounded by a group of bedraggled children.

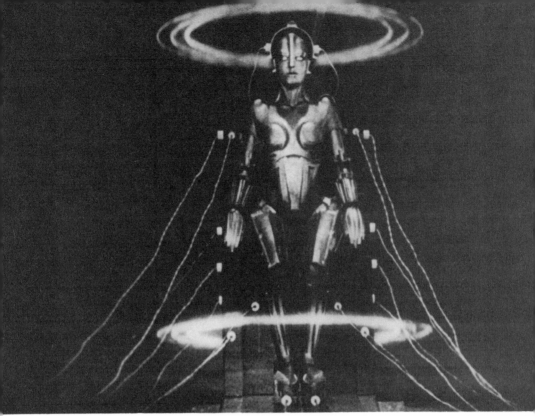

Metropolis: above, the Robot; below, the factory and its workers.

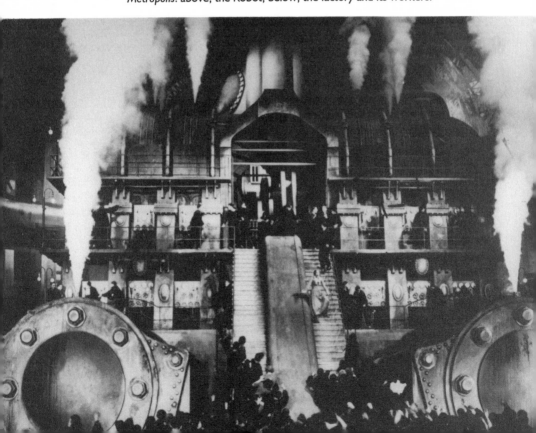

Freder, in close-up, stares in shock at these "phantoms" whom Maria refers to as his "brothers." Grasping his heart, Freder follows her to the "underneath" where he experiences an almost religious conversion, rivaling that of Paul on the road to Damascus.

There Freder witnesses the oppression of the workers who, dressed uniformly in black, contrasting markedly with his purely white attire, march in lock-step up a stairway leading to a gateway. This image, however, suddenly dissolves as the viewer, adopting the POV of Freder, sees the gateway transform itself into the mouth of the god Moloch devouring the workers whole.

Freder now becomes a classic *noir* figure, what Silver-Ward describe as "a complex protagonist with existential awareness." In order to relieve his feelings of guilt and alienation, Freder dons the garb of his "brothers" and even takes one worker's place on the crucifying hands of regulating dial. As he moves the hands rapidly and mind-numbingly from lit bulb to lit bulb, he cries out in direct Biblical allusion to his father above, the Master of Metropolis.

The theme of identity so crucial to *film noir* also appears a primary concern of the science fiction genre from its roots. Through Maria, who tells the workers cautionary parables in the dark and dank catacombs of the cathedral, Lang explores the theme of identity while simultaneously developing an early archetype of the femme fatale, also iconically linked to *film noir*. In order to repress the workers' growing unrest, the Master (Alfred Abel), assisted by the inventor Rothwang (Rudolph Klein-Rogge), develops a robot which takes on the physical appearance of the Madonna-like Maria. He then sends out this cyborg to lead the workers astray, thereby giving him an excuse to "crack down."

However, from the first, the Master's plans go awry. At a lavish party for his rich friends, the Master introduces his creation. From a bejeweled seashell, Maria, a modern Venus, rises, crowned with a tiara and dressed in a diaphanous gown. Performing an erotic dance, she proceeds to whip the Master's guests into a frenzy. At this point any viewer with even a passing acquaintance with either science fiction or *film noir* knows this "feminine principle" will be a force the Master cannot control. Like the heroine of *Gilda* or Phyllis in *Double Indemnity*, this female is a subversive catalyst which will destroy the patriarchal system around her–a primary theme in *film noir*. The robot Maria, like Mary Shelley's creature in **Frankenstein** and its many descendants in the science fiction genre, brings on the destruction of the Master's world as she incites the workers to dismantle the machinery which keeps Metropolis functioning.

Frankenstein (1931) remains seminal to both *noir* science fiction and non-*noir* science fiction. Mary Shelley's novel has always been a source for much of science fiction literature and film with its themes of identity and of human hubris. James Whale's 1931 version, his sequel *Bride of Frankenstein* (1935), and Rowland Lee's

The Frankenstein legend: above, the Monster (Boris Karloff), the Doctor (Basil Rathbone), and, Igor (Bela Lugosi) in *Son of Frankenstein*. Below, Kenneth Branaugh in *Mary Shelley's Frankentein*.

Son of Frankenstein (1939) were the first of many films to unite the science fiction content of the Shelley story with *noir* visual style and themes.

The existential angst in *Frankenstein* is two-fold largely because the focus of Shelley's story was from the beginning schizophrenic, building sympathy for Dr. Frankenstein in his Promethean desire to find the meaning of life by creating it as well as for his Creature in his often violent, yet, at times, tender search for acceptance and identity. Whale telegraphs Dr. Frankenstein's obsessiveness throughout his two movies. *Frankenstein* opens on a graveyard at night as the doctor (Colin Clive) and his assistant (Dwight Frye) dig frantically beneath a gibbet for a newly deceased body to be used in their experiments with "reanimation." As played by

Clive, Frankenstein seems always on the verge of a nervous breakdown and, in fact, suffers such a collapse in both this film and its sequel. In his laboratory, a deserted castle on a gloomy and isolated peak, he abandons his fiancée and family to build a "better monster." When he finally succeeds in reanimating the Creature, the camera cuts from a close-up of the Creature's hand moving almost imperceptibly to a close-up of Frankenstein screaming madly, "It's alive, alive, alive." He is the classic *noir* protagonist, bound by his compulsions, no less than Walter Neff in *Double Indemnity* or the obsessive Johnny in *Gilda*.

But Frankenstein is not alone in his *noir* agony. His Creature (Boris Karloff) also shares his "father's" angst. Like many of the scions of futuristic science in movies, the Creature goes astray, although here more out of child-like innocence and an inability to understand his place in the world than out of evil intentions. As an example, early in the film the Creature, escaping from his master and the cruelty of Frankenstein's assistant who taunts him with fire, comes upon a young girl in the woods. The Creature, happy for once, plays with the young child, throwing flowers in the lake and watching them float. There is an overtly lyrical staging to the scene, suffused in sunlight, free of the ominous shadows which dominate the rest of the film. Associating the beautiful flowers with the little girl, he picks her up gently and tosses her into the water. However, she does not float. Terrified at the result, the Creature runs away, ultimately to meet his fate: to be burned alive in a windmill whose blades resemble a fiery cross, adding another religious layer to the film.

The visual look of these early Frankenstein films draws heavily from *Metropolis* with its deep shadows and expressionistic set design. An example is Frankenstein's laboratory. In both films Whale constructs an expressionistic, Gothic setting with steep stone staircases, bubbling beakers, immense electrical devices,

Below, a new version of the angst-ridden creature: Robert De Niro in *Mary Shelley's Frankenstein*. with a hapless, blind peasant (Richard Briers) who will soon become a victim.

cantilevered operating tables, and electrified kites floating above a tower. The angles he chooses are more often canted while the lighting chiaroscuro in order to disorient the viewer as well as create a mood of suspense and terror.

The third seminal *noir* science fiction work is ***The Strange Case of Dr. Jekyll and Mr. Hyde***, particularly well-adapted in the John Barrymore 1920 version and in the Rouben Mamoulian 1931 version. Robert Louis Stevenson's original novella like Mary Shelley's classic work is a true forerunner of science fiction literature and film. Although neither Stevenson nor Shelley delineate the technology which leads to the protagonist's scientific breakthrough (reanimation of the dead in ***Frankenstein*** and chemically induced schizophrenia in ***Dr. Jekyll***), both authors develop the important theme of the effect of futuristic science on human identity, the *sine qua non* of the science fiction genre. Cinema, however, with its inherent ability to make the abstract concrete, has taken great pains to detail the process of Dr. Frankenstein, as seen earlier, as well as Dr. Jekyll in the filmic adaptations of Stevenson's story.

Dr. Jekyll's laboratory in both the 1920 and 1931 versions exemplifies the *noir* visual style with chiaroscuro lighting and disorienting angles, particularly exaggerated in the 1931 version when the central transformation from good Dr. Jekyll to evil Mr. Hyde occurs. In Mamoulian's film, beakers boil, pots overflow, as the camera spins dizzyingly while Dr. Jekyll (Fredric March) begins to feel the transformational effect of his drug. While he suffers convulsions physically, his DNA altering, the director superimposes images of his angelic fiancee Muriel (Rose Hobart) juxtaposed with his more demonic lover Ivy (Miriam Hopkins) and her gartered thigh, swinging provocatively.

Ivy in the 1931 version and Gina (Nita Naldi) in the 1920 version are classic femme fatales, so inseparably linked to *film noir*'s dramatic construct. Gina is the carnal temptation the saintly Dr. Jekyll (John Barrymore) or, as his friends refer to him, the "St. Anthony of London" must face. When this humanistic physician, whom the spectator sees early on working in a clinic among the poor, watches Gina dancing in a club, she immediately inflames his repressed libidinous side. She is a dark, Mediterranean woman, representative of the "fatal woman" archetype promoted in literature and myth by Anglo-Saxon Victorian culture [cf. ***Woman and the Demon*** by Nina Auerbach]. She is even directly tied to the Borgias by flashback which tells the story of her poison ring. Although Ivy in the 1931 version is much lighter in physical aspect, she too brings out the libidinous desires of the rational, decorous Jekyll as she taunts him with her white, naked thighs.

For Dr. Jekyll's angst in both versions, as opposed to the original novella, is informed by Freudianism. The presence of Ivy and Gina, additions to the Stevenson story, reinforces the interpretation of Jekyll as a man who battles his sexual impulses within the context of a strict Victorian society. The drug he produces releases the "monster of the id" with no superego to direct it into socially acceptable channels. Even Jekyll's physical appearance when he becomes Hyde–

Above, a dark anomaly: Fredric March as the atavistic Mr. Hyde dressed in evening clothes in the 1931 *Dr. Jekyll and Mr. Hyde.*

"troglodytic" (Stevenson's word) with elongated skull and claw-like fingers in the Barrymore version; simian in features and movement in March's rendering–suggests primitive man and unbridled instinct. This violent, voracious evolutionary throwback cannot, of course, continue to exist and so in both versions Jekyll conquers Hyde and redeems himself through his own death.

Commentators agree that the classic period of *film noir* begins around 1940 and ends somewhere in the late 1950s. The two key *noir* science fiction films during this era are *Invaders from Mars* (1953) and *Invasion of the Body Snatchers* (1956). Both films reflect the paranoia and fear common to *noir* films of the period (e.g., *The Window, DOA*, etc.) while also acting as forerunners of contemporary *noir* science fiction like *X-Files*. Most *noir* critics point to the Cold War, McCarthyism, the development of nuclear weapons, post-World War II stress syndrome as causal factors in shaping this paranoia. But whatever the social forces, few can argue with the depth of the paranoia in films like *Invaders from Mars* and *Invasion of the Body Snatchers*.

Invaders from Mars is particularly novel in its exploration of *noir* paranoia from the point of view of a child. David (Jimmy Hunt) awakens from sleep to witness through his telescope the landing of a flying saucer in the sand pit near his house. Lightning streaks across the deep blue of the night sky as David watches with a mix of horror and awe the space vehicle burrow into the sand and disappear. The remainder of the film tracks David's attempts to convince others of the reality of what he saw on the edge of sleep, complicated by the fact that the aliens are sucking individuals into the underground caverns they have blasted away and implanting them with electronic devices to control them.

The central terror here is one common to children, according to psychologists like Bruno Bettelheim (in **Uses of Enchantment**)–fear of abandonment. When David's father (Leif Erickson) returns from the pit, he has changed noticeably in affect. Close-ups of his impassive face, alternating with low angle shots from David's POV of the electronic

Below, John Barrymore's Rasputin-like rather than "troglodytic" Hyde.

implant in the base of his father's skull, reinforce the boy's fear that this is no longer his parent, that somehow these aliens have altered his father's identity. When this suspicion also extends to his other primary caretaker, his mother (Hillary Brooke), who comes to pick him up at the police station where he has sought refuge and help, the boy's world truly collapses. Later he sits at night, alone and distraught, in the sand pit while the army plants charges to destroy the caverns of the aliens. Even though he temporarily adopted a mother surrogate, Dr. Blake (Helena Carter), as well as a father figure, Dr. Kelston (Arthur Franz), he yearns for his real parents.

The stylization of the film, done expertly by designer-director William Cameron Menzies, heightens even further the paranoia while layering the movie with an oneiric patina (for, in the end, the whole film turns out to be but the boy's nightmare). As in much of *film noir*, night scenes abound, here tinted a deep eerie blue. The filmmakers also utilize shadows extensively to convey a mood of fear and mystery. While locked in a jail cell for his own protection, the shadows of the bars crisscross his body and frightened face. When two alien-controlled policemen blow up the research plant, they are apprehended near a wall, tinted red from the flames of the fire with huge human shadows in classic expressionist style.

Menzies also distorts the sets and decor to emphasize the nightmare quality of the movie. As mentioned, many of the shots in the film are from David's POV, a low angle which makes the sets seem more imposing, more ominous than normal, particularly evident in the police station. In addition, Menzies repeats the same running shot of David as he escapes the sand pit and the charges set by the army. As in a dream, he seems to run and yet never to reach his destination.

Invasion of the Body Snatchers, directed by *noir* veteran Don Siegel (*Private Hell 36, The Lineup*, etc.), weaves its paranoid web over the small town of Santa Mira. Using a classic *noir* technique, the first-person narration, Dr. Miles Binnell (Kevin McCarthy) tells the viewer the story of how his quiet town became the "experimental lab" for a new species of "pod people" from space.

Binnell's *noir* angst is evident from the first sequence in which the viewer watches him being restrained by hospital orderlies as he screams out, "I'm not insane" in tight close-up. After calming down, he begins his tale, shown in flashback. He relates how the inhabitants of his town were taken over by "seeds from space" which grew in the form of pods, absorbing the identity as well as the physical appearance of the individual overnight. The result is a species of emotionless, automaton-like beings with a mission to convert others.

Binnell's existential angst is double-edged. First, he must gradually witness with increasing panic his friends and patients becoming "pod people," while at the same time he must protect his own identity. This survival instinct forces him to be suspicious, "I wasn't sure there was anyone I could trust," as well as violate his professional code as a doctor by committing acts of brutality. As an example, when he finds half-formed bodies in a greenhouse, he takes up a pitchfork, hesitating as the camera intercuts between his anxiety-ridden face and the almost human body before him, until finally he musters the strength to drive the weapon into the flesh of the "pod person."

Binnell does achieve his goal of maintaining his human identity but at quite a price. In the climax of the film, Binnell and his love Becky (Dana Wynter) escape the pursuing townspeople by hiding beneath some boards in an abandoned tunnel. Fearing sleep, the time when the pods can absorb human personalities, Becky and Binnell hold on to each other in a tight two-shot, whispering words of encouragement and affection in order to fend off sleep. Binnell, however, makes the fatal mistake of leaving Becky for a few minutes to trace the sound of lyrical voices, siren-like in the distance. When he returns and kisses Becky, the camera cuts back and forth, in a series of unsettling close-ups, between his terrified face and her impassive one. "Accept us," she tells him seductively. Binnell refuses, choosing instead to run into the night and onto a highway where he screams wildly at passing cars as well as straight into the camera in an unnerving close-up, "You're next."

Below, Dr. Miles Binnell (Kevin McCarthy) comforts his fiancée Becky (Dana Winter) in *Invasion of the Body Snatchers.*

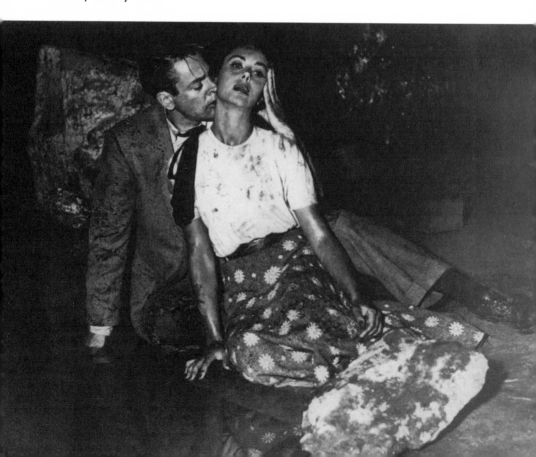

The *noir* classic period extended its life slightly into the 1960s by means of television. Shows like *The Fugitive* and *Twilight Zone* adopted *noir* themes and visuals into the late 1960s when color television rang the death knell for the classic period [cf. my "Angst at Sixty Fields per Second" in the first **Film Noir Reader**]. The most notable *noir* science fiction series of that period was *The Outer Limits* (1963-1964). While *Twilight Zone* only intermittently dealt with science fiction stories, concentrating more on horror of the supernatural and paranormal variety, *Outer Limits* drew most effectively from the well of *noir* science fiction. Utilizing *noir* directors like John Brahm (*Hangover Square*), Gerd Oswald (*A Kiss before Dying*), and Byron Haskin (*I Walk Alone*), the series consistently utilized moody lighting and disorienting angles to subjectify the experiences of a string of alienated, angst-ridden protagonists. One of the most notable episodes is "The Demon with the Glass Hand," written by noted sci-fi author Harlan Ellison and directed by Byron Haskin.

"The Demon with the Glass Hand" is shot almost entirely at that icon of Los Angeles *noir*, the Bradley Building—used to great effect in such *noir* films as *DOA* and Joseph Losey's *M*. Its art deco interior; dark, rich wood banisters; long, dimly lit halls; winding staircase; and centrally located elevator cage are ideal for creating mood as well as for staging action sequences. In "Demon," the basis for the *Terminator* series, the troubled protagonist is a cyborg–Trent (Robert Culp)–unaware of his electronically artificial identity. On the verge of extinction by a race of aliens, humanity has constructed and sent Trent into the past with seventy billion humans stored on an electronic wire in his circuits. He is" the last hope of mankind," humanity's "savior," as the computer in his hand tells him, visually reinforced by the viewer's first high angle glimpse of Trent under a lamp post which casts the shadow of a cross. He must preserve the species for twelve hundred years until it is safe for humanity to re-emerge. The cruel irony of the story, however, is that Trent, like the viewer, only learns of his identity and his fate in pieces throughout the puzzle-like plot as he retrieves the lobes of his computer hand from the aliens who have followed him through the time mirror. Instead he believes for most of the film, as does the viewer, that he is, as a captured alien tells him, "the last man on earth."

Gradually the reasons why he feels nothing, even when stimulated emotionally by Consuelo (Arline Martel), a sweatshop employee he rescues and who falls in love with him, are revealed. He is the "eternal man...Gilgamesh" as the narrator calls him in the first sequence. He proves this description accurate when he walks into a barrage of bullets from the aliens' guns–shot in low angle with strong shadows–and yet manages to rise from the dead in a few hours with direction from his computer hand.

In a final poignant scene, after he destroys the aliens and shatters their time mirror, the now fully functional glass hand confirms his cyborg status. As Consuelo, in close-up, stares at him in horror, Trent stretches his hand out towards her. On his face, also seen in close-up, is the human emotion of anguish. But she can only run away in fear, leaving him alone. As he walks up the winding staircase, automaton-like, resigned to his fate as a cyborg savior, the camera pulls back and the narrator intones, "1200 years without love, without friendship, alone, waiting."

Blade Runner (1982, directed by Ridley Scott) marks the beginning of the "neo-noir period" for the science fiction genre. The revival of interest in film noir in general began with Chinatown (1974) and has continued unabated for more than two decades. The list of neo-noir films to date is quite extensive [cf. the third edition of **Film Noir: An Encylopedic Reference** which features a lengthy essay and filmography of neo-noir films through 1992] and more are being produced as of this writing. However, it is Blade Runner's apocalyptic tone and moody, expressionistic visual design, derived somewhat from Scott's earlier Alien, which, more than any other noir film, left its indelible mark on noir science fiction.

Blade Runner, based on prescient sci-fi writer Philip K. Dick's **Do Androids Dream of Electric Sheep?**, features not just one but three characters haunted by existential anguish. The first is the alienated, dour detective, Deckard (Harrison Ford), a staple of noir stretching back to Philip Marlowe and Sam Spade. The police hire Deckard to eliminate a new, more powerful breed of replicants who have escaped from the human colonies in space and returned to earth to search out, like their antecedant, Frankenstein's Creature, their own "father," industrialist Tyrell (Joe Turkel). Deckard lives by himself in a dimly lit apartment with Aztec designs on the walls. Asleep, he dreams of escaping this apocalyptic earth of constant rain, crowded streets, and huge video billboards. Horses, rare in his decaying world, gallop through his dreams, racing into pure light and space–the diametrical opposite of his dark, claustrophobic earth.

Deckard finds his opportunity for redemption in the unlikeliest of places–the arms of the species he has been hired to destroy–replicants. Rachael (Sean Young) first enters his vision at the offices of Tyrell Corporation where he is to test her electronically to determine if she is a cyborg. An artificial owl flies ominously into frame–a foreshadowing, followed by Rachael who stuns Deckard with her noirish, Joan Crawford-style hair and suit. During the test he discovers her artificial identity which she refuses to believe. Gradually, however, he coldly shatters her self-confidence by showing her how the memories she retains were in fact implanted by Tyrell. After she saves his life in the streets by shooting a fellow replicant Deckard is pursuing, she returns to his apartment where they make love.

The third existential character is the ostensible villain–Roy (Rutger Hauer), the leader of the new breed of replicants. His angst is positively palpable. When he finds his creator Tyrell, he tells him sadly, "It's not an easy thing to meet your maker." But when Tyrell refuses to aid him in stopping his "accelerating decrepitude," Roy kisses him gently and then brutally crushes his skull with his bare hands. Like Milton's fallen angel in **Paradise Lost,** Roy is a muscular, fair-haired

Adonis who recites poetry and cries over the deaths of his fellow replicants. He even turns messiah when in the climactic chase through the Bradbury Building, Roy saves Deckard's life by pulling him up as the detective hangs from a girder of the edifice. Caressing a dove, a symbol of purity, Roy bends his head and dies. This final act of kindness allows Deckard to escape with Rachael and fly away through a bank of clouds into clear light, leaving the claustrophobic future world of Los Angeles far behind.

Twelve Monkeys (1995) is based on *La Jetée* (1964), the short *noir* science fiction classic by Chris Marker. In this large scale remake, director Terry Gilliam continues the exploration of apocalyptic dystopia begun by *Blade Runner*. In this case the world of the future has been ravaged by a man-made virus. The survivors have moved underground, creating there a dark, dirty world which combines old and new technologies. The result is a surreal landscape, in keeping with director Gilliam's own predilections (*Brazil, The Adventures of Baron Munchausen*, etc.), which showcases rows of prisoners in elevated cages, banks of camera eyes and video screens peering like insects, sterile operating rooms where prisoners are interrogated and tortured. Like the workers in *Metropolis* these survivors yearn to return to the world above and so periodically the scientists send "volunteers" above to collect specimens to determine if the earth's surface is safe to inhabit.

Finding little hope that the present will offer them an answer, the scientists develop a method of time travel so that they can prevent the release of the destructive virus in the past and thus change history. They choose a prisoner, James Cole (Bruce Willis), to be their guinea pig. Cole is selected because of a particularly vivid memory he carries from the past in the form of a dream–am image of himself as a young boy (Joseph Melito) witnessing the shooting of a man in an airport and of a beautiful woman running to save the fallen man.

Cole is a brute man, physically powerful yet beaten down psychologically as evidenced by his stooped posture. When he first returns to the past, it is too early, 1990 rather than 1996 when the virus was released. So his Cassandra-like warnings about the destruction of mankind and his efforts to find the source of the virus produce no positive results. Instead he is beaten, institutionalized, and drugged into submission by authorities not far different than the ones in his world.

Cole's angst and confusion only increase when he meets Kathryn (Madeleine Stowe), a psychiatrist at the hospital who resembles the woman in his memory. Cole now, much like the viewer, must solve a complex puzzle: the meaning of his dream and how it relates to finding the source of the man-made virus. He returns twice more to the past, each time becoming more addicted, in the words of the scientists of the future, "to that dying world." Cole, however, finds release in dancing in a stream at night, gazing at the sun in shock, listening to music on the car radio, feeling the rush of air on his face–all experiences he cannot have in the underground world he was raised in. But most of all he has become attached to Kathryn, who starts out as his hostage and ends up his lover and cohort. In a

Above and below, *Gattaca*: 70 years after *Metropolis*, future workers still walk in lock step and strive for genetic rather than mechanistic perfection with Ethan Hawke as Jerome Morrow and Uma Thurman (below, right) as Irene.

sleazy hotel room where he begins to doubt his sanity and looks to her for valida-tion, he confesses emotionally to her: "I want to be whole. I want to stay here with you."

But in order to solve the puzzle of the "army of the twelve monkeys" and find the identity of the scientist who will spread the virus, Cole must relive his trau-matic childhood experience, but from a different perspective. He must repeat the scene in his dream, only no longer as the young boy but as the fallen man. In a tense, almost metaphysical scene shot in slow motion to draw out the agony and enhance the nightmare quality, Cole and Kathryn run through the airport in pur-suit of the scientist who carries the virus–all seen from the POV of the young Cole standing near his mother. The police, however, alerted to the fugitive Cole's presence, shoot him. As he collapses, Kathryn rushes to him. Cradling him she turns in close-up to the boy as if sensing the connection. The sequence ends on a close-up of the boy's eyes filled with tears as he watches his own death.

Gattaca (1997) creates a dystopia which in design owes more to the Bauhaus style than German Expressionism. It is an immaculate, orderly universe–sleek, modern, symmetrical, yet somehow still sinister. The scenes at night are tinted eerily red, blue, or green–disorienting the viewer's color expectations. The day scenes are blazingly bright with rockets flying like meteors over the Gattaca head-quarters at regular intervals. The Gattaca offices are moderne, minimalist with rows of dark-suited employees marching automaton-like through turnstiles, in a clear homage to *Metropolis*.

The central conflict of the film revolves around identity. This "brave new world" will genetically engineer children for the right price, thereby producing a two-tiered society of "valids" and "in-valids." "Valids" occupy the upper echelon positions while "in-valids" perform the menial jobs. As a result the society is ob-sessed with keeping track of its inhabitants' identities through the use of methods like electronic scanning and periodic blood-urine testing.

Vincent (Ethan Hawke) is an "in-valid...conceived in love" who narrates the film in classic *noir* style. His brother Anton (Loren Dean), however, was genetically en-gineered. Vincent's greatest ambition is to travel in space, even though his father (Elias Koteas) tells him, "The only way you'll see the inside of a spaceship is clean-ing it." Although handicapped by poor vision and a weak heart, he is determined to live out his dream. And so he illegally changes his identity with a "valid"–a crip-pled, embittered ex-Olympic athlete, Jerome (Jude Law). In order to maintain this facade, Vincent/Jerome must painfully scrub away his identity every morning–seen in the first shots of the film in a series of close-ups as Vincent washes away every dead cell and follicle he can find. Although he is scheduled to travel to Titan, he lives in a state of constant fear of being discovered, particularly since a murder has occurred at Gattaca which brings in the police, including his own estranged brother.

The key scenes in this movie are the three swimming contests between Vincent and Anton at various ages. These scenes not only crystallize the conflict between the brothers, as well as the class conflict in their society, but it also serves to demonstrate Vincent's perseverance in the face of pain and fear. Although he tells the viewer through his narration that he always lost the contests as a boy to his genetically superior brother, as a teen the spectator sees him outdistance his brother and in fact rescue him from the deep waters. This scene is repeated again, towards the end of the film. This time, however, it is night and the boys are adults. Vincent finally confirms for his doubting brother the superiority of will over genetics as he again beats his brother, rescuing him from the sea. As he pulls Anton's spent body back, Vincent stares up at the stars he so longs to visit.

In the final scene of the movie, the filmmakers construct a powerful montage based on the film's themes of identity and Nietzschean "will to power." The film intercuts between Vincent/Jerome walking through tunnels and boarding the space ship to Titan while the original Jerome, who has become a second brother to Vincent, prepares to immolate himself in a furnace, thereby giving up completely his identity to Vincent: Jerome, "You leant me your dream." The rocket rises. Flames spew forth from the boosters as the fire of the furnace devours Jerome who holds his Olympic medal in a final moment of pride for past accomplishments. The film then cuts to a close-up of Vincent, tears in his eyes, "Every atom in our body was once part of a star...Maybe I'm going home." Sorrow and existential doubt color his final victory as it does the entire film.

Television has finally picked up the mantle of *noir* science fiction dropped in the 1960s by *Outer Limits*. *The X-Files* (1993-present) and its movie offspring in 1998 encapsulate effectively millennial paranoia with its oft-quoted motto of "Trust no one." The obsessive and melancholy Mulder (David Duchovny), a maverick FBI agent marked emotionally by the alien abduction of his sister, finds conspiracies everywhere. Even though tempered by his rationalist partner Scully (Gillian Armstrong), he disregards both personal and professional considerations in his often manic pursuit of "the truth" or, more accurately, *his* "truth." *Star Trek* creator Gene Roddenberry's series *Earth: Final Conflict* (1997-present) mixes paranoia with humanism, much as he did in his former groundbreaking television series. Drawing on *noir* classics like *The Big Heat* (1953) for its basic premise, Roddenberry posits a conflicted protagonist, Detective Boone (Kevin Kilner), who while embittered by the death of his wife in a car bomb explosion agrees to have a control chip implanted in his brain by a highly advanced alien race, the Tælons, who have "persuaded" humans to join them in "improving humanity." Boone does this in order to act as a spy for an underground movement working against the Tælons. But as he grows to understand the aliens, particularly their North American "companion," he can no longer see this as a simplistic battle of good humans versus evil aliens. So he lives with divided loyalties and, because of the Tælon chip, with divided identities as well–half-human, half-Taelon.

The X Files: above, the obsessive and melancholic agent Fox Mulder (David Duchovny, left) confronts the paranoic Dr. Kurtzwell (Martin Landau). Below, Mulder rescues his partner Scully (Gillian Anderson) from an antarctic alien breeding ground.

Dark City (1998) brings us back to the beginning in style and theme. Alex Proyas, who also directed the Gothic *Crow*, constructs a world owing much to German expressionism and, of course, *Metropolis*. On a satellite in the sky a race of dying aliens are conducting a massive lab experiment, seeking there a "cure for mortality," as their human accomplice Dr. Schreber (Kiefer Sutherland) puts it. Each night, from their underground headquarters, the aliens, through an ability called "tuning," destroy and then rebuild parts of the city above, as well as change the identities of the inhabitants in that section of the metropolis.

The viewer does not witness this amazing transformation until mid-way through the film as this city, in which there is never any day, comes to a halt–cars stopping dead on city silent streets, individuals falling asleep in mid-sentence. And as they sleep, new buildings arise like the first shots of *Metropolis*. As in Lang's classic, the city is imposing, stylized, angular, almost Gothic. But in a departure from its model, Proyas, in direct homage to the classic period of *film noir*, has given his dark city a 1940s patina through costuming and set dressing. While the city sleeps, aliens–who resemble Nosferatu with their long black coats, sharp

Dark City: in *Metropolis* revisited, alien "thought police" such as the one portrayed by Richard O'Brien (below) reprogram the memories of their human test subjects.

teeth, bent posture, and bald heads–glide through the streets and hallways, accompanied by the Judas-like Dr. Schreber who implants new memories in the guinea pigs' brains, while the aliens spread new artifacts throughout the humans' abodes.

The film proposes a supremely existential dilemma. On an allegorical level the inhabitants of this city stand for all humanity caught in the web of a seemingly absurd and meaningless existence over which they have no control. The solution to their cosmic dilemma is the classic one put forth by existential writers like Sartre and Camus–consciousness of the absurdity followed by action. The protagonist Murdoch (Rufus Sewell) experiences such an "epiphany" when in close-up he suddenly awakes in his bath to find blood on his forehead from an aborted injection and a dead woman in his apartment.

The remainder of the film tracks Murdoch in his search for his real identity. For the partial injection has erased much of his former memories, leaving him unsure of himself or anyone else, including his own "wife" Emma (Jennifer Connelly) or his "beloved" Uncle Karl (John Bluthal)–who both turn out to be but two more guinea pigs with implanted memories. Pursued by a melancholy detective (William Hurt)–looking much like the classic *noir* sleuths in trenchcoat, fedora and suit–who also begins to doubt the reality of his own identity, Murdoch finds he has assimilated some of the powers of the aliens, most notably, their ability to transform reality by "tuning."

And so the final battle in this Maya-like universe comes down to a contest of wills. Murdoch wins, defeating the aliens at their own game by destroying the underground machinery which operates the city above–recalling a similar destruction by the workers in *Metropolis*. With his victory in hand, Murdoch accepts the unreality of his life and so decides to create a new one. Much like Cole in *Twelve Monkeys* and Deckard in *Blade Runner*, Murdoch is haunted by a vision–a dream, possibly even a memory–of a place called Shell Beach where the sun always shines and the colors are vibrant. Utilizing his "tuning" powers, he decides to construct this beach, flooding the city and then causing the ground to thrust up and create a land's end. In the final scenes he walks down a pier to his waiting "wife" who has now become Anna through yet another memory implant. Together they walk off to Shell Beach, a land of illusion but at least a benign one.

British *Film Noir*

Tony Williams

In contrast to its American cousin, British *film noir* has received relatively little attention except by William K. Everson, Marcia Landy, Laurence Miller, and Raymond Durgnat.[1] This is not surprising. Until recently, British cinema has suffered unduly from disparaging remarks made by international and national critics such as Satyajit Ray, Francois Truffaut, Pauline Kael, Dwight Macdonald, the *Movie* editorial board, David Shipman, James Park, and Gilbert Adair.[2] Furthermore, as Andrew Britton once pointed out, the average British film often exhibits a "blandness and paucity of language which is so striking when one makes the comparison with classical Hollywood, where a vast range of fluctuating, contradictory, inter-related meanings are in process in the materials from which the films are produced and which they in turn inflect." However, despite these factors (and allowing for the fact that there are often exceptions to every rule) Alan Lovell, author of the pioneering 1969 British Film Institute seminar paper, "British Cinema - the Unknown Cinema," recently urged the re-evaluation of a cinema "often most exciting when restraint and excess interact."[3] This is particularly true for British *film noir* whose visual style often parallels American and French *noir* representations.

Britton also noted that directors such as Robert Hamer often utilized "elaborated conventional languages from outside...the *Gothic* in *Dead of Night*, the Hollywood *film noir*/melodrama in *Sundays*, (and) various English comic traditions in *Kind Hearts*." Reviewing a book about a particular British studio popular for depictions of national comedic eccentricity, Britton recognized the presence of a foreign stylistic tradition distinctively inflecting a national cinema usually regarded as bland and conservative. This particular tradition is *film noir*. But its presence is not confined to the examples Britton cited. *Film noir* is a stylistic movement borrowed from outside and given a particular structure of meaning according to certain cultural codes within the British national tradition. Despite traditional definitions categorizing this national cinema within documentary realist paradigms, British cinema actually reveals the presence of many examples involving cross fertilization of formulas. Landy cautions, "The concept of a national cinema is tricky, since cinema is not a hermetic form of representation but is dependent on international influences. The Hollywood influence on British filmmaking is certainly important,

243

but so is the influence of the German cinema of the pre-Nazi era, ... in the pre-World War II films, especially those of Hitchcock and Saville."[4]

Although Everson notes that "British *film noir* is particularly fascinating not only because it has never been officially acknowledged to exist, but because its peak period parallels that of American *noir*," he argues that "it has always been influenced by the French cinema of the 30's rather than the German cinema of the 20's." However, despite recognizing the conservative nature of an industry inimical to the artistic experiments of Hitchcock and The Archers, Everson contradicts himself when he later remarks that "Despite the thematic French influence, cinematographic specialists were often German, especially in the earlier days when Gunther Krampf's skills were much utilized."[5] However, Gunther Krampf was not the only German cinematographer active during the thirties and forties. Several others had fled from Hitler's Germany who had experience of working in a more cosmopolitan Europe. Mutz Greenbaum (later Max Greene) added *noir* elements to *The Green Cockatoo* (1937), *Thunder Rock* (1942), *Wanted for Murder* (1946), *So Evil My Love* (1948), and *Night and the City* (1950). Viennese-born Gunther Krampf was assistant photographer on Murnau's *Nosferatu* (1922) and acted as lighting cameraman on other important German expressionist films such as *The Hands of Orlac* (1925), *The Student of Prague* (1926), and *Pandora's Box* (1929). He also photographed *Kuhle Wampe* (1932) and was obviously familiar with different European cinematic styles. After moving to England and photographing Conrad Veidt in the non-*noir* *Rome Express* (1932), Krampf added expressionist *noir* overtones to films such as *On the Night of the Fire* (1939), *The Night has Eyes* (1942), *Latin Quarter* (1945), and *This Was A Woman* (1947). Prague-born Otto Heller left Germany in 1933 and worked in Europe until 1940. After joining the Czech air force, he later worked on British *noirs* such as *The Dark Tower* (1943), *Temptation Harbor, They Made Me A Fugitive* (both 1947), *The Queen of Spades* (1948), *Now Barabbas* (1949), *The Woman with No Name* (1950), *The Ladykillers* (1955), Robert Siodmak's *The Rough and the Smooth, Peeping Tom* (both 1959), *Victim* (1961), and *West 11* (1963). Erwin Hillier moved to England in 1929 and added distinguished *noir* photography to *The October Man, The Mark of Cain* (both 1947), and *Mr. Perrin and Mr. Traill* (1948). Other non-German cinematographers were also familiar with the style. Australian-born Robert Krasker began his career in France before moving to England in 1930. He photographed *noirs* such as *Odd Man Out* (1946), *Uncle Silas* (1947), *The Third Man* (1949), *Another Man's Poison* (1951), and *The Criminal* (1960). Paris-born Georges Perinal worked in French cinema from 1913 and photographed Cocteau's *Le Sang du Poete* (1930) as well as Rene Clair's *Le Million* and *A Nous la Liberte* (both 1931) before moving to England in 1933. He photographed British *noirs* such as *Nicholas Nickleby* (1946), *The Fallen Idol* (1948), and *Three Cases of Murder* (1954). These foreign cinematographers certainly influenced their British counterparts such as Christopher Challis, Wilkie Cooper, Stephen Dade, and Douglas Slocombe during this period.

The above list not only reveals the importance of recognizing the major role of cinematographers as well as directors in British *film noir* but also suggests that British cinema is often less parochial than its detractors suggest. As a result, hybrid definitions of both national cinema and visual style become indispensable in this area. Despite forties journalistic attacks on certain British directors borrowing from "morbid" elements of German expressionism, such appropriations actually resulted from choosing the correct visual style to express particular problems within the British cultural psyche.

Within its various visual and national cinematic examples, *film noir* is more of a "style" or "movement" rather than a rigidly defined genre. British *film noir* has several parallels to the American model defined by critics such as Paul Schrader, Janey Place and Lowell Peterson.[6] The classical British *film noir* model not only parallels its American counterpart but also occupies a similar historical period. In fact, British *film noir* even begins a few years earlier than its American counterpart with examples such as *The Green Cockatoo* (1937), *They Drive By Night* (1938), *I Met A Murderer* and *On the Night of the Fire* (both 1939) predating Boris Ingster's *Stranger on the Third Floor* (1940). Photographed by Mutz Greenbaum, produced by William K. Howard and directed by William Cameron Menzies, *The Green Cockatoo* exhibits a visual style derived from German expressionism and anticipates American *film noir*. It has definite claims for categorization as the first British *film noir*. Like *On the Night of the Fire*, *The Green Cockatoo* contains a pessimistic score by Hungarian composer Miklos Rosza foreshadowing his music for American films such as *Double Indemnity* (1944), *The Lost Weekend* (1945), *The Killers* and *The Strange Love of Martha Ivers* (both 1946).

Film noir is an amorphous object having many connections to stylistic movements such as gangster films, French "poetic realism," German expressionism, and melodrama. It may even include technicolor films. If Martin Scorsese convincingly argues that *Leave Her to Heaven* (1945) represents a technicolor variant of a style usually regarded as exclusively black and white during its classical period in his video documentary *A Personal History of American Cinema*, the same is true for British examples such as *Blanche Fury* (1947), *Saraband for Dead Lovers* (1948), *Footsteps in the Fog* (1955) and even *Black Narcissus* (1947 which Everson defines as "a *marginal film noir* that nevertheless contains enough key elements to be considered."[7] Like its American contemporary, British *film noir* crosses several genres and styles. If *Pursued* and *Ramrod* (both 1947) merges *film noir* with the western, British *noir* appears in costume films such as *Blanche Fury*, *Saraband*, *Kind Hearts and Coronets* (1949) as well as individual visual sequences in Gainsborough melodramas such as *Fanny By Gaslight* (1944) and *The Magic Bow* (1946). The first film opens with the camera craning down into a London street marking the contrast between the everyday world of Victorian morality and a basement containing a bar proprietor's brothel, Hopwood's Shades, selectively serving clients from the aristocracy and upper middle classes. Most of the film adopts a moody *noirish* style of photography to emphasize the attempts of downwardly mobile Fanny Hopwood (Phyllis Calvert) and her upper-class lover Harry Somerford (Stewart Granger) to escape both the hypocritically repressive world of British class-ridden morality as well as its demonic underside represented by the evil Lord Manderstoke (James Mason). When spurned by his upper-class lover Jeanne (Phyllis Calvert) in *The Magic Bow* (1946), Paganini (Stewart Granger) embarks on a concert tour. As he plays in London, a demure young English aristocratic maiden remarks to her companion, "They say he is the devil! Wouldn't it be exciting to find out?" This remark accompanies a low angle close up of Paganini shot in *noir* lighting making him resemble Christopher Lee's Count Dracula in Hammer horror. Indeed, had not Mason and Granger left for Hollywood, either could have been ideally cast as the evil Count a decade later.

The fluid nature of British *film noir* may cause sleepless nights to critics preoccupied with rigidly statistical and taxonomic definitions but not to those aware of the fluid nature of generic forms. As Mike Nevins commented in a personal e-mail message, *film noir* parallels Ludwig Wittgenstein's comments concerning the supposed essence of games in section 66 of his *Philosophical Investigations*. "Do not say: 'They must have something in common, else they would not be called games' - but look whether all of them have something in common. And the result of this reflection is: we behold a complicated set of similarities which overlap and intersect." Furthermore, Robin Wood's comments concerning American film genres also apply to the stylistic world of British *film noir*. He argues that genres "represent different strategies for dealing with the same ideological tensions" rooted within American society.[8] The same is also true of British *film noir* which visually expresses a continuous interaction between ideology and the material forces of history in which a field of mutually, unevenly determining forces expresses every society's tensions and contradictions.[9] British *film noir*, like melodrama, is a stylistic movement signifying excess. But it is one relevant to social and cultural problems arising during particular disturbances in history. British *film noir* also exhibits two major stylistic influences during its classical period. The first movement features visual elements borrowed from German expressionist photography while post-1945 films borrow many features from American *film noir*.

Miller notes that both Britain and America suffered cataclysmic historical events during the twentieth century such as two world wars and post-war criminal activity[10]. These turbulent events often received indirect cinematic expression ideologically defined by certain cultural perspectives operating within each national society. Schrader divides American *film noir* into three overlapping historical periods: the wartime period of 1941-1946; the post-war realistic period of 1945-1949; and the final phase of 1949-1953 characterized by psychotic action and suicidal impulse. He sees war and post-war disillusionment; post-war realism; the German influence, and the hard-boiled literary tradition represented by writers such as Dashiell Hammett, Raymond Chandler, James M. Cain, and Horace Mc-

Coy as key influences. Schrader does allow for the presence of "stragglers" such as *Kiss Me Deadly, The Big Combo* (both 1955) and *Touch of Evil* (1958) but believes *noir* had virtually ceased by then.[11] The classical British *noir* period contains similarities as well as significant differences from its American counterpart. Everson lists *They Drive By Night* (1938) as the first British *noir*, followed by films such as *I Met A Murderer* and *On the Night of the Fire* (1939), in his cautiously defined "rough (and non-definitive check list) which runs up to 1963 with films such as *Paranoiac, Bitter Harvest, The Haunting* and *Dr. Strangelove*. However, *The Green Cockatoo* is definitely the first British *film noir* in terms of visual style and content. Other examples may also exist both before and after these dates. Everson also notes that 1947-1948 were the peak years of British *film noir* paralleling Hollywood in emphasizing post-war problems, particularly "neuroses of war victims and veterans." [12]

The Haunting and *Dr. Strangelove* were filmed by American directors such as Robert Wise and Stanley Kubrick.[13] But far from complicating the relationship of *noir* to British cinema as a national visual entity this also reveals the style's essential hybridity as well as international continuity. During the 1940's Brazilian Alberto Cavalcvanti directed *Went the Day Well?* (1942), the ventriloquist episode of *Dead of Night* (1945), *Nicholas Nickelby, They Made Me A Fugitive* (both 1947), and *For Them That Trespass* (1949). Cavalcanti began his French 20s career as a set decorator on avant-garden films by Marcel L'Herbier and Ferdinand Leger before moving on to direct documentaries such as *Rien Que Les Heures* (1926) which mingled realism and fantasy anticipating thirties French poetic realism. In 1949, temporary blacklist fugitive Edward Dmytryk directed two British *noirs* - *Obsession* and *Give Us This Day* while Joseph Losey directed several throughout his British career such as *The Intimate Stranger* (1956), *Time Without Pity* (1957), *Blind Date* (1958), and *The Criminal* (1960). Although Everson includes *The Servant* (1963) as a marginal *noir*, he omits *The Damned* (1961) and *King and Country* (1964) which have compelling stylistic claims for inclusion. These Losey films not only display definite *noir* visual images but also contain a key relationship with one of the major cultural ideological meanings frequently appearing in British *film noir-* class barriers. In *The Damned*, Alexander Knox's scientist figure plans for the survival of British society after a nuclear attack by using upper-class children to represent the future British race. Losey's *Blind Date, The Servant,* and *King and Country* examine class issues in several ways as do two color *film noirs Blanche Fury* and *Footsteps in the Fog*. These latter films feature Stewart Granger playing a character driven to murder due to frustration by rigid class barriers. In *Blanche Fury*, he plays a downwardly mobile illegitimate heir to an estate now owned by *nouveau riche* distant relatives. He appears in the latter film as a dependent male who has murdered his older and affluent wife to gain access to her fortune and a business partnership with his father-in-law by marrying his daughter. Granger's character also exists in a symbiotic love-hate relationship with his housekeeper mistress (Jean Simmons) whom he persuades in vain to move to an American New World untrammelled by inhibiting class structures.

Several British *film noirs* feature American actors, some of whom fled to England to escape blacklisting such as Sam Wanamaker and Phil Brown. Wanamaker appeared in Dmytryk's *Give Us This Day*, Everson's listed marginal *noir Mr. Denning Drives North* (1951), and Losey's *The Criminal* while Brown appeared in Dmytryk's *Obsession* and the marginal *noir The Green Scarf* (1954). Two significant *noirs* featuring Americans in the cast are Jules Dassin's *Night and the City* (1950) and Michael Anderson's *1984* (1955). The first film opens with Richard Widmark personifying the archetypal male fugitive of *film noir*. While Gene Tierney and Hugh Marlowe play normal Americans, their dark *noir*ish British counterparts are played by actors who also appeared in British *film noirs* such as Googie Withers, Francis L. Sullivan, and Herbert Lom. Withers's *femme fatale* spider woman is a more dangerous incarnation of roles she had played in British *noirs* such as *Dead of Night, Pink String and Sealing Wax* (1945), and *It Always Rains on Sunday*. Francis L. Sullivan was well known for performances such as the Nazi villain in *Pimpernel Smith* (1941), Dickensian characters in David Lean's *noir*ish *Great Expectations* (1946), *Oliver Twist* (1948) as well as appearing in Gainsborough Studio's *The Man Within* (1947), an adaptation of a Graham Greene novel. Before becoming a comic foil to Peter Sellers's Inspector Clouseau, Herbert Lom had appeared in several British *film noirs* such as *The Seventh Veil* (1945), *Appointment with Crime* (1946), *Dual Alibi* (1947), *Snowbound, Good Time Girl, Portrait from Life* (all 1948). Although directed by an American *Night and the City* is really a good example of an early transnational film, since it combines American, British, and Germanic influences as the cinematography of Max Greene reveals. Both British versions of *1984* star Edmond O'Brien as George Orwell's Winston Smith and Jan Sterling as Julia. While one version follows the pessimistic conclusion of Orwell's novel like the later color neo-*noir* 1984 Michael Radford version, another concludes with Smith shouting "Down with Big Brother" before he and Julia perish under the bullets of the thought police in a manner reminiscent of "the last romantic couple" of Fritz Lang's *You Only Live Once* (1937). Both versions exhibit appropriately bleak visual imagery doing appropriate stylistic justice to the Orwell's vision.[14] During 1947, Burgess Meredith starred in the film version of Nigel Balchin's *Mine Own Executioner*. In 1948, American actress Carole Landis appeared posthumously in a British *film noir The Noose* which also starred Joseph Calleia, an actor well known in Hollywood for his heavy roles. *The Noose* merged *film noir* with the British "spiv" cycle of films such as *Waterloo Road* (1944) and *Brighton Rock* and also featured Nigel Patrick in an accomplished and unusual supporting role as a flashily attired spiv. During the same year, Welsh-born Hollywood actor Ray Milland co-starred with Ann Todd in *So Evil My Love* playing a suave seducer who causes his partner's moral downfall. Milland had starred in American *noirs* such as *The Ministry of Fear* (1944), *The Lost Weekend* (1945) and *The Big Clock* (1947) and would later appear in others such as *Alias Nick Beal* (1950). In 1949, Carol Reed filmed *The Third Man* with American stars such as Orson Welles and Joseph Cotton and British actors such as Trevor Howard and Bernard Lee. Reed's film merged American *noir* traditions in the casting of Welles and Cotton with the Germanic expressionism characteristic of British *film noir*. Both Welles and Cotton had appeared in notable *film noir*s such as *Citizen Kane* (1941), *Journey into Fear, Shadow of A Doubt* (both 1943), *Gaslight* (1944), *The Stranger* (1946), *The Lady from Shanghai, Macbeth* (both 1948), and *Beyond the Forest* (1949). *The Third Man* benefitted from the American *noir* associations both actors brought to this British production shot in Vienna. In 1950 Peter Lorre appeared in Ken Annakin's *Double Confession*. Before Hammer studios launched its successful series of horror films after the mid-fifties, it produced a series of low-budget films featuring American actors in association with Lippert studios. In 1953, Dan Duryea starred in *Thirty-Six Hours*. Although not listed by Everson, the Hammer-Lippert *Murder by Proxy* (1954) featured Dane Clark in a role reminiscent of a Woolrich hero attempting to find out his activities during a mental blackout. Richard Basehart and Mary Murphy appeared in Joseph Losey's *The Intimate Stranger* (1956) while the following year saw Dana Andrews and Jacques Tourneur teamed in *Night of the Demon*. As well as being a masterful horror film, *Night of the Demon* combined the talents of an actor well known for his American *film noir* performances *(Laura, While the City Sleeps,* and *Beyond A Reasonable Doubt)* and a director well versed in the style *(Out of the Past, Nightfall)* which he developed while working in Val Lewton's RKO group with works such as *Cat People* (1942), *I Walked with a Zombie,* and *The Leopard Man* (both 1943). The same year Victor Mature appeared in the British *noir The Long Haul*. His American *noir*s included films such as *I Wake Up Screaming, The Shanghai Gesture* (both 1941), *Kiss of Death* (1947), *Cry of the City* (1948), and *Easy Living* (1949). Although the 1950s saw the end of Rank's attempt to capture the American market by promoting his version of a British national cinema, that decade witnessed the presence of many Hollywood stars appearing in British films to appeal more to the American market. Not all of them were in decline like Dana Andrews, Rod Cameron, Dane Clark, and Dan Duryea. Victor Mature had several years to go as a major star and James Stewart appeared in a non-*noir* 1951 film *No Highway in the Sky*. It would be only natural for British directors and technicians to approximate some of the styles associated with the actors' American films in these productions.

Other films featured Americans long resident in Britain such as Bonar Colleano who often depicted the stereotyped image of the swaggering wisecracking wartime and post-war Yank - "Over here, over paid, and oversexed!" - in *noir*s such as *Wanted for Murder* (1946), *Good Time Girl* (1947), *Give Us This Day,* and *Pool of London* (1950) as well as non-*noir*s such as *The Way to the Stars* (1945), *A Matter of Life and Death* (1946), and *The Sea Shall Not Have Them* (1954). Other actors such as American Diana Decker and Scotsman Hugh McDermott made a career of playing Americans in forties and fifties British cinema. Decker appeared in *San Demetrio London* (1943) and *The Root of All Evil* (1948) as well in the 1956-1957 season of the British *noir* television detective series *Mark Saber* while McDermott featured in *The Seventh Veil* (1945), *Good Time Girl*, and *No Orchids for Miss Blandish* (both 1948) playing untrustworthy characters.

The last film was an adaptation of James Hadley Chase's then-infamous novel (later filmed by Robert Aldrich as *The Grissom Gang*) which featured American actor Jack LaRue among a cast of predominantly British actors playing Americans in a film shot in Britain. Long known for his menacing roles, LaRue had already appeared in a 1939 British gangster film *Murder in Soho*. Shot in deliberate *film noir* style, the opening scenes build up to his dramatic appearance twenty minutes into the film. However, although British popular culture revealed a fascination with American films and hard boiled novels with imitators such as Peter Cheyney with his Slim Callahan and Lemmy Caution novels during the thirties and forties, another significant literary tradition influencing the development of British *film noir* also existed. If British culture proved hostile to the literary *noir* represented by Dashiell Hammett, Raymond Chandler, Horace McCoy, Mickey Spillane, David Goodis and Cornell Woolrich, it did provide fertile seeds for a different type of development represented by novelists such as Graham Greene, Eric Ambler, and Nigel Balchin. Although Ambler both produced and scripted a notable British *noir* such as *The October Man* (1947) and Balchin novels such as *Mine Own Executioner* and *The Small Back Room* (1948) received distinctive *noir* adaptation, Greene is the most significant of the three.

Greene initially appears an odd choice in comparison with an American literary tradition usually associated with hard boiled private eyes such as Sam Spade, The Continental Op, Philip Marlowe, and Mike Hammer. However, we must remember that literary *noir* is as varied as its cinematic counterpart. It may comprise elements of melodrama such as male hysteria and insecurity as the often neglected tradition represented by David Goodis and Cornell Woolrich amply reveals. Although Greene's name often conjures up the names of ambitious works such as **The Power and the Glory** (1940), **The Heart of the Matter** (1948), **The Quiet American** (1955), **The Comedians** (1965-66, **The Honorary Consul** (1973), and **The Human Factor** (1978) his prolific output also includes titles he modestly described as "entertainments" such as **Stamboul Train** (1932), **A Gun for Sale** (1936), **Brighton Rock** (1938), **The Confidential Agent** (1939), **The Ministry of Fear** (1943), and **The Third Man** (1950) which appeared a year after the Carol Reed film version. These titles resemble contemporary thrillers. Greene used the term "entertainments" to distinguish them from what he saw as his more prestigious efforts. However, these books are not only accomplished efforts in their own right but often reveal significant insights into aspects the British cultural tradition. Furthermore, many of Greene's novels, screenplays and treatments were quickly produced and gained expression in cinematic *noir* both in America and Britain such as *Orient Express* (1934), *The Green Cockatoo* (1937/1940), *Twenty-One Days* (1937/1940), *This Gun for Hire* (1942), *Went the Day Well?* (1942), *The Ministry of Fear* (1943), *The Confidential Agent* (1945), *The Man Within, Brighton Rock* (both 1947), *The Fallen Idol* (1948), *The Third Man* (1949), *The Heart of the Matter* (1953), *The Stranger's Hand* (1954), *Across the Bridge, Short Cut to Hell* (both 1957), and *The Quiet American* (1957) within the British classical *film noir* period. Most of these American and British films are visually recognizable as *film noir* while others such as *Twenty-One Days, The Heart of the Matter*, and *Across the Bridge* lack the style but contain *noir* themes of individuals struggling against a hostile universe. Several of the above titles cross various boundaries. *Brighton Rock* (or *Young Scarface* in the US), uses *film noir* cinematography and clothes its gangster protagonists played by Richard Attenborough, William Hartnell, and Nigel Stock in forties spiv suits dating the film a decade after the book's original appearance. *The Quiet American* is not an "entertainment" but the film version used classic *noir* techniques to visualize its murder mystery framework and Greene's theme of guilty protagonist while also emasculating the novel's political critique of early American involvement in Viet Nam. Furthermore, although Greene had no direct involvement in either the direction or screenplay of *The Green Cockatoo* (1937), his story and scenario may have indirectly inspired American director William Cameron Menzies and cameraman Mutz Greenbaum to depict the dangerous London environment using German expressionistic and early *film noir* chiaroscuro lighting imagery. The world of Graham Greene is not unique. It forms an indispensable part of a British cultural tradition providing support to institutional behavior and making life a living hell for those trapped within its boundaries. It actually complements those spiritually debilitating images involving lower middle and working class losers within the British Empire documented in works by George Orwell such as *Keep the Aspidistra Flying, The Road to Wigan Pier*, and *Down and Out in London and Paris*.

Despite Greene's emergence from a privileged background, he intuitively recognized the psychologically crippling nature of a British class structure inhibiting him individually and culturally. Although Greene never engages in a conscious Marxist analysis of the sterility of human existence in British society, the often-maligned but little-understood term "Greeneland" used by critics such as Quentin Falk to characterize the seedy, down-at-heel nature of middle and working-class life in "entertainments" such as **A Gun for Sale, The Ministry of Fear, The Confidential Agent** and other serious works such as **It's A Battlefield** (1934) and **The End of the Affair** (1951), indirectly reflects a cultural and political system still present in Blair's "Cool Britannia" today. Both Greene's works and British *film noir* reflect a particular structure of feeling expressing resentment at a debilitating cultural landscape. As Everson comments, "The British system of life unfortunately conspires to keep a lot of 'little' people in that niche permanently. With a *lot* of talent and persistence one can still rise to the top in England - but the modicum of talent (that would allow a person to succeed in the U.S.) is usually stifled in England by bureaucracy and other restrictions." He further notes the tendency of British characters in real life and fictional situations to deny alternative solutions, "make the best of things," express contentment with one's lot in a world. Everson also states that "Only occasionally does the importance of security and normalcy seem truly tragic, and then usually in a story that does *not* deal with everyday life and where the true tragedy of the final solution is *so* hidden below the surface that it is virtually invisible." [15] His statement may equally apply to *noir* costume melodramas such as *Blanche Fury* and *Saraband for Dead Lovers* containing clearly recognizable issues of institutional class dominance and sexual repression peculiar to British culture. Like American directors choosing westerns and science fiction to depict relevant social issues, their British counterparts returned to the past to depict ideas which could not be countenanced in contemporary depictions. This was a strategy common to Gainsborough melodramas. However, Everson recognizes the strength of a particular British cultural tradition pattern present in other formerly popular novels such as H.G. Wells's **Kipps** and **The History of Mr. Polly** involving ideological issues concerning knowing one's place and being content with one's position in society no matter how demeaning or miserable it may be. Although Everson's comments apply to films such as *Brief Encounter* and *It Always Rains on Sunday*, they also have a wider application. British *film noir* expresses this critique visually.

Everson also notes that, unlike most American *noirs*, class plays a major role in its British counterpart. As he notes, in" British *noirs*, the unsympathetic heavies tend to be uneducated spivs with delusions of belonging to an Upper Class. The trapped *sympathetic* victim-hero usually makes his living in a particularly demeaning and non-profitable job."[16] Although Everson cites the barber occupations of Ralph Richardson and Eric Portman in *On the Night of the Fire* (1939) and *Daybreak* (1946), class factors also appear in two early British *noirs*. In *They Drive by Night* non-English Welsh working class ex-convict Shorty (Emlyn Williams) flees from a British social system he feels certain will convict him on circumstantial evidence for a crime he did not commit. Ironically, the real criminal is an effete, downwardly mobile, abnormal wannabe intellectual character Hoover (Ernest Thesiger) who finds his only audience for his Conan Doyle/Sherlock Holmes intellectual pretensions in a working-class bar whose occupants snigger behind his back. As Landy comments, "The crime for which Shorty might have been wrongly punished is linked to women and sex. His real crime is in being marginal and therefore at the mercy of law and criminals alike." [17] Although *I Met A Murderer* exhibits sparse evidence of *noir* photography and is set in the country, its "man-on-the-run" theme has strong British class overtones. Nagged by his shrewish and snobbish wife (Sylvia Coleridge) for commitment to the agricultural rigors of farm life and despairing at his lazy and drunken brother-in-law (William Devlin), middle-class farmer Mark (James Mason) murders her in a fit of anger and goes on the run. Although Mark is clearly unsuited for the life of a farmer, the domestic and economic pressures he faces accumulate into a crime of passion, the final straw being the wife's murder of a pet dog. His brief idyll with romantic pulp fiction writer Jo (Pamela Kellino) comes to an end when he takes the blame for a killing she accidentally did on his behalf. Although mutilated by an oppressively inappropriate musical score, *I Met A Murderer* clearly traces its protagonist's dilemma to domestic antagonism motivated by the wife's resentment of a lower-class status as a farmer's wife. Although different in scope, the crime of passion resembles the famous act of Dr. Crippen who murdered his wife in 1910 after undergoing a series of domestic humiliations resulting from the American couple's lower-class status in English society.

The same cultural factors also influence cinematic adaptations of British literary classics photographed in distinctively recognizable *noir* style. William K. Everson eliminates films such as Olivier's *Hamlet* (1948) and David Lean's Dickens adaptations such as *Great Expectations* (1946) and *Oliver Twist* (1948) because they did not reflect current *noir* stylistics. If the *noir* mood "was unavoidably dictated by the original literary source," he believes that these "Shakespeare and Dickens originals clearly transcended film fashion, and their *noir* look sprang naturally from their mood and plot." He excludes Cavalcanti's *Nicholas Nickelby* where the director "imposed a *noir* style (especially on the final third) that was not necessarily required by the original."[18] However, this division is too arbitrary because *noir* is

Below, "*Noir* cinematography represents Miss Haversham's bridal chamber as a dark world of decay" in Lean's *Great Expectations*.

Above "...scenes depicting fear, downward mobility, and the loss of secure class and economic status" in Lean's *Oliver Twist*.

noir whatever its origins. Even if the literary originals did dictate a *noir* style, this style would be reproduced very much in terms of contemporary *noir* stylistics. Furthermore, all these films do have a common link in terms of their relevance to a particular British cultural signifier active in both past and present. Although the *noir* style does not occupy a major proportion of either Lean's *Great Expectations* and *Oliver Twist*, it appears predominantly in scenes depicting fear, downward mobility, and the loss of secure class and economic status. This last element has always been used as an instrument of fear in both pre-war British society and the post-war repressive regimes of Thatcher, Major, and Blair in modern England. The opening sequences of both *Great Expectations* and *Oliver Twist* reveal a dark world of insecurity. In the former film, the convict Magwitch terrifies young Pip whom he will later launch on the dubious path towards upward mobility in Victorian society. Unknown to Pip, Miss Havisham trains Estella to be a Victorian femme fatale who will operate as a surrogate avenging figure for her marital betrayal. *Noir* cinematography represents Miss Havisham's bridal chamber as a dark world of decay, frustrated sexuality, and pathological vengeance. *Oliver Twist* opens with the downwardly mobile figure of Oliver's mother walking through a bleak expressionistic landscape before giving birth and dying in the workhouse. Shakespeare's *Hamlet* is a classic text of male insecurity and family dispossession with Olivier's "sweet prince" echoing Woolrich heroes suffering from masculine hysteria and Oedipal conflicts. The *noir* style is an appropriate contemporary visual signifier for such conflicts. Although not a *film noir*, Olivier's *Henry V* contains one color *noir* sequence illustrating the king's doubts and fears about his great burden of responsibility on the night before the Battle of Agincourt. Moody color lighting and close-ups appropriately visualize the significance of lines such as "Upon the king! let us our lives, our souls, Our debts, our careful wives, Our children, and our sins lay on the king! We must bear all." Finally, all three films deal with the British cultural fear of disinheritance and downward mobility which appear in other *noirs* (literary adaptation or otherwise) such as *On the Night of the Fire, Gaslight* (1940), *Uncle Silas, The Mark of Cain* (both 1947), *So Evil My Love, Blanche Fury, No Orchids for Miss Blandish, The Queen of Spades* (all 1948), *Kind Hearts and Coronets, The Rocking Horse Winner* (both 1949), *Night and the City* (1950), *Outcast of the Islands* (1951), and many others. This is not the only theme within British *film noir* but it is a particularly dominant one.

Although British *noir* may stylistically resemble contemporary examples of trans-national cinema at this point, it is important to cite at least one distinctively significant cultural factor peculiar to this area: the British representation of male trauma and insecurity. As Everson points out, both American and British cinema contain an "emphasis on post-war problems and particularly on the neuroses of wartime victims and veterans (*Mine Own Executioner, The Small Back Room*) came to its peak in 1947-49 just as it did in Hollywood in such films as *The Locket*."[19] Although critics such as Durgnat and Murphy recognize the predominant appearance of males undergoing readjustment to civilian life in post-war British films such as *They Made Me A Fugitive, Dancing with Crime, Frieda* (both 1947), *Night*

Below, Laurence Olivier in his *Henvy V.*

Beat, The Flamingo Affair, A Gunman has Escaped, Noose (all 1948), as well as traumatically disturbed males played by Eric Portman in Great Day (1945), Wanted for
Murder, and Corridor of Mirrors (1948) and James Mason in The Night has Eyes
(1942), The Seventh Veil (1945), and The Upturned Glass (1947), the relationship of
these fictional characters to their social environment still remains relatively unex-
plored. Despite medically recorded cases of "shell shock" resulting from World
War I and the later definition of PTSD resulting from the Viet Nam War, the climate of World War II appeared reluctant to admit to the presence of traumatically disturbed soldiers and civilians at the time. The home front also experienced
a world of chaos and traumatic events as evidenced by the precarious nature of
the Blitz, German VI and V2 rockets, unexploded bombs, and a "live now, pay
later" philosophy marked by increasing crime rate, illegitimate births, venereal disease, and transient wartime romances. Both contemporary medical and judicial
opinion tended to ignore the presence of any mitigating factors determining the
criminal activities during this time involving figures such as Elizabeth Jones and
Karl Hulten, Neville Heath, John George Haigh, and Donald Hume. Forties British
society probably experienced the presence of traumatically disturbed individuals
adversely affected by their wartime experiences who would have received medical classification as either schizophrenics or PTSD victims at a later date. However, due to British cultural prohibitions against openly showing emotions and the
gendered attitude of the "stiff upper lip tradition" any males who found it difficult
to adjust to wartime and postwar society were either marginalized, deliberately
forgotten, or coded as criminal if their behavior ever became too uncontrollable.

   As a highly censored entity, British cinema could not comment directly on this
feature. However, as a cinema attuned to the national climate, it would recognize
certain contemporary features but alter them, so that they often appeared unrecognizable in a manner very much akin to the Freudian dream mechanism of con-
densation and displacement.[20] By this means, films would use melodramatic
codes and noir techniques to express reactions to conditions arising from real and
historical problems in society while also denying key materialistic factors. In The
Night has Eyes (1942) James Mason's Stephen Deramid has suffered from his experiences as a veteran in the Spanish Civil War. However, the film disavows this
rare political reference to a taboo factor frequently censored in popular British
cultural representations by explaining Deramid's aberrant behavior as due to a
silly, melodramatic plot on the part of his servants. Ironically, although Francesca
(Ann Todd) suffers mental problems in The Seventh Veil, psychiatrist Dr. Larsen ignores the traumatic condition of her guardian Nicholas (James Mason) who be-
haves in a manner disturbingly akin to a psychotic returning veteran. Although
Gainsborough producer Muriel Box became interested in the theme of insanity
when real-life cases of disturbed veterans came to her attention, the film chose to
focus on an insane female rather than a deranged male. However, if The Seventh
Veil is seen as a film fictionally renegotiating the return of the female wartime role

into one of subordination this gendered ideological use of trauma becomes obvious. Similarly in *The October Man* (1947), although Jim Ackland (John Mills) suffers from traumatic guilt following the death of a friend's child in an accident, his condition could be regarded as a symbolic displacement of wartime "survivor guilt" feelings affecting PTSD victims. In Gainsborough's *Holiday Camp*, filmed a year after the execution of British serial killer Neville Heath in 1946, Dennis Price's fictional surrogate figure becomes transformed into Murphy's definition of an "ineffectual bluffer, a pretentiously middle-class fly in the ointment of working-class harmony, who proves less successful with the ladies than nobby, unglamorous Jimmy Hanley. Had he been played by James Mason, who had something approximating more closely to Heath's murderous charm, he might have posed a more serious threat."[21] However, Murphy forgets the fact that Price does murder one female victim in the film - hapless unglamorous Esma Cannon who parallels both Heath's romantic victims and those female movie audience members who drooled at the sight of James Mason beating Margaret Lockwood to death in *The Man in Grey* (1943), raping her in *The Wicked Lady* (1945), and striking Ann Todd's fingers with his cane in *The Seventh Veil*. Price also begins his murderous seduction in an atmospheric *noir* landscape visually contrasting with the cinematic style in the rest of the film.

Although *Frieda* (1947) deals with the alienation of its title character (Mai Zetterling) by a hypocritical British village society who vilify her because of her German nationality, the film also criticizes her R.A.F husband (David Farrar) for both his failure to adjust to peacetime society as well as his ingratitude to a woman who rescued him in wartime Poland. After the appearance of Frieda's unrepentant Nazi brother (Albert Lieven), it becomes obvious that Farrar's character is just waiting for an excuse to abandon his devoted wife whom he will denigrate as a femme fatale "phantom lady." Ironically, a film poster from Robert Siodmak's 1944 American *noir* appears in the film foreshadowing Frieda's fate in Ealing's 1947 *noir*.

Both Durgnat and Murphy have noted the dark nature of the roles played by Yorkshire-born actor Eric Portman in this period. Described by Murphy as "the most morbidly prolific" of four British actors playing ambiguous roles in this postwar period, Portman's contemporary roles presented a contrast with both his pre-war and post-war work.[22] Despite Murphy's contrast between Portman's *A Canterbury Tale* (1944) inspired-films such as *Great Day* (1945), *Wanted for Murder* (1946), and *Corridor of Mirrors* (1948) and his jealous roles in *Dear Murderer* (1947), *Daybreak*, and *The Mark of Cain* (1948), the two groups of films have deep connections especially involving traumatic depictions. Although Murphy regards *A Canterbury Tale* as the key film influencing Portman's dangerous male roles, *Great Day* has better claims for consideration. In *Great Day*, Portman plays a disturbed World War I hero, Captain Ellis, who can not settle down to civilian life and sustains himself on his illusionary world of past glory. He also resents the more important roles his wife (Flora Robson) and daughter (Sheila Sim) play in the pre-D-Day world awaiting the arrival of Mrs. Eleanor Roosevelt at his village. However, Ellis is also someone suffering from trauma as well as an inability to adjust to World War II society that motivates his temporary act of criminal insanity. The film draws a distinction between Ellis's individual act of aberration and the People's War world of village life characterized by dominant women and the younger generation of soldiers awaiting D-Day. Despite its positive conclusion, *Great Day* makes Ellis a scapegoat figure as if attempting to disavow any evidence of aberrance from a People's War society a year away from Labour's General Election victory. Portman's Ellis functions as a convenient displacement for those real-life cases of trauma affecting people in the home and military fronts. Furthermore, like the real life cases of Jones and Hulton, Heath, and Haigh, Ellis chooses to live in a fantasy world to escape his everyday predicament. Although his crime bears no comparison to the more deadly activities of Heath and Haigh, his motivation also reveals a desire to be caught and punished as revealed by his risk-taking theft in an English pub where he has no desire of succeeding in his goal. Portman's later characters in *Wanted for Murder* and *Corridor of Mirrors* also choose to live in a fantasy world either as sacrificial victimizers or victims acting out their roles in traumatically compulsive ways. In *Wanted for Murder*, Portman plays a wealthy, unmarried, businessman serial killer supposedly haunted by his public hangman father's murderous genes. But he compulsively acts out his murderous desires as a result of undisclosed social factors the film chooses not to explore for censorship reasons. Although set in 1938, *Corridor of Mirrors* again indirectly explores a traumatic dilemma also relevant to post-war society. After

Below, *Wanted for Murder*.

suffering from a shell splinter in World War I Portman's soldier-artist, Paul Mangin, desires to return to the past of renaissance Italy and lives his life according to a hopeless romantic dream incapable of fulfillment. Although Mangin finally occupies the victim role in *Corridor of Mirrors*, he does attempt to kill the reincarnation of his lost love (Edana Romney) until she uses the weapon of mocking female laughter to reveal his impotence. Mangin's male weakness in *Corridor of Mirrors* also parallels Portman's other roles in *Dear Murderer, Daybreak, and The Mark of Cain*. All three films present Portman as a victimized male suffering from traumatic insecurity leading to murderous activities due respectively to a manipulative *femme fatale* wife (Sally Gray), insecure spouse (Ann Todd) forced into adultery by her glamor boy lover (Maxwell Reed), and unrequited desire for his brother's wife (Sally Gray). Despite the different nature of these films, it is hard not to see in them indirect allusions to suspicions of returning veterans concerning both the new independent roles and fidelity of wives while they were away in battle. Finally, although Portman's Thomas Colpepper in *A Canterbury Tale* explains his glueman activities as involving an honorable motivation to preserve female honor during wartime, other explanations are also possible. Despite his physical fitness, Colpepper is not in military service during this crucial pre-D-Day period. His attacks on independent females take place at night photographed in definite *noir* lighting. It is also possible that Colpepper is an insecure male acting out a traumatic rage displacing his feelings of male impotency on independent females as Neville Heath and John George Haigh did in more deadly ways. Like the role of Dennis Price in *Holiday Camp* and those other figures portrayed in *The Upturned Glass* (1947), *The October Man, Mine Own Executioner*, and *The Small Back Room*, these features may represent symbolic fictional displacements of suppressed cases of male trauma and hysteria resulting from wartime conditions.[23]

Nigel Balchin's novels **Mine Own Executioner** and **The Small Back Room** appeared as films during 1948 and 1949 directed respectively by Anthony Kimmins and Michael Powell. As well as depicting more masochistic unheroic aspects of British male identity, both novels and films deal with a form of masculine crisis and trauma related to wartime identity. In *Mine Own Executioner*, unqualified psychologist Felix Milne (Burgess Meredith) unsuccessfully attempts to cure disturbed ex-RAF war veteran Adam Lucian (Kieron Moore). Lucian's problems appear to originate from his experiences as a Japanese POW but both novel and film finally trace the real causes to violent Oedipal aggressive feelings against a mother who has betrayed his father. However, although *Mine Own Executioner* attempts to disavow the real causes which lead Lucian to murder his wife, enough evidence remains in both novel and film to suggest that war trauma plays a major role here.[24] In *The Small Back Room*, Sammy Rice masochistically labors in a government research department under inefficient superiors. Despite support from others, he refuses to take on a leadership role he feels himself incapable of performing. In many ways, Sammy's civilian dilemma echoes Richard Basehart's military trauma in Samuel Fuller's *Fixed Bayonets* (1951). Both novel and film never reveal how Sammy lost his right foot whether in military service or civilian life. However, Sammy (David Farrar) uses his disqualification from wartime service to engage in masochistic feelings of humiliation, aggressive treatment towards his devoted girlfriend Sue (Kathleen Byron), and pathological desire for physical punishment by attempting to provoke a fight with ex-boxer barman Knucksie (Sidney James) in a crowded public house. His attitude mirrors Felix Milne's masochism in *Mine Own Executioner*. Eventually, Sammy conquers his self-induced feelings of male insecurity to defuse an unexploded bomb and recover his self-respect. But while Powell's film version ends on an optimistic note with Sammy offered both military uniform and the leadership of his own government department, Balchin's novel ends pessimistically with Sammy still victimized by his masochistic feelings. The two main heroes of *Mine Own Executioner* and *The Small Back Room* represent fictional displacements of wartime and homefront males who pathologically react against the strains of command and regress into masochistic self-destructive patterns of behavior. Although Lucian's destructive behavior in *Mine Own Executioner* supposedly has its "real" roots in childhood trauma, his wartime experiences as a Japanese POW cracking under interrogation represent a powerful British male humiliation with which he cannot live. The film uses *noir* cinematography to recreate both Lucian's traumatic night-time experiences with the Japanese as well as events leading to the murder of his wife. It ironically employs normal studio lighting for scenes involving Milne whose behavior is clearly not normal throughout the course of the film. By contrast, *The Small Back Room* is often set at night using superb *noir* lighting by cinematographer Christopher Challis. Although later British wartime films concentrated upon stiff upper-lip masculine portrayals of service figures played by Jack Hawkins in *Angels One Five* (1952), *The Cruel Sea, The Malta Story, The Intruder* (all 1953), and *The Bridge on the River Kwai* (1956), Kenneth More in *Appointment with Venus* (1951), *Reach for the Sky* (1956), and *Sink the Bismark!* (1960), and Richard Todd in *The Dam Busters* (1955), *Yangtse Incident* (1957), and *The Long and the Short and the Tall* (1961), figures of veterans facing problems of readjustment to civilian life were not entirely absent. Michael Medwin's role in *The Intruder*, George Baker in *The Ship that Died of Shame* (1955), and even Richard Todd in the shelved film *The Last of the Long-Haired Boys* (1968) proved exceptions to the rule.[25]

In fact, Alfred Hitchcock's *Frenzy* (1970) could have been one of the first postwar neo-*noirs* had it fully employed themes present in the original novel *Goodbye Piccadilly, Hello Leicester Square* by Arthur La Bern. As played by Jon Finch, Hitchcock's former wartime hero appears too young to have fought in the Battle of Britain. Had Hitchcock closely followed the atmosphere in La Bern's novel written in 1966 and set the film in the early sixties, the actual film would not have appeared so anachronistic. La Bern's RAF hero Squadron Leader Blamey suffers from wartime PTSD arising from his involvement in the bombing of Dresden. The novel opens with the suicide of Blamey's rear-gunner who could not adjust to post-war bureaucracy and a changing society in much the same way as his former commander. Blamey's alcoholism directly relates to his traumatic condition. Like his wartime companions he is a fish out of water in sixties Britain. The novel not only contains several references to real-life problems affecting veterans but also compares Blamey's murders with those of the infamous ex-RAF serial killer Neville Heath. As author of novels later filmed such as *It Always Rains on Sunday*, *Good Time Girl*, as well as study of acid-bath murderer John George Haigh which traced his activities to a repressive religious upbringing, La Bern's *Goodbye Picca-dilly. Farewell Leicester Square* (1966) contains several significant insights into offi-cially ignored problems affecting disturbed veterans.[26] Although certain *noirs* such as *Dancing with Crime* (1947), *They Made Me a Fugitive*, and *Nightbeat* (1948) dealt with returning veterans, the problems depicted usually involved criminal activity rather than psychological maladjustment.[27]

However, although its classical form declined, like its American counterpart, *film noir* did not vanish for good. During the 1980s and 1990s, British cinema saw the return of *noir* in a more contemporary stylistic appearance as neo-*noir*. Ap-pearing in an era characterized by the rejection of post-war consensus politics by all major political parties, Mrs. Thatcher's championship of Victorian values, the doctoring of unemployment figures, the unheard-of (at least before 1979) appear-ance of beggars and street people, home dispossessions, greater insecurity in per-sonal and working-life, the return of malnutrition affecting the poorer classes and the high incidence of premature deaths among them, these films returned to the past to treat indirectly dominant cultural and political problems in British society. The vicious "Victorian values" philosophy championed by conservative forces who

Below, *Dancing with Crime*.

demonized both the post-war Welfare State and sixties values led to the appearance of several films implicitly protesting against dominant status quo values. *Dance with A Stranger* (1985), released thirty years following the original events, told the story of Ruth Ellis, the last woman hung in Britain, a theme indirectly treated in J. Lee Thompson's *Yield to the Night* (1957). *Chicago Joe and the Showgirl* (1990) dealt less hypocritically with Britain's 1944 version of Bonnie and Clyde, striptease artist Elizabeth Jones and American deserter Gustav Hulten than *Good Time Girl* (1948). Peter Medak's *The Krays* (1990) dealt with the rise and fall of the terrible twin gangsters who terrorized London in the sixties. The film implicitly suggested that revered British cultural features involving the Blitz and the myth of the People's War may have had some undefined relationship to the Krays brothers criminal activities. *The Krays* also contains an ironic sequence when the brothers meet their American counterparts with whom they have much in common in swinging London. British writer/director Danny Cannon opens his bleak neo-*noir* *The Young Americans* (1993) with seasoned American cop Harvey Keitel watching a scene from the Ealing *noir* *The Blue Lamp* (1950) which ironically foreshadows his introduction to a now unrecognizable British landscape dominated by American drug overlord Viggo Mortensen manipulating young British juveniles by deadly Chicago tactics which offend even traditional British villains. Ealing's cozy world of *The Blue Lamp* and its television spin-off *Dixon of Dock Green* (1955-76) no longer exists except as a nostalgically irrelevant image from a now-obsolete fifties social world. Finally, Medak's *Let Him Have It* (1991) dealt with the judicial murder of Derek Bentley for the killing of a policeman he had no direct involvement with, a crime for which he only received posthumous pardon in August 1998. Acting as a counterpoint to classical juvenile delinquent British *noir* films such as *Good Time Girl* (1948), *The Blue Lamp* and *Cosh Boy* (1952), *Let Him Have It* indicted a vindictive society for an arbitrary execution clearly meant "pour encourager les autres," especially British youngsters traumatically affected by wartime and post-war conditions. Like American *film noir*, British *film noir* and its neo-*noir* versions represent an area worthy of detailed further study.

I wish to acknowledge the pioneering article by William K. Everson frequently cited in the text, the many stimulating suggestions made by Francis M. Nevins in conversations, and the valuable excavation work undertaken by graduate student Eva White in the Department of English of Southern Illinois University during summer 1997 for the purposes of this article.

Notes

1. William K. Everson, "British *Film noir*," *Films in Review* 38.5 (1987): 285-289; "British *Film noir*," *Films in Review* 38.6 (1987): 341-347; Marcia Landy, **British Genres: Cinema and Society, 1930-1960** (New Jersey: Princeton University Press, 1991), 182-183, 229, 257-259, 266-269, 270, 273, 398; Laurence Miller, "Evidence for a British *Film noir* Cycle," **Re-Viewing British Cinema, 1900-1992: Essays and Interviews**, Ed. Wheeler Winston Dixon (New York: State University of New York Press, 1994), 155-

164; Raymond Durgnat "Some Lines of Inquiry into Post-war British Crimes," *The British Cinema Book*, Ed. Robert Murphy, (London: BFI Publishing, 1997), 91-93, 95-96. Durgnat lists four types of British *film noirs* in an article he describes as "a work in progress on British cinema in the Age of Austerity." (90) They are Middle-class *noir*. I: incomes and inheritance; Middle class *noir*. II: The Portman murders; Middle Class *noir*. III: The Gentle Sex; and Thrillers: two fisted/thick ear/hard boiled/tough *noir*. Many of his categorizations overlap not only with material in my own work but also films covered by Robert Murphy in *Realism and Tinsel: Cinema and Society in Britain 1939-49* (London: Routledge, 1989). However, Murphy's chapter "Morbid Burrowings" (a term used to describe contemporary British establishment critical attacks on appropriations of German expressionism and *film noir*) comments that, in contrast to American *film noir*, the "British 'morbid' films are much more diffuse and it is virtually impossible to contain them within a single genre." (169) Murphy also commented that the British equivalent of *film noir* had been confined to the dustbin of cinematic history with the exception of some "discerning scavengers" such as Geoff Brown, "Which Way to the Way Ahead," *Sight and Sound*, 78 (1978): 242-247; Raymond Durgnat, *A Mirror for England*, and Julian Petley, "The Lost Continent," *All Our Yesterdays*, Ed. Charles Barr (London: BFI Publishing, 1986), 98-119.

2. See Satyajit Ray, *Our Films, Their Films* (Bombay: Orient Longman, 1976), 144; Francois Truffaut, *Hitchcock* (London: Secker & Warburg, 1968), 100; Pauline Kael, *Going Steady* (London: Temple Smith, 1970), 180-181; Dwight Macdonald quoted by Charles Barr, "Introduction: Amnesia and Schizophrenia," *All Our Yesterdays*, Ed. Charles Barr (London: British Film Institute, 1986), 2; V.F. Perkins, "The British Cinema" (1962), *Movie Reader*, Ed. Ian Cameron (London: November Books, 1962), 7-11; David Shipman, *The Story of Cinema 2* (London: Hodder & Stoughton, 1983), 558; James Park, *Learning to Dream* (London: Faber, 1984), 13; Gilbert Adair and Nick Roddick, *A Night at the Pictures* (London: Columbus Books, 1985), 14.

3. Andrew Britton, "*Ealing Studios* by Charles Barr," *Framework* 7/8 (1978):47; Alan Lovell "The British Cinema: The Unknown Cinema," British Film Institute Education Department Seminar, 13 March 1969; "The British Cinema: The Known Cinema?" *The British Cinema Book*, Ed. Robert Murphy (London: British Film Institute, 1997), 235-243. The Hammer films Britton refers to are *It Always Rains on Sunday* and *Kind Hearts and Coronets*.

4. Landy 485.

5. Everson 285, 289. For further confirmation of European influence on thirties and forties British cinema see Kevin Gough-Yates, "Exiles and British Cinema," *The British Cinema Book*, 104-113, and Pam Cook, *Fashioning the Nation: Costume and Identity in British Cinema* (London: British Film Institute, 1996), 80-115. Gough-Yates begins his article with a significant sentence, "European exiles dominated British film production in the 1930s" (104) and concludes it with another, "The 1950s was the decade of Ealing and Pinewood, whose very names betoken little England." (112)

6. See Paul Schrader, "Notes on *Film Noir*," "Janey Place and Lowell Peterson, "Some Visual Motifs of *Film noir*," *Film Noir Reader*, Eds. Alain Silver and James Ursini, (New York: Limelight Editions, 1996), 53-77. In her examination of the *noir* style in *The Third Man*, Landy also quotes the following section from Janey Place, "Women in *film noir*,"

Women in Film Noir, Ed. E. Ann Kaplan (London: British Film Institute, 1978). Like many British *noir* films such as *The October Man, Daybreak, Obsession, Blanche Fury*, and *Saraband for Dead Lovers*, Landy describes the world vision of *The Third Man* as "paranoid, claustrophobic, hopeless, doomed, predetermined by the past, or moral or personal identity... The visual style conveys this mood through expressive view of darkness, both real, in predominantly underlit and night-time scenes, and psychologically through shadows and claustrophobic compositions which overwhelm the character in exterior as well as interior settings." (182)

7. Everson 343. Furthermore, Landy also sees *film noir* as a visual style influencing several different genres such as the post-war crime film (*The Third Man*), the woman's film (*Bedelia*), tragic melodramas (*On the Night of the Fire, Daybreak, Dear Murderer, The October Man, The Spider and the Fly*), and Gothic horror (*Uncle Silas*). British *film noir* is as much a transformative hybrid visual style as its counterparts in other national cinemas. For example, she notes that the "mid- and late 1940s provide striking instances of the transformation of the woman's film into *film noir*" and cites *Bedelia* (1946) as a key example. *Bedelia* not only opens with a portrait reminiscent of Fritz Lang's *The Woman in the Window* (1944) and a voice-over leading to a flashback but also represents a British adaptation of a novelist whose books became American *noir* films such as *Laura* (1944) and *Leave Her to Heaven* (1945) - Vera Caspary. However, as opposed to the original novel's pre-World War I American setting, Lance Comfort's film version places the film in a recognizably contemporary British social and historical context. This change is not accidental.

8. Robin Wood, "Ideology, Genre, Auteur," *Film Comment* 13.1 (1977): 46-51.

9. See here Raymond Williams, **Marxism and Literature** (New York: Oxford University Press, 1977) for a description of this process.

Below and opposite, *The Third Man*: "...claustrophobic compositions which overwhelm the character in exterior as well as interior settings."

10. Miller, 156-157. In his survey, "Some Lines of Inquiry into Post-war British Crimes," Durgnat draws attention to certain relevant cultural attitudes influencing British *noir* films such as *Blanche Fury*, a film combining inheritance and social rise themes, "thus appealing to spectators in *both* the threatened upper *and* the rising lower classes" (91) in an era affected by both World War II bankruptcy and Labour's Age of Austerity. He also notes that "Whereas Hollywood *noir* between 1945 and 1949 is driven by an optimism/cynicism split, the British mood owes more to a more gradual, uneasy shift of the balance between older, more traditional suspicions about human nature and more modern, lenient attitudes, spreading fastest among the middle classes, some of whom regarded Victorian harshness as a main cause of evil." Ironically, the former element would return with a vengeance as a result of Thatcher's electoral victory in 1979 which also influenced British neo-*noir*. Despite optimistic hopes fueled by Labour's 1945 electoral victory for a better society, the post-war period soon became characterized by disillusionment, a mood which certainly contributed to British *film noir*. See Arthur Marwick, **Britain in the Century of Total War** (Boston: Little, Brown and Company, 1968), 328-342; **British Society Since 1945** (London: Penguin Books, 1982), 13-111; Robert Hewison, **In Anger: Culture in the Cold War 1945-60** (London: Weidenfeld and Nicholson, 1981); **Society and Literature, 1945-1970**, Ed. Alan Sinfield (London: Methuen, 1983), 13-19, 237, 240-241; Alan Sked and Chris Cook, **Post-War Britain: A Political History**, Second Edition (New York: Penguin Books, 1984), 96-100; Marwick, **Culture in Britain Since 1945** (London: Basil Blackwell, 1991), 13-64; and Neil Nehring, **Flowers in the Dustbin: Culture, Anarchy, and Postwar England** (Ann Arbor: The University of Michigan Press, 1993). Despite wartime romances, any type post-war attempts at sexual freedom faced Britain's long-standing repressive cultural and historical tradition as seen in films such as *Good Time Girl* and *The Blue Lamp* where "wild youngsters" face the disapproval of authoritarian figures played by Flora Robson, Jack Warner and surrogate son Jimmy Hanley. See also Stephen Humphries, **A Secret World of Sex: Forbidden Fruit: The British Experience, 1900-1950** (London: Sidgwick and Jackson, 1988).

11. Schrader, 54-61. Significantly, Schrader does not list either David Goodis or Cornell Woolrich amongst his literary ensemble. This is not suprising in terms of the future director's role in masculine cinematic depictions. Also, television *noir* such as the 60s *Outer Limits* series forms another category deserving another exploratory article.

12. Everson, 287, 289. Petley (90) also notes the existence of several "exotic late blooms" such as Cy Endfield's *Hell Drivers* (1958) and "stragglers" such as Val Guest's *Hell is a City* (1960), Sidney Hayers's *Payroll* (1961), and Anthony Simmons's *Four in the Morning* (1965) which do not appear on Durgnat's list.

13. Everson, 344-346.

14. Two different endings were shot for the film. The American ending concludes with Winston defiantly condemning Big Brother before police shoot him and Julia. The other follows Orwell's original conclusion.

15. Everson, 287-288.

16. Everson, 288.

17. Landy, 251-252.

18. Everson, 341, 342.

19. Everson, 289, see also 343.

20. See here Charles Eckert, "The Anatomy of a Proletarian Film: Warner's *Marked Woman," Movies and Methods Volume II* (Berkeley: University of California Press, 1985), 407-429.

21. Murphy, *Realism and Tinsel*, 179.

22. Murphy, 186. The other three were James Mason, Robert Newton, and David Farrar. Before his death in 1969, Portman played generally positive characters such as the commanding officer in *The Colditz Story* (1954) and Jess Oakroyd in *The Good Companions* (1957). However, although he also played occasional sinister roles such as the psychotic murderer in *The Naked Edge* (1961), the immediate post-war period saw his most prolific appearances as dangerous male characters.

23. Although the aftermath of World War I brought cases of shell shock to public attention, different cultural and historical circumstances affected definitions of trauma affecting both soldiers and civilians during World War II. Studies did appear in America recognizing the psychological effects of war on soldiers. But they generally tended to move towards optimistic conclusions by regarding such problems as merely temporary. See, for example, Frank Joseph Sladen Ed., *Psychiatry and the War: A Survey of the Significance of Psychiatry and its Relation to Disturbances in Human Behavior to Help Provide for the Present War Effort and For Post War Needs* (Springfield, Il.: C.C. Thomas, 1943); George Kenneth Pratt, *Soldier to Civilian: Problems of Readjustment* (New York: McGraw-Hill Book Company, 1944); and Therese Benedek, *Insight and Personality Adjustment: A Study of the Psychological Effects of War* (New York: The Ronald Press Company, 1946). We must remember that this era saw the suppression of any unpleasant facts concerning wartime experience as shown by the banning for public exhibition of John Huston's documentary dealing with traumatized soldiers, *Let There Be Light* (1946) and the rapid lack of interest in war neuroses after 1945. See Allan Young, *The Harmony of Illusions: Inventing Post-Traumatic Stress Disorder* (New Jersey: Princeton University Press, 1995), 91-94. Young (224) also notes Hitchcock's comparison of the act of recovering a traumatic memory with watching a film in *Spellbound*, one made by others both before and after his film. Recent medical research now recognizes that PTSD did affect World War II servicemen. It also documents the reasons for its contemporary neglect. Like many recent researchers, British psychologist Joan Busfield notes the pervasive changing historical influence of cultural and gender factors affecting medical discourse. She points out that "whilst mental breakdowns in the Second World War were not uncommon, they do not seem to have been quite so frequent or to have attracted so much public attention, although there is reference in the literature to so-called 'battle fatigue'." But after the war attention focussed on the traumas of prisoners, especially those in concentration camps, rather than service personnel or homefront civilians. Busfield also comments on relevant gender factors motivating medical definitions whereby men are less likely to be labelled mentally disordered than women even if they are disturbed resulting in male problematic behavior being categorized as wrongdoing or criminality rather than the result of mental instability. See Joan Busfield, *Men, Women, and Madness: Understanding Gender and Mental Disorder* (New York: New York University Press,

1996), 212-213, 99-100, 232. For recent medical evidence recognizing PTSD as a World War II disablilty in America, Australia, and Britain see Roderick J. Orner, Post-Traumatic Stress Disorder and European War Veterans," *British Journal of Clinical Psychology*, 31 (1992): 387-403; Raul Cuervo-Rubio, "The Secret War: Don't Miss Post-Traumatic Stress Disorder in World War II Veterans,"*Geriatrics* 50.11 (1995): 51-52, 55-56; Christopher Krasucki, D. Bandyopadhay, and Emily Hooper,"Post World War II Stress Syndrome," *The Lancet*, 345, May 13 (1995): 1240; Kimberly A. Lee, George E. Voillant, William C. Torrey, and Glen H. Elder,"A 50 Year Prospective Study of the Psychological Sequels of World War II Combat,"*American Journal of Psychiatry*, 152. 4 (1995): 516-522; E.J. Wiseman, "World War II: Its Effects after 50 Years," *American Journal of Psychiatry*, 153.4 (1996): 584-585; G.H. Elder Jr and M.J. Shanahan, "Linking Combat and Physical Health: The Legacy of World War II in Men's Lives," *American Journal of Psychiatry*, 154.3 (1997): 330-336; John T. Ellard,"The Epidemic of Post-Traumatic Stress Disorder: A Passing Phase? *Medical Journal of Australia* 166 (1997): 84-87; Alexander McFarlane,"Post-Traumatic Stress Disorder: The Importance of Clinical Objectivity and Systematic Research,"op. cit, 88-90; and "Elderly Veteran is Treated for Battle Stress," *Electronic Telegraph* (U.K.) # 1164 Web site, Sunday 2 August 1998. The last citation concerns a Bomber Command veteran who had witnessed devastation and suffering caused by strategic bombing of England's industrial cities while in his late teens. After volunteering for Bomber Command, he became a POW after parachuting from a burning plane and later suffered from classic PTSD symptoms. Another report has recently noted that some 750,000 women of a "forgotten generation" still suffer from World War II homefront trauma, a condition which may also have affected their children. See"Women Still Bear Wounds of the War," *Electronic Telegraph*, op.cit.

24. Despite *Mine Own Executioner*'s attempt to deny the real causes of Lucian's condition, the novel contains significant references to real-life cases of trauma. When replying to a Regent Street retailer's comments about"A *war case, a fighter pilot. One of the Few,* eh?" Milne responds, "No. One of the many, I'm afraid. There are a lot of these boys about who're only just showing what the war really did to them". Milne later decides to use pentothal on Lucian to make him remember his traumatic war experiences. "We used it quite a bit in the war." After Lucian's suicide another character comments, "I often think that's one of the worst aspects of war...Not only the tragedies that it causes, but the tragedies it leaves behind it."See Nigel Balchin, ***Mine Own Executioner*** (Boston: Houghton Mifflin Company, 1946), 130, 157, 295. Critic Anthony Boucher also recognized the grim nature of comments about wartime home front society in his review of *The Small Back Room* in *The San Francisco Chronicle*, April 15, 1945. "This is a distinguished job–and not the least of its distinctions is the fact that it could be published in wartime." I'm grateful to Francis M. Nevins for supplying me with this reference.

25. For Todd's comments on this very elusive film see Tony Williams,"An Interview with Richard Todd," *Films in the Golden Age* 14 (1998): 94. "I could understand the character. He was quasi-military in that he was an ex-pilot. A lot of his mental disturbance and his problems arose out of his war service. I've seen chaps like that. I can understand them, and I felt a certain sympathy with him...He was just one of the people who had been badly affected."

26. Paralleling Roland Culver's disgruntled demobilized criminal officer figure comments against post-war British bureaucracy in *The Ship that Died of Shame*, a character in **Goodbye Piccadilly, Farewell Leicester Square** (New York: Stein and Day, 1966) comments, "The guys in jackboots don't worry me half as much as the striped pants in our own country." (40) Busfield has recently noted that "One group of the military vulnerable to mental breakdowns were the members of the air force squadrons whose missions were highly dangerous, but who had to spend long periods of inactivity waiting for the call to action - again a situation characterized by powerlessness." See **Men, Women, and Madness**, 221. As Arthur La Bern reveals in his study of the acid-bath murderer John George Haigh, contemporary judicial opinion preferred legalistic definitions of criminality as opposed to complicated medical and psychological evidence. La Bern regards Haigh as a disturbed schizophrenic who should never have been executed and whose repressively religious upbringing turned him into a callous psychopath. Haigh also resembled Hitchcock's Uncle Charlie in *Shadow of A Doubt*, both in his devil-may-care attitude and an "enthusiasm for the Edwardian era, about which he could have known very little." See Arthur La Bern, **Haigh: The Mind of A Murderer** (London: W.H. Allen, 1973). 139. Significantly, enough Blamey's historical nemesis Neville Heath "never exhibited any sign of mental abnormality, or rather of disordered conduct, when he was young. His offenses began after the time of joining the Army" but they never resembled the sadistic sexual serial killer activities which followed his four year tour of duty with the South African Air Force. Although Heath's defence counsel did raise the question as to whether his air service may have contributed to his sadistic activities, this motivation is later dropped. His speech also has relevance to people affected by the Blitz and V rockets on the homefront. "You will remember, perhaps, that this man has taken many risks. He is one of thousands of young men who has taken his life in his hands and risked one of the most painful of deaths, by burning, on your behalf and on mine...The human frame was not built to fly in machines and be fired at. The human frame and human people have had to put up with shocks and risks and dangers which were unknown up to the present generation....The human frame and the human mind were not intended to meet with such awful shocks as they have had to meet with in the past few years, and it may be that they have not yet evolved such an immunity as to leave them normal after they have gone through those sorts of experiences. You may yourselves come to the conclusion that that kind of experience may have something to do with the outburst, the admitted outburst, of sadism in this man after the war was over." See **The Trial of Neville George Clevely Heath**, Ed. Macdonald Critchley, M.D. (London: William Hodge and Company, Limited, 1951), 27, 187-188. This certainly suggests that trauma was not unknown during this period. In La Bern's novel, Blamey has been drastically affected by his traumatic memories of the infamous Dresden bombing raid. Heath also used the pseudonym of Rupert Brooke, the World War I poet, and also suggested that a "Jack" (Jack the Ripper?) was responsible for his crimes.

27. Ironically, the star of *They Made Me A Fugitive*, Trevor Howard, had left wartime service due to mental problems and became identified with upright military characters for most of his career in films such as *The Third Man*, *Odette* (1950), *Cockleshell Heroes* (1955), *Operation Crossbow*, *Von Ryan's Express* and *Morituri* (all 1965). According to *The Sunday Times* Website of August 23, 1998, Howard came under police investigation for claiming medals he had not actually earned in combat.

Above, Johnny Prince (Dan Duryea) peddles the work of Kitty March, which is actually painted by her "sugar daddy," the hapless Chris Cross in *Scarlet Street*.

Peinture Noire:
Abstract Expressionism and *Film Noir*

Kent Minturn

Introduction

While much has been written on *film noir*'s indebtedness to American Scene painting–in particular, to the cityscapes of Reginald Marsh and Edward Hopper [Figure 1]–little, if any, attention has been given to the significant formalistic and thematic similarities between *film noir* and the art of the next generation of American painters, the Abstract Expressionists.[1] Michael Leja's **Reframing Abstract Expressionism: Subjectivity and Painting in the 1940s** (1993) stands as the only in-depth study of this phenomenon.[2] "Art history," he convincingly argues, "has assigned New York School painting an aggressively transcendental and highbrow classification, which has isolated that art from the contemporary popular cultural forms with which it had so much in common."[3] Following Leja's lead, my aim in this paper is to examine Abstract Expressionist painting within its often-ignored popular cultural context; specifically, in relation to the dominant visual milieu established by *film noir* in the 1940s.

Let us begin, therefore, by noting that during the late 1930s and early 1940s film found its way into New York City's artistic *mélange* through such organizations and institutions as The Film and Photo League, The Eighth Street Cinema, and The Museum of Modern Art. In 1955, William C. Seitz, Abstract Expressionism's first chronicler, wrote:

> How can the colossal impact of The Museum of Modern Art be estimated? It was a center–a "cathedral" of art if ever one existed–within which direct experience of the greatness of Cezanne, Gauguin, van Gogh, Picasso, Seurat, and Braque fired young men, most of them "uncultured" in the academic meaning of the word, and defiant of middle-class respectability, to paint with modern forms.... The masterpieces of modern art were available almost gratis, with a special artist's card of membership–along with free movies at four o'clock![4]

According to Seitz, Abstract Expressionist painters went to The Museum of Modern Art to see masterpieces of modern art *and* films. During the 1940s, the

271

Above, Figure 1: Edward Hopper's etching Night Shadows. Below, the escape of the "Merry Widow" killer in Hitchcock's *Shadow of a Doubt* (1943).

visual traditions of film and painting (and photography) coalesced at the MoMA; Fritz Lang's pioneering *films noirs*, it is important to remember, were "displayed" under the same roof as Picasso's *Les Demoiselles d'Avignon*.

In addition to presenting the reader with an accurate description of the artists' affinities toward (and personal identifications with) anti-academic, anti-bourgeois forms of art that were thought by many to reside outside of the realm of high culture, Seitz's passage reminds us of two important facts: Abstract Expressionism's development coincided with the cultural fusion of modern painting and film in America, and the MoMA, an art museum, was largely responsible for the dissolution of high culture's long-standing contempt for cinema.

In June 1935, the museum's young director, Alfred H. Barr, officially opened the Film Department in hopes of legitimizing what he dubbed "the most important twentieth century art: motion picture films."[5] Internationally renowned art historian, Erwin Panofsky, played an important role in furthering Barr's cause. The following year (1936), Panofsky gave a lecture entitled "The Motion Picture as an Art" to a crowd of more than 300 at the Metropolitan Museum of Art. In this lecture he outlined his general film theory and showed films from the collection of the Museum of Modern Art Film Library. Historian Thomas Levin recapitulates:

> In 1936, the notion of any scholar lecturing anywhere on film (much less this particular scholar speaking...at that particular museum) was nothing short of remarkable.... What made this event so newsworthy, besides the incongruous union of the plebeian medium of the movies with such an austere institution and famous art historian, was the rather unusual cultural legitimation of the cinema that it implied.[6]

Panofsky's theory of film provides us with a crucial touchstone in that it addresses the "unique aesthetic capacities" of film which Abstract Expressionist painting came to challenge, and because it directly affected cinema's status in the New York City art world during the late Thirties and early Forties.

In his essay "Style and Medium in the Moving Pictures" (a revision of the lecture he gave at the Metropolitan Museum of Art) Panofsky posits that it took time for viewers of this new art form to master the "rather extensive repertoire of formal cinematic devices...which constitute the seemingly automatic (because habitualized) 'cinematic literacy' of the contemporary movie goer." He writes that

> the silent movies developed a definite style of their own, adapted to the specific conditions of the medium. A hitherto unknown language was forced upon a public not yet capable of reading it, and the more proficient the public became the more refinement could develop in the language.[7]

Influenced by Walter Benjamin's ideas about the historicity of perceptual skills in relation to reigning modes of representation (as described in "The Work of Art in the Age of Mechanical Reproduction"), Panofsky argues that cinema not only stages new visual epistemes, but simultaneously schools new modes of vision.[8] In film, as in painting, Panofsky is concerned with the way in which images communicate meaning within a given context. In order to ensure that meaning would be grasped, Panofsky suggests in "Style and Medium in the Moving

Pictures," early cinema utilized a "fixed iconography," of specific character types, cinematic devices, and forms.

During the 1940s film noir filmmakers developed their own set of iconographic character types (e.g., the noir protagonist and the femme fatale), cinematic devices (e.g., the subjective camera), and forms (e.g., the web, the labyrinth, the vortex, and the noir city).[9] Elements of film noir's specific iconography later appeared in Abstract Expressionist painting. By expanding the visual literacy of mass audiences, it can be argued, film noir also paved the way for a popular reading, understanding, and acceptance of Abstract Expressionist painting–especially the "mature" works of Jackson Pollock, Mark Rothko, Willem de Kooning, and Franz Kline. Film noir, therefore, can be used to help us see and account for better Abstract Expressionism's specific forms, its trajectory, and its reception.[10]

Through an examination of certain elements which the Abstract Expressionist painters knowingly or unknowingly appropriated from film noir I hope to answer, at least in part, the perennial question of how Abstract Expressionism, a movement ostensibly opposed to (and ignored by) America's ruling class, came to be popularized, institutionalized, and ultimately, as Serge Guilbaut has demonstrated in How New York Stole the Idea of Modern Art, utilized in the "cultural Cold War."

Though the boundaries of Abstract Expressionist painting and film noir extend well beyond the six year period 1944-1950, this window encompasses the crucial developments in each movement. The heyday of film noir, or film noir's first full-blown "cycle," occurred between 1944-1948. During this time over 150 films noirs saturated American visual culture. In the postwar economic boom cinema attendance rose to an all-time high–the weekly average in the United States was about 90,000,000.[11] In 1946, one out of every five films produced in Hollywood was a film noir. Orson Welles' Lady from Shanghai (1948), characterized above all by its iconographic self-consciousness and formulaic acknowledgment of the films noirs that came before, signaled the end of the first cycle. Concentrating on life in the modern metropolis, film noir's second cycle emphasized realism and themes of urban decadence.

Film noir's first cycle developed contemporaneously with Abstract Expressionism's emergence as a distinct entity within the New York City art world (beginning with Mark Rothko, Adolph Gottlieb, and Barnett Newman's self-proclaimed status as "a band of Mythmakers" in 1945). The two overlapped briefly during the three year period, 1947-1950 in which the four seminal artists in question arrived at what are now regarded as their signature styles–Jackson Pollock's "dripped" paintings, Mark Rothko's "multiforms," Willem de Kooning's "Women," and Franz Kline's black-and-white abstractions. Accurately described by April Kingsley as the movement's "turning point," 1950 stands as the year Abstract Expressionism effectively moved into the limelight. In New York, Pollock, de Kooning, Rothko, and Kline each had breakthrough one-man exhibitions of the very works which eventually made them famous. More importantly, perhaps, 1950 was the year Jackson

Pollock, the Abstract Expressionist *par excellence*, received extensive coverage in *Life* magazine, and sold his first drip painting to the Museum of Modern Art.[12]

Film Noir

Film noir, like Abstract Expressionism, is a contentious subject. No one is sure if the films in question constitute a period, a genre, a cycle, a style, or simply a "phenomenon."[13] As its name suggests, *film noir* is about the flip side of the ordered, optimistic view of life presented in classical Hollywood films. The term itself was coined in 1946 by French critics struck by the dim lighting and dark mood of five films initially released in Paris after the war—John Huston's *The Maltese Falcon* (1941), Otto Preminger's *Laura* (1945), Edward Dmytryk's *Murder, My Sweet* (1944), Billy Wilder's *Double Indemnity* (1945), and Fritz Lang's *The Woman in the Window* (1945).

From these films it is possible to come up with a working definition of *film noir*, at least at the level of narrative structure. At the core of each film there is a triangular relationship which involves a male protagonist, a *femme fatale*, and a crime—a theme reminiscent of the Surrealist concept of *l'amour fou*, a love that finds justification only in death. In *"Film noir*: A Modest Proposal," James Damico elaborates:

> Either he is fated to do so or by chance, or because he has been hired for a job specifically associated with her, a man whose experience in life has left him sanguine and often bitter meets a not-innocent woman of similar outlook to whom he is sexually and fatally attracted. Through this attraction, either because the woman induces him to it or because it is the natural result of their relationship, the man comes to cheat, attempt murder or actually murder a second man to whom the woman is attached (generally he is her husband or lover), an act which often leads to the woman's betrayal of the protagonist, but which in any event brings about the sometimes metaphoric, but usually literal destruction of the woman, the man to whom she is attached, and frequently to the protagonist himself.[14]

In addition to those films listed above, this narrative model fits the following first-cycle *films noirs*: *Scarlet Street* (1945), *The Postman Always Rings Twice* (1945), *Detour* (1945), *The Killers* (1946), *The Strange Love of Martha Ivers* (1946), *The Blue Dahlia* (1946), *Out of the Past* (1947), *Pitfall* (1948).

Like Abstract Expressionist painting, *film noir* attempted to give shape to times that were out of joint. Not surprisingly, *film noir* deals with feelings of postwar alienation and disillusionment, the veteran's reintegration into society, the social ramifications of the entrance of women into the work force, and the portent of nuclear destruction. In short, *film noir* is about the confusion, fear, anxiety, and paranoia that existed at a specific moment in American history. The identical, or nearly identical, titles of *films noirs* and Abstract Expressionist paintings completed between 1945-1947 are indicative of the artists' and filmmakers' similar preoccupations: Alfred Zeisler's *Fear* (1945) and Clifford Still's *Fear* (1946), Robert Siodmak's *The Dark Mirror* (1946) and William Baziotes' *Night Mirror* (1947), Delmar Daves' *Dark Passage* (1947) and Willem de Kooning's *Labyrinth* (1946), Jacques Tourneur's *Out of the Past* (1947) and Jackson Pollock's *Something of the Past* (1946), Edwin L. Marin's *Nocturne* (1946) and William Baziotes' *Nocturne* (1945), Jean Negulesco's *Nobody Lives Forever* (1946) and Mark Rothko's *Entombment* (1946), Robert Florey's *Danger Signal* (1945) and Adolph Gottlieb's *Evil Omen* (1945).

At one level, it can be argued, there are significant differences in the ways in which Abstract Expressionist painters and *film noir* filmmakers handled their shared material. Michael Leja notes that while *film noir* filmmakers chose to use iconographic elements and story lines relevant to immediate historical circumstances, the Abstract Expressionist artists utilized a set of remote symbols and pictographs to "project the problematic materials they addressed into an abstract and timeless realm."[15] However, there are instances where the opposite holds true. It seems to me that many of the quintessential films noirs effectively depict an ahistoric, atemporal realm that has little to do with the immediate present (*The Shanghai Gesture* [1941] even goes so far as to open with the disclaimer, "Our story has nothing to do with the present"), and conversely, that some of the Abstract Expressionists' universalizing "symbols and pictographs" reflect "immediate historical circumstances," real or imagined.

It is here, I think, that we arrive at one of *film noir* and Abstract Expressionism's most important shared characteristics; namely, a sense of *in medias res* or "in-betweeness," that is indicative of modernism's inherent apocalyptic discourse.[16] The Abstract Expressionists claimed that through their art they were making a schismatic break with the past, and that, in Pollock's famous words, "the modern painter cannot express this age, the airplane, the atom bomb, the radio, in the old forms of the Renaissance or of any other culture."[17] However, with every genesis myth comes its necessary correlative, an impending apocalypse. In "Painting: The Task of Mourning," art historian Yves-Alain Bois writes:

> The whole enterprise of modernism, especially abstract painting, which can be taken as its emblem, could not have functioned without an apocalyptic myth.... The pure beginning, the liberation from tradition, the "zero degree" that was searched for by the first generation of abstract painters could not but function as an omen of the end. One did not have to wait for the "last painting" of Ad Reinhardt to be aware that through its historicism (its linear conception of history) and through its essentialism (its idea that something like the essence of painting existed, veiled somehow,

and waiting to be unmasked), the enterprise of abstract painting could not but understand its birth as calling for its end.[18]

It is this, T.J. Clark contends, that we should focus on if we are to truly understand Abstract Expressionist paintings, their "incessant courting of Death," and ultimately, their "petty bourgeois pathos."[19] Again, the similarity between the titles of certain *films noirs* and Abstract Expressionist paintings completed at this time is quite telling—frequently, they rely on modernism's rhetoric of beginnings and endings: Mark Rothko's *The Source* (1946) and Barnett Newman's *The Beginning* (1946), necessarily complement Harold Clurman's *Deadline at Dawn* (1946) and Jean Negulesco's *Nobody Lives Forever* (1946).

Surprisingly, there is little evidence which suggests that *film noir* filmmakers and Abstract Expressionist painters communicated with each other directly. However, their biographical histories are similar, and the genealogies of their respective movements are, in many ways, one and the same. Many of *film noir's* finest filmmakers—Fritz Lang, Robert Siodmak, Billy Wilder, Otto Preminger—were first generation European immigrants, as were Mark Rothko, Arshile Gorky, Willem de Kooning, and Hans Hofmann. Abstract Expressionist painters and *film noir* filmmakers alike synthesized elements of Existentialism, German Expressionism, and Surrealism in their work. In their move away from Regionalism and American Scene painting, the Abstract Expressionists turned to European modernists and Surrealists (many of whom arrived in New York in 1940) for inspiration, while *film noir* filmmakers were influenced by, and eventually integrated their artistic heritage with, purely American productions such as Depression-era and gangster films.

Through its emphasis on "the mark, the stroke, the brush, and the drip," Meyer Schapiro observed, Abstract Expressionist painting emphasizes "the artist's active presence."[20] Similarly, *film noir* pulls the curtain on the "omniscient narrator" of classical Hollywood cinema and reveals the "active presence" of the filmmaker through its overt emphasis on filmic processes and techniques. Such self-reflexivity is another hallmark of modernism. *Film noir* filmmakers, like the Abstract Expressionist painters, laid bare processes of their art—or, if we apply Clement Greenberg's credo, they used "the characteristic methods of [their] discipline to criticize the discipline itself."[21] *Film noir* filmmakers, in essence, came out from behind the camera and began to demonstrate their art profilmically. In a voice-over sequence in *Double Indemnity*, protagonist Walter Neff seems to be speaking for director Billy Wilder when he confesses his crime:

> You know how it is... You're like the guy behind the roulette wheel, watching the customers so they don't crook the house. And then one night you get to thinking how you could crook the house yourself—and do it smart. Because you've got that wheel right under your hands; you know every notch of it by heart. And you figure, all you need is a plant out front; a shill to put down the bet.

The ongoing debate that surrounds *film noir* opposes its formal qualities, that is, its unprecedented combination of filmic techniques such as low-key lighting, oblique camera angles, flashbacks, and voice-overs, to the philosophical underpinnings of its subject matter—existentialism, alienation, and fatalism. *Film noir* scholarship is characteristically divided between "stylistics" and "themes." Similarly, critical response to Abstract Expressionism, from the beginning, has been divided into two opposing camps: the formalists (led by Clement Greenberg) and the esoteric, melodramatic, anti-formalists (e.g., Harold Rosenberg). Art historical scholarship has suffered, Leja posits, because it fails to observe the degree to which these categories "represent two sides of a single coin."[22] The same holds true for the analysis of *film noir*. In each case, form is inseparable from content.

Jackson Pollock's Dripped *Noirs*

In the final pages of ***Abstract Expressionism: Painting and Subjectivity in the 1940s***, Michael Leja acknowledges three of the most common (and closely related) visual metaphors which appear in both *film noir* and Jackson Pollock's drip paintings: the labyrinth, the web, and the vortex. In March of 1950, film critic Parker Tyler wrote one of the first articles on Pollock's drip paintings entitled "Jackson Pollock: The Infinite Labyrinth." In it Tyler explains that Pollock's "labyrinths," are visual metaphors which even "the most unprepared spectator would immediately grasp."[23] Through them, he adds, Pollock is able to create a "a deliberate disorder of hypothetical hidden orders." Although Tyler does not elaborate on why he thinks the "labyrinth" is something that an unprepared gallery visitor would "immediately grasp," we can infer from his statement that it existed as a widely recognized visual metaphor *before* it was adopted by Pollock.

　Film noir is largely responsible for the labyrinth's dissemination throughout postwar visual culture. *Film noir* filmmakers set out to fabricate a "deliberate disorder" in their works to achieve a specific emotional effect. In "Towards a Definition of *Film noir*," Raymond Borde and Etienne Chaumeton propose that calculated confusion resides "at the core of *film noir*." They write:

> All components of *film noir* yield the same result: disorientating the spectator, who can no longer find the familiar reference points. The moviegoer is accustomed to certain conventions: a logical development of the action, a clear distinction between good and evil, well-defined characters, sharp motives, scenes more showy than authentically violent, a beautiful heroine and an honest hero. At least these were the conventions of American adventure films before the War.[24]

With his drip paintings, Pollock similarly shattered the established conventions of prewar American painting. Presented with a Pollock painting, the only "familiar reference points" in the visual vocabulary of the postwar observer were the iconic labyrinths, webs, and vortices of *film noir*. In this sense, the seasoned *film noir* viewer was preconditioned to grasp Pollock's drip paintings.

The *film noir* filmmaker's ability to disorient the viewer in his medium paved the way for Pollock and his attempts to render the experience of living in the modern world "in terms of painting—not as an illustration of—(but *the equivalent*)."[25] In the paintings done during his "transition" period (1947-1950), such as *Untitled [Composition with Black Pouring]* (1947), *Cut Out* (1948), and *Out of the Web: Number 7, 1949* (1949), Pollock waffles between controlled figuration and dripped abstraction. The figures in these paintings, like the characters in a typical *film noir*, find themselves trapped in a chaotic web. While the idea of being trapped in a web is alluded to in a number of *film noir* titles—*The Web* (1947), *Trapped* (1949), *No Way Out* (1950)—the web also appears as a reoccurring visual motif. One of the first instances of this can be seen in Edward Dmytryk's *Murder My Sweet* when the protagonist, Philip Marlowe (Dick Powell), confesses that he feels caught in a "web woven by a thousand spiders."

Earlier, in a fantasy sequence, Marlowe is shown spiraling out of control toward the heart of a vortex suggested by the recession of concentric spurts of water. While vortices appear also in *Mildred Pierce* (1945), *Conflict* (1945), *The Spiral Staircase* (1946), and *DOA*

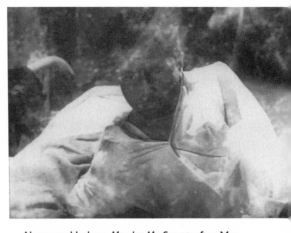

Above and below, *Murder My Sweet*: after Marlowe (Dick Powell) is drugged his dizziness is epxressed by optical effect. Then his POV illustrates what he imagines is a dark whirlpool opening in the floor. Bottom, Figure 2: Jackson Pollocks' *Vortex*.

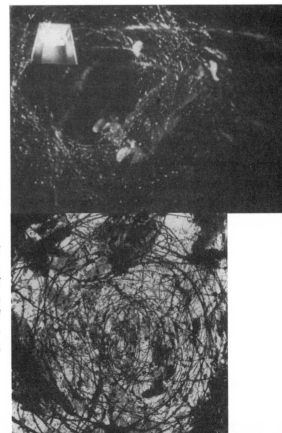

(1950), this example is particularly suited for a comparison with one of Pollock's earliest drip paintings, *Vortex* (1947) [Figure 2]. In this painting, Pollock relies on what Janey Place and Lowell Peterson have described as "the archetypal *noir* shot...the extreme high-angle long shot."[26] Paradoxically, the viewer finds himself in a perpendicular relationship to the vortex–in Leja's words, "the spatial axis normally experienced as vertical [i.e., the axis of recession] has been turned to the horizontal."[27] The vortex, therefore, can be seen as the most important visual metaphor that Pollock adopted from *film noir* insofar as it prefigured his attempts to disorient the viewer more directly through the horizontal/vertical duality of his mature drip paintings 1947-1950.

The trajectory of Pollock's artistic development from 1947 forward is worth reviewing. After experimenting briefly with liberating the figures in his webs of dripped paint through the violent process of literally "knifing" them out of the canvas, Pollock abandoned representation of the figure altogether. Instead, he chose to implicate himself as the subject of the painting–that is, as the figure trapped in the labyrinth, web, or vortex. Pollock, in essence, moved from "illustrating" to "enacting" his visual metaphors. (A similar shift from figurative representation to gestural automatism can be seen in Pollock's so-called "psychoanalytic drawings.") Pollock's wish to "literally be in the painting" resulted in his decision to tack large unstretched canvases on the floor onto which he poured, flung, or dripped paint. "What was to go on the canvas," Harold Rosenberg observed in 1952, "was not a picture but an event."[28])

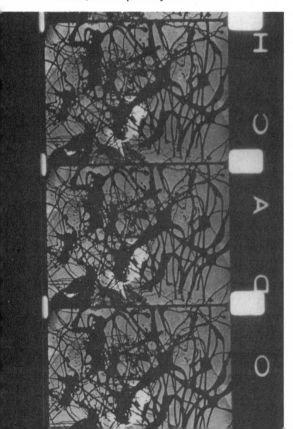

Below, film strip from *Jackson Pollock*.

Pollock's labyrinths, webs, and vortices, therefore, are not "wholly optical"; they have a deeper significance. As Rosalind Krauss has pointed out in Chapter Six of the ***Optical Unconscious***, Pollock's drips signify, above all, the artist's process–which in turn, becomes the painting's subject and content. Pollock's drip paintings, as iconic as they may be, are not antithetical to story-telling, or the narrative traditions he embraced during the thirties. Krauss picks up on this as well, asserting that Pollock's paintings require the viewer to actively participate in the unraveling of a "murder mystery"–an experience not unlike the viewing of a typical *film noir*.

In *film noir* we are presented first with the corpse; the rest of the film we move with the hero towards this known fatality. (Here, Krauss' analogy seems particularly helpful.) Presented with a finished drip painting (a corpse), viewing becomes a process of reasoning backwards, moving from the "clues" (the drips) to the "cause" (Pollock's painting process). Thus, the viewer is pulled into the painting at a dramatic level; ultimately he is forced to experience for himself Pollock's *noir*-ish drama of being "in" the painting at the time it was being painted.[29] Perhaps this explains why Pollock always maintained that there was "no chaos" in his painting process. Pollock's mature paintings, like the best *films noirs*, are calculated attempts at disorienting the spectator through technique and form.

Pollock's drip paintings, it can be argued, possess other "cinematic" qualities. Their grand scale and approximate 2:35:1 "aspect" ratio elicit comparison to "the big screen." In relation to the other arts, Panofsky claims (in anticipation of Deleuze), cinema's "unique and specific possibilities can be defined as *dynamization of space* and, accordingly, *spatialization of time*."[30] Through an emphasis on drama and recording movement, Pollock's drip paintings accomplish both. In 1950, Pollock admitted to interviewer William Wright that he worked primarily "with space and time."[31] Dore Ashton suggests that Pollock held a long standing grudge against Abstract Expressionism's rival media, and that he may have been trying to out-do cinema when he painted.[32]

Given Ashton's claim, Pollock's next major step as an artist–his decision to literally "paint" a film–seems logical. In 1950, Hans Namuth and Paul Falkenberg (who also edited Fritz Lang's *noir* masterpiece, *M*) made the now-famous film of Pollock painting.[33] By pouring paint onto a sheet of glass horizontally suspended above Namuth's camera, Pollock, in effect, returned his vortices, webs, and labyrinths to the medium from which they were borrowed. Moreover, he reintroduced the figure (himself) into his paintings. In the film, Pollock's face can be seen through the translucent surface he paints on; he is "in" the painting and the film, simultaneously [Figure 3]. The viewer, consequently, is presented with an image of Pollock that recalls the aforementioned scene in *Murder My Sweet* (1944), only this time around Pollock is the *noir* protagonist "caught in a web woven by a thousand spiders."[34] The question is: to what extent is Pollock's similarity to a *film noir* protagonist more than just contingent here? His biographers remind us:

> Inspired by his sessions with Namuth, Jackson became obsessed with the subject of the artist as an actor. Frequently...he quizzed friends like John Little, Clement Greenberg, and Harold Rosenberg on the "persona" of the modern artist, collecting fragments of a portrait like pieces of a puzzle to be assembled at the next session before Namuth's lens.[35]

The Abstract Expressionist Artist as a *Film Noir* Protagonist

The typical *film noir* protagonist is portrayed as a heroic loner; a man who lives by no other code but his own. Invariably, he wrestles with internal or external forces beyond his control. In response to the chaotic universe in which he resides, however, he displays (as did the literary "hard-boiled" detective before him) an "impassive toughness in the face of inescapable tragedy."[36] This description also fits for any number of the Abstract Expressionist painters. A specific notion of "self" seems to be one of the most obvious forms that Jackson Pollock and other Abstract Expressionist artists borrowed from first cycle *films noirs*. In *Reframing Abstract Expressionism*, Leja notes:

> The personas projected by some of the Mythmakers, as well as by many of the other New York School artists, reeked of *noir*, strong evidence of the essential congruence of the two notions of self. Tough-talking, morose, troubled, hard-drinking, and two-fisted, the public image and sometimes the self-image of the New York School artists made their careers into *noir* dramas. Sometimes even the formal strategies of their public presentation overlapped strikingly with conventions of *film noir*.[37]

Leja offers two examples of this phenomenon—a *noir*-ish photographic portrait of Mark Rothko taken by Bert Stern, and Arnold Newman's *Life* magazine picture of Jackson Pollock next to a skull (I would add also Robert Frank's 1951 portrait of Franz Kline), but fails to investigate how and why this may have happened.

Fascinating is the idea that *film noir* prepared a niche in America's psyche which the Abstract Expressionists and their art came to haunt. Or, that the lives (and violent deaths or suicides) of the Abstract Expressionist artists were somehow pre-scripted by *film noir*. What should not be overlooked are the inordinate number of first cycle *films noirs* in which the protagonist or another lead character *is an artist*. These films include: *Bluebeard* (1944), *Phantom Lady* (1944), *Scarlet Street* (1945), *Danger Signal* (1945), *The Locket* (1947), *The Two Mrs. Carrolls* (1947), *The Big Clock* (1948), *So Evil My Love* (1949).[38]

At the popular level, these films revived the nineteenth century Romantic notion of the artist as a tortured genius, a trope essential to the rise of modernism in both Europe and America. At the core of this trope is a tendency to associate creativity with mental illness, which predates even the Romantic era. In their seminal study of evolving notions of artistic genius, **Born Under Saturn** (1963), Rudolf and Margot Wittkower trace the conflation of insanity and creativity to Plato's theory of the *furores*, which holds that the true artist creates in a state of inspired madness. When this notion surfaced again in the Renaissance, it was coupled with the medieval idea of the *divino artista*, a corporeal version of God the Architect of the universe, creator and destroyer.[39] By the late nineteenth century, however, morbidity and death were added to the beliefs about the unique temperament of the artist.[40] Consumed by uncontrollable passions, artists were seen as individuals likely to murder or commit suicide. In *Therese Raquin* (1868), Emile Zola, personal friend of the original *peintres maudits*, even suggests that murder is capable of enhancing artistic talent.

The *film noir* artist/protagonist is borne of these pre-existing mythologies. In each case he suffers from some sort of psychosis, and often, he is portrayed as a murderer. For example, in *The Two Mrs. Carrolls*, Humphrey Bogart plays a deranged painter who murders for artistic inspiration, and in *Bluebeard*, the painter/protagonist is an estranged murderer of young women. At certain points in the latter film, however, the protagonist's evil means seem to justify a higher artistic end. *Bluebeard*, *Phantom Lady*, *Scarlet Street*, and *The Locket* each tell the story of an artist who ends (or attempts to end) his life in suicide.

In Fritz Lang's *Scarlet Street*, Edward G. Robinson plays Christopher Cross, an unhappily married bank cashier and struggling painter. After murdering his mistress in fit of jealousy, and he can no longer paint (as it would implicate him in the murder), Cross hangs himself. "There is pity in Lang's *noir* vision of this character," writes Julie Kirgo in **Film Noir: An Encyclopedia to the American Style**, "*Scarlet Street* conveys the attitude that those who live by the imagination can become helpless victims in a cruelly realistic world."[41] In the final scene of *Scarlet Street*, Lang pulls out all stops. After Cross's limp body is taken down, the viewer is presented with a cinematic pieta, wherein the artist is substituted for Christ. Parenthetically speaking, Lang's sympathetic portrayal of the struggling artist may stem from his own failed attempts at being a painter in Munich and Paris from 1910-1913.

The *film noir* artist is often compared to or identified with Vincent van Gogh who, by the late 1930s (thanks in part to the MoMA's retrospective show in 1936 which capitalized on the melodramatic features of van Gogh's life), had come to epitomize *the* tortured genius. Jack Marlow (Franchot Tone), the mad artist in *Phantom Lady*, is purposefully associated with a van Gogh self-portrait. In *The Two Mrs. Carrolls* the association is taken even further. The mad artist's precocious daughter questions him about the relationship between artistic genius and insanity while looking at a book on van Gogh.

Below, *Scarlet Street*: left, Edward G. Robinson as bank clerk-turned-struggling-painter Chris Cross. Right, a mock pieta.

The van Gogh "persona" of the modern artist, revitalized and popularized in *film noir*, spread to *Tiger's Eye*, a widely read artist-run magazine which regularly featured contributions from the Abstract Expressionists.[42] In 1949, the year after Arshile Gorky hanged himself (Abstract Expressionism's first suicide), passages from Antonin Artaud's "Van Gogh, the Man Suicided by Society" appeared in *Tiger's Eye* 7. Evinced in following excerpts is a shift in culpability from artist to society:

> He is a man who has preferred to go mad, in the social sense of the term, rather than forfeit a certain loftier idea of human honor.
>
> Van Gogh sought his own self all his life, with a strange energy and determination. And he did not commit suicide in a fit of madness, in the terror of being unsuccessful, but on the contrary he had just succeeded and had just discovered what he was and who he was, when the general consciousness of society, in order to push him for having torn himself away from it, suicided him.
>
> One does not commit suicide by oneself...but, in the case of suicide, there has to be an army of evil beings to impel the body to the unnatural gesture, to deny itself its own life.[43]

The four Abstract Expressionist painters whose mature works arguably have the most in common with *film noir* visually–Pollock, Rothko, de Kooning, and Kline–are the same artists whose lives, careers and projected public personas most resemble those of artists depicted in *film noir*.[44] While Leja suggests that their adopted *noir* personas were "more important in the culture's absorption of the New York School artists than was their work,"[45] it is more plausible that the two elements worked synergistically.

While *film noir* influenced the Abstract Expressionist's notion of "self" in relation to his public, it also had an opposite effect: educating mass audiences on society's relation to the modern artist and the world of modern art. In this regard, *Crack-Up* (1945) and *Dark Corner* (1946), should be added to those films listed above. As Diane Waldman has observed, films of the forties generally view modern art with hostility and suspicion. Charges against it include: its incomprehensibility, its appeal to a narrow elite, its ugliness, its similarity to the work of children and the mentally deranged, and its political subversiveness.[46] Though predominately negative, this attention ultimately helped to explain and popularize modern art and the modern artist–modern art, it seems, had to be acknowledged before it could be denigrated.

In *Crack-Up*, George Steele (Pat O'Brien), a curator at the "Manhattan Museum," lectures on modern art to group of skeptical museum-goers. He considers himself to be a "people's defender"–and argues that modern art belongs to the "masses," not "sophisticated snobs" like the museum's Director, Mr. Barton (read: Mr. Barr). Also, he attempts to debunk the notion expressed by one minor character that "artists are a no-good bunch." In the end, the film puts the blame on the corrupt world of "high" art and culture, not the modern artist.[47] A similar sort of villainy is attributed to "high" culture in *Dark Corner*. The eventual destruction of the elitist art dealer, Hardy Cathcart (Clifton Webb), who keeps his greatest paintings in a vault, equates to a victory of art "for the people" over art "for the ruling elite."

The notion of the artist as a disturbed loner, an anti-establishmentarian, and a champion of "art for the people" is precisely what was later exploited for political purposes and used in America's cultural Cold War. The American "avant-garde artist" was transformed into the American "individualist." In the final pages of *How New York Stole the Idea of Modern Art*, Serge Guilbaut uses the example of Pollock to explain:

> Pollock was transformed into a symbol, a symbol of man, free but frail.... In contrast to [the totalitarian man] the free world offered the exuberant Jackson Pollock, the very image of exaltation and spontaneity. His psychological problems were but cruel tokens of the hardships of freedom. In his "extremism" and violence Pollock represented the man possessed, the rebel transformed for the sake of the cause into nothing less than a liberal warrior in the Cold War.[48]

As an epilogue to this section, however, I should note Paul Watson's made for BBC docudrama of Mark Rothko's life, *The Rothko Conspiracy* (1983). It is here that the *film noir* protagonist/Abstract Expressionist artist connection is seen in its fullest teleological manifestation–it comes full circle. Baker's film, complete with flashbacks, voice-overs, and low-key lighting, is a true neo-*noir*. Furthermore, Rothko is associated with van Gogh from beginning to end. In short, the film gives dramatic form to Lee Seldes' claim in *The Legacy of Mark Rothko* that Rothko's suicide was the "ultimate work of art, the final dramatic gesture, the true, most poignant action painting."[49]

Willem de Kooning's *Femmes Fatales*

From 1950-1953 Willem de Kooning devoted himself exclusively to painting the female figure. Art history has sought to connect de Kooning's *Women* series to ancient female representations such as Mesopotamian fertility figures or the *Venus of Willendorf*. This in part has to do with de Kooning's comments on his *Women*, which are frequently taken out of context, and consequently, misconstrued. In an interview with David Sylvester, de Kooning admitted that his *Women* "had to do with idea of the idol and the oracle–the hilariousness of it."[50]

What, exactly, is so hilarious about the idea of the "idol and the oracle?" It is likely that de Kooning is making a reference to the work of the early Abstract Expressionists (i.e., the Mythmakers). What de Kooning loathed was their insistence on using a set of archaic symbols and forms to express modern man's condition, as well their pompous transcendental rhetoric about their "spiritual kinship with primitive art." De Kooning made it clear that he had no "nostalgia" for their "idols or oracles." Forms, he insisted, should express "the emotion of concrete experience," and his own female figures, he said, were "wrapped up in the melodrama of vulgarity."[51] De Kooning's "oracles," by his own admission, were women of popular culture and imagination.

An ardent cinema fan, de Kooning turned to film (specifically, the representation of women in film) for inspiration.[52] After interviewing de Kooning in 1953, William Seitz wrote: "De Kooning's heroine is not wife, mother, or even mistress but...*the ideal of a million cinema going males*–the indulgent strumpet, a carnal product of wish fulfillment and commercialism, frightening in its orgiastic gaiety."[53] Without saying the word, Seitz describes De Kooning's *Women* as prototypical *femmes fatales*. De Kooning frequently referred to his *Women* (in the gritty lingo of *film noir*) as "big city dames."

A comparison of the typical *film noir femme fatale*, epitomized by Phyllis Dietrichson (Barbara Stanwyck) in *Double Indemnity* de Kooning's *Woman I* [Figure 4] reveals several overt formalistic and thematic similarities. Both women are characterized by their devious smiles, protruding breasts, and scant clothing. Introduced to the spectator through a low-angle shot, Mrs. Dietrichson, like *Woman I*, dominates the observer below. Dietrichson's face is framed by patches of darkness, as is *Woman I*'s. Here, de Kooning mimics the effects of low-key lighting. Also, de Kooning's *Woman I* seems to be historio-specific insofar as she wears an ankle bracelet, a popular accessory for women in the Forties. In *Double Indemnity* Mrs. Dietrichson wears one which Walter Neff (the protagonist) admits he "can't stop thinking about."

Through its depiction of the *femme fatale, film noir* gave shape to what E. Ann Kaplan has referred to as the "crisis in masculinity" that came with the entrance of women into the work force during World War II. Film historian Frank Krutnik writes:

Left, Phyllis Dietrichson (Barabara Stanwyck) on an interior balcony in *Double Indemnity*.

Opposite, Figure 4: Willem de Kooning's *Woman, I*.

> With the mass drafting of men into the armed services, one of the consequences of the war time expansion of the national economy was that women were overtly encouraged, as part of their "patriotic duty," to enter the work force rather than devoting themselves exclusively to home and family. During the war years, the female labor force increased by 6.5 million (or 57 percent), and by 1945 there were almost 20 million women workers in the USA. The new prominence of women in the economic realm was matched by a wide-scale and rapid redefinition of their place within culture. These changes set into motion a temporary confusion in regard to traditional conceptions of sexual role and sexual identity, for both men and women, but this in itself was not allowed any significant articulation in the war-directed ideological consolidation.[54]

The first "significant articulation" of the changing "conceptions of sexual role and sexual identity" caused by World War II occurred in *film noir*.

It is possible, however, that de Kooning's *femme fatales* issued forth from a more personal "crisis in masculinity." Elaine, Willem's wife, had begun writing for *Art News* in 1949 under the sponsorship of Tom Hess (with whom she was rumored to be having an affair) and was on the verge of becoming a real art world power. At the time Willem was painting his *Women*, Elaine's career as a painter was also taking off–she had been selected for the Koontz "New Talent" show in May 1950, and her early expressionistic sports paintings were large, forceful, and well received.[55]

As mentioned in the previous section, art is a common gambit in first cycle *films noirs*. Comprising a significant subsection of these films are *films noirs* in which the *femme fatale is also a painting*–e.g., *I Wake Up Screaming* (1942), *Experiment Perilous* (1944), *Woman in the Window* (1945), *Laura* (1945), *Dark Corner* (1946). The common motif of the painted portrait, occurring within the film's diegetic space, was acknowledged early on in Raymond Durgnat's seminal article, "Paint it Black: The Family Tree of *Film noir*" (1970), but it was not until Janey Place's "Women in *Film noir*" (1978) that it began to receive the kind of attention it deserves.[56] These films play off the inherent duality of art–it is unclear if the woman in the portrait is an illusion (frequently oneiric), or real. The woman in the portrait remains elusive and unattainable throughout the duration of the film. De Kooning is after the same effect–his *Women* play off of, and ultimately, derive their emotional strength from, a manipulation of this unresolved ambiguity. Above all, de Kooning wanted to paint, in his own words, "something that I can never be sure of, and no one else can either."[57]

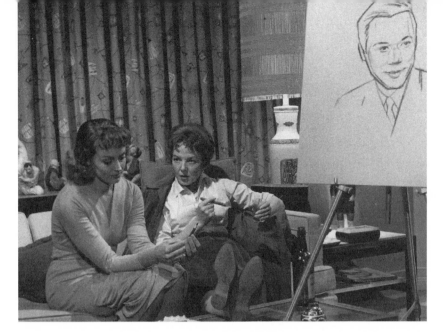

Above, woman as artist, next to a sketch for a portrait of her Asian lover, Christine Downs (Victoria Shaw) seeks advice from Mac (Anna Lee) in Samuel Fuller's *The Crimson Kimono*. Below, cops and psychiatrists obsessed with paintings.

Left, Lt. Ed Cornell (Laird Cregar) gazes at Vicky (Carole Landis) in *I Wake Up Screaming*.

Above, psychiatrist Richard Wanley (Edward G. Robinson) meets Alice Reed (Joan Bennett) in *Woman in the Window*.

Left, Det. Mark McPherson (Dana Andrews) is haunted by the painting of murder victim Laura Hunt (Gene Tierney) in *Laura*.

Mark Rothko's Troubled Vision

In the 1940s, Michael Leja posits, American society's "dominant models of subjectivity were losing credibility."[58] The Abstract Expressionist painters' initial experiments with new "models of subjectivity" involved the evocation of primitive forms, allusions to Greek myths and dramas, and Jungian archetypes. In their mature works, however, they discarded these mediating symbols in hopes of connecting with the spectator more directly. The Abstract Expressionist artist most obsessed with this idea was Mark Rothko. In 1949, he wrote: "The progression of a painter's work as it travels in time from point to point, will be toward clarity: toward the elimination of all obstacles between the painter and his idea and between the idea and the observer."[59] Rothko thought that a painting should "command" the observer's visual experience. Moreover, he felt the best way to experience his paintings was to be surrounded by them. Rothko wanted the observer, upon seeing one of his paintings, to have the same experience he had while making the painting.

Art history has failed to investigate the possibility that popular visual culture—specifically, *film noir*—may have provided Rothko with an impetus.[60] In 1947, Panofsky observed:

> Movies have the power...to convey psychological experiences by directly projecting their content on the screen, substituting, as it were, the eye of the beholder for the consciousness of the character (as when the imaginings and hallucinations of the drunkard in the otherwise overrated *Lost Weekend* appear as stark realities instead of being described by mere words).[61]

That Panofsky should choose a scene from an immensely popular first cycle *film noir* to illustrate his point is not surprising. *Film noir* introduced to mass audiences artistic attempts at conveying "psychological experiences" more directly, through the use of "subjective camera." By aligning the camera with the protagonist's point-of-view, the subjective camera grants the observer a first-person perspective, a privileged position both "in" the film, and "in" the mind of the character. In addition to the *Lost Weekend* (1945), the most striking examples of subjective camera can be seen in *Murder My Sweet* (1944), *My Name is Julia Ross* (1945), *The Spiral Staircase* (1946) *Dark Passage* (1947), *Lady in the Lake* (1947), *Possessed* (1947), *The High Wall* (1947), and *The Dark Past* (1948).

Film noir's subjective camera, writes film historian J. P. Telotte, "was developed primarily as a way of more forcefully involving viewers in the narrative; but as a side effect it also suggested an alternative to the way we usually see."[62] The questioning of visual experience, or "the way we usually see," is central also to modernist painting. T. J. Clark's thoughts on this subject are worth quoting at length:

Something decisive happened in the history of art around Manet which set painting and the other arts upon a new course. Perhaps the change can be described as a kind of skepticism, or at least an unsureness, as to the nature of representation in art...the steadfast gaze rather quickly gave way to uncertainty. Doubts about vision became doubts about almost everything involved in the act of painting; and in time the uncertainty became a value in its own right; we could almost say that it became an aesthetic.[63]

Rothko's multiform paintings are formal explorations of modern painting's preoccupation with the uncertainty of vision. In these paintings Rothko makes the act of seeing his actual subject. His goal, he once claimed, was to "convey a new vision."[64] It is not surprising that Rothko chose to title a 1946 abstracted self-portrait *Tiresias*, after the prophet of Greek mythology who began to see only after he was blinded by Hera. The revelatory nature of blinded sight was a theme embraced by French Surrealists in the Thirties, and it reappears in *film noir*. For example, in the opening scene of *Murder My Sweet* (1944), a blinded Philip Marlowe (Dick Powell) sits at a small desk, while others in the room accuse him of murder. Prompted by policemen, he begins to recount his story. Blindness has allowed him to see things more clearly; it is only after losing his sight that he is able to put things "in perspective." Other titles allude to *film noir*'s fascination with

Below, "pure abstraction": the smoke-filled spotlight before a performance in *Gilda*.

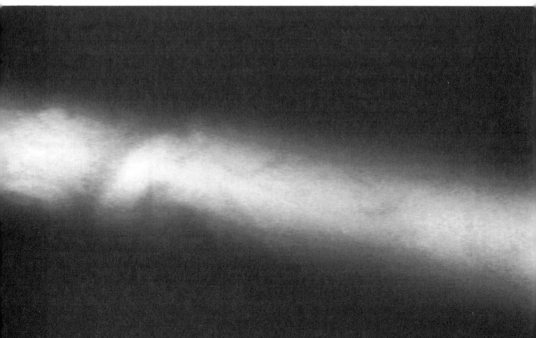

blindness or challenged sight: *Gaslight* (1944), *Strange Illusion* (1945), *The Unseen* (1945), and *Blind Spot* (1947).

When looking at Rothko's paintings, it is helpful to keep in mind Michael Baxandall's notion of the "period eye," which, essentially, refers to "the visual skills of an audience at any given time and place."[65] The subjective camera expanded the visual skills of American audiences in the forties by frequently presenting them with visions that were unclear–blurred images, wavy patterns, or out-of-focus distortions. Often, these occur at climatic transitional moments when the protagonist experienced loss of consciousness, reverie, or sudden terror.[66] Occasionally, audience members were even asked to revel in pure abstraction. However, since these abstractions were embedded within the overall narrative structure of a film, they were quickly explained, and given meaning. The significance of this is twofold: *film noir* symbolized and codified subjective processes and, in so doing, it converted abstraction into a language legible to mass audiences.

Rothko relied on a similar "soft-focus" effect when he painted his multiforms. Through his nebulous abstractions, Rothko attempted to convey "basic human emotions–tragedy, ecstasy, doom, and so on." In the end, he accomplished this by relying on the same strategy as *film noir* filmmakers. His forms possess the same "in-betweeness" as the shots that *film noir* filmmakers used to challenge the observer's efforts to see clearly. As Jaques Lacan and other post-Freudians have emphasized, the act of seeing plays an essential role in an individual's construction of his sense of self. When the way in which one sees is challenged, it follows, then one's identity is called into question. In this sense, the *film noir*'s subjective camera and Rothko's multiforms accomplish similar ends: they frustrate our desire to see clearly, and consequently, cause us to look into the depths of ourselves. *Film noir* inspired Rothko's attempts to connect with his audience at the level of self by making the subjective processes of seeing the subject of his art. Moreover, it engendered formalistic devices for the visual representation of subjectivity.

Franz Kline's Black-and-White Abstractions and the *Noir* City

As mentioned in the introduction, around 1948 a new trend began to appear in *film noir*. Inspired by Italian neo-realist dramas like Rossellini's *Open City* and De Sica's *Bicycle Thief* (which emphasized on-location photography, sunlit urban landscapes, and deteriorating architectural forms) *film noir* filmmakers focused their efforts on capturing the essence of life in the American metropolis. In numerous instances, this neo-realist influence merged with a residual German Expressionistic devotion to oblique angles, menacing shafts of light and dark, and claustrophobic spaces. *Film noir*'s finest examples from this period include: Jules Dassin's *The Naked City* (1948), Robert Siodmak's *Cry of the City* (1948), Henry Hathaway's *Call Northside 777* (1948), Ted Tetzlaff's *The Window* (1949), Rudolph Maté's *Union Station* (1950), and Vincent Sherman's *The Damned Don't Cry* (1950).

The urbanization of *film noir* prefigured the urbanization of Abstract Expressionist painting. In 1950 Franz Kline moved to the forefront of the Abstract Expressionist movement with his gestural black-and-white paintings. Initially, contemporary critics separated Franz Kline's black-and-white abstractions from the popular cultural forms with which they had so much in common by associating them with Japanese calligraphy. However, Kline quickly took steps to deny associations of this sort. "Calligraphy is writing," he told one interviewer, "and I'm not writing." He maintained that his paintings were not two-dimensional—but rather, "finite spaces."[67] Kline's "finite spaces," it can be argued, describe the same urban space that appears repeatedly in *films noirs* made from 1948-1950.

"Since the time of the Ashcan School," William Seitz reminds us, "the appearance and the spirit of New York City, as subject-matter and conditioning milieu, has been instrumental in forming American painting."[68] Early on, Clement Greenberg acknowledged Abstract Expressionism's involvement with the idea of the modern metropolis. In his 1947 article, "The Present Prospects of American Painting and Sculpture," he claimed that Pollock's art was full of "Gothic-ness, paranoia, resentment...violence, exasperation and stridency...." In other words, it was "an attempt to cope with urban life."[69] Kline's mature works are most accurately seen as a continuation of the influence of New York City on American painting. In the Thirties and early Forties Kline was an American Scene painter of local landscapes, portraits, and trains. Sometime in 1948, however, Kline began to devote himself to capturing the "spirit" of New York City. Commenting on Kline's representational New York scenes after his death, Elaine de Kooning wrote:

> The extraordinary memory for essential gesture, structure, and detail that made him a great mimic, enabled him to reconstruct sweeping cityscapes in his studio—the old Ninth Avenue El, Chatham Square, Hudson Street, the Fulton Fish Market—in characterizations so keen that any New Yorker would immediately recognize the specific neighborhood, from its feel rather than from any circumstantial detail.[70]

Increasingly, Kline experimented with ways of evoking the city through (in de Kooning's words) an "essential gesture," "structure" or "detail." After limiting his palette to black and white, he turned to the visual traditions of film (and photography) for inspiration. Kline finally arrived at the condensed visual metaphor of the city popularized by *film noir*; namely, the distorted and imperfect black-and-white grid. His cityscapes, expressed through this visual metaphor, took on a drastically different feel. Through this new visual metaphor Kline was able to express a kinetic energy that hitherto belonged exclusively to the medium of film.

Kline went to the movies "at least once per week—usually twice." One of his favorite movies was the *film noir* forerunner, *I am a Fugitive From a Chain Gang*.[71]

Mervyn LeRoy's film is a stylistic *tour de force*; his use of line for purposes of disturbing the viewer is relentless. From 1948-50 *film noir* filmmakers utilized line in a similar manner. In their films, the protagonist or other leading characters frequently find themselves imprisoned by girders, bridges, fire escapes, or radio towers. These structures, seen through extreme high-angle or low-angle shots, are juxtaposed against white backgrounds of sky or city street. They have the typical *noir* effect of disorienting and disturbing the viewer. They immediately bring to mind Kline's *Mahoning* (1951-1956) [Figure 5]. Kline always maintained that he did not paint specific "bridge constructions" or "sky scrapers;" rather, he said, he painted "experiences."[72] Translated to the viewer through violent black and white configurations, these "experiences" had much in common with those facing the typical *film noir* protagonist. Kline sounds more like a *film noir* director than a painter when he says, "to think of ways of disorganizing can be a way of organizing, you know."[73]

David Anfam points out that "as much, if not more, of Kline's art from 1950 onwards belongs to photography's New York School as it does to that other New York School of painting."[74] The New York School photographers frequented screenings at the Museum of Modern Art and were influenced also by the prevailing *noir* aesthetic. In **The New York School: Photographs 1936-1963**, Jane Livingston writes:

Below, Figure 5: *Mahoning* by Franz Kline.

Opposite, a man in flight on a steel staircase in *The Naked City*.

> If there is a single artistic phenomenon with which these photo-
> graphers are identified, it was the short-lived and hard-to-define
> movement in American cinema known as *film noir*. Those among
> our photographers who grew up in New York were practically
> weaned on movies.... The emergence of *film noir* during and after
> World War II...fed into the sources assimilated by these
> photographers.... Not only the visual look of *film noir*, but its
> themes of corruption in high places and the vulnerability and dignity
> of the little man, are more naturally allied to the belief system of
> these photographers than is the superficially mythic Hollywood fair
> of the standard classical cinema.[75]

This connection is relevant to our present study because it supports the argument
that during the 1940s, contrary to Greenbergian claims of media "purity" and
"uniqueness," the boundaries of painting, *film noir*, and photography were
blurred—artistic attitudes, subjects and forms overlapped. Franz Kline's close
friendship with the New York School photographers Aaron Siskind and Robert
Frank facilitated this sort of artistic interchange.

Conclusion:

> Today there is no denying that narrative films are not only
> "art"—not often good art, to be sure but this applies to other media
> as well—but also, besides architecture, cartooning, and "commercial
> design," the only visual art entirely alive. The "movies" have
> reestablished that dynamic contact between art production and

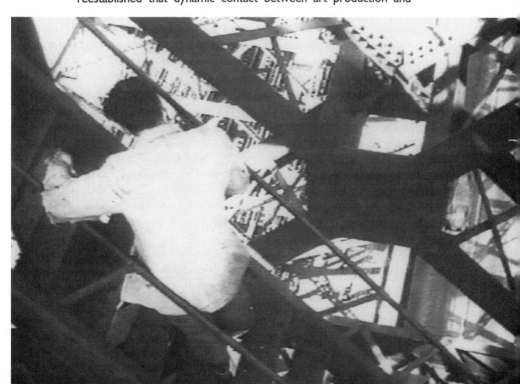

consumption which...is sorely attenuated, if not entirely
interrupted, in many other fields of artistic endeavor. Whether we
like it or not, it is the movies that mold, more than any other single
force, the opinions, the tastes, the language, the dress, the
behavior, and even the physical appearance of a public comprising
more than 60 per cent of the population of the earth.[76]

—Erwin Panofsky (1947)

If art history is to more accurately locate Abstract Expressionist painting within its
social and (popular) cultural context, it must take into consideration the ubiquity
of "the movies" in the world from which it emerged. *Film noir*, the dominant style
of movie from 1944-1950, is largely responsible for "molding" the visual
"language" and "taste" of the Abstract Expressionist painters and viewing public
alike. In 1944, Robert Motherwell (Abstract Expressionism's mouthpiece)
articulated the dilemma facing the modern American artist. "The artist's
problem," he wrote "is with what to identify himself.... The popular association
with modern art is its remoteness from the symbols and values of the majority of
men."[77] In their search for "the symbols and values of the majority of men,"
Abstract Expressionist painters turned to film for inspiration. Eventually, they
incorporated elements of *film noir's* pre-established iconography—of character
types (e.g., the *noir* protagonist and the *femme fatale*), cinematic devices (e.g.,
subjective camera) and forms (e.g., the web, the labyrinth, the vortex, and the
city)—in hopes of communicating their subject matter more directly.

The influence of *film noir*, therefore, is not only crucial to our understanding of
Abstract Expressionism, it sheds light on the perennially neglected give-and-take
relationship between cinema and American painting. Also, Abstract Expressionism's relation to *film noir* provides strong evidence that popular visual culture can
stimulate avant-garde art, and, accordingly, challenges common notions about
how the latter engenders the former.

Abstract Expressionism, while standing as the epitome of high modernism,
should be recognized as pointing the way in some important respects toward the
artistic development of postmodernism.[78] Moreover, Pop Art does not represent
a clean break from Abstract Expressionism. Art history should take its lessons
from Andy Warhol's response to Abstract Expressionism. Warhol, perhaps more
than anyone, saw (what T.J. Clark has described as) the "vulgar" aspects of Abstract Expressionism—its affinities to the medium of film, its courting of melodrama, its commodity of forms, its "celebrity artists," and so on. Warhol's earliest
publicly displayed silk-screen "paintings" (which were simply enlarged film stills)
can be seen as an attempt to reestablish painting's priority over the medium of
film, not vice versa. And if Abstract Expressionism did, as I have tried to demonstrate, transfer some of the "unique and specific possibilities of film" to painting,
then it was Warhol who reversed the process and gave film those qualities tradi-

tionally associated with painting. His film *Empire* (1964), a single static eight-hour shot of the Empire State Building, defies description as a "motion" picture.[79]

The subject matter of Warhol's work from 1961-1964 is also worth noting. "What this body of painting adds up to," Thomas Crow has observed:

> is a kind of *peinture noire* in the sense that we apply the term to the *film noir* genre of the forties and early fifties–a stark, disabused, pessimistic vision of American life, produced from the knowing rearrangement of pulp materials by an artist who did not opt for the easier paths of irony or condescension.... By 1965, of course, this episode was largely over: the flowers, cow wallpaper, silver pillows, and the like have little to do with the imagery under discussion here. Then the clichés began to ring true. But there was for a time, in the work of 1961-1964, a threat to create a true "pop" art in the most positive sense of that term–a pulp-derived, bleakly monochrome vision that held, however tenuous the grip, to an all-but-buried tradition of truth telling in American commercial culture.[80]

The question that I have tried to open space around is: To what extent can Abstract Expressionist painting be thought of as the first example of *peinture noire*?

Appendix A:

Early *films noirs* in which either the protagonist or one of the main characters is a painter:

The Big Clock (John Farrow, 1948)

Bluebeard (Edgar G. Ulmer, 1944)

Body and Soul (Robert Rossen, 1947)

Crossfire (Edward Dmytryk, 1947)

Danger Signal (Robert Florey, 1945)

Dark Passage (Delmar Daves, 1947)

Destination Murder (Edward L. Cahn, 1950)

The Locket (John Brahm, 1947)

Scarlet Street (Fritz Lang, 1945)

So Evil My Love (Lewis Allen, 1949)

The Two Mrs. Carrolls (Peter Godfrey, 1947)

Whiplash (Lewis Seiler, 1948)

The Woman on the Beach (Jean Renoir, 1947)

Other Artists:

Angels Over Broadway (Ben Hecht, 1940) Playwright.

Black Angel (Roy Chanslor, 1946) Songwriter.

Blindspot (Robert Gordon, 1947) Mystery writer.

Blues in the Night (Anatole Litvak, 1941) Blues musician.

Daisy Kenyon (Otto Preminger, 1947), Fashion designer.

Deception (Irving Rapper, 1946) Music teacher.

Detour (Edgar G. Ulmer, 1945) Pianist and nightclub singer.

A Double Life (George Cukor, 1948) Actor.

Hangover Square (John Brahm, 1945) Composer.

Hollywood Story (William Castle, 1951) Director.

House by the River (Fritz Lang, 1950) Writer.

Humoresque (Jean Negulesco, 1947) Violinist.

In a Lonely Place (Nicholas Ray, 1950) Hollywood screenwriter.

I Wake Up Screaming (H. Bruce Humberstone, 1941) Actress.

Jealousy (Gustav Machaty, 1945) Writer.

The Man I Love (Raoul Walsh, 1946) Torch singer.

The Mask of Diijon (Lewin Landers, 1946) Vaudeville magician.

The Mask of Dimitrios (Jean Negulesco, 1944) Mystery writer.

Mystery Street (John Sturges, 1950) Architect.

Nightmare (Maxwell Shane, 1956), Musician.

Night Without Sleep (Roy Ward Baker, 1952) Songwriter.

Nocturne (Edwin L. Marin, 1946) Composer.

Above, eccentric artist Louise Patterson (Elsa Lancaster) in *The Big Clock*. Opposite, Hugo Haas as pianist Paul Marvan and Cleo Moore as Margo in *Strange Fascination*.

Phantom Lady (Robert Siodmak, 1944) Sculptor.
The Second Woman (James V. Kern, 1951) Architect.
Secret Beyond the Door (Fritz Lang, 1948) Architect.
Shakedown (Joseph Pevney, 1950) Photographer.
Specter of the Rose (Ben Hecht, 1946) Ballet dancer.
Strange Fascination (Hugo Haas, 1952) Pianist.
The Strip (Leslie Kardos, 1951) Jazz musician.
Sudden Fear (David Miller, 1952) Actor.
Sunset Boulevard (Billy Wilder, 1950) Hollywood screenwriter.
The Velvet Touch (John Gage, 1948) Actress.
Vicki (Harry Horner, 1953), Actress.
Voice in the Wind (Arthur Ripley, 1944) Concert pianist.
Young Man with a Horn (Michael Curtiz, 1949) Jazz musician.

Paintings and Portraits:

The Big Clock (John Farrow, 1948)
The Big Heat (Fritz Lang, 1953)
The Dark Corner (Henry Hathaway, 1946)
The Dark Mirror (Robert Siodmak, 1946)
Experiment Perilous (Jacques Tourner, 1944)

I Wake Up Screaming (H. Bruce Humberstone, 1942)

Kiss Me Deadly (Robert Aldrich, 1955)

Laura (Otto Preminger, 1944)

Night and the City (Jules Dassin, 1948)

The Paradine Case (Alfred Hitchcock, 1948)

The Picture of Dorian Gray (Albert Lewin, 1945)

Portrait of Jennie (William Dieterle, 1948)

Rebecca (Alfred Hitchcock, 1940)

Scarlet Street (Fritz Lang, 1946)

Suspicion (Alfred Hitchcock, 1941)

The Two Mrs. Carrolls (Peter Godfrey, 1947)

The Unsuspected (Michael Curtiz, 1947)

While the City Sleeps (Fritz Lang, 1956)

Woman in the Window (Fritz Lang, 1945)

A Woman's Vengeance (Zolton Korda, 1948)

Vertigo (Alfred Hitchcock, 1958)

Notes

1. For a related, prefatory account of the merging of American painting with Hollywood, popular culture, and certain modes of mass production see: Erika Doss, **Benton, Pollock, and the Politics of Modernism: From Regionalism to Abstract Expressionism** (Chicago: University of Chicago Press, 1991). For more on Hopper's relationship to film noir see Gail Levin, "Edward Hopper: The Influence of Theater and Film," *Arts Magazine* 55 (October 1980); Erika Doss, "Edward Hopper, Nighthawks, and *Film Noir*" in *Postscript: Essays in Film and the Humanities* 2 no. 2 (Winter 1983); 14-36; Slavoj Zizek's brief discussion in **Enjoy Your Symptom: Jaques Lacan in Hollywood and Out** (London and New York: Routledge, 1992), 152-54; Beth Venn's exhibition brochure for **Edward Hopper and the American Imagination** (New York: Whitney Museum of American Art, 1995) or Kate Rubin's article of the same name in *Antiques* (August 1995), 166-175; and more recently, Nicholas Christopher's **Somewhere in the Night: Film Noir and the American City** (New York: Henry Holt, 1997), 15-16, 60, 103, 148. Christopher recounts the anecdote of the time when director Abraham Polonsky, dissatisfied with the filming of *Force of Evil* (1948), took his Director of Photography, George Barnes, to an Hopper exhibit and demanded, "This is how I want the picture to look." (p.15) For more on Reginald Marsh's influence see: Foster Hirsch, **Film Noir: The Dark Side of the Screen** (New York: Da Capo Press, 1981), 79-83.

2. Art historian David Anfam has written on Abstract Expressionism and *film noir*, albeit at a more cursory level. See **Abstract Expressionism** (London: Thames and Hudson, 1990), p. 131; "Beginning at the End: The Extremes of Abstract Expressionism," in **American Art in the 20th Century: Painting and Sculpture 1913-1993**, eds., Christos M. Joachimides and Norman Rosenthal (Munich: Prestel-Verlag, 1993), 85-91, "Interrupted Stories: Reflections on Abstract Expressionism and Narrative," in **American**

Above, *Portrait of Jennie*: struggling artist Eben Adams (Joseph Cotten) is haunted by a girl whose portrait he must paint.

Abstract Expressionism, ed., David Thistlewood (Liverpool: Liverpool University Press, 1993), 21-39, and his review of Leja's book in *Art in America* (October 1994), 37-39. Also see Caroline A. Jones' ***Machine in the Studio: Constructing the Postwar American Artist*** (Chicago: The University of Chicago Press, 1996), 35, 384n., 72-80, and Ann Eden Gibson's ***Abstract Expressionism: Other Politics*** (New Haven: Yale University Press, 1997), 53.

3. Michael Leja, ***Reframing Abstract Expressionism: Subjectivity and Painting in the 1940s*** (New Haven: Yale University Press, 1993), 110-11.

4. William C. Seitz, *Abstract-Expressionist Painting in America: An Interpretation Based on the Work and Thought of Six Key Figures*. Ph.D dissertation, Princeton University (May 1955), 422.

5. Thomas Y. Levin, "Iconology at the Movies: Panofsky's Film Theory," *The Yale Journal of Criticism* 9 no. 1 (1996), 27. For more on the history of The Museum of Modern Art's Film Department and Film Library see Mary Lea Bandy's "Nothing Sacred: 'Jock Whitney Snares Antiques for Museum:' The Founding of The Museum of Modern Art Film Library" in *The Museum of Modern Art at Mid-Century: Continuity and Change (Studies in Modern Art 5)* (New York: The Museum of Modern Art, 1995), 75-103. In passing, Bandy mentions the MoMA's 1940 film series, "Abstract Films." The relation of these films to Abstract Expressionist painting warrants further investigation. Perhaps the best place to begin is at the end of William Moritz's "Abstract Film and Color Music" in *The Spiritual in Art: Abstract Painting 1890-1985* (New York: Abbeville Press, 1986), 309-10.

6. Levin, p. 27.

7. Erwin Panofsky, "Style and Medium in the Motion Pictures," *Critique* 1:3 (1947), 27-28, reprinted in *Film Theory and Criticism*, eds. Gerald Mast, Marshall Cohen, and Leo Braudy (New York and Oxford: Oxford University Press, 1992), 240.

8. Levin, p. 32.

9. See Lawrence Alloway's *Violent America: The Movies 1946-1964* (New York: the Museum of Modern Art, 1971), 41-61, and Colin McArthur's *Underworld USA* (New York: Viking, 1972). Alloway and McArthur are the first writers who speak of *film noir* in terms of its specific iconography.

10. Michael Leja, *Reframing*, 202. At this point, the relation of my argument to Leja's requires some clarification. Leja, employing structuralism and post-structuralism, is chiefly concerned with how knowledge and art are affected by prevailing ideologies. Consequently, he situates both Abstract Expressionist painting and *film noir* in the context of an all-pervasive "cultural production" he calls "Modern Man discourse"—a dominant ideology of the 1940s which developed in and around literature (popular texts on anthropology, psychology, and philosophy) focusing on "the nature, mind, and behavior of 'modern man.'" (p.7) The strength of Leja's argument is its premise that the Abstract Expressionists incorporated preexisting popular cultural forms and ideas into their art. However, in my opinion, Leja runs into problems when he tries to combine intellectual history with art history. While his Modern Man discursive frame works effectively as "a portmanteau device for wrapping disparate goods" (the description is David Anfam's), it inevitably "frames" out some the most important *visual* similarities that exist between Abstract Expressionist painting and *film noir*. Unfortunately, Leja treats paintings and films as "texts" instead of objects of visual experience. *Film noir* and Abstract Expressionist painting, I think, have more in common with each other than either has with the popular literature that Leja uses to construct his Modern Man discursive frame. Moreover, two of the texts he cites—James Harvey Robinson's *The Mind in the Making* (1921) and Horace Carncross' *The Escape from the Primitive* (1926)—seem somewhat anachronistic to the art in question. I am not denying that both *film noir* and Abstract Expressionism were connected to an extant "dominant ideology"—what concerns me here is the extent to which *film noir* and Abstract Expressionist painting translated

this ideology into a similar set of widely recognized visual metaphors. For this reason I have chosen to focus first and foremost on the visual evidence (i.e., film stills and paintings).

11. Paul Kerr, "Out of What Past? Notes on the B *film noir*," in **Film Noir Reader**, eds. Alain Silver and James Ursini (New York: Limelight Editions, 1996), 119. Also, during this period there was, more generally speaking, an expanding interest in the artistic relationship of painting and film. See, for example, **Art in Cinema**, edited by Frank Stauffer (San Francisco: Art in Cinema Society, San Francisco Museum of Art, 1947).

12. April Kingsley, **The Turning Point: The Abstract Expressionists and the Transformation of American Art** (New York: Simon and Schuster, 1992), 29.

13. James Naremore, "American *Film noir*: The History of an Idea," *Film Quarterly* 49 no. 2, (Winter 1995), 12-27. Also see David Bordwell, Janet Staiger, and Kristin Thompson, **The Classical Hollywood Cinema: Film Style and Mode of Production to 1960** (New York: Columbia University Press, 1985). On the difficulty of defining *film noir* the authors write: "The problem resembles one in art history, that of defining 'non-classical' styles. Gombrich reminds us that most style terms—Gothic, Mannerist, Baroque—originally characterized a new style solely by its repudiation of a norm. Such terms of exclusion cannot be translated into a set of traits for the style in question because the original epithet intended no more than negative characterization. ('Gothic' simply meant 'barbarous'.) Historically, however, critics tend to take the term as a positive definition and try to find the essential traits of the style." (p. 75)

14. James Damico, "*Film noir*: A Modest Proposal," in **Film Noir Reader**, 103.

15. Michael Leja, **Reframing**, 112.

16. This part of my essay is indebted to David Anfam's discussion of *in medias res* in "Beginning at the End: The Extremes of Abstract Expressionism" in **American Art in the 20th Century: Painting and Sculpture 1913-1993**, 85-91.

17. Quoted in **Abstract Expressionism: A Critical Record** Eds. David and Cecile Shapiro (Cambridge: Cambridge University Press, 1990), 358.

18. Yves-Alain Bois, "Painting: The Task of Mourning," in **Painting as Model** (Cambridge: MIT Press, 1990), 230. Modern painting's inevitable apocalypse is the underlying theme of Robert Aldrich's *noir* swan song, *Kiss Me Deadly* (1955).

19. T.J. Clark, "In Defense of Abstract Expressionism." *October* 69 (Summer 1994), 24-48.

20. Meyer Schapiro, "Abstract Art," reprinted in **Modern Art: 19th and 20th Centuries** (New York: George Braziller, 1979), 218.

21. Clement Greenberg, "Modernist Painting," *Arts Yearbook* 4 (1961), 109-116. From the newsreel scenes in Lang's *Fury* (1936) to the final moments of Wilder's *Sunset Boulevard* (1950), *film noir* has taken as its subject an implicit self-reflexive critique of the medium of film. See, for example, J.P. Telotte's "Self-Portrait: Painting and the *Film noir*," *Smithsonian Studies in American Art* 3:1 (Winter 1989); Laurence E. Soroka's unpublished Ph.D. dissertation, **Hollywood Modernism: Self-Consciousness and the Hollywood-on-Hollywood Film Genre**, Emory University (1983); and Richard Dorfman's article, "Conspiracy City," in the *Journal of Popular Film and Television* 7:4 (1980), in which he concludes, "*film noir* is the clearest example of the self-reflexive practices of

advanced European narrative ineluctably influencing the more intelligent filmmaker working within the Hollywood system." (p. 47)

22. Michael Leja, **Reframing**, 34.

23. Quoted in Leja, p. 313. Tyler was not the only film critic drawn to Pollock's paintings. See, for example, Manny Farber's article in *New Republic*, June 25, 1945, pp. 871-72, in which he uses a series of *noir*-ish adjectives to praise Pollock's "masterful violence," "hectic action," "bleeding" paint, and "emphatic contrasts." Or Gregory Thomas Taylor's unpublished Ph.D. dissertation, **Constructive Criticism: Manny Farber, Parker Tyler and the Emergence of an American Film Culture**, University of Wisconsin-Madison (1993).

24. Raymond Borde and Etienne Chaumeton, "Towards a Definition of *Film Noir*," Trans. by Alain Silver in **Film Noir Reader**, 24.

25. Quoted in Michael Leja, **Reframing**, 323.

26. Janey Place and Lowell Peterson, "Some Visual Motifs of *Film noir*." Reprinted in **Film Noir Reader**, 68.

27. Leja, **Reframing**, 308. Also, this play between the horizontal and the vertical is characteristic of the aerial footage included in World War II newsreels regularly shown before feature films. It is not surprising that critic Henry McBride, writing in 1950 (*New York Sun*, December 23), described one of Pollock's drip paintings as "a flat, war-shattered city, possibly Hiroshima, as seen from a great height." Quoted in Krauss' **Optical Unconscious** (p. 245).

28. Harold Rosenberg, "The American Action Painters." *Art News* (December 1952), 23.

29. For Krauss, Pollock's violent painting process takes on a specific dramatic form—one which happens to fit our working definition of *film noir*. This drama involves Pollock (the protagonist), Fame (the seductive object of Pollock's desire) and Picasso (Pollock's rival in his quest for Fame). In Pollock's case, Krauss maintains, "the cast of characters eventually narrowed to one," and consequently, his painting process becomes "a violent rivalry with himself." (p. 278) Like the typical *noir* protagonist, Pollock participates in his own demise.

30. Erwin Panofsky, "Style and Medium in the Motion Pictures," reprinted in **Film Theory and Criticism**, 235. Also see, Herbert Read's "Towards a Film Aesthetic," *Film Quarterly* 1 (Autumn 1932), 7-11, in which he writes: "The film is the art of space-time; it is a space-time continuum."

31. William Wright, "An Interview with Jackson Pollock," in **Abstract Expressionism: A Critical Record**, 359.

32. Dore Ashton, **Abstract Expressionism: A Cultural Reckoning** (New York: Viking Press, 1973), 38.

33. For more on Falkenberg's role see, "Notes on the Genesis of an Art Film," in Barbara Rose, ed., **Pollock Painting** (New York: Agrinde Publications Ltd., 1980).

34. This is not the only *noir*-derived scene in the Namuth/Falkenberg film. In **Machine in the Studio: Constructing the Postwar American Artist** (Chicago: University of Chicago Press, 1996) Caroline Jones observes that after the opening scene, "Namuth and Falkenberg next show a spooky silhouette of Pollock, apparently painting—but the black

and white image of his shadow thrown upon a sheet is laden with associations to the murderous mayhem of *film noir*. Presumably casting paint, the silhouette makes stabbing motions through the air, and the sense of voyeurism and terror is inescapable. The sequence is over in a few seconds, as if it were a flashback or momentary interruption of the repressed giving way to a lengthy set of close-ups, pans, and dissolves of Pollock's paintings. Then Pollock is shown (in clean clothes) tacking a canvas to the wall of a pristine, white-walled room, and the camera pans left to show the back of a seated woman, apparently studying the paintings mounted on the wall." (pp. 73-74)

35. Steven Naifeh and Gregory White Smith. ***Jackson Pollock: An American Saga*** (New York: Harper Perennial, 1991), 621.

36. Michael Leja, ***Reframing***, 111.

37. Ibid., p. 113.

38. The *film noir* artist/protagonist is frequently, but not always, a painter. In *Hangover Square*, (1945) *Deception* (1946), *Black Angel* (1946), the artist is a musician; in *The Mask of Dimitrios* (1944) and *House By the River* (1950), writers; in *A Double Life* (1948), an actor; and in *Specter of the Rose* (1946), a dancer–see Appendix A. For more examples, literary antecedents, and general commentary on *film noir*'s stance toward art,

Below, Victorian composer and pianist George Bone (Laird Cregar) is taken with "singer" Netta Longdon (Linda Darnell) in *Hangover Square*.

see: John Schultheiss, "The *Noir* Artist," *Films in Review* 40 no. 1 (January 1989), 33-35. The mad artist trope coincided also with popular myths about jazz musicians. See, for example, the article, "Be-bop Be-bopped," in *Time* (March 25, 1946), 52, Ann E. Gibson's *Abstract Expressionism: Other Politics* (New Haven: Yale University Press, 1997), 31-32, or the depiction of jazz musicians in *Blues in the Night* (1941), *Phantom Lady* (1944), *Young Man with a Horn* (1949), *DOA* (1950), and *The Strip* (1951).

39. Rudolf and Margot Wittkower, ***Born Under Saturn; The Character and Conduct of Artists: A Documented History from Antiquity to the French Revolution*** (New York: Random House, 1963).

40. Griselda Pollock, "Artists' Mythologies and Media Genius, Madness and Art History." *Screen* 21:3 (1980), 69. For a brief history of the myth of the mad artist in 19th century American literature, see Neil Harris' ***The Artist in American Society: The Formative Years 1790-1860*** (Chicago: The University of Chicago Press, 1982), 218-251.

41. Alain Silver, Elizabeth Ward and James Ursini, eds. ***Film Noir: An Encyclopedic Reference to the American Style*** (Third Edition, New York: The Overlook Press, 1992), 248. For more commentary on the image of the artist in *Scarlet Street* see Parker Tyler's "The Artist Portrayed and Betrayed" *Art News* 52 (February 1954), 30-33, 55-56, or Jeanne Hall's "'A Little Trouble With Perspective': Art and Authorship in Fritz Lang's *Scarlet Street*," *Film Criticism* 21 no. 1 (Fall 1996), 34-47.

42. Ann Gibson, ***Issues in Abstract Expressionism: The Artist Run Periodicals*** (Ann Arbor: UMI Research Press, 1990), 25-32.

43. Ibid., pp. 181-204.

44. Although none of the Abstract Expressionist artists committed murder (Jackson Pollock would have been charged had he survived the August 11, 1956 car crash that killed him and Edith Metzger), many, it has been argued, suffered from psychopathic disorders. See Schildkraut, Joseph J., M.D., et. al. "Mind and Mood in Modern Art, II: Depressive Disorders, Spirituality, and Early Deaths in the Abstract Expressionist Artists of the New York School." *The American Journal of Psychiatry* 151 no. 4 (April 1994), 482-488.

45. Michael Leja, ***Reframing***, 113.

46. Diane Waldman, "The Childish, the Insane, and the Ugly: The Representation of Modern Art in Popular Films and Fiction of the Forties." *Wide Angle* 5 no. 2 (1982), 53.

47. *Crack-Up* is an unjustly underestimated *film noir*. It directly reflects the controversial case of Hans van Meegeren (see David Anderson's "Old Masters to Order: Forgery as a Fine Art" in the *New York Times* December 23, 1945 VI, p.10), and touches on timely issues relating to patronage, connoisseurship, and Nazi art thefts. For more on the idea of the art historian as a detective, see Carlo Ginzburg's "Morelli, Freud, and Sherlock Holmes: Clues and Scientific Method" in ***The Sign of Three***, edited by Umberto Eco and Thomas A. Sebeok (Bloomington: Indiana University Press, 1983), 81-118.

48. Serge Guilbaut, ***How New York Stole the Idea of Modern Art: Abstract Expressionism Freedom, and the Cold War***. Trans. by Arthur Goldhammer (Chicago: University of Chicago Press, 1983), 201-202. For more on the history of this type of "individualism" see T.J. Clark's "In Defense of Abstract Expressionism" *October* 69 (Summer 1994), 24-48 or Nicholas Green's, "Art History and the Construction of Individuality"

The Oxford Art Journal 6:2 (1983), 80-82, a review of C. M. Zemel's **The Formation of a Legend: Van Gogh Criticism 1890-1920** (Ann Arbor: UMI Research Press, 1981.

49. Lee Seldes, **The Legacy of Mark Rothko** (New York: Penguin Books, 1979), 111. For an in-depth analysis of The Rothko Conspiracy see Howard Singerman's "Tainted Image: Rothko on TV," *Art In America* (November 1983), 11-15. Singerman's uses Ernst Kris and Otto Kurz' important study, **Legend, Myth, and Magic in the Image of the Artist** (New Haven: Yale University Press, 1979), to show how Rothko is portrayed as the stereotypical mad artist–"a culturally conditioned role that preexists and supersedes Rothko." (p. 11)

50. David Sylvester, "De Kooning's Women: Interview with Willem de Kooning." Reprinted in **Abstract Expressionism: A Critical Study**, 225-28.

51. Willem De Kooning, from, respectively, Clifford Ross, ed., **Abstract Expressionism: Creators and Critics, An Anthology** (New York: Harry N. Abrams, 1990), 47 and "What Abstract Art Means to Me," in **Abstract Expressionism: A Critical Record**, 1990), 223.

52. According to de Kooning, *Excavation* (1950) was inspired by image of women in a rice field in *Bitter Rice* (1949), a neo-realist film by the Italian director Giuseppe de Saints. Also, Elaine de Kooning spoke of Willem's admiration of *film noir*, especially The Maltese Falcon. See Ann E. Gibson's **Abstract Expressionism: Other Politics**, 53.

53. Seitz, Ph.D. Dissertation, 342.

54. Frank Krutnik, **In a Lonely Street: Film Noir, Genre, Masculinity** (New York: Routledge, 1991), 57.

55. April Kingsley, **The Turning Point: The Abstract Expressionists and the Transformation of American Art** (New York: Simon and Schuster, 1992), 222.

56. See Durgnat's essay reprinted in **Film Noir Reader**, 37-51, and Place's in **Women in Film Noir**, ed. E. Ann Kaplan (London: BFI, 1978), 35-54. For a Lacanian interpretation see Reynold Humphries, **Fritz Lang: Genre and Representation in His American Films** (Baltimore: The John Hopkins University Press, 1989), 48-51.

57. From an interview conducted by Harold Rosenberg (1972), reprinted in **Abstract Expressionism: A Critical Record**, 253. Indeed, De Kooning's *Women* are threatening because they exist in a middle ground, somewhere between naturalism and abstraction, wholeness and fragmentation, figuration and disfiguration. Deborah Thomas uses a similar set of oppositions to define the threatening aspects of the *film noir femme fatale*. See, "Psychoanalysis and *Film noir*," in Ian Cameron, ed. **The Book of Film Noir** (New York: Continuum, 1993), 71-87.

58. Leja, **Reframing**, 7.

59. Mark Rothko, "Statement on His Attitude Towards Painting," *Tiger's Eye* I no. 9 (October 1949), 114.

60. Rothko, a onetime drama student and life-long theater fan, may have been influenced also by Fredrick Kiesler, a popular figure in the New York city art community who, as a theater director, was interested in breaking down conventional boundaries between stage, actor, and the audience. Also, Kiesler invented "100% Cinema" which entailed showing a film "both in front of the theater and on its side walls." See Dore Ashton,

Abstract Expressionism: A Cultural Reckoning (New York: Viking Press, 1973), 29. Robert Profirio discusses the influence of radical theater on *film noir* in Chapter 4 of his pioneering Ph.D dissertation *The Dark Age of American Film: A Study of the American Film Noir*, Yale University (1979).

61. Erwin Panofsky, "Style and Medium in the Motion Pictures," reprinted in *Film Theory and Criticism*, 236.

62. J.P. Telotte, *Voices in the Dark: The Narrative Patterns of Film Noir* (Urbana and Champaign: University of Illinois Press, 1989), 88. Telotte's book also explores the limitations of language. *Film noir*, he argues, reflects a world in which alienated individuals "always find communication difficult or simply irrelevant." (p. 45) An interesting parallel can be found in Ann Gibson's article "Abstract Expressionism's Evasion of Language," in *Art Journal* 47 (Fall 1988), in which she discusses the Abstract Expressionists' collective resistance to explain or communicate what their paintings "meant." The most reluctant, she adds, was Mark Rothko.

63. T.J. Clark, *The Painting of Modern Life* (New Jersey: Princeton University Press, 1984), 11-12.

64. Quoted in James Breslin, *Mark Rothko: A Biography* (Chicago: University of Chicago Press, 1993), 270. Rothko is not the only Abstract Expressionist artist who spoke of this. De Kooning was interested in "glimpses," and Clifford Still wanted to explore "new ways of seeing." For more on this, see: David Anfam's review of Leja's book in *Art in America* (October 1994), 37-39.

65. See Baxandall's *Painting and Experience in Fifteenth-Century Italy* (Oxford: Oxford University Press, 1972). The description is Svetlana Alpers' in *October* 77 (Summer 1996), 26.

66. Anfam, *Abstract Expressionism*, p. 86.

67. Quoted in David Anfam, *Franz Kline: Black & White 1950-1961* (Houston: Houston Fine Art Press, 1994), 19.

68. Seitz, Ph.D. dissertation, 348.

69. Quoted in T.J. Clark's "Jackson Pollock's Abstraction," reprinted in *Reconstructing Modernism: Art in New York, Paris, and Montreal 1945-1964*, ed. Serge Guilbaut (Cambridge: MIT Press, 1995), 178.

70. Elaine De Kooning, "Franz Kline: Painter of His Own Life." Reprinted in *Abstract Expressionism: A Critical Record*, 304-15.

71. Harry F. Gaugh, "Franz Kline: The Man and the Myths." *Artnews* (December 1985),61-67

72. Katherine Kuh, *The Artists Voice: Talks With Seventeen Artists* (New York: Harper & Row, 1962), 144.

73. Quoted in David Anfam, *Franz Kline: Black & White 1950-1961*, 9.

74. Ibid., p. 24.

75. Jane Livingston, *The New York School Photographs 1936-1963* (New York: Stewart, Tabori, and Chang, 1992), 260-70. Also see Ann Elizabeth Sass' unpublished Ph.D. dissertation on Robert Frank and *film noir*, *Robert Frank's Photography 1942-1959*, Co-

lumbia University (1991), and Kerry Brougher's essay in the exhibition catalog**Hall of Mirrors: Art and Film Since 1945** (Los Angeles: The Museum of Contemporary Art/New York: The Monacelli Press, 1996), 37-41.

76. Erwin Panofsky, "Style and Medium in the Motion Pictures,"reprinted in **Film Theory and Criticism**, 234.

77. Quoted in Seitz, Ph.D. dissertation, 348.

78. Leja, **Reframing**, 331.

79. See Douglas Fogle's"Cinema is Dead, Long Live Cinema." *Frieze* (Summer 1996), 32.

80. Thomas Crow, "Saturday Disasters: Traces and Reference in Early Warhol." In **Reconstructing Modernism: Art in New York, Paris, and Montreal 1945-1964** Edited by Serge Guilbaut (Cambridge: MIT Press, 1990), 324.

Below, *Daisy Kenyon*: Dan O'Mara (Dana Andrews) looks over materials with aspiring fashion designer Daisy Kenyon (Joan Crawford).

Above, Theresa Russell as Det. Lottie Mason in *Impulse*.

Girl Power: Female-Centered Neo-*Noir*

William Covey

Women-centered neo-*noir* films of the 1980s and 1990s showcase tough women cops and detectives operating with action, clarity, and decisiveness in a male-centered world. There were very few female investigators and no female detectives in classic *film noirs*. Two central roles, the strong-willed, femme fatale versus the bland but moral wife or girlfriend at home dominated classic *noir* films. With the lone exception of Ida Lupino, there were also no female directors of classic *noir*. These limitations have altered some since the 1980s. In neo-*noir* women usually fill three roles: the femme fatale, the female investigator/detective, and though still marginalized, the female director or writer. A short list of contemporary women directors of neo-*noir* includes: Kathryn Bigelow, Lizzie Borden, Tamra Davis, Mary Lambert, Sondra Locke, Dorothy Ann Puzo, Katt Shea Ruben, and Lili Fini Zanuck. Two key contemporary hardboiled detective writers are Sue Grafton and Sara Paretsky.

Woman-centered neo-*noirs* intermingle both new and old *noir* themes within new critiques of patriarchy and analyses of female identity. Complex psychoanalytic points including androgyny, sexuality, voyeurism, and women's physical strength compete with political issues concerning women as professionals. Each of these sociopolitical topics is presented from a woman's perspective. Further, female-centered neo-*noir* films proffer integrationist, separatist, and backlash positions for their women's roles. These elements taken together illustrate that there is no essential woman's neo-*noir* film. The best approach then is to map the parameters for female-centered neo-*noir* by analyzing as many female-driven neo-*noirs* as possible.

While most neo-*noirs* directed by a woman and/or featuring a woman in their lead roles are positive both in aesthetic/cultural terms, for expanding the parameters of neo-*noir* discourse, and also in economic terms, for providing employment for women into spaces that have been dominated by white men, there still remain retrograde women's neo-*noirs*. Thus, not every woman's neo-*noir* intends a message of female empowerment or resistance to the male-dominated status quo. In fact, a mainstream Hollywood-friendly trade magazine like *Premiere*, which featured two cautious "special issues" about "Women in Hollywood" for both 1993's Year of the Woman and 1996, reveals how slowly the Hollywood system has changed since the times of classic *film noir*. In a statistical chart on directors in the

311

1993 issue one learns that, of the 7,332 feature films released from 1949-79, there were 7,318 directed by men and 14 films directed by 7 different women. From 1983-1992, of the 1,794 feature films released, 1,713 were directed by men and 81 were directed by women.[1] "Year of the Woman" or not, these numbers make clear that, as recent as in 1993, women were still marginalized forces in United States filmmaking. Ironically, despite such numbers, the female audience for movies continues to increase. The first "Women In Hollywood" special issue of *Premiere* makes clear that, "Women 25 and older...control more movie-ticket dollars than any other segment of the audience. If this group likes a movie, they will go again and again."[2] Whether these viewers will also pressure companies to add female directors, especially if producers listen to demographics as much as the popular press implies, remains to be seen. As more and more female detectives populate neo-*noirs*, the jury is similarly out on whether a larger female audience for characters and films born of male-centered pulp novels will also continue to grow.

Women's neo-*noirs* in the 1980s first called for changes in depicting the gender of criminal investigators, and then began uncovering women's crime issues such as discussions of female violence. As Elayne Rapping makes clear in her summary of the politics of women's issues, "Feminism assumes that society itself needs to change in important, democratizing ways."[3] Analyzing a selection of current films proves seminal for neo-*noir's* continuing redefinition, opening up neo-*noir* discourse away from the singular concerns of male-centered classic *film noir*. Female-centered neo-*noirs* carve out a niche for tough investigators, expand cultural roles for women, and paradoxically, in backlash films, may also reinscribe traditional gender roles.

In other words, is a film technique like voiceover discourse challenged or altered when a woman narrates instead of a man? Additionally, one might inquire whether we are able to read classic films like *Double Indemnity* (1944) and *D.O.A.* (1950) differently once we have seen Mary Lambert's *Siesta* (1987). Does Diane's (Ellen Barkin's) nightmare narrative in the latter film, told from her moments both before and after death and spoken in voiceover, add the "woman's voice" to *noir* filmmaking? *Siesta* may do just this. Diane's voice over at least offers a subversion of the theory of voiceover as "generally male"[4] and Diane's strong character both updates and responds to the parallel male characters in the two classic films just mentioned. In its similar plotting and narration devices, the viewer recognizes the *noir* pattern of the dying protagonist trying to make sense of her/his life once it is already too late. However, whether Diane's discovery that Dell (Martin Sheen) is exploiting her daredevil, skydiving skills for personal monetary gain, or that she still loves her trainer Augustine (Gabriel Byrne), is more essentially feminine than Walter Neff's (Fred MacMurray's) male confession about falling for Phyllis Dietrichson (Barbara Stanwyck) or Frank Bigelow's (Edmond O'Brien's) explanation to the cops about his poisoning is debatable. Still, a film which allows a woman to narrate the demons of her inner psyche, all the while confessing her true romantic feelings in a voiceover stream-of-consciousness style over the entire length of a feature film, is certainly startling, perhaps overtly feminist, compared to typical *noir* films. Diane is defined neither as a femme fatale nor as a long suffering girlfriend for the male protagonist. Rather, she is the protagonist, complete with a host of contradictory feelings and impulses. Therefore, Diane is long suffering in that she is compelled to return to Augustine to try to reclaim his discarded love. Yet, in a way, she responds to and redefines other traditional *noir* female roles—she remains a dangerous woman toward Augustine and his new, lawful wife as well as a rebel to the legal bonds of her marital relationship with Dell.

A female protagonist who narrates a film is powerful because, "Ways of looking are inevitably linked to ways of speculating, of theorizing...and...to ways of representing oneself"[5] In *Siesta*, Diane controls the narration and the plot by her voiceover and actions, representing herself more accurately because she controls these technique. Discourse analysis is most convincing when it reveals how subtle variations on gender roles, within a film such as *Siesta*, revise classic *noir* thematics and narrative patterns.

Consequently, Diane's control of filmic technique also focuses critical analyses on thematics that reflect her perspective. The connection between love and money, the hopelessness of romantic love in contemporary society, and the use of flashback in order to try to redeem a doomed life all work together to undercut the assumption that these are "essentially" male thematics of *film noirs*. In Diane, a strong woman on a mental and psychic quest, *Siesta* reveals neo-*noirs* aesthetic discourse as constantly shifting and open to issues of women's identity. Mary Ann Doane argues that when a woman-centered film "insistently and sometimes obsessively attempts to trace the contours of female subjectivity and desire within the traditional forms and conventions of Hollywood narrative...certain contradictions within patriarchal ideology become more apparent"[6] Even though a male-identified formalistic *noir* narrative device is retained by the use of voiceover in *Siesta*, gender identity and cultural codes are illustrated as shifting and fluid. This neo-*noir* woman's film reveals that the voiceover device is no more owned by the male than the female. *Siesta* decenters the paradigm for analyzing *noir* voiceover, proving that the aesthetic device is not a fixed mechanism, but rather just another site where new discourses may contest the old. In *Siesta*, Diane's existential journey, mirroring but also differing from the male narrative pattern, is coded as specifically female, demonstrating that stylistics and thematics are malleable terms in neo-*noir* and they should, therefore, always be discussed in conjunction with surrounding cultural influences.

Katt Shea Ruben's *Stripped to Kill* (1987) offers an additional unusual challenge for neo-*noir* criticism. The director co-wrote the screenplay with her husband about a female cop named Cody (Kay Lenz) who must go undercover and pose as a topless dancer in order to locate the criminal inhabiting the world of nightclub

stripping who is brutally murdering various dancers. The film is challenging to analyze in at least two ways. Firstly, it is a hybrid genre film. Titled as it is and produced by Roger Corman, the film was made cheaply and carried the imprimatur
of an exploitation film. Yet, the film is also teeming with *noir* elements. Secondly,
the movie problematizes the assumption of the camera as essentially phallic, a
crucial element of the "male gaze" theory. The film levies its critique by its consistently pro-women's community stance and by the fact that the gaze watching
these strippers is most often constructed as female. Together, the gaze and the
composition of *Stripped to Kill* work to oppose Laura Mulvey's theory that "mainstream film coded the erotic into the language of the dominant patriarchal order."[7] While the film is far from a radical feminist tract, it is also more than simple
sexploitation images presented for the enjoyment of male adolescent viewers.

Katt Shea Ruben seems to be arguing that the conventions of "realism" are not
as important as getting her ideas of the thematic and creative aspects of each
woman's dance sequence shown in a proper manner. The film de-emphasizes
stripping's economic relationship to men in order to emphasize erotic dancing as
a profession where women, who may have entered the club out of various economic needs, instead develop a subcultural resistance to their profession's traditional meaning. The dancers develop strong bonds amongst themselves and a
deep appreciation for the creativity of their fellow workers. The impetus that
drives these dancers is impressing other women with one's own creativity, rather
than the clientele or male owners who are concerned more with flesh, money,
and the economics of dance. Despite the contradiction of satisfying the male heterosexual gaze for cash, the women actually develop and improve their professional skills for the approval of their own subcultural women's community.

Because we are introduced to the individual strippers, rather than to their club
audiences, Katt Shea Ruben allows the viewer's sympathies to favor the women's
growing empowerment and skills in place of the leers and money of the men in
the club's audience. Therefore the typical relationship between stripper and voyeur is broken down. By demystifying the strippers, the movie turns the women
into human beings. Viewers who are looking for a traditional sexploitation film are
asked to rethink their responses to female nudity. The female director constructs
an antihegemonic mise-en-scene that emphasizes how much athletic and creative
ability these dancers possess. In fact, the one dancer named Cinnamon who uses
drugs and tumbles off stage during her overtly vulgar routine is looked down upon
by the other dancers as a "has been." She even loses her economic support when
she is fired by Ray because of her lack of discipline. In *Stripped to Kill*, topless
dancing is a profession neither rudimentary nor inherently degrading.

In contrast, by roughing up local street criminals and labeling a local guy named
Pocket both a "pervert" and his prime suspect because he watches every topless
show with his left hand in his pocket and gifts some girls with paper flowers he
makes, Heineman (Greg Evigan) gets nowhere with his part in this murder investi-

gation. Repeatedly, he strikes macho poses, is caught snooping in apartments, or follows false leads. On the other hand, his female partner Cody begins to make friends with the other dancers, discovers that Pocket is not masturbating at shows but rather is missing his hand, which is why he always hides his stub in his pocket, and she becomes obsessed with mastering both her undercover dancing and solving this case. When Heineman tells Cody that "the brass" has found out what she is doing and has ordered her to "hang up [her] G-string," Cody yells angrily at Heineman for tricking her into breaking police rules and dancing in the first place. She then decides to perform a final dance both in order to get closer to solving the case and to provide a kind of answer to Heineman's trick on her. For the first time in the film, Cody demonstrates for Heineman both her sexual power and her ability to do good work. Heineman busts back stage afterwards, flustered and angry. He yells, asking her what the hell she is doing and pulls rank on Cody–"You were ordered NOT to come back here. You are a COP", and, in frustration, begs her, "Don't flake out on me."

Cody's response shows how this film often attempts to construct male/female attraction differently than standard Hollywood fare. As Laura Mulvey has made clear concerning classic Hollywood narrative, "In a world ordered by sexual imbalance, pleasure in looking has been split between active/male and passive/female. The determining male gaze projects its fantasy onto the female figure, which is styled accordingly."[8] Cody points out that Heineman has only gotten romantically interested in her because he subconsciously accepts Mulvey's theory that Cody has value because other men sexualized her body when she was dancing on stage, and sharing her sexuality with others makes him jealous. Heineman also seems to realize that her good dancing and investigating has freed her from her mentee position under him.

But, Cody's intentions do not buy into the binary relationship implied by Mulvey's theory. Cody strips as a professional obligation, in order to solve a murder case. Her dancing deconstructs the active/passive binary. She strips (acts) in the capacity of female investigator solving a crime and she improves her dancing in order to be appreciated professionally by her fellow female dancers, not merely to "turn on" the male crowd. Despite the fact that the crowd responds to her, Cody's active pleasure in her power to both arouse Heineman and be complimented by her female cohorts complicates the lone male sexual fantasy of gazing at women that Mulvey's theory argues for. Unsure of how to react to this new kind of subject positioning, Heineman can only respond as a passive voyeur and ineffectual male action hero.

Throughout *Stripped to Kill* Cody is the more professional of the two cops. While arguing with Heineman, she continues to do her job, discovering that Pocket is innocent by getting to know him and, even though she is ordered out of the club, announcing she has to go back and finish solving the case. Because Heineman stalks off in disgust to find the killer on his own, he potentially jeopardizes his partner's life. Obviously, the film would have had a more clearly female-empowered ending had Heineman remained out of the picture. Cody would have survived on her own, ready to solve future cases. Still, the film makes clear that Cody is the better professional investigator, able to handle cases without a man's help. Cody's mastery of stripping offers rebellion against status quo women's roles, establishing "performative pleasure based on the satisfaction of maintaining a sense of subcultural difference, a social identity that is *not* constructed by and for the interests of the dominant"[9] as a kind of sex positive feminism. Without becoming friends and being respected by her fellow dancers, Cody could never have learned the information about this subculture that allows her to solve the case. Cody's ability to capture and contain the male murderer ultimately proves she has even learned how to knife fight and is no longer dependent on Heineman's guidance.

In the way that one woman gets initiated into crime investigation originating from some other walk of life, *Stripped to Kill* is very much in line with other woman-centered neo-*noirs* of the 1980s. The following women all become *noir* investigators even though they begin their films defined in other ways: Judith Singer (Susan Sarandon) in *Compromising Positions* (1985), and Katie Phillips/Cathy Weaver (Debra Winger) in *Betrayed* (1988) are housewives; Alex Sternbergen (Jane Fonda) in *The Morning After* (1986) is an actress; and Katya Yarno (Diane Lane) in *Lady Beware* (1987) is a window designer.

To use the last film as an example, Katya Yarno (Diane Lane) goes from a lonely fashion designer with a low self-esteem to a hardened crime investigator no longer fearful of the city in Karen Arthur's *Lady Beware* . Katya's improving investigative skills parallel her growing confidence and daring with her "day job" as a window display artist. As her window displays become more daring and risqué, she is first terrorized by a stalker who has fetishized her work and then empowered by her pursuit and capture of the stalker.

No longer a "small-town girl," Katya ends the film excelling at both of her jobs, an accomplished professional able to take care of herself. As neo-*noirs* move into 1990s, a confluence of competing issues concerning female employment and identity continue to be worked out within woman-centered movies.

For example, there are plenty of recent films like *Impulse* (1990) that seem more intent on reversing this trend toward female independence found in 1980s neo-*noirs*, in order to return women to more traditional roles. For example, in Sondra Locke's *Impulse*, Lottie (Theresa Russell) plays a working-class undercover vice cop who acts as either a prostitute or escort in order to make vice squad busts. Because of problems Lottie has had before the film opens, she is forced to see a psychiatrist once a week, who will decide whether Lottie should be allowed to continue working. Lottie reveals what attracts her to vice to her uptight, black female shrink, admitting, "Working in vice. Strangers. The way they look at you. Feel all that power over them. Make 'em pay. It excites me." Lottie's experience with vice customers has made her cynical about any kind of romantic relationship in her own life, paralleling Bree Daniel's (Jane Fonda's) feelings about heterosexual romance in the sur-text about murder mysteries and prostitution, *Klute* (1971). In fact, later in the film, Lottie claims that she really only wants a man who has a lot of money.

She spends the movie being pursued by two men with whom she works: Morgan (George Dzundza), an overweight and crude working-class cop who is her boss, and Stan (Jeff Fahey), a thin and refined lower middle-class, assistant district attorney. When Stan is assigned to her precinct, he immediately recognizes the harassment Morgan inflicts on Lottie. During their first meeting, Stan prods her with questions about her job, asking "It must be difficult working for a man like Morgan." Lottie replies casually, "I think I can handle him.... Friction is normal." Stan counters with, "Is it 'normal' police procedure for a male officer to frisk a female?," referring to Morgan's actions toward Lottie on an earlier faked bust where he did not want to give away her real identity to the crook. Lottie says, "Morgan just likes to harass people, I don't take it personally."

In a surprising moment where the male has to define sexual harassment for the female perhaps because, as a middle-class person, he has more "knowledge" of legal argot than the working-class woman, Stan tells her she should take it personally because Morgan's actions are wrong. Stan's ethics lesson allows Lottie to offer her first impression of Stan, saying she thinks Stan is an unhappy, tight-assed reactionary who will spend the rest of his life spitting into the wind. He accepts Lottie's summary of himself, but her nerve and toughness also helps him to become romantically infatuated with her. Perhaps Morgan is only treating Lottie like "one of the guys," expressing his appreciation of her good work through sarcasm and contempt. Yet, because of Morgan's fondling of her, the viewer is supposed to take Stan's side and see him as an unethical cop. In contrast, Stan's respectful treatment of women is "sophisticated" and more appropriate for the workplace. As the film continues and he becomes increasingly jealous of Stan and Lottie's blooming relationship, Morgan is made to look more and more like a bad guy who may even be responsible for the film's primary murder.

The film builds up suspense near the end when the audience questions whether Lottie, once she discovers she holds the key to the million dollar stash of a government-protected witness named Peron, will take the money and run away from both her low-paying job and the kind of men with whom she is surrounded. Also at this point in *Impulse* we do not know the identity of the killer or whether he will discover that Lottie was in Peron's place during the murder. Morgan quickly figures out that Lottie was the mystery woman with Peron, and leaks the information to Stan. Lottie confesses what happened to Stan, and, because they each now share romantic inclinations, she weeps her way into admitting that she did not have sex with Peron stating, "I didn't. I stopped because I don't know what the hell I was doing there in the first place." While Stan warns her that she

Above, a wounded Officer Megan Turner (Jamie Lee Curtis) in *Blue Steel*.

should be worried because the killer knows there was a survivor, Lottie says, "Right now, I'm more scared about us than anything." Lottie switches from a loner detective to a desperate lover, placing her against the grain of hardboiled detectives and in line with the typical Hollywood damsel in distress. Still, in the climax, Lottie shoots the killer Vic (another government witness who needed to shoot Peron to get off the hook), and Stan gives her a chance to leave the country with the million dollars he now knows she has confiscated.

In *noir* fashion, Lottie quits the police force with the intention of leaving town. Stan and Morgan have another confrontation as Morgan is now also sure that Lottie has Peron's money, though he can not prove it. He yells at Stan, "she'll fuck you over for that money," setting up a unique ending for the movie where the female cop may become a femme fatale worthy of a character like Matty Walker in *Body Heat* (1981). Instead of heeding Morgan's advice, Stan follows Lottie to the airport and gives her a chance to leave alone. She walks off, perhaps thinking about what her life will be like as a rich woman, only to return to him in the bar a few minutes later. She returns Peron's key and money, saying "Turn it in." Stan finishes the film with a toast and seals Lottie's new life as an ex-cop and his new lover. The film ends with a Kim Carnes song whose refrain repeats "Everybody Needs Someone to Lean On...To Love" which encourages viewers to assume that this female detective has handed in her badge for a solid heterosexual relationship with a successful and honest young man.

Impulse, contains all the elements of the neo-*noir,* including the provocative addition of a tough white female cop, only to reinscribe patriarchal gender relations by film's end. The unhappy, wild-willed woman is merely redomesticated. The cultural message of the film implies that women should only work at a profession until the right man comes along and asks them to give up their careers for a domestic home life.

Still, there are also recent neo-*noir*s that celebrate independent women. Certain 1990's female detectives and investigators advance the possibilities for women's representation in neo-*noir*s. The following female-centered films expand the acceptable parameters for the hardboiled detective character in neo-*noir*. Women, however, do not have a similar cinematic history of tough action heroes, or detectives to build upon as males. Consequently, much of the professional anxiety expressed by the female-centered neo-*noir*s of the 1980s may have to do with the pioneering status of those women portraying such detective roles.

Many critical circles champion *Blue Steel* (1990) as perhaps the key contemporary female neo-*noir*. While it is truly a fine action thriller, its critical reception may have been aided by Kathryn Bigelow's strong script and the fact that she has been educated at Columbia college by film scholars like John Belton and Sylvère Lotringer. Her knowledge of film and genre history is clear in her comments on making this film. In an interview just before *Blue Steel* was released, Bigelow admits that she intended to do a "woman's action film," and that she was fascinated by *film noir*s because "they delve into a darkness and talk about the demons that exist in all of us."[10] Critics have responded to *Blue Steel* with almost universal admiration and also from a wide array of critical perspectives, including: psychoanalysis (Cora Kaplan,[11] Nickolas Pappas,[12] and Bob Self[13]), feminism and institutional critique (Linda Mizejewski[14]) and identity politics (Pam Cook). Like Mizejewski, I see *Blue Steel* as illustrating a cultural moment, marking both a continuation and improvement upon the shifting placement of female professionals as representatives of the law and as enemies to misogyny.

Robert Self makes a case for *Blue Steel*'s status as neo-*noir*, uncovering ambiguities and disturbances in its narrative pattern: "The representation of the woman as the law constitutes a major destabilization of the symbolic order in which gendered subjectivity is a central project."[15] In other words, like most classic *noirs*, the story has an uneasy relationship with institutions like the justice system, yet, unlike those older films, this story does not end happily nor resolve the gender and sexuality contradictions it posits. In fact, typical femininity is altered in the film in terms of the cultural construction of femininity and desire. Megan (Jamie Lee Curtis) is androgynous-looking, but markedly heterosexual even though many critics have tried to use her "butch" look to find a lesbian subtext within the film—with her short slicked-back hair and, wearing a uniform and hat, "hiding the breasts with the uniform,...[designating the] disappearance of the woman into the law, of her positioning as subject to the law and the subject of its enforcement."[16] Megan uncovers double standards within the milieu of typical law enforcement when she forces the law to examine women's issues. While *V.I. Warshawski* (1991)talks tough, still she captures the most attention from her red high heels and sexy legs. In *Blue Steel*, Megan scares off potential suitors by either dressing androgynously or admitting to men that she is a cop. None of Megan's working-class male friends have any use for such an apparent "butch femme." The lone exception in the film is Eugene (Ron Silver), the homme fatale and psychosexual deviant, who fetishizes and identifies with phallic women. The viewer may also see Megan as attractive and heroic, based in part on Curtis's previous film roles, even though this role marks a break with her previous mainstream depictions of standard female beauty.

Beyond these issues of identity politics, Cora Kaplan reads this film through a lens that combines social class with gender issues. Megan, detective Nick Mann (Clancy Brown), and most of Megan's New York world is ethnic and working-class. Part of her initial attraction to Eugene the stock broker are his class markers (they dine in elegant restaurants and take helicopter rides over the city as part of their dates) and his ethnic difference from the men she has grown up around. Eugene is Jewish, dark-skinned, and successful—quite the opposite of her Catholic, overweight, and unhappy father as well as her working-class male friends in her neighborhood, each of whom are embarrassed that Megan has become a cop. Her father stays home and slaps around his wife to relieve his almost constant depression. As Cora Kaplan makes clear, while Megan is aggressive and independent around men of her own kind (at one point handcuffing her father and taking him toward the police station after one of his spousal abuse incidents), she is "both feminine and deferential"[17] around Eugene. Thus, *Blue Steel* introduces a female detective who acts differently according to people's social class. Because Megan represents the law, this implies the law may also be preferential. In other words, preferential treatment of people of economic advantage is an important subtext within *Blue Steel*.

In terms of neo-*noir* as a changing generic category, "the nihilism of the ending"[18] with Megan staring off into space alone in a squad car, as well as the emphasis on social class and detection, and the positioning of women's issues as key criminal issues, each work together by using gender to redefine classic neo-*noir* concerns. Because traditional *noir* criticism privileges men, the use of male/female role reversals place women within general neo-*noir* discourse. In other words, *Blue Steel* illustrates that when a woman is the hero of the film and the man is evil, the assumptions that we normally make about detectives and dangerous adversaries no longer match traditional gender assumptions.

Linda Mizejewski labels these newest neo-*noir*s as "female dick" movies. Despite contrary mainstream generic and cultural pressures, Mizejewski believes *Blue Steel* delineates "the feminist fantasy of woman as powerful within the law and the male fantasy of the law-woman as fetish."[19] Mizejewski implies sarcasm in her label, but I believe Megan's character illustrates how altering *noir* discourse is influential, allowing concerns like domestic violence to be her ethical and woman-centered guide for law enforcement . *Love Crimes* (1992) continues this cultural dialogue begun in *Blue Steel*, as another tough investigative cop forces the law to discover the existence of women's issues as legitimate criminal issues.

As director Lizzie Borden makes clear in her 1992 *Cineaste* interview, the version of *Love Crimes* she intended for release can only be found on the unrated videocassette. Borden explains that the disastrous theatrical reception resulted from the company's intentionally edited theatrical release of the film because various scenes in the film "made some of the executives feel uncomfortable."[20] Borden also admits that her pledged audience is always "women over thirty" but that "I'm not a separatist. I hope that men can see my films through eyes colored by female characters they have to identify with–just as women have had to do in watching film with male characters."[21] *Love Crimes* is intended as a female-empowering neo-*noir*.

In the film, district attorney Dana Greenaway (Sean Young) discovers a legal "gray area" when she begins to look into her case against "David Hanover" (Patrick Bergin), a man who poses as a famous soft-core fashion photographer whose photographic style is not unlike real-life photographers Herb Ritts or Helmut Newton. Hanover uses his alias, with its accompanying baggage of his abilities to construct beautiful images of women, to "con" various everyday women into posing for him. When they do pose, he gets pleasure by forcing them into taking more and more of their clothes off, often leading to some sort of physical assault and usually culminating in consensual sex. Because the women agree to his actions and because he comforts them afterwards, telling them how "great" they were in

Above, District Attorney Dana Greenway (Sean Young) is terrorized by serial rapist "David Hanover" (Patrick Bergin) in *Love Crimes*.

the photos, even though each woman feels violated, Hanover has broken no law. Borden claims in her interview that Love Crimes plays on women's need to feel beautiful, it "presents women who think that they are going to be legitimized by a fashion photographer."[22] Dana's anger at this loophole in the legal system is the just cause she needs to anger her fellow male DAs. As the case intensifies, Dana is warned by her ex-lover boss that "it's not your job to write the laws, it's to uphold it (sic)"–something Dana can not comply with until she feels the law begins to take woman's issues more seriously.

Typical of other strong women investigators in contemporary neo-noirs, Dana is presented early on as asexual and androgynous, with slicked-back short hair, gray business suits, and the lifestyle of a loner who adopts such a serious business-like tone with people and is so aggressive that she develops no romantic relationships. Neo-noir films continue to struggle with what the proper "look" is which can represent a tough female investigator. Dana's effeminate male secretary admires her attitude and look but, at one point, Maria (Arnetia Walker) a black, fellow female detective advises her to remember, "I'm your only friend."

Dana's appearance is important because most of the film deals with various female fantasies, identifying the cultural importance that female beauty and sexual appeal impose on all men and women. David recognizes this power and uses it for his own distorted psychosexual pleasures. Dana, on the other hand, has to learn about her feelings through her captivity by David. Borden's intention, according to her interview, is that the film be troubling, "it's about someone who's so unconscious about herself that she puts herself in a dangerous situation."[23] Though lack of self-knowledge has been used many times in many classic and neo-noirs about males, many female critics feel that when a male jeopardizes a strong female, the resulting film sends out anti-feminist messages. The challenge for Lizzie Borden was to avoid such a message.

The combination of Dana's strengths and unconscious weaknesses manifest themselves during her captivity in David's cabin in the woods. Once David has seen her unclothed and still has not tried to have sex with her, Dana admits in the general depression and confusion of her captivity, that she has never had an orgasm, does not like to be touched, and has slept with her boss though she did not like it. The film builds to this point where it focuses equally on both Dana's psychosexual makeup and on David's sex crimes. Through flashback, the viewer discovers that Dana's father used to lock her in a closet after Dana caught him in the midst of one of his many affairs with various women while her mother (his wife) was at work. The movie suggests that Dana is troubled by Hanover because she sees in David's photographs the kind of erotic ecstasy she saw on her father's and his lover's faces during his infidelities.

At one point when Maria and Dana are investigating some of David's Polaroids of various women, Maria says to Dana, "This joker is shit as a photographer.... The women are enjoying the hell out of themselves. [This is] more than a simple con going on here. It's some sort of mutual fantasy. Can't you see it?.... Damn straight you can see it!" While the art film aspects of this film such as the use of flashback and the skipping around in time of the narrative seem to have turned off a popular audience, the fact that Dana begins fantasizing about David offends most of the usual independent film and feminist audience. Neither satisfying the erotic thriller crowd in its depictions of sexuality nor the art film crowd in its non-traditional women's politics, *Love Crimes* has been almost universally dismissed. Yet, Borden's thematic obsessions are worth examining and her technical innovations signify Dana's scattered psyche in this brave film.

For example, when Dana is put on extended leave of absence for not dropping the "Hanover thing," she is told by Maria that he has been caught. At home later, Maria calls to tell Dana that the cops got the wrong guy and suddenly Dana's phone goes dead. The suspense builds, she gets hold of her gun, and David confronts her in the darkness of her living room, whispering "We were close to something." He admits they were building a mutual erotic fantasy and asks, "Don't let [your] gun come between us." He then flashes his photographer's bulb as a weapon, recalling Hitchcock's *Rear Window* (1954), by using its light to temporarily blind Dana's eyes in her attempt to get a "bead" on him. The bulb's flash triggers another psychic flashback for Dana where it is revealed that her father accidentally shot her mother during a domestic fight. In anger, Dana breaks a heavy glass object over David's head. While he lies in her living room bleeding, his flash-bulb continues to flash like a weapon, and the police arrive to apprehend him.

Maria (the black detective) finishes the film as it began, being taped and interrogated by two white Internal Affairs men. They tell her that David is calling his bust entrapment—Hanover has claimed, "she invited him in. She wanted it." But Maria sides with Dana against these claims. She responds with a classic *noir* line, now marked as different because it is used to justify a feminist ideology, accomplishing critic Griselda Pollock's call for a flip-flopping of conventional ideas to show their ideological power.[24] When Maria says, "Who cares what line she [Dana] crossed, she caught him," a defense that has been used by countless males to justify all sorts of activities in detective thrillers, the line now resonates with female empowerment. For this one time, a woman espouses bending a law in elucidation of the ethics of a woman's issue. Maria next assures the men that Dana is not hiding anything from them.

The film ends with Maria and Dana, in secret friendship, burning the lone compromising nude photo of Dana standing in a bathtub that David took while he was harboring her. Maria has confiscated the photo earlier from the abduction sight and never turns it in as evidence. The audience is meant to see this as a small victory for women against a still unfair and still patriarchal justice system. Dana and Maria break the law, concealing evidence, compromising their positions as law officers in order to more surely get a bust against David's "love crimes." Dana learns to express her sexuality by reliving the nightmares of her father's love crimes through the erotic consequences of David's twisted view of sexuality. For the first time in neo-*noir*, a feminist detective expresses confused sexual fantasies and unconventional views of male and female-centered fantasies throughout the length of a feature film.

While this essay necessarily de-emphasizes the neo-*noir* femme fatale movies, because her character has not changed much since the classic period, she remains a key player in neo-*noirs* which emphasize sexuality, particularly in: *Body Heat* (1981), *Against All Odds* (1984), *The Hot Spot* (1990), *Basic Instinct* (1992), *Guncrazy* (1992), *Poison Ivy* (1992), *White Sands* (1992), *Blown Away* (1993), *Body of Evidence* (1993), *The Crush* (1993), *Point of No Return* (1993), *True Romance* (1993), *The Wrong Man* (1993), *China Moon* (1994), *Disclosure* (1994), *Dream Lover* (1994), *Love and a .45* (1994), *Romeo is Bleeding* (1994), *Jade* (1995), *Heaven's Prisoners* (1996), *Palmetto* (1998) and *Wild Things* (1998). Despite the femme fatale's increased display of nudity, fluid sexual interest in either men or women, and the occasional substitution of teenage girls in roles originally designed for "experienced" women, these film's stories continue to center around how an innocent, unintelligent, lonely, or desperate man gets caught up in the spider's web spun by the black widow. The conventionalized film character of the femme fatale continues to provide non-traditional roles for strong women and garner lots of popular attention. Hence, Sharon Stone was literally invented as a movie star based on her "controversial" role in *Basic Instinct*. Within the world of the new *noir* films, the femme fatale remains dangerous by knowing how to both tote and use the latest weaponry. In just the past few years, characters like Lane (Mary Elizabeth Mastrantonio), Maggie (Bridget Fonda), Alabama (Patricia Arquette), Zoe (Julie Delphy), Starlene (Renee Zellweger) and Mallory (Juliette Lewis) are willing and able to take an active role in murder either for themselves or for their men in their respective films, *White Sands* (1992), *Point of No Return* (1993), *True Romance* (1993), *Killing Zoe* (1994), *Love and a .45* (1994) and *Natural Born Killers* (1994). Yet, most femme fatale movies continue to reinscribe patriarchy. Thus, the easiest way to tame aggressive women in conserva-

Below, Ellen Barkin as Diane in *Siesta*

tive femme fatale films is to kill them off. *Mortal Passions* (1989), *The Grifters* (1990), and *Consenting Adults* (1992) also make the destruction of the transgressive female the main point of their films. The recent crop of neo-*noir* women outlaws on the run, including such films as *Mortal Thoughts* (1991), *Guncrazy* (1992), *Thelma and Louise* (1992), *Kalifornia* (1993), *Love and a .45* (1994), *Natural Born Killers* (1994), and *Jackie Brown* (1997) also differ from older outlaw films concerning heterosexual couples in their "projections of masculine arrogance and contempt [as arousing women] to physical violence."[25] The toughest, least sentimental outlaw may just as easily be the woman as the man in these neo-*noirs* and they add further variations for cultural analysis when one ponders what such female fantasies reflect about contemporary women's feelings and frustrations with traditional heterosexual romances. A critical supposition of this essay, that "the drama of sexuality and [gender] difference...[is a]...primary text for cultural interpretation"[26] has guided my mapping of the history and cultural issues surrounding woman-centered neo-*noir* films of the 1980s and 1990s.

Since the emergence of female directors in the 1980s and 1990s, films that have concentrated on women detectives and thematics have become more acceptable to the genre. Unlike classic *film noir*, women can inhabit lead, investigative roles and pursue various women's cultural, legal, and political issues. That such cultural issues have become a larger part of neo-*noir* discourse, illustrates that many neo-*noir* movies will remain women-centered, shifting, "the epistemic problem of crime films from that of a subject eager to know, chasing his prey, to that of a subject already possessing all the facts, needing rather herself to be known–acknowledged as a subject."[27] Women are finally being depicted as tough professional investigators who welcome danger and solve tough mysteries. The growing number of woman's neo-*noirs* builds an argument against the overgeneralized summary of labeling all contemporary *film noirs* as anti-woman, backlash movies. The various films discussed here also problematize basic views of detective films as essentially male gendered. Critics need no longer ignore woman-centered neo-*noir*, but instead should further describe and expand issues of female identity, professionalism, and violence that have been introduced here. Neo-*noir* is an everchanging and vibrant cultural discourse that can also point out both theoretical problems and role limitations in viewing hardboiled detectives movies as merely male-centered identity films.

Notes

1. Susan Lyne, Ed.. "Women in Hollywood." *Premiere*, Special Issue 1993, p. 35.

2. Ibid., p. 120.

3. Elayne Rapping, ***Media-tions: Forays into the Culture and Gender Wars*** (South End Press, 1994), p. 37.

4. Christine Gledhill, "*Klute* 1: a contemporary *film noir* and feminist criticism." in ***Women in Film Noir***. Ed. E. Ann Kaplan, Ed. (BFI, 1978), p. 16.

5. Mary Ann Doane, *The Desire to Desire: The Woman's Film of the 1940s*, (Indiana, 1987), p. 37.

6. Ibid., p. 13.

7. Laura Mulvey, *Visual and Other Pleasures*, (Indiana, 1989), p. 16.

7. Ibid., p. 19.

8. John Fiske, *Reading the Popular*, (Unwin Hyman, 1989), p. 118.

9. Cook, Pam. "Blue Steel." *Monthly Film Bulletin* 57.682 (November 1990), p. 313.

10. Cora Kaplan, "Dirty Harriet/*Blue Steel*: Feminist Theory Goes to Hollywood," *Discourse*, 16.1 (Fall, 1993), pp. 50-70.

11. Nickolas Pappas, "A *Sea of Love* Among Men," *Film Criticism*, 14.3 (Spring, 1990), pp. 14-26.

12. Robert T. Self, "Redressing the Law in Kathryn Bigelow's *Blue Steel*." *Journal of Film and Video*, 46.2 (Summer, 1994), pp. 31-43.

13. Linda Mizejewski, "Picturing the Female Dick: *The Silence of the Lambs* and *Blue Steel*," *Journal of Film and Video*, 45.2-3 (Summer-Fall, 1993), pp. 6-23.

15. Self, p. 33.

16. Ibid., p. 35

17. Kaplan, p. 57.

18. Ibid., p. 66.

19. Mizejewski, pp. 16-17.

20. Cynthia Lucia, "Redefining Female Sexuality in the Cinema: An Interview with Lizzie Borden," *Cineaste*, 19.2-3 (1992), p. 7.

21. Idem.

22. Ibid., p. 9.

23. Ibid., p. 10.

24. Griselda Pollock, "What's Wrong With 'Images of Women'? *The Sexual Subject*," (Routledge, 1992), pp. 135-45.

25. Kathleen Murphy, "Only Angels Have Wings: Women in Revolt," *Film Comment*, 27.4 (July-August 1991), p. 26

26. Kaplan, p. 59.

27. Pappas, p. 24.

SHOCK STORY
of a crime-filled romance!
ROBERT MITCHUM
JANE GREER
KIRK DOUGLAS
RHONDA FLEMING
IN
'Out of the Past'
Re-released by
RKO RADIO PICTURES
Directed by JACQUES TOURNEUR • Screenplay by GEOFFREY HOMES • Produced by WARREN DUFF

Noir 101

Philip Gaines

While I normally teach production classes to students whose interest in the "history" of movies ranges from slim to none, I have on several occasions forced some reluctant observers to endure an entire term of *film noir*. And while these dark retrospectives were initially met with the kind of enthusiam usually reserved for a dead mackerel, within a few class sessions all of these reluctant film historians, whose incoming attitudes were either down on Hollywood or apathetic about any films but their own, were hooked on *noir*. When the Editors of this book approached me about quickly synthesizing my course approach (apparently they lost the rights to another piece) and presenting my outline for a sort of *Film Noir* 101, I wasn't sure how well my free form approach would work when experienced purely on paper. You'll have to judge that for yourself.

I've found that many of the overview books on film noir (and there must be more than a dozen of them by now) are pretty useless. Of course, if I had to pick my ideal point of view, it would have to be one that tackles the noir phenomenon like most of its heroes tackled their travails, making it up as they went along. Since that's a hard method to sustain over an entire academic term, the "text" I previously used was just a selection of photocopied essays. Then I discovered that almost all of them were reproduced in *Film Noir Reader*, which is now my basic text. (Of course, I expect that in the future I will bookend the original *Film Noir Reader* with this volume featuring my own prose.)

I won't bother to take a position in the style versus content, movement versus genre debate. I have one, but flogging it in a lecture is usually counter-instructive for students who would rather hear the crisp report of a gats in a dark alley than dogma. Besides *Noir* 101 is about gats going off in dark alleys first and about postwar angst, the residues of German Expressionism, and the dialectic between patriarchal structures and Leibniz's monads second, sixth, and three hundred and forty-third respectively.

Possible Introductory Essays (all reprinted in ***Film Noir Reader***)

Borde and Chaumeton, "Towards a Definition of *Film Noir*"

Raymond Durgnat, "Paint it Black"

Paul Schrader, "Notes on *Film Noir*"

1. Opening with a Bang: *Double Indemnity*

I'd certainly get more laughs with *Detour* (someday fate points that finger at you) and definitely put more people to sleep if I opened with *The Postman Always Rings Twice* (tried it. Once). I've also used *Laura* as the introductory movie, but *Double Indemnity* is a lot funnier and a lot grimmer. It also exemplifies more aspects of *noir* than just about any other film. It was based on a hard-boiled novel (by James M. Cain), co-written by a major hardboiled guy as well (Raymond Chandler), directed by a refugee not from German Expressionism but German Fascism (Billy Wilder), and shot and scored by preeminent *noir* craftsmen, John Seitz and Miklós Rósza, at a major studio (Paramount). So in introductory comments on *film noir*, one can touch on the source literature, earlier film movements, the political context in the world (war in Europe) and in Hollywood (the first *film noir* nominated for an Academy Award®), or visual and aural styles and have examples right at hand. In terms of the narrative, which is the aspect of *film noir* that is readily accessible to most students, *Double Indemnity* really packs a wallop: *femme fatale* (in spades); flashback; first person narration (heavily ironic to boot); ace investigator; more greed than Von Stroheim could throw at you; hetero- and a soupçon of homo-eroticism; and, even without the cut scene of Keyes watching Neff entering the gas chamber, some pretty harsh shuffling off this mortal coil by assorted characters. It's even got pompous company owners, proletarian figures who go bowling, statistics, and a sweet young thing, whom the hapless hero discovers too late.

An excellent alternate title is *Out of the Past* for most of the same reasons as those above.

Possible Additional Reading

Cain's original novella (it's short and Cain gives up nothing to Woolrich or even Jim Thompson in evoking thoroughly twisted people with spare prose)

Richard Schickel, BFI Monograph on *Double Indemnity*

Claire Johnston's essay in **Women in Film Noir**

Maurice Zolotow's description of Wilder/Chandler set-tos in **Billy Wilder in Hollywood** (also recapped in Ward/Silver, **Raymond Chandler's Los Angeles**)

2. Pre-*noir*

There are few images from early cinema more striking than the faces of Griffith's *Musketeers of Pig Alley* and a short film such as this quickly demonstrates the depth of *noir*'s roots. It's simple to explain that the style and content of pre-*noir* ranges from the tilted chiaroscuro of German Expressionism to E.G. Robinson's mouthing "Mother of Mercy, can this be the end of Rico" in *Little Caesar*. When one actually considers the key films of German Expressionsm, from *Caligari* to *The Last Laugh*, it's clear that American gangster films are the best bet. If one insists on opening with something German, the choice is M. Sternberg's *Underworld* captures qualities of both antedents, but I usually show *Scarface* and refer to Universal horror films, *I Was A Fugitive from a Chain Gang*, and a list ranging from *King Kong* to *Citizen Kane* for further research.

Possible Additional Reading

The texts on pre-*noir* are limited but include the introductory comments from Schrader's "Notes" and Carlos Clarens' book *Crime Movies*

3. The Classic Period: *The Maltese Falcon*

Schrader's "Notes" first proposed and Silver/Ward et al in their subsequent books have established a concensus on what they call the "classic period" of *film noir*: it begins with *The Maltese Falcon* and it ends with *Touch of Evil*. Not long really, less than two decades; and nobody agrees on all the pictures in between. Even if one opts for the suggestion of Porfirio and a couple of others that *The Stranger on the Third Floor* is the first *noir* film, *The Maltese Falcon* is a much more appropriate and compelling introduction to classic *noir*. Bogart's still got it, and while I don't require the Hammett book be read, I recommend it and/or one of the first four Chandler novels. The context is the development of *noir* inside and outside the hard-boiled tradition. Hammett, Graham Greene, Raymond Chandler, and Cornell Woolrich provide a wide choice of literary sources, so alternate film

Below, Alan Ladd as the hired killer Phillip Raven in *This Gun For Hire*.

selections are *This Gun for Hire, Murder My Sweet* and *The Phantom Lady* all of which feature heavy-handed visuals but the latter two may draw some snickers for their graphic excesses.

Possible Additional Reading

Carl Richardson, *"Film Noir* in the Studio: *the Maltese Falcon"* in **Autopsy: an Element of Realism in Film Noir**

4. Post-war angst: *Nobody Lives Forever*

The clichéd assumption about post-World War II *noir* is that it dramatized the post-traumatic stress syndrome (masquerading under some less enlightened name such as "battle fatigue") of the the combat veteran. In fact, *noir* had plenty of alienation going for it before World War II came along. There are some memorably disturbed veterans, for instance, William Bendix as the manic Buzz Wanchek who loses control whenever he hears "jungle music" in *The Blue Dahlia*. But even though it boasts a Chandler screenplay and has Alan Ladd and Veronica Lake as its key protagonists, the real post-war irony is this film is not the steel plate in Buzz's head but the infidelity of the Ladd character's wife, who stepped out on him while he was off killing the enemy. Whatever the psychological disturbance,whether it's as explicit as the amnesiac ex-Marine George Taylor (John Hodiak) in *Somewhere in the Night* or as subtle as the perpetually sneering Gagin (Robert Montgomery) in *Ride the Pink Horse*, the hardest thing for many returning veterans to face is not what they did in the war but what they missed at home. In that sense the best example I've found is the 1946 *Nobody Lives Forever* (a script by W.R Burnett directed by Jean Negulesco), where John Garfield portrays a pre-war criminal, a gambler whose budding career was stunted by the draft.

A significant side effect of such characterizations is that the occasional and re-strained Freudianism of early *noir* explodes into unrestrained psychosis in such titles as the *The Dark Mirror* and *The Dark Past,* where inky cases of the fantods splatter across *film noir* like an unrestrained Rorschach. Whatever the feature selection, I usually add as short subject the John Huston documentary *Let There be Light*, which provides a segue to the next segment.

5. Docu-*noir: The Naked City*

We all know that post-war *noir* also adapted new technologies: high speed film, faster lenses, smaller cameras and other equipment. Still the "shot on actual location" De Rochement productions at Fox were pretty stodgy affairs, as is *Call Northside 777*, despite James Stewart's performance in it. And should one sit through Lang's *Blue Gardenia* just to comment on its crab dolly work? Fortunately there is a perfect example: *The Naked City*.

Naked City ends with the catch phrase popularized in the TV spin-off of the Fifties: "There are eight million stories in the naked city. This has been one of them." It opens with a voiceover intoned by that most extraordinary of *noir* producers Mark Hellinger (whose death in 1947 cut short a credit list of *noir* that already included *Brute Force*, *The Two Mrs. Carrolls*, and *The Killers*). Over aerial shots of Manhattan, Hellinger solemnly promises that "It was not photographed in a studio. Quite the contrary...the actors, played out their roles on the streets, in the apartment houses, in the skyscrapers of New York itself." Despite the showboating, *Naked City* is remarkably undated (or perhaps has endured beyond that perception). While somewhat intrusive, eventually Hellinger's commentary, which is kept up throughout the film and often slips into second-person mode where he talks to the characters, creates a snide, pseudo-documentary tone that is truly *noir*. "Take it easy, Garza," Hellinger warns a fugitive, "Don't run. Don't call attention to yourself." The montages of "real" behind-the-scenes events won the big prize for editing in 1948 but seem old hat now after the method became obligatory for so many cop shows. Some examples, such as the PBX board labels tracing the phone calls from the discovery of a body to the notification of the homicide squad, are still effective if no longer novel.

Two excellent alternate choices are by Anthony Mann, *Border Incident* and *T-Men*, both of which were shot by the legendary John Alton, whose lighting of locations yields an eerie blend of the chiaroscuro and the hyper-real.

Possible Additional Reading

Malvin Wald, "The Making of *The Naked City*," reprinted in **The Big Book of Noir**

Below, *The Naked City:* Detective Halloran (Don Taylor) questions Ruth Morrison (Dorothy Hart).

J.P. Telotte, "The Transparent Reality of Documentary *Noir*," in **Voices in the Dark**

The shots of the city recall the sardonic freeze-frames of WeeGee the Famous [Ed. Note: cf. Linda Brookover's essay *"Blanc et Noir*: Crime as Art" earlier in this volume] and a compilation book of his photographs is a good addition to the reading list.

6. Fugitive Couples: *Gun Crazy*

"Thrill Crazy, Kill Crazy, Gun Crazy"–what more needs to be said? The fugitive couple is a rich tradition in *film noir*, and Joe Lewis' classic brings it all home. Whether or not a closeted John Dall ever really drooled over Peggy Cummins' gams in black stockings, his heavy-lidded leering makes him the perfect low-budget *noir* everyman, intoxicated by the pistol-packing con-woman, Annie Laurie Starr. Shot on actual locations (a King Brothers production couldn't afford to build sets), *Gun Crazy* easily cross-refers to docu-*noir*, B-*noir*, and even, neo-*noir*, getting a nod from the 1992 *Guncrazy* and overt homage from the American *Breathless*. The celebrated long take shot from the back seat of the car, as the couple rob a bank while dressed in cowboy costumes, ends with Cummins' post-orgasmic glance over her shoulder. Of course, *Gun Crazy*'s car scenes can be strip-mined for over-blown comments such as "The passengers are traveling between two sets of emotional or existential situations...in which the automobile's interior can carry the same charged or clautrophobic atmosphere as the *noir* city itself." (**Somewhere in the Night**) In plain talk, wherever the spectator is situated, *Gun Crazy* is about the sexual dynamics of mixing guns, gals, and high performance engines.

Possible Additional Reading

Jim Kitses, BFI Monograph on *Gun Crazy*.

Astonishingly the only decent piece out there is Brookover/Silver "What is This Thing Called *Noir*?" in **Film Noir Reader**

7. Psychological Melodrama: Auld Lang *Noir*

Fritz Lang's dry melodramas of hopeless entrapment make him, for many critics, the uber-auteur of *noir*. Samuel Fuller or Bob Aldrich, he ain't; and the deterministic subtleties of *Human Desire* or *Beyond a Reasonable Doubt* can make the most resolute *noir* freak nod off. There is certain Yeats-like symmetry to his parables of middle-class mayhem, a sardonic undertone to the impeccably groomed Tom Garrett (Dana Andrews) in *Beyond a Reasonable Doubt* moving smoothly from the world of crime journalism and burlesque joints to courtroom in a double-twist plot. But there's not much "va-va-voom" here.

There are some Lang characters with a lot of intensity, most notably Glenn Ford's relentless cop out for revenge in *The Big Heat* or the small-town Joes (Paul Douglas and Robert Ryan) in *Clash by Night*. But the Langian hero par excellence is Edward G. Robinson and his remarkable performances in *Woman in the Window* and *Scarlet Street*, a double take on obsession with Joan Bennett as the obscure object of his desire. Whether its the psychology and dream states of *Woman in the Window* or the artist-meets-cons and debasement of *Scarlet Street*, either of these examples probes the melodramatic aspects of *noir* pretty deeply.

The alternate choice for "sturm und drang" meets *noir* is Otto Preminger, not *Laura* but the "Angel" movies: *Fallen Angel* and *Angel Face*. Outside the context of falling in love with a picture, Andrews in the former and Mitchum in the latter are hooked by a bad girl a la Preminger. One survives, the other doesn't.

<u>Possible Additional Reading</u>

Alfred Appel, Jr., "Frint Lang's American Nightmare" in *Film Comment* (November-December, 1974)

Robin Wood on Lang's *Big Heat* and Aldrich's *Kiss Me Deadly* in *CineAction* No. 21/22 [Ed. Note: reprinted earlier in this volume]

Florence Jacobowitz, "The Man's Melodrama: *Woman in the Window* and *Scarlet Street*" reprinted in **The Book of Film Noir**

8. The A's, B's, and Z's of *Noir*: *Detour* and *DOA*

It not news that *film noir* was mostly <u>not</u> mainstream stuff. Still early examples like *Maltese Falcon* and *Double Indemnity* were strictly "A" pictures. There were also "B" studio (RKO) and "B" unit *noir* films from the beginning. A final post-war effect was the emergence of the "poverty row" *noir*. But the "Z" grade efforts, made for budgets of less than $150,000, were not limited to PRC and Monogram.

Below, *Beyond a Reasonable Doubt*: Tom Garrett (Dana Andrews) still has a starched shirt in jail where he reaffirms his innocence to his socialite fiancée Susan Spencer (Joan Fontaine).

As the 1940s ended and the blacklist forced many *noir* writers to work cheaply for independent producers such as the King Brothers or Harry Popkin, pictures such as *Detour* and *DOA* were made on a shoestring.

The problem with *Detour* as an example is its mannered script and acting. Where else in *film noir* is a there a death as outrageous as that of the hitchhiking Vera (Ann Savage), who ends up strangled by a man pulling on a phone cord from another room. This is, after all, a movie that embodies the fickle finger of fate, and some laughs in that regard from contemporary audiences are unavoidable. For that reason, *DOA*, despite its wacky concept of "luminous toxin," is easier to swallow as an archetype of mischance. The hapless Frank Bigelow (Edmund O'Brien), an accountant away from his small-town girl friend, leering at anything in skirts and kicking up his heels in San Francisco, may be guilty of some mild lechery but does nothing to deserve a fatal dose. Knowing he will shortly die, his relentless pursuit of the his unknown killers drips with dark irony without straining the limits of its budget or of credulity in the *noir* world.

Possible Additional Reading

Paul Kerr, "Out of What Past? Notes on the B *film noir*" in **Film Noir Reader**

Andrew Britton, "*Detour*" in **The Book of Film Noir**

9. Apocalypse *Noir: Kiss Me Deadly*

It may be that more has been written about *Kiss Me Deadly* than any other *film noir*—unfortunately much of it is drivel. If Nick the Mechanic were to read about his latently homosexual relationship with Hammer, he'd lay somebody out with a wicked "pretty pow." So Hammer's an asshole, Hammer's a mysogynist, Hammer's in the closet—little could Mickey Spillane have suspected that this distorted rendering of his mindless macho divorce dick would become all things to all critics.

In his original *Film Comment* essay in 1974, Alain Silver first suggested that Hammer was on "a quest for a *noir* grail"; and never have the streets of Los Angeles been more steeped with quasi-mythic, quasi-operatic, quasi-hard-boiled characters who keep popping up as if in some crazed reverse rendering of Twain's Connecticutt Yankee: damsels in distress, atomic-powered wizards, Lily Carver-cum-Gabrielle-cum-Pandora-cum-Morgan le Fey with a, yes, I'll admit it, phallic roscoe in her hand asking Mike for "the liar's kiss." Perhaps the most phenomenal aspect of *Kiss Me Deadly*, its literally explosive conclusion, recently restored to include long-missing shots of Hammer watching the "great what's-it," his grail, consumed in an atomic inferno, is also the most powerful distortion of Spillane. His pulp endings usually find a snide Hammer watching some treacherous bitch breath her last. In turning macho myth upside down, Aldrich's Hammer sputters helplessly in the surf, out-smarted, out-gunned and out-classed, hoisted on his own smug petard by some ditzy dame.

Above, "Apocalypse *Noir*": Gabrielle/Lily Carver (Gaby Rodgers) opens the great what's-it and unleashes an atomic firestorm in *Kiss Me Deadly*.

<u>Possible Additional Reading</u>

Telotte, "Talk and trouble; *Kiss Me Deadly*'s Apocalyptic Discourse" in ***Voices in the Dark***

Silver, "*Kiss Me Deadly*: Evidence of a Style" reprinted in ***Film Noir Reader***

10. The Classic Period Ends: *The Killing* and *Touch of Evil*

As Schrader suggested in 1972 and Silver/Ward elaborated in their 1979 introduction for the real big book of *noir*, *The Encyclopedic Reference*, whether you think it's a movement or a genre or, like David Bordwell, a mass hallucination, *noir* is not really about auteurs. At the same time, as Schrader was quick to note, a lot of marginal auteurs did their best work in *noir*. While no one could dispute concluding a survey of the classic period with *Touch of Evil*, my experience has been that, after a steady diet of mainstream *noir* for so many weeks, *Touch of Evil* can actually end up seeming like a cheesy pastiche. There is a compelling irony to watching a massive Orson Welles lumbering through this film (which was to be his swan song as a Hollywood director) under the full weight of his uncontrolled gastronomy. The manic performances of Welles, Akim Tamiroff, and even Dennis Weaver are an apt coda for *noir*, a last, Münch-like scream of unfettered, expressionistic excess. But what does *Touch of Evil* really say? There's a new sheriff in town, a drab, play-by-the-rules, poker-up-the-ass detective in a shiny pressed suit—not very *noir* and not very interesting.

The caper gone nightmarishly awry is not a new concept. But the time-distorted overlay of events in *The Killing* is as compelling as it was over forty years ago. Sterling Hayden's Johnny Clay is a natural progression from his characer in

Below, Timothy Carey as sharpshooter Nikki Arane in *The Killing*.

The Asphalt Jungle, smarter, meaner, and *noir* to the core. Kubrick breaks down the archetype and reveals "the skull beneath the skin" with visuals as spare but precise as T. S. Eliot's prose. This is the ultimate evolution of classic *noir*: surrounded by such icons of menace, psychosis, and exploitation by *femme fatales* respectively as the hulking Ted de Corsia, the deranged Timothy Carey, and the cuckolded Elisha Cook, Jr., Clay's careful scheme disintegrates. This time when Hayden's character expires there is no ironic allusion in the manner of *The Asphalt Jungle*, but rather the complete dissolution of his life and dreams, blown away like the money from the heist.

Possible Additional Reading

Richardson, "*Film Noir* in Limbo: *Touch of Evil*" in **Autopsy**

I I. TV *Noir*

While a survey of TV *noir* is probably not in the cards at those institutions of higher learning where the film snobs rule, the soft-boiled, *noir*-inspired television homicide squads and private eyes are worth a look. The transition from docu-*noir* is unmistakable not just in the television series versions of *The Naked City* or *The Line-up*, but in the granddaddy of by-the-book cop shows, *Dragnet*. While the laconic style of creator and star, Jack Webb, may have long ago succumbed under the weight of countless parodies, the style of exposition continues to inspire imitators. It may be four decades later, but it'still just a small step from Sgt. Friday to the protagonists of *Law and Order*, where time and location sub-titles and a single ominous chord open every sequence, or the de rigueur hand-held in *Homicide*.

While they may be a little harder to find, besides the ubiquitous *Dragnet*, it's worth tracking down one or two more samples from the 50s, if not *Naked City* or *The Line-up* (both of which hold up quite well), *Peter Gunn*, *Richard Diamond*, or best of all, the remarkable *Johnny Staccato*, created by John Cassavetes before he went for high art. Easier to find and also worth a look are Michael Mann's first forays into neo-*noir* by way of TV, *Miami Vice* and the very dark, period series *Crime Story*.

Possible Additional Reading

James Ursini, "Angst at Sixty Fields per Second" in **Film Noir Reader**

Jeremy Butler, "*Miami Vice*: The Legacy of *Film Noir*" reprinted in **Film Noir Reader**

12. Neo-*noir*

Where does this phenomenon begin? Some could argue for Don Siegel's remake of *The Killers* released theatrically in 1964, just six years after *Touch of Evil*, because it was too violent for television. It does feature Ronald Reagan slapping Angie Dickinson; but even with that it seems pretty tame today. *Chinatown*?

Richard Jameson was calling that "son of *noir*" twenty-five years ago [Ed. Note: in the article reprinted earlier in this volume]. If one is to believe Silver and Ursini in their extended essay on neo-*noir* in the latest edition of their big book, this phenomenon took off in Hollywood in the 1980s. It's easy to read through their Addendum filmography of nearly 200 titles and cull one's favorite examples, such as *Body Heat*; *The Hot Spot*; *Kill Me, Again*; or *Sea of Love*. In a spin-off article, Silver makes an interesting point about how bloated, star-driven and big budget neo-*noir*s violate the classic tradition at their peril, often resulting in really bad movies, especially compared to new examples still working in the no-money, B-through-Z picture milieu. So it may be worth sampling one of these under $1 million efforts, such as *Guncrazy*, *Delusion*, or the strictly micro-budget (hence dear to my heart) *Horseplayer*.

Chances are there will be some high, medium or low-budget neo-*noir* just released to theaters, cable, or video respectively wherever a *film noir* course is offered. Why not roll the dice and assign one sight unseen as supplementary viewing? I've found that, armed with a deeper perception at the end of so many weeks of study, would-be filmmakers *noir* are quick to discern the cheap and/or superficial knock-off trying to pass themselves off as the genuine article.

<u>Possible Additional Reading</u>

Silver/Ursini, "Appendix E: Neo-*Noir*" in ***Film Noir: An Encyclopedic Reference***

Todd Erickson, "Kill Me Again: Movement becomes Genre" in ***Film Noir Reader***

Below, the 1964 "Enest Hemingway's*The Killers*," orginally made for TV; but the methods of its title figures (Lee Marvin, left, and Clu Gulager with Angie Dickinson) were deemed too violent.

Alain Silver, "Son of *Noir*: Neo-*Film Noir* and the Neo-B Picture" in **Film Noir Reader**

For many students, particularly mine, the ultimate question is not what *noir* was, but what it might be. They see *film noir* as an open-ended experience. Of course, with the short-sightedness of the young, they also see their own times–where slow internet access can be a most grievous fate–as more angst-ridden than any previous. The encapsulation effect, a selective view of the 1940s and 1950s through a *noir* filter, is not an easy read for those whose parents were not yet born when *The Maltese Falcon* was released. Still the through-line of *film noir* is undeniable and, in what may be the greatest irony, can be exhilarating to perceive for the first time at the turn of millennium.

Below, *Chinatown*: Jake Gittes (Jack Nicholson) searches for dark conspiracies while parked in an orange grove.

Above, conducting the coda to *film noir*: Robert Aldrich directs an uncertain Gaby Rodgers as Lily Carver/Gabrielle regarding the opening of the great "whats-it" in *Kiss Me Deadly*.

Notes on Contributors

Linda Brookover is a researcher and writer who has worked extensively in the fields of multi-cultural education. She has written on a variety of American Indian/ethnographic subjects and *The Crocodile Files* for *oneWorld*, an on-line magazine which she co-edited. Previously a corporate communications specialist and electronic toy designer, she now works as a social science researcher and educator. Since her essay in the first ***Film Noir Reader***, she wrote the screenplay for the family feature *Time at the Top* which recently aired on Showtime Networks and contributed an essay on Weegee to ***The Noir Style***.

Sharon Y. Cobb is an award-winning former journalist and magazine editor who is currently working as a screenwriter in Hollywood. She is co-author, with U.C.L.A. screenwriting instructor Neill D. Hicks, of ***Secrets of Selling Your Script to Hollywood*** and has lectured on *film noir* at U.C.L.A. and the Directors Guild of America. Her neo-*noir* Comedy, "Baja Triangle," is in development with Stir Fry Films, and she also co-wrote with suspense screenwriter William Kelley, "The River & The Knife," a *noir*-style suspense drama.

William B. Covey is an English Instructor at Slippery Rock University of Pennsylvania where he teaches film studies, literature and composition. His dissertation, "Compromising Positions: Theorizing American Neo-*Noir* Film" (Purdue, 1996) discusses thirty years of neo-*noir* film production from a cultural studies perspective. He has published reviews of books on *film noir* in *Analytical and Enumerative Bibliography, Film Criticism, The Journal of Film and Video, Postscript,* and *Style*.

Dale Ewing, Jr. was, according to his 1988 bio, writing a book on alienation and spiritual recovery in *film noir*. He has an M.A. in History from the University of Kansas and works [or worked] in the technical services department of the Kansas City Library system.

Stephen Farber is currently the film critic and contributing editor for *Movieline* magazine. His books include ***The Movie Rating Game*** (1972), ***Hollywood Dynasties*** (1984), ***Outrageous Conduct: Art Ego and the Twilight Zone Case*** (1988), and ***Hollywood on the Couch*** (1993). He has also written reviews and articles for numerous publications including *The New York Times, The Los Angeles Times, Esquire, New York, New West, Harper's Bazaar, Film Comment, Film*

Quarterly, and *The Hudson Review*. He has lectured at several American universities, the J. Paul Getty Museum, the Swedish Film Institute, the Norwegian Broadcasting Corp., in a program sponsored by Australian Film and Television School and the New Zealand Film Commission, and on an ongoing basis at UCLA Extension.

Tom Flinn began his work as a frequent contributor and editor for *The Velvet Light Trap* while still a student and film programmer at the University of Wisconsin, Madison. His essays and interviews on *film noir* have also been reprinted in ***Kings of the Bs*** and ***The Big Book of Noir*** (which features his piece on *Out of the Past*).

Philip Gaines has produced a number of low-budget independent features (several of which he co-wrote) and also teaches moviemaking and, occasionally, movie history at a local [that is, situated in Hollywood] institute of technology. His interest in *film noir* developed when he was a film student and has continued to the neo-*noir* project he currently has in development. He also wrote the production guides ***Hollywood on 5, 10, and $25,000 a Day*** and ***Micro-Budget Hollywood***, a term he coined with co-writer David Rhodes.

Richard T. Jameson programmed and wrote notes for university and institutional film series, co-founded and operated several film societies, managed and co-programmed an art theater in the Greater Seattle area (1967-71), and designed and taught cinema courses at the University of Washington (1969-84). His writings on film have appeared in *Film Comment, Film Quarterly, Take One, The Velvet Light Trap, American Film,* and the *Seattle Film Society's Movietone News,* which he edited for most of its history (1971-81). He was film critic of *The Weekly* (Seattle, 1976-78 and 1979-86), *Pacific Northwest* (1986-90), and *7 Days* (1989-90), and has been editor of *Film Comment* magazine since the beginning of 1990. Until he moved to New York, he has enjoyed the distinction of being "the only member of the National Society of Film Critics west of Chicago and north of San Francisco."

Kent Minturn is a Ph.D candidate in art history at Columbia University.

Francis M. Nevins is a professor at St. Louis University School of Law and the author of five mystery novels: ***Publish and Perish*** (1975), ***Corrupt and Ensnare*** (1978), ***The 120-Hour Clock*** (1986), ***The Ninety Million Dollar Mouse*** (1987), and ***Into the Same River Twice*** (1996). He has also written about forty short stories which have appeared in *Ellery Queen, Alfred Hitchcock* and other national magazines and many of which have been reprinted in leading mystery anthologies. He has edited more than fifteen mystery anthologies and collections and has written articles, book reviews, similar short pieces on movies and mystery fiction and book-length nonfiction studies on the genre, two of which, ***Royal Bloodline:***

Ellery Queen, Author And Detective (1974) and **Cornell Woolrich: First You Dream, Then You Die** (1988), were awarded Edgars from the Mystery Writers of America. During 1994 he served as Awards Chair for Mystery Writers of America.

Robert Porfirio began his extensive work on *film noir* while in the Master's program at U.C.L.A. which culminated in his 1979 dissertation for Yale University *The Dark Age of American Film: A Study of American* **Film Noir** *(1940-1960)*. His articles include contributions to *Continuum, Dialog, Literature/Film Quarterly,* and *Sight and Sound.* As co-editor of **Film Noir: An Encyclopedic Reference to the American Style** (1979), he wrote over sixty entries on individual films. He was formerly assistant professor of American Studies at California State University, Fullerton and is presently a real estate broker in Southern California. He contributed several "modules" to **The Noir Style**, and, when pressed, he occasionally lectures on *film noir.*

Alain Silver wrote, co-wrote and co-edited the books listed in the front. Forthcoming later in 1999, **The Noir Style** is the first full-length study of the movement's complex iconography. Shorter pieces have appeared in *Film Comment, Movie, Literature/Film Quarterly, Wide Angle, Photon,* the *DGA Magazine,* the *Los Angeles Times,* and the on-line magazines *Images* and *oneWorld.* He has co-written two feature films (*Kiss Daddy Goodbye* and *Time at the Top*) and produced several others (*Beat, Palmer's Pick-up, Cyborg^2, The Night Visitor*), as well as documentaries, music videos, and over sixty soundtrack albums for the Bay Cities and Citadel labels. He has lectured on film production at UCLA Extension and the Directors Guild of America and consulted on the recent restoration of the ending of *Kiss Me Deadly.*

Grant Tracey is an Assistant Professor of English at the University of Northern Iowa where he teaches Film, Popular Culture, and Creative Writing. He has published stories in a variety of literary magazines including *Aethlon: The Journal of Sport Literature, Farmer's Market,* and *Kansas Quarterly.* He has an article on James Cagney and ethnicity forthcoming in *The Journal of Film and Video.* He is also the editor of *Images: The Journal of Film and Popular Culture* and *Literary Magazine Review.*

James Ursini is the co-author, with Alain Silver, of the forthcoming **The Noir Style** and **Roger Corman: Metaphysics on a Shoestring** and the completed volumes listed in the front. He has also contributed articles to *Mediascene, Cinema* (U.S.), *Photon, Cinefantastique, Midnight Marquee,* and the *DGA Magazine.* He has produced Oral Histories and been a researcher for the American Film Institute and has also been associate producer and producer on feature films and documentaries for various school districts and public broadcasting. He has lectured on filmmaking at UCLA and other colleges and continues to work as an educator in Los Angeles.

Elizabeth Ward is co-editor of *Film Noir: An Encyclopedic Reference to the American Style* and co-wrote and co-photographed *Raymond Chandler's Los Angeles* (1987), on which she has also lectured. She also co-authored with Alain Silver, *The Film Director's Team* (2nd Edition, 1992) and *Robert Aldrich: a guide to references and resources* (1979). Other of her articles and interviews related to film noir have appeared in *Movie*, the *Los Angeles Times*, and the reference volumes *Dictionary of Literary Biography* (on Leigh Brackett) and *Survey of Cinema*. She worked extensively as a production manager, assistant director, and stage manager in motion picture and television production for Paramount Pictures and ABC on such series as *Cheers, Family Ties*, and *Moonlighting*. She was formerly assistant editor of publications for AFI West and is currently a primary school educator.

Tony Williams is the co-author **of *Italian Western: Opera of Violence*** (1975), co-editor of ***Vietnam War Films*** (1994) and ***Jack London's "The Sea Wolf": A Screenplay by Robert Rossen*** (1998). He is the author of ***Jack London: the Movies*** (1992); ***Hearths of Darkness: the Family in the American Horror Film*** (1996); ***Larry Cohen: Radical Allegories of an American Filmmaker*** (1997); and the forthcoming ***Structures of Desire: British Cinema 1949-1955***. His articles have appeared in *Cinema Journal, CineAction, Wide Angle, Jump Cut, Asian Cinema, Creative Filmmaking*, and the first ***Film Noir Reader***. He is an Associate Professor and Area Head of Film Studies in the Department of English, Southern Illinois University at Carbondale.

Robin Wood, whose numerous books on motion pictures include seminal English-language *auteur* studies of Alfred Hitchcock, Howard Hawks, Ingmar Bergman, and Arthur Penn and most recently *Hollywood from Vietnam to Reagan*, is now writing fiction. He is a former Professor of Film Studies at Queen's College and York University and remains a founding member of the collective which edits the film journal *CineAction!*